MW00788925

Fundamental Ephemeris Computations

For use with JPL data in PowerBasic and C

Paul J. Heafner

Published by

Willmann-Bell, Inc.

P.O. Box 35025 • Richmond, Virginia 23235 ☎ (804) 320-7016 • www.willbell.com

Published by Willmann-Bell, Inc.
P.O. Box 35025, Richmond, Virginia 23235

Copyright ©1999 by Willmann-Bell, Inc.
First English Edition

All rights reserved. Except for brief passages quoted in a review, no part of this book may be reproduced by any mechanical, photographic, or electronic process, nor may it be stored in any information retrieval system, transmitted, or otherwise copied for public or private use, without the written permission of the publisher. Requests for permission or further information should be addressed to Permissions Department, Willmann–Bell, Inc. P.O., Box 35025, Richmond, VA 23235.

Printed in the United States of America

92 93 94 95 96 97 98 9 8 7 6 5 4 3 2

Preface

Within the last decade there have been many books dealing with the application of personal computers to general problems in celestial mechanics, astrometry, astrodynamics, and spherical astronomy. So, the reader may ask, "Why one more?"

The most evident reason is the use of approximations. Usually a full verbal explanation of a procedure is given, but when the algorithm is programmed, approximations are often made that, in the final analysis, defeat the power of a computer. Modern microcomputers are wonderful machines, never tiring of performing the same computations over and over again until the user is satisfied with the result. While it is true that efficient coding often reduces the execution time, the point is that there is no need to make any great approximations until the very end of the computation. For instance, it is generally accepted that it is useless to compute times of sunrise and sunset to an accuracy greater than one minute of time because of the uncertain nature of atmospheric refraction near the horizon and the constantly changing local meteorological conditions. However, why not let the computer perform the computation to the full precision of the machine and then let the user round the result to the nearest minute of time? Computer gurus may argue that this will slow down the computation substantially, but I propose that for the user who has a 80486 or Pentium computer (both of which are the mainstream machines today), there will be no practical decrease in computation speed. This is the general approach adopted for this book.

Another major problem with existing computer-oriented astronomical books is that there has been little or no effort to adopt the computational algorithms used for the preparation of data in the national almanacs, particularly the U.S. Naval Observatory's *Astronomical Almanac*. The *Explanatory Supplement to the Astronomical Ephemeris*, which is now out of print, was a computational bible for those wishing to delve into the world of precise ephemerides, tables, and data reductions. It has been superseded, as of 1992, by the *Explanatory Supplement to the Astronomical Almanac*, which, while still a definitive reference work, lacks the detailed numerical examples of its predecessor. However, as of 1984 an entire new system of fundamental and derived constants has been implemented to form the basis of new and improved planetary and lunar ephemerides and computation procedures. Of course, these new procedures also form the basis for the data presented in the *Astronomical Almanac*. To my knowledge, there is no *widely available* library of routines in any language that implements the new algorithms or fully exploits the existing ones. The software probably exists in the form of FORTRAN code hidden away in the mainframe computers at the Jet Propulsion Laboratory (JPL) or the Naval Observatory, but none of this software is available to the public. So, the primary goal of this book is to present a library of useful PowerBASIC and C subprograms and functions that can be combined to make powerful application programs. I also hope that this book will find its way into the classroom, teaching astronomy students how to perform astronomical calculations and how to program them effectively. I find it a shame that celestial mechanics and spherical astronomy are no longer considered important enough to be included in the astronomy programs of many colleges and universities.

Many factors influenced the choice of PowerBASIC as the main language with which to build this library. First, BASIC itself is a rich and powerful language, full of commands that no other language offers. While most professional programmers laugh at the idea of using any dialect of BASIC for software development, I contend that in the hands of a skilled programmer a modern implementation of BASIC can do anything that any other language can do. I do not profess to be a "computer scientist" of any sort, but I do know that today's PowerBASIC is a virtually untapped source of power for programming scientific applications. Numerous third-party developers are just now beginning to realize this, and there is finally a small but growing market for PowerBASIC scientific programming tools. The second influence is that PowerBASIC is inexpensive and can usually be purchased from software dealers for around $100 to $150. At this price, every computer owner who wants to learn BASIC programming can afford PowerBASIC. Furthermore, the recent introduction of a privately published journal, *Celestial Computing*,[1] presenting professional quality QuickBASIC software for astrodynamics, celestial mechanics, fundamental astronomy, and numerical methods, only strengthens the arguments for the adoption of PowerBASIC as a serious tool. This means that BASIC is more widespread than ever before, and the days of GW-BASIC, line numbers, `GOTO` statements, and `GOSUB` statements (even though I have used `GOSUB` in a couple of strategic places anyway because it simply works) have been replaced with software containing highly structured subprograms and functions just like Pascal, FORTRAN, or even C.

---

[1] At the time of this writing *Celestial Computing* is on an indefinite hiatus.

I hope that this book will demonstrate both the power and ease of use of PowerBASIC as a viable language for developing astronomical software. In addition, the reader will find explanations of topics which have been glossed over or even totally ignored in other works. Great care has been taken to put hard-to-find bits of information from widely scattered sources into one convenient place. For example, many authors state that there are different time scales in use for astronomical computations, but most never incorporate the conversion procedures into their software. True, most authors stress the difference between Universal Time (without explaining the different UT time scales in use) and Ephemeris or Dynamical Time, but when a typical Julian day number algorithm is programmed, there is no provision for computing the Julian day number on *all* of the available time scales. The Julian day number routine developed in Chapter 2 will allow the user to obtain a Julian day number on *any* desired time scale. I would also like to point out that I am not advocating a programming language "holy war." FORTRAN is not dead, C is a standard programming language in many fields, but BASIC is not dead either. If the reader does not like BASIC, my source code should be portable to other languages.

Lest the reader think I am too dogmatic in my praise of PowerBASIC, I have, with the assistance of Charles Gamble, ported the software to C. This code appears in Appendix A and on the accompanying disk.

As for the scope of the software itself, the routines I present cover both elementary and advanced topics in computational celestial mechanics and spherical astronomy. Primarily, the topics covered include time systems, precession, nutation, coordinate transformations, orbital elements and ephemerides, reduction to apparent place, rise/transit/set times for celestial objects, and use of the JPL ephemerides. Care has been taken to present the results of computations in the same form as the corresponding data in the *Astronomical Almanac* and at least to the same precision. To my knowledge, this book is the only one describing how to obtain, process, and use the official Jet Propulsion Laboratory ephemeris data files. The JPL ephemerides form the basis of practically all of the national astronomical almanacs, including the *Astronomical Almanac*. Many readers will be surprised to learn that these data files are available free from JPL via the Internet or via a CD-ROM prepared by JPL and published by Willmann-Bell ($24.95 plus shipping). In this book I give explicit instructions on how to retrieve them from JPL and put them into a usable form. In addition, I also supply with this book a disk that includes enhanced PowerBASIC and C versions of the original JPL FORTRAN processing software that manipulates the data files. Today, these ephemerides are considered to be the final word on planetary ephemerides, and now the serious non-professional who wants to make use of them can do so. In no way should my software be considered a replacement for JPL's ephemeris export package. Many years of development have gone into that package and I respect that. My package is simply an alternative. I should also add that I assume that the reader is familiar with standard astronomical terminology, probably at the level of a junior/senior astronomy or physics student. A familiarity with elementary matrix methods would also be helpful, but is not required.

Early in the development of this book, Microsoft QuickBASIC was the language used for program development. However, I stopped using it because Microsoft stopped supporting it. QuickBASIC has many wonderful features, but a product without technical support is a product not worth using for a project such as this one. PowerBASIC is constantly being improved (up to version 3.2 at the time of this writing) and is supported by a conscientious technical staff, members of whom even make their presence known on the Internet in the BASIC-related Usenet groups. All of these programs presented here and on the book's companion disk were developed with the latest version of PowerBASIC running on a generic 80486DX-33 machine with 8 megabytes of RAM. The operating system used was OS/2 Warp (another wonderful product). Occasionally, I booted to DOS 6.22 (via OS/2's dual boot feature) to test the software under DOS, but no problems were encountered running the programs under OS/2's DOS emulation. The programs have been tested under Microsoft DOS, Windows 3.11 and Windows 98. I also employed a Compaq Contura Aero 4/33C laptop for program development. The text for this book was written with emTeX[2] running on the desktop system and on the laptop.

The programs have been extensively tested. However, I am sure that some bugs have crept in here and there. If any bugs are encountered, do not hesitate to inform me of them. The most efficient way to contact me is via the Internet (heafnerj@interpath.com) or via www.willbell.com. With the assistance of my publisher I intend to maintain any errata as part of this book's web page at www.willbell.com. I hope you find this book instructive and useful, and I look forward to hearing from readers.

Paul J. Heafner
May, 1999

---

[2]emTeX is a freely available PC implementation of the TeX typesetting system.

Table of Contents

Acknowledgements

The majority of this book was written during the spring semester of 1991, from January to May, while I was a second-year graduate student at the University of North Carolina at Greensboro. My fellow residents in South Spencer Graduate Center were supportive of the project from the beginning. They are too numerous to list, but I would like to thank them for their friendship, understanding, and encouragement. Many thanks to Dr. Stephen Danford, who served as my advisor for the independent study course in which I wrote much of the text. He provided many remarks and suggestions during the process and helped me focus my efforts.

A great deal of appreciation goes to David Eagle, editor-in-chief of *Celestial Computing*, for whom I have written many articles, reviews, and programs for publication. David introduced me to the marvels of BASIC as a serious computational tool and provided me with many resources. I originally developed the desire to write this book when I was an undergraduate at the University of North Carolina at Chapel Hill, but I almost abandoned the idea until David encouraged me to pursue the project. It is safe to say that I would not have completed the book without David's support. I find it amusing that although I have written many articles for *Celestial Computing* and had hundreds of telephone and e-mail conversations with David, I have yet to meet him in person. Hopefully, we will meet in the near future.

I would also like to thank Roger Mansfield and Rex Shudde for taking the time to proofread portions of the book. Their expert opinions were greatly appreciated. Also Perry Remaklus of Willmann-Bell for his endless patience and desire to pursue this project and Robert Zale and his staff for creating and supporting PowerBASIC.

This software was originally written in BASIC and then ported to ANSI C. The ANSI C version would not have been possible without the help of Charles Gamble, who basically took my poor attempt at porting code from BASIC to C and made it all work correctly. Charles lives and works in Great Britain and we have only "spoken" via e-mail over the Internet. I sincerely hope that someday, we have to the opportunity to meet because I want to personally thank him for taking the time to help me with this project. From the beginning, my dream was to have a suite of programs that would compile unchanged on various platforms and allow users to generate binary data files that would also be portable, unchanged, across the same platforms and still maintain compatibility with the original BASIC software. Thanks to Charles' skill, this dream is now a reality. Until you are better paid, my friend, thank you.

Varian Swieter helped me get started with the porting project and did most of the initial work on ASC2EPH.C. Thank you too, Varian.

Joel Wright introduced me to the wonders of TeX and LaTeX. Eberhard Mattes created emTeX (which was used to typeset my book) and the EMX program development system, including a port of gcc. My software would not exist without these vital tools. Thank you, Eberhard.

My thanks also go to Myles Standish of the Jet Propulsion Laboratory for all his help regarding the JPL ephemerides. On more than one occasion, Dr. Standish cleared up errors in my thinking and helped me understand the JPL ephemeris data files.

My family has been consistently supportive of this project, and I extend thanks to them as well. Finally, thanks to God for giving me an appreciation for the science of, as well as the sheer beauty of, astronomy and for giving me the ability to understand something well enough to explain it to others.

Chapter 1

Introduction

1.1 What is a Fundamental Ephemeris?

For the purposes of this book, an *ephemeris* is a table giving the positions (and maybe velocities) of a celestial object. To present an ephemeris of, say, a major planet in our solar system requires many "behind the scenes" computations. Depending on just how precise the ephemeris needs to be these can be quite involved—but the basic computations are the same from one ephemeris to the next. Today, even the desktop computers can be instructed to carry out these tedious, but fortunately repetitive, mathematical details for us with any modern programming language to very high levels of precision.

There are two basic types of fundamental ephemerides: analytical and numerical. Analytical ephemerides are based on closed-form algebraic expressions which yield the object's position and velocity components for a given instant of time. These expressions must be derived from an algebraic solution to the equations of motion for the object. When mutual gravitational perturbations and relativistic perturbations (and there are many others to consider) are taken into account, the expressions necessarily become more complicated. Computer algebra systems such as Mathematica and Maple can be employed to remove some of the drudgery, but the final expressions must be derived explicitly. The primary benefit of analytical ephemerides is that they express the positions and velocity components as explicit functions of time. In general, analytical ephemerides are no longer used in most applications, but a group of astronomers at the Bureau des Longitudes in Paris, France has continued to make advances in this area.

Numerical ephemerides, as the name suggests, rely on a numerical solution to the equation of motion. The output of such a computation is a table of numbers giving the positions and velocities at the desired times. A potential drawback of this method is the sheer size of the tables when the object's position and velocity components are required for a large number of times—for example, a one day interval over several centuries. In practice, the positions and velocities may be "compressed" by fitting them with a well-behaved mathematical function which can replicate the original values to within a very small tolerance for any desired instant of time. This is the approach taken in the production of the Jet Propulsion Laboratory (JPL) planetary ephemerides. Such ephemerides are extremely compact and the effort required to extract the data is minimal for a computer. For the user, not having an explicit algebraic expression may take some getting used to though. Generally speaking, numerical ephemerides have replaced analytical ephemerides. They are the basis for the U.S. Naval Observatory *Astronomical Almanac*.

The positions and velocities obtained from either type of ephemeris are generally not in a form for use by Earth-based observers. Several transformations and correctons may be necessary to reduce the data to a form which can actually be compared to the observed values. These transformations and corrections are the subject of this book.

I have chosen to concentrate on the process of generating the actual ephemeris rather than on specific applications. Ten different persons may have ten different reasons for wanting precise planetary coordinates. A book that attempts to deal with each of these would rapidly become huge. Rather, I have directed my efforts in this book to describing how you can acquire precise starting data and then maintain that precision throughout the creation of a basic ephemeris. Therefore, the concepts of time, coordinate transformations, precession, nutation, aberration, relativistic corrections, and atmospheric refraction are presented here in a rigorous modular form that suggests use as modifiers to the original data. Keplerian two-body motion is also presented as a means of generating ephemerides for objects not included in the JPL ephemeris data files. A generalized suite of routines, based on the JPL export software and suitable for processing any JPL ephemeris data file, is developed, as is an explanation of the data file format. This section conveniently pulls together tidbits of information that previously had to be gleaned from several sources. I have also included a toolbox of matrix, vector, and numerical routines that has been useful. Finally, in Chapter 10 all the concepts developed earlier in this book are brought together in the development of a powerful, easy to use command-line ephemeris program which can serve as a starting point for more advanced applications. Suggestions for enhancements are included as programming exercises.

Nowhere do I give algorithms for finding planetary conjunctions, oppositions, lunar or solar eclipses, lunar phases, or other such events. I consider these to be applications whose existence depends on having suitable positional data. Excellent books, like Jean Meeus' *Astronomical Algorithms* already provide this information. I do, however, include an algorithm for finding rise/transit/set times because I see these as fundamental applications on nearly the same footing as the ephemerides themselves. Conceptually, these times determine whether or not a particular event will be visible from a given location on Earth.

So, this book shows you how to create precise basic ephemerides for celestial bodies ready for modification by the user to meet his or her specific needs. It is the reference and text which I wished was available when I began learning about astronomy and how to compute the positions of the planets.

1.2 The Software Source Code

Software source code is distributed with this book and is to be found in a plastic pouch located on the inside back cover. This source code includes all of the primary subprograms described in the book, including the driver programs, utility routines and functions in PowerBasic and C. The files are organized into three subdirectories, one for the PowerBASIC files, one for the ANSI C files, and one for (PowerBASIC) executables only. The files are distributed in compressed form and are found in a file titled `Fund_eph.ZIP`, this file in turn contains the following directory structure which will be created when expanded to your hard drive:

```
\exec\
\fecsoftb\
\fecsoftc\
```

The `exec` folder holds executable programs. The `fecsoftb` folder contains BASIC source code. The `fecsoftc` contains ANSI C source code.

1.2.1 Program Requirements

The BASIC Code

The BASIC programs were created and compiled with PowerBASIC 3.2 from PowerBASIC, Inc. The PB language system is not required to run the executables, but is needed if you wish to modify and recompile the programs. Information on PowerBASIC can be found on the World Wide Web at the URL http://www.powerbasic.com. The programs will run under MS-DOS, Windows 3.1, Windows 98, and OS/2 Warp 3 and 4.

The driver programs are tersely written and they make extensive use of PowerBASIC's `$include` metastatement—this means that when an external routine is needed, it is included in the main program via an `$include` metastatement. Notice that each such metastatement contains the full path to the required routine's source code file. These metastatements may, of course, be modified by the user in the event that he or she decides not to use the provided directory structure. Consult the PowerBASIC documentation for more details.

The C Code

In order to build the executables, you must have an ANSI C compiler, a make utility, and the GNU file utilities installed on your computer. GNU make was used extensively for testing. After expanding the archive to your hard drive, change to the directory on your hard disk where you installed the code, and type the following at the system prompt:

```
C:\>make -f makefile.XXX
```

where **XXX** is either 'dos' (for DJGPP systems), 'os2' (for EMX systems), or 'unx' (for UNIX or LINUX systems). This will build the executables, leaving the object files intact for later use. The sources were compiled and the resulting executables were tested on the following computer platforms:

1. Compaq AERO 4/33C running MS-DOS 6.2/Win31 (DJGPP)

2. Sony VAIO PCG-731 200Mhz Pentium running Windows 98 (DJGPP)

3. Gateway Pentium P5-90 running MS-DOS 6.22/Win31 (DJGPP)

4. Intel Pentium 166MHz, 32Meg RAM, running OS/2 Warp 4 (EMX, DJGPP)

5. Gateway Pentium Pro 200, 48Meg RAM, running Windows NT (MS Visual C++ 5)

6. LINUX (gcc)

7. Sun SPARC 5 running Solaris and SunOS 4.1.3

1.2.2   Modifying the Source Code

The reader is free to modify the source code and to experiment with it. Indeed, there are even suggestions for such experimentation provided throughout the book. Under no circumstances, however, should the original or modified code be distributed. It is copyrighted and your purchase only entitles you to personal use without written permission from Willmann-Bell. Certain modifications have purposely not been made to the software so that the user can learn more by experimenting.

1.2.3 Programming Conventions

Let me emphasize that I am **not** a professional computer programmer. I consider both the computer and the chosen programming language as tools for solving problems. I also do not claim that my software is always written in the most efficient manner. That is the main reason I decided to make the source code available to users of this book. While many readers will be content with the programs as they stand, others will feel the need to experiment with the source code and to build applications that meet specific needs. I wholeheartedly recommend this form of experimentation.

Chapter 2

Astronomical Time Systems

2.1 Introduction

In this chapter, we demonstrate the computation of the Julian day number or the modified Julian day number on any of the currently used astronomical time scales. We also present two useful subprograms that perform conversions to and from Julian or Besselian epochs and one that carries out the computation of mean and apparent sidereal time.

2.2 The Various Time Scales

Of all the concepts embraced by astronomy, the concept of time is perhaps the most misunderstood. There are numerous "clocks" one could use to measure time and numerous units in which to express these measurements. Couple this with the inclusion of some general relativity and you can see that asking the simple question "What time is it?" becomes a non-trivial matter. There also seems to be some confusion in the literature as to the nature of certain astronomical time scales, so it would be beneficial at this point to clear up some of the misunderstandings. For our purposes, we can classify time into the four categories of dynamical time, atomic time, sidereal time, and universal time.

2.2.1 Dynamical Time

Dynamical time is the uniform time that appears in an object's equation of motion. When we write, for example, Newton's second law of motion for a mass m under the influence of a one-dimensional net force F_x in the conventional form

$$F_x = ma_x = m\frac{d^2x}{dt^2} \tag{2.2.1}$$

7

we assume that the time t is a free-flowing time. It always passes at a constant rate, but the numerical value of this rate is not the same for all observers due to the effects of general relativity.

General relativity is far beyond the scope of this book, and no attempt will be made to cover the details. An excellent discussion of how general relativity affects the role of time, particularly in astronomy, can be found in [Green 1985]. The basic concept, however, may be understood by considering an inertial reference frame S' moving in the x−direction at a constant velocity v with respect to another inertial reference frame S. The familiar Lorentz transformation

$$x' = \gamma(x - vt)$$
$$y' = y$$
$$z' = z$$
$$t' = \gamma\left(t - \frac{v}{c^2}x\right) \tag{2.2.2}$$

(where $\gamma = (1 - v^2/c^2)^{-\frac{1}{2}}$ and c is the speed of light in vacuum) specifies how to calculate the coordinates of an object (in general, of any event) in the S' frame given its coordinates in the S frame. Although dynamical time is derived within the framework of general relativity, the special relativistic Lorentz transformation illustrates an important physical principle quite simply. The expression for time in the S' frame, t', depends on a spatial quantity x and on a temporal quantity t in the S frame. Similarly, the expression for position in the S' frame x' depends on both spatial and temporal quantities in the S frame. Time in the S frame is not the same as time in the S' frame. The two times run at different rates. From the Lorentz transformation, we see that time itself is **not** independent of reference frame. This concept is important because the time appearing in Newton's second law depends on one's reference frame. For this reason, there is more than one type of dynamical time.

For solar system bodies, the time appearing in the equations of motion is symbolized as T_{eph} and is very loosely referred to as *ephemeris time*, although this is not the same as the ET traditionally referred to in the astronomical literature. To add to the confusion, T_{eph} has mistakenly received many names over recent years in an attempt to clearly define this time scale. We shall now examine the many time scales that have been defined in dynamical astronomy.

2.2.2   Barycentric Dynamical Time

T_{eph} was once referred to as Barycentric Dynamical Time (TDB). However, the IAU (International Astronomical Union) definition of TDB was quite

different. According to the IAU, TDB was defined to differ from Terrestrial
Time (TT, defined in Section 2.2.4) by only periodic terms which account
for a general relativistic difference between the two time scales. TDB was
intended to be a coordinate time, but according to the mathematics of general relativity, a coordinate time cannot differ from TT (a proper time) by
only periodic terms. Therefore, TDB is not a physically realizable time scale
[Standish 1998]. Analogous to the Lorentz transformation of special relativity, there is a transformation that allows one to calculate coordinate time
from proper time[1] or vice versa, but it is significantly more complex than the
Lorentz transformation. For something no more accurate than present day
optical observations, the transformation may be put into the useful form

$$\text{TDB} = \text{TDT} + 0\overset{s}{.}001658 \sin g + 0\overset{s}{.}000014 \sin 2g \qquad (2.2.3)$$

where g is the Earth's mean anomaly. It suffices to take $g = 357\overset{\circ}{.}53 +
0\overset{\circ}{.}98560028(\text{JD}-2451545)$ where $\text{JD} = $ Julian day number (on the TDT scale)
of the time of observation. This is only an approximation, and higher order
terms have been neglected. Additional higher order terms are required for
non-optical sources of observational data (radio, laser or radar ranging, pulsar timing, etc.). This particular form of the conversion from TDT to TDB is
derived in [Green 1985] using an undergraduate-level approach to general relativity. A much more complicated (and more accurate) expression can be found
in [Moyer 1981]. This topic is also discussed in [Murray 1983]. A modern discussion of the relativistic derivation of TDB is given by [Fukushima 1995].

2.2.3 Atomic Time

Atomic time is essentially time kept by a network of atomic clocks. The
clocks are synchronized and their rates are adjusted to account for relativistic
difference. The basic unit is the SI second, which is defined as the duration
of 9192631770 oscillations between two hyperfine levels of the ground state
of the cesium 133 atom. The formal name for this time scale is International
Atomic Time or TAI for short.

2.2.4 Terrestrial Dynamical Time

Terrestrial Dynamical Time (TDT, recently renamed to just Terrestrial
Time and symbolized as TT) is defined, for historical reasons, as TAI +
32\overset{s}{.}184 (SI seconds) and is used as the time argument for apparent geocentric
(which is somewhat redundant as explained in Chapter 6) ephemerides of
solar system bodies. This is not the same as the time argument in the object's

---

[1]In relativity theory, a proper time is time measured by a clock at rest in the observer's
reference frame.

equation of motion. Since we are observers and we are located on the Earth, we can also think of TT as a *proper time* in the relativistic sense. That is, TT is the time measured in the rest frame of the observer's clock.

2.2.5   Sidereal Time

As every astronomy student has learned, sidereal time is "time kept by the stars." Rigorously, sidereal time is governed by the Earth's (irregular) rotation with respect to the inertial reference frame of distant radio sources such as quasars. Sidereal time is determined from measurements of Earth's orientation with respect to this inertial frame.

2.2.6   Universal Time

There are two types of universal time and they are designated UT1 and UTC.[2] UT1 is merely a measure of Earth's (irregular) rotation with respect to the mean sun. The mean sun is a fictitious body that moves around our sky at a rate at which the actual Sun would move if the Earth's orbit were a perfect circle and not an ellipse. UT1 is defined by a mathematical formula in terms of sidereal time, which is just a measure of the Earth's rotation with respect to inertial space (see Section 2.5). UTC, the abbreviation for Coordinated Universal Time, is basically what we live our lives by. UTC is the "zone time" as kept at the Greenwich meridian and is always kept to within 0.9s of UT1 by the periodic insertion of leap seconds. Theoretically, one can measure sidereal time observationally, compute UT1 from the mathematical formula, and compare it with UTC to see whether or not leap second adjustments are needed. All time zones in the world are based on integral or half-integral hour offsets from UTC.

2.2.7   Ephemeris Time

Ephemeris time, denoted by ET, was an early attempt at defining T_{eph} in terms of the existing dynamical theories of the motions of the Sun and the Moon. However, the theories were not perfect and neither was ephemeris time. The intent was a freely-flowing time scale.

2.2.8   Barycentric Coordinate Time

Barycentric Coordinate Time, TCB, is the IAU's latest attempt at realistically defining T_{eph}. The result is a physically realizable time scale that

---

[2]We include UT2 here because the formula for obtaining it from UT1 is available from the *IERS Bulletin A*.

is related to TT through a relativistic correction. TCB is defined to be measured in SI units whereas T_{eph} is not. TCB departs from TT at the rate of 0.5s per year. The relationship between TDB and TCB in seconds is

$$\text{TCB-TDB} = 1.550506 \times 10^{-8}(\text{JD} - 2443144.5)86400.$$

2.3 Relationships Between the Time Scales

UTC is readily available from any standard time radio station such as WWV or CHU. Other such stations operate in other parts of the world. TAI is kept by atomic clocks. All observatories, and certainly amateur astronomers, are not equipped with such clocks so there must be another way to ascertain the time on the TAI scale at any given instant. There is, and the relationship is that TAI differs from UTC by an integral number of seconds ΔAT. The value of ΔAT is readily available from the *International Earth Rotation Service Bulletin A*. As of August 1996, ΔAT = 30.0 seconds.

The relationship between UTC and UT1 is

$$\text{UT1} = \text{UTC} + \Delta\text{UT1} \qquad (2.3.1)$$

but the precise value of ΔUT1, published in the *IERS Bulletin A* is usually not known in advance of any observations. An approximation to ΔUT1, called DUT1, is transmitted with the standard UTC radio time signals. The value of DUT1 is encoded in the transmission as follows: UT1 leads UTC, the second markers of each minute are doubled beginning at the 1^s mark. The number of doubled markers indicates the number of tenths of a second UT1 is ahead of UTC. If UT1 lags UTC, the doubling of the second markers begins at the 9^s mark [RASC 1990]. This encoding applies to WWV and CHU as well as to most other time stations. As of 8 August 1996, DUT1 = +0.1 seconds and as of 3 October 1996, DUT1 = 0.0 seconds.

The precise relationship between TDT and UT1 is

$$\text{TDT} = \text{UT1} + \Delta\text{T} \qquad (2.3.2)$$

where ΔT is determined from Earth's motions through VLBI (Very Long Baseline Interferometry) or LLR (Lunar Laser Ranging). For optical observations, we can approximate ΔT by recalling that TDT differs from TAI by a constant offset of $32^s_.184$ so we can write

$$\text{TDT} = \text{UTC} + \Delta\text{AT} + 32^s_.184. \qquad (2.3.3)$$

But recall that UTC = UT1 − ΔUT1 so now we can finally write

$$\text{TDT} = \text{UT1} - \Delta\text{UT1} + \Delta\text{AT} + 32^s_.184 \qquad (2.3.4)$$

from which we can see that $\Delta T = \Delta AT + 32\overset{s}{.}184 - \Delta UT1$. Thus, at the time of this writing (August 1996), $\Delta T = 62\overset{s}{.}0$. The relationship between TDT and TDB is described in Section 2.2.2.

We can also approach the time scale relationships from the point of view of T_{eph} being Nature's most fundamental time scale. Take an atomic clock which measures SI seconds and put it at rest at the solar system barycenter (center of mass of the solar system) and shield it from the planets' gravitational potentials. The clock would keep TCB if synchronized with TT in 1977.0. If we now adjust the rate of the clock to keep time with TT, it will keep T_{eph}. It no longer measures SI seconds, but a different number of cesium 133 transitions per second.

Strictly speaking, all formulae in this book that require a uniform time scale should use T_{eph}. But we will (knowingly) erroneously use TDB instead, primarily for two reasons. First, TCB differs from T_{eph} by only a constant offset and a constant rate but the two are physically equivalent. TCB and TDB differ only slightly. Second, all published formulae still name the freely-flowing time argument TDB when they really should name it T_{eph}. For the purposes of this book, we shall neglect the very small differences between the two scales and adopt TDB as our freely-flowing time scale while keeping in mind that TDB is not actually a physically realizeable time scale at all. This approximation will suffice for all the most absolutely meticulous applications. The reader is directed to [Standish, 1998] and [Seidelmann, 1992a] for details.

2.4   Julian Day Numbers and Calendar Dates

The Julian day number is simply a continuous count of days (and fractions thereof) since Greenwich noon on 1 January 4713 BC. Note that the Julian day begins at noon, so at 0^h the fractional part of the Julian day number is 0.5. Technically, the time scale to which the Julian day number is referred should also be specified. This is because none of the above time scales coincide exactly. It follows that 2448990.5 TDT and 2448990.5 UT1 do **not** correspond to the same instant of time. One may also see the term *modified Julian day number* (MJD), which is defined as follows:

$$MJD = JD - 2400000.5. \qquad (2.4.1)$$

The MJD is a commonly used quantity in studies of Earth rotation and time systems. When the Julian day number is calculated on the TDT or TDB time scale, it is sometimes referred to as the *Julian ephemeris date* or JED.

When calculating the Julian day number on any time scale, one must take into account whether the given calendar date is on the Julian calendar or the Gregorian calendar. The Julian calendar was introduced by Julius Caesar in 46 BC to replace the Roman calendar. Every fourth year in the Julian calendar was a leap year of 366 days, while all other years had 365 days. The Gregorian calendar was introduced by Pope Gregory XIII in 1582 to replace the Julian calendar.[3] In this system, every year that is evenly divisible by four is a leap year with the exception of centurial years. Centurial years are leap years only if evenly divisible by 400. Any algorithm used to compute the Julian day number should be able to reconcile the difference between the two calendar systems.

Now we present the first subprogram for this chapter. It is called `Cal2JED` and its purpose is to take a date and time on the UTC time scale and to compute the JD or MJD on the UT1, UT2,[4] TDT, TDB, or UTC time scale. The source code listing for `Cal2JED` is as follows:

```
sub Cal2JED (m as integer, d as integer, y as integer, utc as double,_
             s as integer, tai_utc as double, ut1_utc as double,_
             w as integer, jed as double)

'----- Subprogram to compute the Julian date on the
'----- specified time scale.  The Julian day algorithm
'----- of Meeus is used, and the algorithm for converting
'----- to TDB is due to Hirayama et al. and can be found
'----- in REFERENCE FRAMES IN ASTRONOMY AND GEOPHYSICS ed.
'----- by Kovalevsky et al., 1989, pp. 439-442.
'----- Input:     m          month
'-----            d          day
'-----            y          year
'-----            utc        UTC as hh.mmssss
'-----            s          = 1 for UT1
'-----                       = 2 for UT2
'-----                       = 3 for TDT
'-----                       = 4 for TDB
'-----                       = 5 for UTC
'-----            tai_utc    TAI-UTC in seconds
'-----            ut1_utc    UT1-UTC in seconds
'-----            w          = 1 for MJD
'-----                       = 0 otherwise
'----- Output:    jed        appropriate JED
'-------------------------------------------------------------------

dim time   as double
dim datnum as double
dim a      as double
dim b      as double
dim term1  as double
dim corr   as double
dim t      as double

'----- Convert to decimal hours
time = deg(utc)

if m = 1 or m = 2 then
   y = y - 1
   m = m + 12
end if
```

---

[3]The whole story behind the Gregorian calendar reform is beyond the scope of this book.

[4]We include UT2 here because the formula for obtaining it from UT1 is available from the *IERS Bulletin A*.

```
'----- Test to see if date is in Gregorian calendar
'----- Converts date to a number of the form YYYY.MMDD
datnum = cdbl(y) + 0.01# * cdbl(m) + 0.0001# * cdbl(d)

if datnum >= 1582.1015# then    '----- Gregorian calendar
  a = fix(0.01# * cdbl(y))
  b = 2# - a + fix(0.24# * cdbl(a))
else                            '----- Julian calendar
  a = 0#
  b = 0#
end if
if y < 0 then  '----- Handles negative years
  term1 = fix(365.25# * cdbl(y) - 0.75#)
else
  term1 = fix(365.25# * cdbl(y))
end if

jed = term1 + fix(30.6001# * (cdbl(m) + 1#)) + cdbl(d)_
      + time / 24# + 1720994.5# + cdbl(b)

if s = 1 then                          '----- Convert to UT1
  corr = ut1_utc / 86400#
elseif s = 2 then                      '----- Convert to UT2
  '----- First convert to UT1
  corr = ut1_utc / 86400#
  jed = jed + corr
  '----- Compute date in Besselian years
  t = 2000# + (jed - 2451544.5333981#) / 365.242198781#
  corr =   0.022# * sin(2# * PI * t)_
          -0.012# * cos(2# * PI * t)_
          -0.006# * sin(4# * PI * t)_
          +0.007# * cos(4# * PI * t)
  corr = corr / 86400#
elseif s = 3 then                      '----- Convert to TDT
  corr = (tai_utc + 32.184#) / 86400#
elseif s = 4 then                      '----- Convert to TDB
  '----- First convert to TDT
  corr = (tai_utc + 32.184#) / 86400#
  jed = jed + corr
  t = (jed - J2000.0) / JulCty
  '----- Now compute the new correction in microseconds
  corr = 1656.675#       * sin((35999.3729# * t +  357.5287#) * D2R)_
       +   22.418#       * sin((32964.467#  * t +  246.199#)  * D2R)_
       +   13.84#        * sin((71998.746#  * t +  355.057#)  * D2R)_
       +    4.77#        * sin(( 3034.906#  * t +   25.463#)  * D2R)_
       +    4.677#       * sin((34777.259#  * t +  230.394#)  * D2R)_
       +   10.216# * t * sin((35999.373#  * t +  243.451#)  * D2R)_
       +    0.171# * t * sin((71998.746#  * t +  240.98#  )  * D2R)_
       +    0.027# * t * sin(( 1222.114#  * t +  194.661#)  * D2R)_
       +    0.027# * t * sin(( 3034.906#  * t +  336.061#)  * D2R)_
       +    0.026# * t * sin((  -20.186#  * t +    9.382#)  * D2R)_
       +    0.007# * t * sin((29929.562#  * t +  264.911#)  * D2R)_
       +    0.006# * t * sin((  150.678#  * t +   59.775#)  * D2R)_
       +    0.005# * t * sin(( 9037.513#  * t +  256.025#)  * D2R)_
       +    0.043# * t * sin((35999.373#  * t +  151.121#)  * D2R)

  '----- Convert from microseconds to seconds
  corr = corr * 0.000001#

  '----- Convert to days
  corr = corr / 86400#
elseif s = 5 then                      '----- Convert to UTC
  corr = 0#
end if

jed = jed + corr

'----- Return modified JED if requested
if w = 1 then jed = jed - 2400000.5#
```

```
end sub
```

While the subprogram is fully commented, some remarks are in order before we proceed. First, note that the time is *not* input as separate variables containing the hour, minute, and second. Instead, it is input as a *double precision number* in the form `hh.mmss`. A user-written function called `deg` converts a time in this format to the format `hh.hhhh`. In other words, `deg` performs a conversion from sexagesimal measure to decimal measure. Another user-written function called `dms` performs the reverse transformation. Source listings for these two functions are given in Chapter 9. Remember that the input time *must* be on the UTC time scale. UTC was chosen as the starting point for time conversions since it is immediately available from a range of sources (WWV, CHU, etc.). Furthermore, UTC often only varies from one's local time by an integral number of hours (sometimes, but rarely, half-hours).

The integer variable `S` indicates the time scale on which the JD is to be computed. For conversions to any time scale other than UTC, the double precision variables `TAI_UTC` and `UT1_UTC` must also be specified. Again, these are available from *IERS Bulletin A*. The integer variable `W` indicates whether the full JD or the MJD is to be computed. Finally, the required JD or MJD is returned in the double precision variable `JED`. The variable `PI` is the constant π, and the variable `D2R` is the conversion factor for converting degrees to radians. Note that the correction from TDT to TDB implements more terms than are necessary. In fact, for the purpose of using the JPL planetary ephemerides for optical observations, the first term is all that is needed. However, more terms are included here to illustrate the simplicity of the programming.

Since we now have a powerful routine for converting a calendar date to a Julian day number, we should be able to carry out the reverse computation. That is, we need a routine to convert a Julian day number to a calendar date. This is what the subprogram `JED2Cal` does. The source code listing for this subprogram is as follows:

```
sub JED2Cal(jed as double, yr as integer, mo as integer,_
            dy as integer, ti as double) static

    '----- Subprogram to convert a JED to an ordinary calendar date.
    '----- The algorithm is that of Meeus.
    '----- Input:   jed   Julian day number
    '----- Output:  yr    year
    '-----          mo    month
    '-----          dy    day
    '-----          ti    time of day in decimal hours
    '-----------------------------------------------------------------------

    dim jedz     as double
    dim z        as double
    dim f        as double
```

```
dim a         as double
dim b         as double
dim c         as double
dim d         as double
dim e         as double
dim alpha     as double
dim daywtime as double

if jed = jedz then exit sub

jedz = jed

z = fix(jed + 0.5#)
f = (jed + 0.5#) - z
if z < 2299161# then
  a = z
else
  alpha = fix((z - 1867216.25#) / 36524.25#)
  a = z + 1# + alpha - fix(0.25# * alpha)
end if

b = a + 1524#
c = fix((b - 122.1#) / 365.25#)
d = fix(365.25# * c)
e = fix((b - d) / 30.6001#)
daywtime = b - d - fix(30.6001# * e) + f
dy = fix(daywtime)
ti = 24# * (daywtime - cdbl(dy))

if e < 13.5# then mo = fix(e - 1#)
if e > 13.5# then mo = fix(e - 13#)
if mo > 2.5# then yr = fix(c - 4716#)
if mo < 2.5# then yr = fix(c - 4715#)

end sub
```

Note that JED2Cal does *not* perform any time scale conversions. Its only
purpose is to convert a Julian day number into a calendar date and time.
Also, note that the time returned in variable TI is expressed in decimal hours.
That is, it has the form hh.hhhh.

Following is a sample driver program illustrating how to use subprogram
Cal2JED. It is called JDTEST, and the source code listing is as follows:

```
'----- JDTEST.BAS

defdbl a-z

$include "\fecsoftb\astrolib.dec"
$include "\fecsoftb\constant.inc"
$include "\fecsoftb\cal2jed.bas"
$include "\fecsoftb\deg.bas"

dim month    as integer
dim day      as integer
dim year     as integer
dim utc      as double
dim tai_utc as double
dim ut1_utc as double
dim s        as integer
dim jed      as double
dim w        as integer
dim m        as string
dim jd(1 to 5) as double
```

```
cls
print "EXAMPLE DRIVER FOR Cal2JED"
print
input "month, day, year          ", month, day, year
input "enter UTC as hh.mmssss    ", utc
input "TAI-UTC in seconds        ", tai_utc
input "UT1-UTC in seconds        ", ut1_utc
input "Do you want MJD's (y/n)? ", m

if ucase$(m) = "Y" then
  w = 1
else
  w = 0
end if

for s = 1 to 5
  call Cal2jed(month,day,year,utc,s,tai_utc,ut1_utc,w,jed)
  jd(s) = jed
next s

print
if ucase$(m) = "Y" then
  print "MODIFIED JULIAN DATES ON ALL FIVE TIME SCALES:"
else
  print "JULIAN DATES FOR DIFFERENT TIME SCALES:"
end if
print
print using "#######.######## UT1"; jd(1)
print using "#######.######## UT2"; jd(2)
print using "#######.######## TDT"; jd(3)
print using "#######.######## TDB"; jd(4)
print using "#######.######## UTC"; jd(5)

print
print "OK"

end
```

Below is a typical screen created by JDTEST.

```
EXAMPLE DRIVER FOR Cal2JED

month, day, year        8,24,1995
enter UTC as hh.mmssss  5.3428123
TAI-UTC in seconds      29
UT1-UTC in seconds      -0.2
Do you want MJD's (y/n)? n

JULIAN DATES FOR DIFFERENT TIME SCALES:

2449953.73226763 UT1
2449953.73226742 UT2
2449953.73297809 TDT
2449953.73297808 TDB
2449953.73226994 UTC

OK
```

Notice that this program makes use of PowerBASIC's $include metastatement for loading the source code for subprograms. Also note that the path to each file is included. The absence of an explicit drive letter (e.g. d:)

implies that the directory `fecsoftb` is located off the current drive's root directory. This convention is followed throughout the book.

Before leaving this subject, we present two more useful subprograms that perform unique functions:

1. Subprogram `Epoch2JED` accepts as input a string that represents a Julian or Besselian epoch[5] and converts the string to the epoch's corresponding Julian day number. For example, J2000 would be converted to 2451545.0, and

2. Subprogram `JED2Epoch` performs the reverse computation. The user inputs a Julian day number, and a switch indicating whether a Julian epoch or a Besselian epoch is required. Then `JED2Epoch` returns a string representing the required epoch. For example, computing the Julian epoch corresponding to JD 2447344.625 would result in the string J1988.5 being returned.

The source code listings for `Epoch2JED` and `JED2Epoch` are as follows:

```
sub Epoch2JED(epoch as string, jed as double) static

    '----- Subprogram to convert an epoch to its corresponding JED.
    '----- Input:    epoch    J or B epoch
    '-----                    e.g. J2000
    '----- Output:   jed      appropriate JED
    '-------------------------------------------------------------------

    dim date as double

    epoch = ucase$(epoch)
    date = val(mid$(epoch, 2))

    if left$(epoch, 1) = "J" then
        '----- Julian epoch
        jed = (date - 2000#) * 365.25# + 2451545#
    else
        '----- Besselian epoch
        jed = (date - 1900#) * 365.242198781731# + 2415020.31352#
    end if

end sub

sub JED2Epoch(jed as double, s as string, epoch as string) static

    '----- Subprogram to convert a given JED to its corresponding Julian
    '----- or Besselian epoch.
    '----- For example, 2451545.0 becomes J2000.
    '----- Input:    jed      Julian day number
    '-----           s        J or B, whichever is desired
    '----- Output:   epoch    J or B epoch as a string
    '-------------------------------------------------------------------

    dim d    as string
    dim date as double
```

---

[5] A Besselian epoch is an instant specified by a system in which the year has a slowly varying number of days. Contrast this with a Julian epoch, which is an instant in a system in which a year has exactly 365.25 days and 100 such years is exactly 36525 days, or one Julian century.

```
if ucase$(s) = "J" then
   date = 2000# + (jed - 2451545#) / 365.25#
   d = str$(date)
else
   date = 1900# + (jed - 2415020.31352#) / 365.242198781731#
   d = str$(date)
end if

epoch = ucase$(s) + ltrim$(d)

end sub
```

2.5   More On Sidereal Time

Technically, sidereal time is the hour angle of the equinox. If the hour angle is referred to the Greenwich meridian, the sidereal time is called *Greenwich sidereal time*, which is abbreviated GST. If the hour angle is referred to the observer's local meridian, the sidereal time is called *local sidereal time*, abbreviated LST. For a given value of GST, one can compute one's LST by *algebraically adding* one's longitude (in hours) to the GST. Keep in mind that east longitudes are positive and west longitudes are negative. Sidereal time is affected by *nutation* (discussed in Chapter 3), and when this correction is taken into account, the sidereal time is called *apparent sidereal time*, in contrast to *mean sidereal time*, which is not corrected for nutation. This means that we can specify four different types of sidereal time: Greenwich mean sidereal time (GMST), Greenwich apparent sidereal time (GAST), local mean sidereal time (LMST), and local apparent sidereal time (LAST).

There are two beginning points for computing sidereal time. First, there is what may be called *"universal" sidereal time*, which is defined in terms of UT1 by a standard formula [Aoki 1982], which is written as follows:

$$\text{GMST at } 0^h UT1 = 24110\overset{s}{.}54841 + 8640184\overset{s}{.}812866T + 0\overset{s}{.}093104T^2 \\ - 6\overset{s}{.}2 \times 10^{-6}T^3. \tag{2.5.1}$$

In this formula, T is the time in Julian centuries since JD 2451545.0 UT1. In other words, $T = (\text{JD} - 2451545.0)/36525$ with JD being on the UT1 scale. Strictly, 2451545.0 should be 2451545.0 UT1 as well. Equation (2.5.1) has two minor inconveniences. First, it requires a knowledge of the UT1 time scale for any future date for which the Greenwich sidereal time is required.

Second, the equation only yields the GMST at 0^h UT1 on the given date. If one wants the GMST at 5^h UT1 on a certain date, one must first calculate the GMST at 0^h UT1 from equation (2.5.1), convert the remaining solar time interval between 0^h UT1 and 5^h UT1 to a sidereal interval through multiplication by a conversion factor, and then add this sidereal interval to the GMST at $0^{\rm h}$ UT1. Would it not be more expedient to have a single formula that yields the GMST at *any* time on a given date? Of course, the answer is "yes." However, such a formula comes with a minor complication. The time variable must be expressed on the TDB time scale. This is really not such an inconvenience, since all precession and nutation quantities, as well as ephemeris information, are also specified on the TDB scale. The required formula is from [Aoki 1982]:

$$\text{GMST} = 67310\overset{s}{.}54841 + (876600^{\rm h} + 8640184\overset{s}{.}812866)T + 0\overset{s}{.}093104T^2$$
$$- 6\overset{s}{.}2 \times 10^{-6}T^3.$$

$$(2.5.2)$$

Note again that in this equation, the variable T represents time in Julian centuries since JD 2451545.0 TDB. Since T is on the TDB scale, the GMST given by equation (2.5.1) is called *dynamical sidereal time*. This dynamical sidereal time is numerically equal to the corresponding "universal" sidereal time at a given instant, and the only advantage of equation (2.5.2) over equation (2.5.1) is that it is valid for all values of T, not just those that correspond to $0^{\rm h}$ UT1. By using equation (2.5.1) in a computer routine, one or two steps are eliminated, and thus time is saved.

The correction for nutation to be applied to mean sidereal time in order to derive apparent sidereal time is called the *equation of the equinoxes* and takes the form

$$\Delta\psi \cos\epsilon \qquad\qquad (2.5.3)$$

where $\Delta\psi$ is the *nutation in longitude* and ϵ is the *true obliquity of the ecliptic*. Both of these quantities are defined in Chapter 3.

We now present a subprogram called GetGST that accepts as input a Julian day number on the TDB scale and returns the dynamical sidereal time. A calling parameter s can also be specified. This parameter indicates whether mean or apparent sidereal time is computed. The source code listing for GetGST is as follows:

```
sub GetGST(jed as double, s as integer, gst as double) static

    '----- Subprogram to compute the Greenwich mean or
    '----- Greenwich apparent sidereal time, depending
    '----- on which is required.  Strictly speaking, the
    '----- computed time is the DYNAMICAL SIDEREAL TIME,
    '----- but for all practical purposes is the same as
    '----- the observed sidereal time.
    '----- Input: jed    Julian day number on TDB scale
    '-----         s       = 0 for mean sidereal time
    '-----                 = 1 for apparent sidereal time
    '----- Output: gst    GMST or GAST in radians
    '-------------------------------------------------------------------

    dim jedz    as double
    dim sz      as double
```

```
dim t          as double
dim dpsi       as double
dim deps       as double
dim dpsidot    as double
dim depsdot    as double
dim MeanEps    as double
dim TrueEps    as double
dim MeanEpsDot as double
dim TrueEpsDot as double
dim EqEqnx     as double
dim EqEqnxDot  as double

if ((jed = jedz) and (s = sz)) then exit sub

jedz = jed
sz = s

t = (jed - J2000.0) / JulCty

'----- Compute GMST in seconds
gst = 67310.54841# + t * ((876600# * 3600# + 8640184.812866#)_
            + t * (0.093104# + t * (-0.0000062#)))

'----- Convert to radians
gst = amodulo(gst / 3600#, 24#) * H2R

if s = 1 then
    '----- get nutation quantities
    call GetDpsiDeps(jed, dpsi, deps, dpsidot, depsdot)

    '----- get mean obliquity
    call Obliquity (J2000.0, jed, 0, MeanEps, MeanEpsDot)

    '----- get true obliquity
    call Obliquity (J2000.0, jed, 1, TrueEps, TrueEpsDot)

    '----- get equation of the equinoxes
    EqEqnx    = dpsi * cos(TrueEps)
    EqEqnxDot = dpsidot * cos(TrueEps) - dpsi * TrueEpsdot * sin(TrueEps)
    gst       = gst + EqEqnx
end if

gst = amodulo(gst, TWOPI)

end sub
```

Note that the underscore in the first line of the equation for GST simply indicates a continuation of that line. Also, the expression for ST will fit on one line within the PowerBASIC editor and is included here for typesetting purposes. Otherwise, the line would run off the printed page and would be difficult to read in a text editor or in the PowerBASIC editor. If apparent sidereal time is desired, the subprogram GetDpsiDeps, which computes the nutations in longitude and in obliquity along with their rates, is called. The equation of the equinoxes (and its rate) is calculated and stored in the variable EqEqnx. This correction is then applied to obtain the apparent sidereal time.

This routine uses a utility function called amodulo that reduces a given number to the range 0 to N, where N is the maximum value the number can have. For example, time is normally expressed in hours ranging from 0 to 24, so amodulo(27, 24) would reduce to 3. It also works for negative

arguments as well. For example, amodulo(-10, 360) would evaluate to 350.
The source code listing for amodulo is provided in Chapter 9. Note that the
variables R2A, H2R, and TWOPI are unit conversion constants and are declared
and initialized in the file constant.inc. R2A is the conversion factor from
radians to arcseconds. H2R is the conversion factor from hours to radians, and
TWOPI is the value of 2π.

Following is a sample driver program for subprogram GetGST. It is called
SIDTEST, and the source code listing is as follows:

```
'----- SIDTEST.BAS

defdbl a-z

$include "\fecsoftb\astrolib.dec"
$include "\fecsoftb\constant.inc"
$include "\fecsoftb\amodulo.bas"
$include "\fecsoftb\dround.bas"
$include "\fecsoftb\fmtdms.bas"
$include "\fecsoftb\funarg.bas"
$include "\fecsoftb\getgst.bas"
$include "\fecsoftb\nutation.bas"
$include "\fecsoftb\obliquty.bas"

dim i        as integer
dim jdate    as double
dim numsteps as integer
dim inc      as double
dim gmst     as double
dim gast     as double
dim f        as string

cls
print "EXAMPLE DRIVER FOR GetGST"
print

input "Enter starting Julian date on TDB scale  ", jdate

numsteps = 21
while numsteps > 15
  input "Enter number of steps (<= 15)  ", numsteps
wend

if numsteps > 1 then
  input "Enter increment in days  ", inc
else
  inc = 0#
end if
print

f = "JED #######.#  GMST \              \  GAST \              \"

i = 0
do
  call GetGST(jdate,0,gmst)
  gmst = gmst * R2H
  call GetGST(jdate,1,gast)
  gast = gast * R2H
  print using f; jdate; FmtDms(gmst,4,2); FmtDms(gast,4,2)
  incr jdate, inc
  incr i
loop until i = numsteps

print
print "OK"
```

end

This driver makes use of two other functions: amodulo and FmtDms. These are utility routines and are described in detail in Chapter 9. This is our first encounter with the function FmtDms. Its job is to convert decimal hours into hours, minutes, and seconds and decimal degrees into degrees, minutes, and seconds and properly format the output into a string variable. It even adds the appropriate unit symbols. The included file nutation.bas contains the routine for computing the nutations in longitude and obliquity, quantities to be described in detail in the next chapter. The included file funarg.bas is used by the nutation routine. Finally, obliquty.bas contains a subprogram that computes the mean obliquity of the ecliptic. The nutations and the mean obliquity are stored in global variables declared in the file constant.inc. A sample output screen for this program follows.

```
EXAMPLE DRIVER FOR GetGST

Enter starting Julian date on TDB scale    2447390.5
Enter number of steps (<= 15)   10
Enter increment in days   1

JED 2447390.5   GMST 21h42m21.2736s   GAST 21h42m21.5964s
JED 2447391.5   GMST 21h46m17.8290s   GAST 21h46m18.1458s
JED 2447392.5   GMST 21h50m14.3844s   GAST 21h50m14.6974s
JED 2447393.5   GMST 21h54m10.9397s   GAST 21h54m11.2517s
JED 2447394.5   GMST 21h58m07.4951s   GAST 21h58m07.8093s
JED 2447395.5   GMST 22h02m04.0505s   GAST 22h02m04.3698s
JED 2447396.5   GMST 22h06m00.6058s   GAST 22h06m00.9326s
JED 2447397.5   GMST 22h09m57.1612s   GAST 22h09m57.4960s
JED 2447398.5   GMST 22h13m53.7166s   GAST 22h13m54.0582s
JED 2447399.5   GMST 22h17m50.2719s   GAST 22h17m50.6171s

OK
```

Chapter 3

Precession and Nutation

3.1 Introduction

In this chapter, we demonstrate how to write compact, efficient, and accurate subprograms that provide coordinate corrections for general precession and nutation. Several subprograms, along with sample drivers, will also be detailed.

3.2 Obliquity of the Ecliptic

Put simply, the *obliquity of the ecliptic* is the angle measured *from* the plane of the celestial equator *to* the plane of the ecliptic. On the average, the obliquity of the ecliptic has a value of about $23°.5$, but it slowly changes with time. The following formula from [Lieske 1977] is used to compute the obliquity of the ecliptic for any time:

$$\bar{\epsilon} = 23°26'21''.448 - 46''.8150T - 0''.00059T^2 + 0''.001813T^3 \qquad (3.2.1)$$

where T is the time in Julian centuries from J2000.0 TDB. Mathematically, $T = (\text{JD} - 2451545)/36525$. Note that the JD should be on the TDB time scale.

The value of $\bar{\epsilon}$ given by equation (3.2.1) is called the *mean obliquity of the ecliptic*, and is strictly defined as the angle between the plane of the ecliptic of date and the plane of the mean equator of date. The adjective *mean* refers to the fact that corrections for nutation are not taken into account. In order to correct for nutation, we must add the quantity $\Delta\epsilon$ to the value of $\bar{\epsilon}$ given by equation (3.2.1). The resulting obliquity is called the *true obliquity of the ecliptic*. The quantity $\Delta\epsilon$, the *nutation in obliquity*, is discussed in Section 3.4 of this chapter.

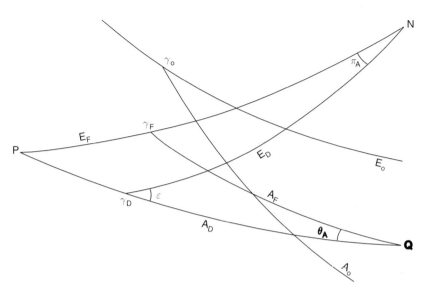

Figure 3.1. *Quantities related to precession:* T_o T_F T_D = *base epoch, arbitrary epoch, and epoch of date.* E_o E_F E_D = *ecliptics at the same epochs.* A_o A_F A_D = *equators at the same epochs.* γ_o γ_F γ_D = *equinoxes at the same epochs.* ϵ = *mean obliquity of ecliptic of date on equator of date.* z_A = $arc(\gamma_D Q - 90°)$, ζ_A = $arc(90° - \gamma_F Q), \theta_A$ = *angle between* A_F *and* A_D. π_A = *angle between* E_F *and* E_D, Π_A = arc $\gamma_F N$.

The following subprogram used to compute ϵ is called `Obliquity`, and its source code listing is as follows:

```
sub Obliquity(jed1 as double, jed2 as double, m as integer, obl as double,_
              obldot as double) static

    '----- Subprogram to compute the mean obliquity of the ecliptic
    '----- and its derivative using Lieske's formula.
    '----- Input:    jed1      initial Julian Date on the TDB scale
    '-----           jed2      final Julian Date on the TDB scale
    '-----           m         = 0 for mean obliquity
    '-----                     = 1 for true obliquity
    '----- Output:   obl       obliquity of the ecliptic in radians
    '-----           obldot    derivative in radians/day
    '-----------------------------------------------------------------------

    dim t1 as double
    dim t2 as double
    dim e0 as double
    dim e1 as double
    dim e2 as double
    dim e3 as double
    dim e4 as double
    dim e5 as double
    dim e6 as double
    dim EpsBar  as double
    dim dpsi    as double
    dim deps    as double
    dim dpsidot as double
    dim depsdot as double
```

```
t1 = (jed1 - J2000.0) / JulCty
t2 = (jed2 - jed1) / JulCty

e0 = 84381.448#
e1 =    -46.815#
e2 =     -0.00059#
e3 =      0.001813#
EpsBar = e0 + e1 * t1 + e2 * t1 * t1 + e3 * t1 * t1 * t1
e1 = -46.815#
e2 =    0.00117#
e3 =    0.005439#
e4 =   -0.00059#
e5 =    0.005439#
e6 =    0.001813#
obl = EpsBar + (e1 + t1 * (e2 + t1 * e3)) * t2 _
             + (e4 + e5 * t1) * t2 * t2 _
             + e6 * t2 * t2 * t2
obldot = e1 + t1 * (e2 + t1 * e3) _
            + 2# * (e4 + e5 * t1) * t2 _
            + 3# * e6 * t2 * t2

if m = 1 then
 '----- need true obliquity
   call GetDpsiDeps(jed2,dpsi,deps,dpsidot,depsdot)
   '----- unit conversion is needed because obl is
   '----- in arc seconds, nutations are in radians.
   obl = obl+deps*R2A
   obldot = obldot + depsdot*R2A
end if

'----- Convert to radians and radians/day
obl = obl * A2R
obldot = obldot * A2R / JulCty

end sub
```

Again, note that the underscored characters indicate a continuation of the current line. Obliquity requires two input parameters, the initial Julian day number and the final Julian day number, both of which must be on the TDB scale. The value of the mean obliquity of the ecliptic is returned in the double precision variable Obl. The time derivative of the mean obliquity is also computed and stored in OblDot. Since Obl has units of radians, its derivative has the units of radians per day.

3.3 Precession

Precession is one of the most important factors to consider in positional astronomy. To complicate matters, there are many variables associated with precession, and sometimes, as with the time systems, the terminology can get confusing. The best reference on the subject is the paper [Lieske 1977] which gives precise definitions of all the associated precessional quantities, as well as numerical expressions for all of the quantities. This paper is especially important because all of the numerical formulae in it are based on the 1976 IAU System of Astronomical Constants. A later paper by Lieske [Lieske 1979] introduces a small correction to one of the expressions in the 1977 paper. Both of these papers contain much practical information, and the author strongly urges the reader to refer to them for terminology and physical explanations.

There are two ways to handle precessional computations: 1) the trigonometric method and 2) the matrix method. Both methods rely on three parameters, which are denoted by ζ_A, z_A, and θ_A. These parameters have simple power series representations and are explicit functions of time. The numerical expressions for the precessional parameters are as follows [Lieske 1979]:

$$\zeta_A = (2306\rlap{.}''2181 + 1\rlap{.}''39656T - 0\rlap{.}''000139T^2)t \\ (+\ 0\rlap{.}''30188 - 0\rlap{.}''000344T)t^2 + 0\rlap{.}''017998t^3 \tag{3.3.1}$$

$$z_A = (2306\rlap{.}''2181 + 1\rlap{.}''39656T - 0\rlap{.}''000139T^2)t \\ (+\ 1\rlap{.}''09468 + 0\rlap{.}''000066T)t^2 + 0\rlap{.}''018203t^3 \tag{3.3.2}$$

$$\theta_A = (2004\rlap{.}''3109 - 0\rlap{.}''85330T - 0\rlap{.}''000217T^2)t \\ +\ (-0\rlap{.}''42665 - 0\rlap{.}''000217T)t^2 - 0\rlap{.}''041833t^3 \tag{3.3.3}$$

where
$$T = \frac{JD_1 - 2451545.0}{36525} \tag{3.3.4}$$

$$t = \frac{JD_2 - JD_1}{36525}. \tag{3.3.5}$$

With these definitions of T and t, we compute the precessional parameters for precessing *from* JD_1 to JD_2. Note that all Julian day numbers in these formulae should be on the TDB time scale.

We do not give the trigonometric formulae for precessional corrections because at best, these formulae are cumbersome to work with and even more cumbersome to program on a computer. Every popular programming language is capable of handling them, but the use of the trigonometric functions creates an undesirable effect—trig functions in a program take a relatively long time to evaluate. Furthermore, these transformation equations are in terms of equatorial polar coordinates, and it is much more convenient to work with equatorial rectangular coordinates. Hence, these equations are not the most efficient ones to use. Let us define a 3×3 *precession matrix* with the following elements [Lieske 1979]:

$$\mathbf{P}_{11} = \cos z_A \cos \theta_A \cos \zeta_A - \sin z_A \sin \zeta_A \tag{3.3.6}$$

$$\mathbf{P}_{12} = -\cos z_A \cos \theta_A \sin \zeta_A - \sin z_A \cos \zeta_A \tag{3.3.7}$$

$$\mathbf{P}_{13} = -\cos z_A \sin \theta_A \tag{3.3.8}$$

$$\mathbf{P}_{21} = \sin z_A \cos \theta_A \cos \zeta_A + \cos z_A \sin \zeta_A \qquad (3.3.9)$$

$$\mathbf{P}_{22} = -\sin z_A \cos \theta_A \sin \zeta_A + \cos z_A \cos \zeta_A \qquad (3.3.10)$$

$$\mathbf{P}_{23} = -\sin z_A \sin \theta_A \qquad (3.3.11)$$

$$\mathbf{P}_{31} = \sin \theta_A \cos \zeta_A \qquad (3.3.12)$$

$$\mathbf{P}_{32} = -\sin \theta_A \sin \zeta_A \qquad (3.3.13)$$

$$\mathbf{P}_{33} = \cos \theta_A. \qquad (3.3.14)$$

In the terminology of rotation matrices, this precession matrix can be elegantly defined in terms of the elementary *rotation matrices* with the formula

$$\mathbf{P} = \mathbf{R}_3(-90° - z_A)\mathbf{R}_1(\theta_A)\mathbf{R}_3(90° - \zeta_A) \qquad (3.3.15)$$

$$= \mathbf{R}_3(-z_A)\mathbf{R}_2(\theta_A)\mathbf{R}_3(-\zeta_A) \qquad (3.3.16)$$

where $\mathbf{R}_1, \mathbf{R}_2$, and $\mathbf{R}_3$ are matrices corresponding respectively to rotations about the x, y, and z axes in a right-handed coordinate system.

Recall that the rectangular coordinates of an object can be derived from the polar coordinates via

$$x = \cos \alpha \cos \delta \qquad (3.3.17)$$

$$y = \sin \alpha \cos \delta \qquad (3.3.18)$$

$$z = \sin \delta, \qquad (3.3.19)$$

where α and δ are, respectively, the object's right ascension and declination. These components form a unit vector in the direction of the object. Using matrix formulation, the equation that corrects for precession now becomes

$$\mathbf{r}_2 = \mathbf{P}\mathbf{r}_1 \qquad (3.3.20)$$

where the subscripts denote, respectively, the position vectors referred to the original and final equinoxes. The inverse transformation is rigorously given by

$$\mathbf{r}_1 = \mathbf{P}^{-1}\mathbf{r}_2 = \mathbf{P}^T\mathbf{r}_2. \qquad (3.3.21)$$

Because the precession matrix is orthogonal, its inverse is its transpose.[1] These simple matrix equations are much more straightforward to program than the trigonometric equations mentioned earlier. The corresponding computer code executes faster as well. The only trigonometric functions that must be used are the ones in the expressions for the elements of the matrix **P**.

Our subprogram GetPrecesParams accepts as input an initial Julian day number, JED1, and a final Julian day number, JED2, and computes the values of the precessional parameters for precession *from* JED1 *to* JED2. GetPrecessParams also computes the derivatives of the precessional quantities. Quantities and their derivatives are stored in global variables. The source code listing for GetPrecessParams (PRECESS.BAS) is as follows:

```
sub GetPrecessParams (jed1 as double, jed2 as double, zeta as double, z as _
    double, theta as double, zetadot as double, zdot as double, thetadot as _
    double) static

    '----- Subprogram that computes the general precession
    '----- parameters and their derivatives for precessing
    '----- equatorial rectangular coordinates and velocities
    '----- from jed1 to jed2.
    '----- Input:  jed1      initial Julian Date
    '-----         jed2      final Julian Date
    '----- Output: zeta      equatorial precession parameter
    '-----         z         equatorial precession parameter
    '-----         theta     equatorial precession parameter
    '-----         zetadot   derivative in rad/day
    '-----         zdot      derivative in rad/day
    '-----         thetadot  derivative in rad/day
    '-------------------------------------------------------------------

    dim t1   as double
    dim t2   as double
    dim c1   as double
    dim c2   as double
    dim c3   as double
    dim c4   as double
    dim c5   as double
    dim c6   as double
    dim p1   as double
    dim p2   as double
    dim x    as double
    dim xdot as double

    t1 = (jed1 - J2000.0) / JulCty
    t2 = (jed2 - jed1) / JulCty

    '----- Compute zeta, z, theta, zetadot, zdot, thetadot
    c1 = 2306.2181#: c2 =   1.39656# : c3 = -0.000139#
    c4 =    0.30188#: c5 = -0.000344#: c6 =   0.017998#
    gosub Evaluate
    zeta = x * A2R
    zetadot = xdot * A2R / JulCty
```

---

[1] The reader not familiar with these terms should consult any mathematical textbook in which matrices are discussed.

```
c1 = 2306.2181#:  c2 = 1.39656#  : c3 = -0.000139#
c4 =    1.09468#:  c5 = 0.000066#: c6 =   0.018203#
gosub Evaluate
z = x * A2R
zdot = xdot * A2R / JulCty

c1 = 2004.3109#:  c2 = -0.85330#  : c3 = -0.000217#
c4 =   -0.42665#:  c5 = -0.000217#: c6 = -0.041833#
gosub Evaluate
theta = x * A2R
thetadot = xdot * A2R / JulCty

exit sub

Evaluate:
    p1 = c1 + c2 * t1 + c3 * t1 * t1
    p2 = c4 + c5 * t1
    x = p1 * t2 + p2 * t2 * t2 + c6 * t2 * t2 * t2
    xdot = p1 + 2# * p2 * t2 + 3# * c6 * t2 * t2
    return

end sub
```

GetPrecessParams does not actually carry out the transformation of coordinates from JED1 to JED2. Rather, it computes the angles needed in the matrix that will transform the original position vector into the final one. Another subprogram is needed to evaluate the precession matrix, and yet another subprogram is needed to do the actual matrix/vector multiplication.

We now give a source code listing that illustrates how to incorporate GetPrecessParams into a program. Instead of explicitly computing the elements of the precession matrix, we adopt another method of carrying out the transformation. The following program makes use of the routine MRotate, which accepts as input an initial position vector, an integer specifying a coordinate axis (1 for x−axis, 2 for y−axis, and 3 for z−axis), and an angle in radians. The output is the original position vector rotated about the specified axis by the specified angle. Note from the program listing that the input and output position vectors can have the same name. Here is the source code listing for sample program PRETRAN:

```
'----- PRETRAN.BAS

defdbl a-z

$include "\fecsoftb\astrolib.dec"
$include "\fecsoftb\constant.inc"
$include "\fecsoftb\epoc2jed.bas"
$include "\fecsoftb\mrotate.bas"
$include "\fecsoftb\precess.bas"

dim pmat(1 to 3, 1 to 3)     as double
dim pmatdot(1 to 3, 1 to 3) as double
dim r1(1 to 3)               as double
dim r2(1 to 3)               as double
dim epoch1                   as string
dim epoch2                   as string
dim jed1                     as double
dim jed2                     as double
dim zeta                     as double
```

```
dim z                        as double
dim theta                    as double
dim zetadot                  as double
dim zdot                     as double
dim thetadot                 as double

cls
print "EXAMPLE DRIVER FOR GetPrecessParams"
print

input "Enter initial epoch or Julian date  ", epoch1
epoch1 = ucase$(epoch1)
input "Enter final epoch or Julian date    ", epoch2
epoch2 = ucase$(epoch2)

if left$(epoch1,1) = "J" or left$(epoch1,1) = "B" then
  call Epoch2JED(epoch1,jed1)
else
  jed1 = val(epoch1)
end if

if left$(epoch2,1) = "J" or left$(epoch2,1) = "B" then
  call Epoch2JED(epoch2,jed2)
else
  jed2 = val(epoch2)
end if

print "Enter initial position vector components (x,y,z)"
input "", r1(1), r1(2), r1(3)
print

print "INITIAL POSITION VECTOR COMPONENTS"
print using "+#.######### +#.######### +#.#########";r1(1);r1(2);r1(3)
print

'----- Compute the precessional angles
call GetPrecessParams(jed1,jed2,zeta,z,theta,zetadot,zdot,thetadot)

'----- Perform the matrix rotations one at a time.
'----- Note the order of application of the matrices.
call MRotate (r1(), 3, -zeta      , r1())
call MRotate (r1(), 2, theta      , r1())
call MRotate (r1(), 3, -z         , r2())

print "PRECESSED POSITION VECTOR COMPONENTS"
print using "+#.######### +#.######### +#.#########";r2(1);r2(2);r2(3)

print
print "OK"

end
```

This program prompts the user for the initial and final epochs. These quantities can be entered as Julian day numbers or as epochs such as J2000 or B1900. The user is then prompted to input the initial position vector components. The program then displays the initial position vector components and the precessed position vector components. In the source code for the MRotate, notice that the elements of the precession matrix are never explicitly evaluated. Instead, a direct application of the proper rotation matrices is employed. A typical output screen for program PRETRAN is shown below.

```
EXAMPLE DRIVER FOR GetPrecessParams

Enter initial epoch or Julian date   B1950
Enter final epoch or Julian date     J2000
Enter initial position vector components (x,y,z)
0.249874234, -0.42434984, -0.9987987

INITIAL POSITION VECTOR COMPONENTS
+0.2498742340 -0.4243498400 -0.9987987000

PRECESSED POSITION VECTOR COMPONENTS
+0.2594526176 -0.4215028652 -0.9975612445

OK
```

This numerical example is the one presented in [Lieske 1979]. The largest error in our example, compared to Lieske's numbers, is two digits in the last decimal place.

PROGRAMMING EXERCISE: Modify PRETRAN to print out the elements of the precession matrix. This will require some other routines for matrix multiplication discussed in Chapter 9.

3.4 Nutation

Closely related to precession is the phenomenon known as *nutation*, which arises from external gravitational forces acting on the Earth's pole. There are two components of nutation, which are termed the *nutation in obliquity* (denoted by the symbol $\Delta\epsilon$) and the *nutation in longitude* (denoted by the symbol $\Delta\psi$). Thus, nutation affects the value of the obliquity of the ecliptic by requiring that the quantity $\Delta\epsilon$ be added to the mean obliquity to derive the *true obliquity of the ecliptic*. The quantity $\Delta\psi$ must be added to the celestial longitude of an object in order to derive the apparent longitude of that object. Nutation has no effect on the ecliptic latitude of an object.

As mentioned in Chapter 2, nutation also affects the sidereal time such that the quantity $\Delta\psi\cos(\bar{\epsilon} + \Delta\epsilon)$ must be added to the mean sidereal time in order to derive the *apparent sidereal time*. The quantity $\Delta\psi\cos(\bar{\epsilon} + \Delta\epsilon)$ is termed the *equation of the equinoxes* or the *nutation in right ascension*.

As with precessional corrections, there are two methods of applying the corrections due to nutation to a given position vector—the trigonometric method and the matrix method. Again, the trigonometric method is cumbersome and inefficient, and the relevant formulae will not even be given here.[2] The matrix method is preferred, and in this case we will make use of

---

[2]To see them, the reader is advised to consult a textbook such as [Green 1985].

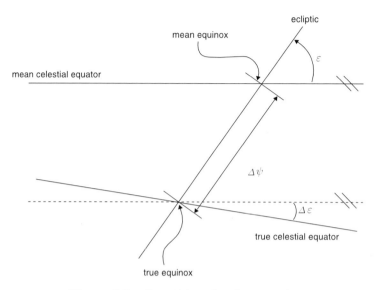

Figure 3.2. *Quantities related to nutation.*

a 3×3 *nutation matrix* which, when it operates on a position vector, will correct for nutation. The elements of the nutation matrix are functions of $\Delta\epsilon$, $\Delta\psi$, and $\bar{\epsilon}$. For their derivation, the reader is again referred to page 233 of [Green 1985]. Alternatively, the elements of the nutation matrix may be derived in a straightforward manner from the rigorous definition of the nutation matrix in terms of the elementary rotation matrices. The nutation matrix is defined as

$$\mathbf{N} = \mathbf{R}_1(-\bar{\epsilon} - \Delta\epsilon)\mathbf{R}_3(-\Delta\psi)\mathbf{R}_1(\bar{\epsilon}) \qquad (3.4.1)$$

where the elementary rotation matrices $\mathbf{R}_1, \mathbf{R}_2$, and $\mathbf{R}_3$ are defined in the previous section and in Chapter 4.

Subprogram `GetDpsiDeps` accepts as input a Julian day number on the TDB time scale and then computes the nutations in obliquity and longitude and their derivatives. All angular quantities are returned in radians, and the rates are in radians per day. The full precision IAU 1980 theory of nutation [Kaplan 1981] is utilized.

The source code listing for `GetDpsiDeps` (`NUTATION.BAS`) is as follows:

```
sub GetDpsiDeps(jed as double, dpsi as double, deps as double, _
           dpsidot as double, depsdot as double) static

   '----- Subprogram to compute dpsi, deps, dpsidot,
   '----- and depsdot.
   '----- Input:   jed        Julian day number on TDB scale
   '----- Output:  dpsi       nutation in longitude
   '-----          deps       nutation in obliquity
   '-----          dpsidot    derivative of dpsi in
```

```
'-----                          radians/day
'-----              depsdot    derivative of deps in
'-----                          radians/day
'--------------------------------------------------------------------------

dim jedZ          as double
dim NutTermsRead  as integer
dim nc(min,2)     as double
dim FunArg(min,1) as double
dim j             as integer
dim k             as integer
dim L             as double
dim Ldot          as double
dim lp            as double
dim lpdot         as double
dim f             as double
dim fdot          as double
dim d             as double
dim ddot          as double
dim n             as double
dim ndot          as double
dim LL            as double
dim LLdot         as double
dim t             as double
dim c1            as double
dim c2            as double
dim c3            as double
dim c4            as double
dim c5            as double
dim lamp          as double
dim oamp          as double
dim ls            as double
dim os            as double
dim arg           as double
dim argdot        as double

'----- Read the coefficients from the data statements
'----- only if not already done.
if (NutTermsRead = 0) then
  redim nc(1 to 106, 1 to 9)
  redim FunArg(1 to 12)
  restore Terms
  for j = 1 to 106
    for k = 1 to 9
      read nc(j,k)
    next k
  next j
  NutTermsRead = 1
end if

t = (jed - J2000.0) / JulCty

call FunArgIAU(jed, FunArg())
L  = FunArg(1) : Ldot  = FunArg(7)
lp = FunArg(2) : LPdot = FunArg(8)
f  = FunArg(3) : fdot  = FunArg(9)
d  = FunArg(4) : ddot  = FunArg(10)
n  = FunArg(5) : ndot  = FunArg(11)
LL = FunArg(6) : LLdot = FunArg(12)

'----- evaluate the series
dpsi = 0#        '----- initialize to zero
deps = 0#
dpsidot = 0#
depsdot = 0#
for j = 1 to 106
  lamp = nc(j,1)
  oamp = nc(j,3)
```

```
    ls = nc(j,2)
    os = nc(j,4)
    c1 = nc(j,5)
    c2 = nc(j,6)
    c3 = nc(j,7)
    c4 = nc(j,8)
    c5 = nc(j,9)
    arg = c1 * L + c2 * LP + c3 * F + c4 * D + c5 * N
    arg = amodulo(arg, TWOPI)
    dpsi = dpsi + (lamp + ls * t) * sin(arg)
    deps = deps + (oamp + os * t) * cos(arg)
    argdot = c1 * Ldot + c2 * LPdot + c3 * fdot + c4 * ddot + c5 * ndot
    argdot = amodulo(argdot, TWOPI)
    dpsidot = dpsidot + (lamp + ls * t) * argdot * cos(arg)_
                      + ls * sin(arg) / JulCty
    depsdot = depsdot - (oamp + os * t) * argdot * sin(arg)_
                      + os * cos(arg) / JulCty
  next j

  '----- normalize and convert units
  dpsi = dpsi * 0.0001# * A2R
  deps = deps * 0.0001# * A2R
  dpsidot = dpsidot * 0.0001# * A2R
  depsdot = depsdot * 0.0001# * A2R

'----- coefficients for IAU 1980 nutation theory
Terms:
  data -171996#, -174.2#, 92025#, 8.9#,  0#, 0#, 0#, 0#, 1#
  data    2062#,    0.2#,  -895#, 0.5#,  0#, 0#, 0#, 0#, 2#
  data      46#,      0#,   -24#,   0#, -2#, 0#, 2#, 0#, 1#
  data      11#,      0#,     0#,   0#,  2#, 0#,-2#, 0#, 0#
  data      -3#,      0#,     1#,   0#, -2#, 0#, 2#, 0#, 2#
  data      -3#,      0#,     0#,   0#,  1#,-1#, 0#,-1#, 0#
  data      -2#,      0#,     1#,   0#,  0#,-2#, 2#,-2#, 1#
  data       1#,      0#,     0#,   0#,  2#, 0#,-2#, 0#, 1#
  data  -13187#,   -1.6#,  5736#,-3.1#,  0#, 0#, 2#,-2#, 2#
  data    1426#,   -3.4#,    54#,-0.1#,  0#, 1#, 0#, 0#, 0#
  data    -517#,    1.2#,   224#,-0.6#,  0#, 1#, 2#,-2#, 2#
  data     217#,   -0.5#,   -95#, 0.3#,  0#,-1#, 2#,-2#, 2#
  data     129#,    0.1#,   -70#,   0#,  0#, 0#, 2#,-2#, 1#
  data      48#,      0#,     1#,   0#,  2#, 0#, 0#,-2#, 0#
  data     -22#,      0#,     0#,   0#,  0#, 0#, 2#,-2#, 0#
  data      17#,   -0.1#,     0#,   0#,  0#, 2#, 0#, 0#, 0#
  data     -15#,      0#,     9#,   0#,  0#, 1#, 0#, 0#, 1#
  data     -16#,    0.1#,     7#,   0#,  0#, 2#, 2#,-2#, 2#
  data     -12#,      0#,     6#,   0#,  0#,-1#, 0#, 0#, 1#
  data      -6#,      0#,     3#,   0#, -2#, 0#, 0#, 2#, 1#
  data      -5#,      0#,     3#,   0#,  0#,-1#, 2#,-2#, 1#
  data       4#,      0#,    -2#,   0#,  2#, 0#, 0#,-2#, 1#
  data       4#,      0#,    -2#,   0#,  0#, 1#, 2#,-2#, 1#
  data      -4#,      0#,     0#,   0#,  1#, 0#, 0#,-1#, 0#
  data       1#,      0#,     0#,   0#,  2#, 1#, 0#,-2#, 0#
  data       1#,      0#,     0#,   0#,  0#, 0#,-2#, 2#, 1#
  data      -1#,      0#,     0#,   0#,  0#, 1#,-2#, 2#, 0#
  data       1#,      0#,     0#,   0#,  0#, 1#, 0#, 0#, 2#
  data       1#,      0#,     0#,   0#, -1#, 0#, 0#, 1#, 1#
  data      -1#,      0#,     0#,   0#,  0#, 1#, 2#,-2#, 0#
  data   -2274#,   -0.2#,   977#,-0.5#,  0#, 0#, 2#, 0#, 2#
  data     712#,    0.1#,    -7#,   0#,  1#, 0#, 0#, 0#, 0#
  data    -386#,   -0.4#,   200#,   0#,  0#, 0#, 2#, 0#, 1#
  data    -301#,      0#,   129#,-0.1#,  1#, 0#, 2#, 0#, 2#
  data    -158#,      0#,    -1#,   0#,  1#, 0#, 0#,-2#, 0#
  data     123#,      0#,   -53#,   0#, -1#, 0#, 2#, 0#, 2#
  data      63#,      0#,    -2#,   0#,  0#, 0#, 0#, 2#, 0#
  data      63#,    0.1#,   -33#,   0#,  1#, 0#, 0#, 0#, 1#
  data     -58#,   -0.1#,    32#,   0#, -1#, 0#, 0#, 0#, 1#
  data     -59#,      0#,    26#,   0#, -1#, 0#, 2#, 2#, 2#
  data     -51#,      0#,    27#,   0#,  1#, 0#, 2#, 0#, 1#
```

```
data      -38#,       0#,      16#,      0#,     0#,   0#,   2#,   2#,   2#
data       29#,       0#,      -1#,      0#,     2#,   0#,   0#,   0#,   0#
data       29#,       0#,     -12#,      0#,     1#,   0#,   2#,  -2#,   2#
data      -31#,       0#,      13#,      0#,     2#,   0#,   2#,   0#,   2#
data       26#,       0#,      -1#,      0#,     0#,   0#,   2#,   0#,   0#
data       21#,       0#,     -10#,      0#,    -1#,   0#,   2#,   0#,   1#
data       16#,       0#,      -8#,      0#,    -1#,   0#,   0#,   2#,   1#
data      -13#,       0#,       7#,      0#,     1#,   0#,   0#,  -2#,   1#
data      -10#,       0#,       5#,      0#,    -1#,   0#,   2#,   2#,   1#
data       -7#,       0#,       0#,      0#,     1#,   1#,   0#,  -2#,   0#
data        7#,       0#,      -3#,      0#,     0#,   1#,   2#,   0#,   2#
data       -7#,       0#,       3#,      0#,     0#,  -1#,   2#,   0#,   2#
data       -8#,       0#,       3#,      0#,     1#,   0#,   2#,   2#,   2#
data        6#,       0#,       0#,      0#,     1#,   0#,   0#,   2#,   0#
data        6#,       0#,      -3#,      0#,     2#,   0#,   2#,  -2#,   2#
data       -6#,       0#,       3#,      0#,     0#,   0#,   0#,   2#,   1#
data       -7#,       0#,       3#,      0#,     0#,   0#,   2#,   2#,   1#
data        6#,       0#,      -3#,      0#,     1#,   0#,   2#,  -2#,   1#
data       -5#,       0#,       3#,      0#,     0#,   0#,   0#,  -2#,   1#
data        5#,       0#,       0#,      0#,     1#,  -1#,   0#,   0#,   0#
data       -5#,       0#,       3#,      0#,     2#,   0#,   2#,   0#,   1#
data       -4#,       0#,       0#,      0#,     0#,   1#,   0#,  -2#,   0#
data        4#,       0#,       0#,      0#,     1#,   0#,  -2#,   0#,   0#
data       -4#,       0#,       0#,      0#,     0#,   0#,   0#,   1#,   0#
data       -3#,       0#,       0#,      0#,     1#,   1#,   0#,   0#,   0#
data        3#,       0#,       0#,      0#,     1#,   0#,   2#,   0#,   0#
data       -3#,       0#,       1#,      0#,     1#,  -1#,   2#,   0#,   2#
data       -3#,       0#,       1#,      0#,    -1#,  -1#,   2#,   2#,   2#
data       -2#,       0#,       1#,      0#,    -2#,   0#,   0#,   0#,   1#
data       -3#,       0#,       1#,      0#,     3#,   0#,   2#,   0#,   2#
data       -3#,       0#,       1#,      0#,     0#,  -1#,   2#,   2#,   2#
data        2#,       0#,      -1#,      0#,     1#,   1#,   2#,   0#,   2#
data       -2#,       0#,       1#,      0#,    -1#,   0#,   2#,  -2#,   1#
data        2#,       0#,      -1#,      0#,     2#,   0#,   0#,   0#,   1#
data       -2#,       0#,       1#,      0#,     1#,   0#,   0#,   0#,   2#
data        2#,       0#,       0#,      0#,     3#,   0#,   0#,   0#,   0#
data        2#,       0#,      -1#,      0#,     0#,   0#,   2#,   1#,   2#
data        1#,       0#,      -1#,      0#,    -1#,   0#,   0#,   0#,   2#
data       -1#,       0#,       0#,      0#,     1#,   0#,   0#,  -4#,   0#
data        1#,       0#,      -1#,      0#,    -2#,   0#,   2#,   2#,   2#
data       -2#,       0#,       1#,      0#,    -1#,   0#,   2#,   4#,   2#
data       -1#,       0#,       0#,      0#,     2#,   0#,   0#,  -4#,   0#
data        1#,       0#,      -1#,      0#,     1#,   1#,   2#,  -2#,   2#
data       -1#,       0#,       1#,      0#,     1#,   0#,   2#,   2#,   1#
data       -1#,       0#,       1#,      0#,    -2#,   0#,   2#,   4#,   2#
data        1#,       0#,       0#,      0#,    -1#,   0#,   4#,   0#,   2#
data        1#,       0#,       0#,      0#,     1#,  -1#,   0#,  -2#,   0#
data        1#,       0#,      -1#,      0#,     2#,   0#,   2#,  -2#,   1#
data       -1#,       0#,       0#,      0#,     2#,   0#,   2#,   2#,   2#
data       -1#,       0#,       0#,      0#,     1#,   0#,   0#,   2#,   1#
data        1#,       0#,       0#,      0#,     0#,   0#,   4#,  -2#,   2#
data        1#,       0#,       0#,      0#,     3#,   0#,   2#,  -2#,   2#
data       -1#,       0#,       0#,      0#,     1#,   0#,   2#,  -2#,   0#
data        1#,       0#,       0#,      0#,     0#,   1#,   2#,   0#,   1#
data        1#,       0#,       0#,      0#,    -1#,  -1#,   0#,   2#,   1#
data       -1#,       0#,       0#,      0#,     0#,   0#,  -2#,   0#,   1#
data       -1#,       0#,       0#,      0#,     0#,   0#,   2#,  -1#,   2#
data       -1#,       0#,       0#,      0#,     0#,   1#,   0#,   2#,   0#
data       -1#,       0#,       0#,      0#,     1#,   0#,  -2#,  -2#,   0#
data       -1#,       0#,       0#,      0#,     0#,  -1#,   2#,   0#,   1#
data       -1#,       0#,       0#,      0#,     1#,   1#,   0#,  -2#,   1#
data       -1#,       0#,       0#,      0#,     1#,   0#,  -2#,   2#,   0#
data        1#,       0#,       0#,      0#,     2#,   0#,   0#,   2#,   0#
data       -1#,       0#,       0#,      0#,     0#,   0#,   2#,   4#,   2#
data        1#,       0#,       0#,      0#,     0#,   1#,   0#,   1#,   0#
'----- end of IAU 1980 nutation coefficients

end sub
```

There are some noteworthy points about this subprogram. First of all, it makes use of the function `amodulo`. In this case, `amodulo` is used to reduce angular variables to the range 0 to 2π radians. Second, `GetDpsiDeps` calls subprogram `FunArgIAU` to compute the fundamental angles that appear in the expressions for `DPSI` and `DEPS`. Also, just like `GetPrecessParams`, `GetDpsiDeps` only computes the angles required for the rotation matrix needed to correct for nutation. Finally, the `DATA` statements are read only one time, and that is on the initial call to this routine. On subsequent calls, the coefficients are retained in memory because of the `static` keyword in the subprogram's first line.

It is important to remember that `GetDpsiDeps` is only used to compute angles needed for the nutation matrix to correct equatorial, not ecliptic, coordinates. If we wish to work instead in the ecliptic system, the correction for nutation takes on an especially simple form. If we look at equation (3.4.1) and remember that matrix equations should be interpreted from right to left, we see that the equatorial nutation correction consists of a rotation about the x-axis through the angle ϵ, a rotation about the z-axis through the angle $-\Delta\psi$, and a final rotation about the x-axis through the angle $-(\bar{\epsilon} + \Delta\epsilon)$. The first and third rotations respectively serve to rotate into and out of the ecliptic system, where the middle rotation actually takes place. Therefore, we can see that the ecliptic nutation correction consists of only one simple rotation, and the expression for the corresponding nutation matrix becomes

$$\mathbf{N} = \mathbf{R}_3(-\Delta\psi). \qquad (3.4.2)$$

Below is the listing for a simple driver for `GetDpsiDeps`, which prompts the user for a Julian day number (on the TDB scale of course) and then displays the various nutation parameters. The mean and true obliquities are also displayed. The listing for program `NUTTEST` is as follows:

```
'----- NUTTEST.BAS

defdbl a-z

$include "\fecsoftb\astrolib.dec"
$include "\fecsoftb\constant.inc"
$include "\fecsoftb\amodulo.bas"
$include "\fecsoftb\dround.bas"
$include "\fecsoftb\fmtdms.bas"
$include "\fecsoftb\funarg.bas"
$include "\fecsoftb\nutation.bas"
$include "\fecsoftb\obliquty.bas"

dim jdate     as double
dim NumSteps  as integer
dim inc       as double
dim Which     as integer
dim i         as integer
dim m         as string
dim t         as string
dim dpsi      as double
dim deps      as double
dim dpsidot   as double
```

```
dim depsdot   as double
dim MeanEps   as double
dim TrueEps   as double
dim MeanEpsDot as double
dim TrueEpsDot as double
dim TEps      as double
dim MEps      as double
dim de        as string
dim dp        as string

cls
print "EXAMPLE DRIVER FOR GetDpsiDeps"
print

input "Enter Julian date on TDB scale  ", jdate
do
   input "Enter number of steps (<= 15)   ", NumSteps
loop until NumSteps <= 20

if NumSteps >= 1 then
   input "Enter increment in days  ", inc
else
   NumSteps = 0
end if

print        "  JED        Mean Obl.   True     dpsi      deps"
print        "----------------------------------------------------------"

i = 0
do

   '----- get nutation parameters
   call GetDpsiDeps(jdate,dpsi,deps,dpsidot,depsdot)
   '----- get mean obliquity
   call Obliquity(J2000.0,jdate,0,MeanEps,MeanEpsDot)
   '----- get true obliquity
   call Obliquity(J2000.0,jdate,1,TrueEps,TrueEpsDot)

   TEps = TrueEps * R2D
   MEps = MeanEps * R2D
   dpsi = dpsi * R2D
   deps = deps * R2D

   m = FmtDms(MEps,3,1)
   t = right$(FmtDms(TEps,3,1),7)
   dp = FmtDms(dpsi,4,1)
   dp = left$(dp,1)+right$(dp,8)
   de = FmtDms(deps,4,1)
   de = left$(de,1)+right$(de,8)

   print using "#######.# \          \ \    \ \       \ \       \"; _
        jdate, m, t, dp, de

   jdate = jdate + inc
   incr i

loop until i = NumSteps

print
print "OK"

end
```

The program is straightforward and will reproduce the same data given in Section B of the *Astronomical Almanac*. Note that NUTTEST makes use of utility routines amodulo and FmtDms. The source code listings for these rou-

tines are given in Chapter 9. Below is a typical input screen from program
NUTTEST.

```
EXAMPLE DRIVER FOR GetDpsiDeps

Enter Julian date on TDB scale   2447780.5
Enter number of steps (<= 15)    15
Enter increment in days   1
   JED        Mean Obl.    True    DPSI      DEPS
-----------------------------------------------------
2447780.5  +23d26'26.273"  34.162"  +10.2869"  +07.8892"
2447781.5  +23d26'26.272"  34.209"  +10.3343"  +07.9374"
2447782.5  +23d26'26.270"  34.267"  +10.3328"  +07.9966"
2447783.5  +23d26'26.269"  34.323"  +10.2702"  +08.0536"
2447784.5  +23d26'26.268"  34.361"  +10.1514"  +08.0929"
2447785.5  +23d26'26.267"  34.369"  +10.0006"  +08.1019"
2447786.5  +23d26'26.265"  34.342"  +09.8560"  +08.0768"
2447787.5  +23d26'26.264"  34.288"  +09.7550"  +08.0241"
2447788.5  +23d26'26.263"  34.221"  +09.7206"  +07.9587"
2447789.5  +23d26'26.262"  34.160"  +09.7535"  +07.8980"
2447790.5  +23d26'26.260"  34.116"  +09.8349"  +07.8562"
2447791.5  +23d26'26.259"  34.099"  +09.9358"  +07.8404"
2447792.5  +23d26'26.258"  34.108"  +10.0266"  +07.8503"
2447793.5  +23d26'26.256"  34.137"  +10.0840"  +07.8802"
2447794.5  +23d26'26.255"  34.177"  +10.0936"  +07.9215"

OK
```

The program MICA[3] confirms these values for this date. Note the form of
the values of the mean and true obliquity. Note that when the program is
actually executed, the d's will actually appear as degree symbols.

In actual applications, the corrections for precession and nutation can be
combined into a single correction that involves only one matrix instead of
both $\mathbf{P}$ and $\mathbf{N}$. This matrix is denoted by $\mathbf{R}$ and is defined as the product
$\mathbf{NP}$. Note that this is a matrix multiplication. Careful consideration reveals
this combination to be rather intuitive. In practice, one first corrects for
precession to refer the coordinates to the mean equator and equinox of date.
Then, one corrects for nutation to refer the coordinates to the true equator
of date. Thus, one first operates on the initial coordinate vector with $\mathbf{P}$
and then with $\mathbf{N}$. As defined above, $\mathbf{R}$ performs these same two operations
on the initial vector. Recall that, in general, matrix multiplication is *not
commutative*. In other words, the product $\mathbf{PN}$ is not, in general, equal to the
product $\mathbf{NP}$; care must be taken to define $\mathbf{R}$ as $\mathbf{NP}$ and not as $\mathbf{PN}$.

With these thoughts in mind, we can write an efficient subprogram that
will compute the elements of the $\mathbf{R}$ matrix, the $\mathbf{P}$ matrix, or the $\mathbf{N}$ matrix
as specified by the user. The elements of the $\mathbf{R}$ matrix are also presented
in Section B of the *Astronomical Almanac*. This subprogram is GetRPNmat
(GETRPN.BAS), and its source code listing is as follows:

---

[3]MICA is the *Multiyear Interactive Computer Almanac 1990–2005* program developed by
the U.S. Naval Observatory for both the IBM-PC and Macintosh computers and published
by Willmann-Bell.

```
sub GetRPNmat(jed1 as double, jed2 as double, rpn as integer, d as _
              integer, m3() as double, m6() as double) static

    '----- Subprogram to compute the nutation matrix, the
    '----- precession matrix, or the combined R matrix
    '----- for equatorial coordinates.
    '----- Input:  jed1    initial JED on TDB scale
    '-----         jed2    final JED on TDB scale
    '-----         rpn     = 1 for precession matrix
    '-----                 = 2 for nutation matrix
    '-----                 = 3 for R matrix
    '-----         d       = 1 for 3X3 matrix
    '-----                 = 2 for 6X6 Qmatrix
    '----- Output: m3()    requested 3X3 matrix
    '-----         m6()    requested 6X6 matrix
    '-------------------------------------------------------------------------

    dim p1mat(min,2)  as double
    dim p2mat(min,2)  as double
    dim p3mat(min,2)  as double
    dim pmat(min,2)   as double
    dim n1mat(min,2)  as double
    dim n2mat(min,2)  as double
    dim n3mat(min,2)  as double
    dim nmat(min,2)   as double
    dim rmat(min,2)   as double
    dim p(min,2)      as double
    dim n(min,2)      as double
    dim dpsi          as double
    dim deps          as double
    dim dpsidot       as double
    dim depsdot       as double
    dim MeanEps       as double
    dim TrueEps       as double
    dim MeanEpsDot    as double
    dim TrueEpsDot    as double
    dim zeta          as double
    dim zetadot       as double
    dim z             as double
    dim zdot          as double
    dim theta         as double
    dim thetadot      as double

    select case rpn
      case 1
        '----- compute precession matrix
        redim p1mat (1 to 6, 1 to 6)
        redim p2mat (1 to 6, 1 to 6)
        redim p3mat (1 to 6, 1 to 6)
        redim pmat  (1 to 6, 1 to 6)

        call GetPrecessParams(jed1,jed2,zeta,z,theta,zetadot,zdot,thetadot)
        call GetQMatrix(-zeta,-zetadot,3,0,p1mat())
        call GetQMatrix(theta,thetadot,2,0,p2mat())
        call GetQMatrix(-z,-zdot,3,0,p3mat())
        call MatXMat(p2mat(),p1mat(),pmat(),6,6,6)
        call MatXMat(p3mat(),pmat(),m3(),6,6,6)

      case 2
        '----- compute nutation matrix
        redim n1mat (1 to 6, 1 to 6)
        redim n2mat (1 to 6, 1 to 6)
        redim n3mat (1 to 6, 1 to 6)
        redim nmat  (1 to 6, 1 to 6)

        call GetDpsiDeps (jed2, dpsi, deps, dpsidot, depsdot)
        call Obliquity(jed1,jed2,0,MeanEps,MeanEpsDot)
```

```
      call Obliquity(jed1,jed2,1,TrueEps,TrueEpsDot)
      call GetQMatrix(MeanEps,MeanEpsDot,1,0,n1mat())
      call GetQMatrix(-dpsi,-dpsidot,3,0,n2mat())
      call GetQMatrix(-TrueEps,-TrueEpsDot,1,0,n3mat())
      call MatXMat(n2mat(),n1mat(),nmat(),6,6,6)
      call MatXMat(n3mat(),nmat(),m3(),6,6,6)

   case 3
      '----- compute R matrix
      redim p1mat (1 to 6, 1 to 6)
      redim p2mat (1 to 6, 1 to 6)
      redim p3mat (1 to 6, 1 to 6)
      redim pmat  (1 to 6, 1 to 6)
      redim n1mat (1 to 6, 1 to 6)
      redim n2mat (1 to 6, 1 to 6)
      redim n3mat (1 to 6, 1 to 6)
      redim nmat  (1 to 6, 1 to 6)
      redim rmat  (1 to 6, 1 to 6)
      redim P     (1 to 6, 1 to 6)
      redim N     (1 to 6, 1 to 6)

      call GetPrecessParams(jed1,jed2,zeta,z,theta,zetadot,zdot,thetadot)
      call GetQMatrix(-zeta,-zetadot,3,0,p1mat())
      call GetQMatrix(theta,thetadot,2,0,p2mat())
      call GetQMatrix(-z,-zdot,3,0,p3mat())
      call MatXMat(p2mat(),p1mat(),pmat(),6,6,6)
      call MatXMat(p3mat(),pmat(),p(),6,6,6)
      call GetDpsiDeps (jed2,dpsi,deps,dpsidot,depsdot)
      call Obliquity(jed1,jed2,0,MeanEps,MeanEpsDot)
      call Obliquity(jed1,jed2,1,TrueEps,TrueEpsDot)
      call GetQMatrix(MeanEps,MeanEpsDot,1,0,n1mat())
      call GetQMatrix(-dpsi,-dpsidot,3,0,n2mat())
      call GetQMatrix(-TrueEps,-TrueEpsDot,1,0,n3mat())
      call MatXMat(n2mat(),n1mat(),nmat(),6,6,6)
      call MatXMat(n3mat(),nmat(),n(),6,6,6)

      call MatXMat(n(),p(),m3(),6,6,6)

   end select

 end sub
```

This is a complicated subprogram, and it would be beneficial to point out some details at this time. First, notice that the input consists of initial and final Julian day numbers on the TDB time scale, an integer flag to specify which matrix is to be returned, and another integer that specifies whether a 3×3 or a 6×6 matrix is to be returned. The use of a 6×6 matrix is covered in Chapter 9. Basically, the ordinary 3×3 matrices we have discussed up to this point are sub-matrices of the larger matrices. The specific purpose of the 6×6 matrices is in the application of precessional and nutational effects to *state vectors* as opposed to *position vectors*. The state vector of an object is a six-dimensional vector in which the first three elements are the position components and the final three elements are the velocity components. Again, this is covered in detail in Chapter 9. Second, note the extensive use of routines designed for matrix manipulation. The subprograms GetQMatrix and MatXMat are also presented and discussed in Chapter 9.

Here is a driver program that makes use of GetRPNmat. The user enters the appropriate Julian day numbers and selects which matrix to return and the requested 6×6 matrix is computed and displayed. The listing for program RPNMAT is as follows:

```
'----- RPNMAT.BAS

defdbl a-z

$include "\fecsoftb\astrolib.dec"
$include "\fecsoftb\constant.inc"
$include "\fecsoftb\amodulo.bas"
$include "\fecsoftb\funarg.bas"
$include "\fecsoftb\getqm.bas"
$include "\fecsoftb\getrpn.bas"
$include "\fecsoftb\matxmat.bas"
$include "\fecsoftb\nutation.bas"
$include "\fecsoftb\obliquty.bas"
$include "\fecsoftb\precess.bas"
$include "\fecsoftb\rotmat.bas"

dim jed1                 as double
dim jed2                 as double
dim pmat(1 to 6,1 to 6)  as double
dim m6(1 to 6,1 to 6)    as double
dim i                    as integer
dim Which                as integer

cls
print "EXAMPLE DRIVER FOR GetRPNmat"
print

input "enter JED1 on TDB scale  ", jed1
input "enter JED2 on TDB scale  ", jed2
input "[1] Precession [2] Nutation [3] Combined  ", Which
print

call GetRPNmat(jed1,jed2,Which,1,pmat(),m6())

for i = 1 to 6
  print using "+#.######## +#.######## +#.######## +#.######## +#.########_
  +#.########";    pmat(i,1);pmat(i,2);pmat(i,3);pmat(i,4);pmat(i,5);pmat(i,6)
next i

print
print "OK"

end
```

Here is a sample output screen from three different runs of program RPNMAT showing the computation of all three matrices for a given Julian day number.

```
EXAMPLE DRIVER FOR GetRPNmat

enter JED1 on TDB scale  2451545
enter JED2 on TDB scale  2447160.5
(1)Precession (2)Nutation (3)Combined  1

+0.99999572 +0.00268422 +0.00116649 +0.00000000 +0.00000000 +0.00000000
-0.00268422 +0.99999640 -0.00000157 +0.00000000 +0.00000000 +0.00000000
-0.00116649 -0.00000157 +0.99999932 +0.00000000 +0.00000000 +0.00000000
+0.00000000 +0.00000000 +0.00000000 +0.99999572 +0.00268422 +0.00116649
+0.00000000 +0.00000000 +0.00000000 -0.00268422 +0.99999640 -0.00000157
+0.00000000 +0.00000000 +0.00000000 -0.00116649 -0.00000157 +0.99999932

OK
```

```
EXAMPLE DRIVER FOR GetRPNmat

enter JED1 on TDB scale   2451545
enter JED2 on TDB scale   2447160.5
(1)Precession (2)Nutation (3)Combined   2

+1.00000000 -0.00000458 -0.00000199 +0.00000000 +0.00000000 +0.00000000
+0.00000458 +1.00000000 -0.00004134 +0.00000000 +0.00000000 +0.00000000
+0.00000199 +0.00004134 +1.00000000 +0.00000000 +0.00000000 +0.00000000
+0.00000000 +0.00000000 +0.00000000 +1.00000000 -0.00000458 -0.00000199
+0.00000000 +0.00000000 +0.00000000 +0.00000458 +1.00000000 -0.00004134
+0.00000000 +0.00000000 +0.00000000 +0.00000199 +0.00004134 +1.00000000

OK

EXAMPLE DRIVER FOR GetRPNmat

enter JED1 on TDB scale   2451545
enter JED2 on TDB scale   2447160.5
(1)Precession (2)Nutation (3)Combined   3

+0.99999573 +0.00267964 +0.00116450 +0.00000000 +0.00000000 +0.00000000
-0.00267959 +0.99999641 -0.00004290 +0.00000000 +0.00000000 +0.00000000
-0.00116461 +0.00003978 +0.99999932 +0.00000000 +0.00000000 +0.00000000
+0.00000000 +0.00000000 +0.00000000 +0.99999573 +0.00267964 +0.00116450
+0.00000000 +0.00000000 +0.00000000 -0.00267959 +0.99999641 -0.00004290
+0.00000000 +0.00000000 +0.00000000 -0.00116461 +0.00003978 +0.99999932

OK
```

The values for the combined (**R**) matrix may be confirmed from page B45 of the 1988 *Astronomical Almanac*.

A final point: Notice that we have not addressed the problem of updating a star's position and proper motion components from one epoch and equinox to another epoch and equinox due to the effects of general precession and proper motion. The reason is that this process is somewhat subsumed under the computation of a star's apparent place from its mean place at J2000.0, and this is covered in Chapter 6. However, sometimes it may be necessary to update a star's positional data, and this topic is covered elsewhere in spherical astronomy textbooks and in the *Explanatory Supplement to the Astronomical Almanac*.

Chapter 4

Coordinate Systems and Transformations

4.1 Introduction

We now turn our attention to the various astronomical coordinate systems and how they are related. Compact routines that perform conversions among the various systems will be developed. Rotation matrices will be used extensively in the development of coordinate transformation software.

4.2 Preliminary Explanations

The study of coordinate systems is without a doubt one of the most important aspects of celestial mechanics and positional astronomy. Several different "standards" are in use for naming the various systems, and we shall base our development on the explanations given in Chapter 3 of [Taff 1985] and in Chapter 3 of [Mueller 1969].

To begin with, we shall attempt to deal exclusively with *rectangular coordinates* instead of *polar coordinates*. We define the *direction* to an object in space to be the following vector:

$$\hat{\mathbf{r}} = \begin{pmatrix} \cos\lambda\cos\phi \\ \sin\lambda\cos\phi \\ \sin\phi \end{pmatrix} = \begin{pmatrix} x \\ y \\ z \end{pmatrix} \qquad (4.2.1)$$

where λ is the longitudinal polar coordinate and ϕ is the latitudinal polar coordinate. Recall that λ may lie in the range $0 \le \lambda \le 2\pi$ radians and ϕ may lie in the range $-\pi/2 \le \phi \le \pi/2$ radians. Notice that the *direction vector* is a unit vector. When we multiply this position vector by the object's distance, we obtain what we will call the object's *position vector*. Mathematically, we will have:

$$\mathbf{r} = \rho \begin{pmatrix} \cos\lambda\cos\phi \\ \sin\lambda\cos\phi \\ \sin\phi \end{pmatrix} = \rho \begin{pmatrix} x \\ y \\ z \end{pmatrix} = \rho\hat{\mathbf{r}} = \begin{pmatrix} \xi \\ \eta \\ \zeta \end{pmatrix} \qquad (4.2.2)$$

where ρ is the distance to the object from the coordinate system origin. From these definitions, we can now define the transformation equations that allow us to convert from polar coordinates to rectangular coordinates and vice versa. Therefore, given the polar coordinates ρ, λ, ϕ we can transform them to rectangular coordinates ξ, η, ζ using equation (4.2.2). If we are given a set of rectangular coordinates ξ, η, ζ we can transform them into their corresponding polar coordinates via the following formulae:

$$\rho = \sqrt{\xi^2 + \eta^2 + \zeta^2} \qquad (4.2.3)$$

$$\lambda = \tan^{-1}\left(\frac{\eta}{\xi}\right) \qquad (4.2.4)$$

$$\phi = \tan^{-1}\left(\frac{\zeta}{\sqrt{\xi^2 + \eta^2}}\right). \qquad (4.2.5)$$

At first glance, equation (4.2.5) may seem cumbersome until we realize that we can alternatively compute ϕ from the arcsine of the quantity (ζ/ρ). However, an angle is always determined more accurately from its tangent than from either its sine or cosine alone. Also, note that the factor of ρ cancels out of the expression for ϕ. When one uses the tangent function to determine an angle, an ambiguity arises that may cause an error of π or 2π in the value of the determined angle. The problem is that the tangents of angles in the first and third quadrants are equal because the sine and cosine in either of these quadrants have the same *algebraic sign*. So, the ratio $\sin\theta/\cos\theta$, which defines the tangent, is always positive in these two quadrants. A similar problem exists for angles in the second and fourth quadrants. In this case, the sine and cosine are of opposite algebraic sign, so the tangent is always negative. To take this ambiguity into account, we must look at the algebraic sign of the sine and of the cosine and make sure we place the resulting angle in the correct quadrant.

There are two subprograms that can be used to transform from rectangular coordinates to polar coordinates and back again. These routines are called `Rec2Pol` and `Pol2Rec`. Note that `Rec2Pol` makes use of another utility function called `atan2` that will correct for the quadrant ambiguity described above. The source code listing for `atan2` is given in Chapter 9, while the source code listings for `Rec2Pol` and `Pol2Rec` are as follows:

```
sub Rec2Pol(a() as double, b() as double) static

    '----- Subprogram to convert a cartesian state vector into
    '----- a polar state vector.
    '----- Input:  a()  cartesian state vector
    '----- Output: b()  polar state vector
    '----- NOTE:   THE POLAR VELOCITY VECTOR IS THE TOTAL VELOCITY,
    '----- CORRECTED FOR THE EFFECT OF LATITUDE.
    '---------------------------------------------------------------------

    dim x          as double
    dim y          as double
    dim z          as double
    dim x_dot      as double
    dim y_dot      as double
    dim z_dot      as double
    dim rho        as double
    dim r          as double
    dim lambda     as double
    dim beta       as double
    dim lambda_dot as double
    dim beta_dot   as double
    dim r_dot      as double

    x = a(1)
    y = a(2)
    z = a(3)
    x_dot = a(4)
    y_dot = a(5)
    z_dot = a(6)

    rho = sqr(x * x + y * y)
    r = sqr(rho * rho + z * z)

    lambda = atan2(y, x)
    beta   = atan2(z, rho)
    if (z < 0#) then beta = beta - TWOPI

    if rho = 0# then
       lambda_dot = 0#
         beta_dot = 0#
    else
       lambda_dot = (x * y_dot - y * x_dot) / (rho * rho)
         beta_dot = (z_dot * rho * rho - z * (x * x_dot + _
                    y * y_dot)) / (r * r * rho)
    end if

    r_dot = (x * x_dot + y * y_dot + z * z_dot) / r

    '----- Position vector components
    b(1) = lambda
    if b(1) >= TWOPI then b(1) = b(1) - TWOPI

    b(2) = beta
    b(3) = r
    '----- Total velocity vector components
    b(4) = r * lambda_dot * cos(beta)
    b(5) = r * beta_dot
    b(6) = r_dot

end sub

sub Pol2Rec(a() as double, b() as double) static

    '----- Subprogram to convert a polar state vector into a cartesian
    '----- state vector.
    '----- Input:   a()   polar state vector
    '----- Output:  b()   cartesian state vector
```

```
'----- NOTE:  THIS ROUTINE EXPECTS THE POLAR VELOCITY VECTOR TO
'----- BE THE TOTAL VELOCITY CORRECTED FOR THE EFFECT OF LATITUDE.
'-------------------------------------------------------------------

dim lambda     as double
dim beta       as double
dim r          as double
dim v_lambda   as double
dim v_beta     as double
dim v_r        as double
dim lambda_dot as double
dim beta_dot   as double
dim r_dot      as double
dim cosl       as double
dim sinl       as double
dim cosb       as double
dim sinb       as double


lambda   = a(1)
beta     = a(2)
r        = a(3)
v_lambda = a(4)
v_beta   = a(5)
v_r      = a(6)

'----- Separate the angluar derivatives from the
'----- total velocity components
cosl = cos(lambda)
sinl = sin(lambda)
cosb = cos(beta)
sinb = sin(beta)

lambda_dot = v_lambda / (r * cosb)
beta_dot = v_beta / r
r_dot = v_r

'----- Position vector components
b(1) = r * cosl * cosb
b(2) = r * sinl * cosb
b(3) = r * sinb

'----- Velocity vector components
b(4) = r_dot * cosl * cosb _
     - r * lambda_dot * sinl * cosb _
     - r *    beta_dot * cosl * sinb
b(5) = r_dot * sinl * cosb _
     + r * lambda_dot * cosl * cosb _
     - r *    beta_dot * sinl * sinb
b(6) = r_dot * sinb + r * beta_dot * cosb

end sub
```

Before we move into a detailed discussion of the various coordinate systems, we need to consider *rotation matrices*. The study of rotation matrices is an interesting branch of classical mechanics, and the reader is referred to the textbook by Goldstein [Goldstein 1980] for what is perhaps the best treatment of the subject. Simply put, a *rotation matrix* is the matrix which, when operating on a vector in an original coordinate frame, will refer the components of the original vector to the axes of a new coordinate frame. We will deal with three elementary rotation matrices that correspond to rotations about the *x*-, *y*-, and *z*-axes in a *right-handed coordinate system*. These elementary matrices are defined as follows:

$$\mathbf{R}_1(\theta) = \begin{pmatrix} 1 & 0 & 0 \\ 0 & \cos\theta & \sin\theta \\ 0 & -\sin\theta & \cos\theta \end{pmatrix} \qquad (4.2.6)$$

$$\mathbf{R}_2(\theta) = \begin{pmatrix} \cos\theta & 0 & -\sin\theta \\ 0 & 1 & 0 \\ \sin\theta & 0 & \cos\theta \end{pmatrix} \qquad (4.2.7)$$

$$\mathbf{R}_3(\theta) = \begin{pmatrix} \cos\theta & \sin\theta & 0 \\ -\sin\theta & \cos\theta & 0 \\ 0 & 0 & 1 \end{pmatrix} \qquad (4.2.8)$$

Equation (4.2.6) represents the matrix for a rotation about the x-axis through the angle θ. Equation (4.2.7) represents a rotation about the y-axis through the angle θ. Finally, equation (4.2.8) represents a rotation about the z-axis through the angle θ. These rotation matrices were employed in the precession and nutation algorithms in the previous chapter. Almost all coordinate system transformations in which all the involved reference frames share the same origin can be defined as successive applications of these three rotation matrices. We will demonstrate this principle in the following sections.

4.3 The Astronomical Coordinate Systems

We are now in a position to define the various fundamental coordinate systems in use in positional astronomy. These fundamental systems are the *horizon system*, the *equatorial system*, the *ecliptic system*, and the *observer's geocentric system*. One other, the *galactic system*, will not be discussed since we are only concerned with solar system applications. We present these definitions with the assumption that the reader has already encountered them in one form or another in the study of elementary astronomy. The descriptions here will emphasize the subtleties in the precise definitions of astronomical coordinate systems.

4.3.1 The Horizon System

The horizon system is a left-handed system centered on the observer in which the x-axis points toward the north point on the observer's horizon. The y-axis points toward the east point on the observer's horizon, while the z-axis points toward the observer's zenith (the point directly above the observer). The longitudinal coordinate (denoted by A) for an object in this system is called *azimuth* and is defined as the angle from the north point of the horizon to the foot of the object's hour circle, measured *through the east point of the horizon*. Note that some authors, such as Taff and Meeus, prefer to measure the azimuth from the *south* point of the horizon. Such a convention still yields a left-handed system, but this practice is awkward, and we will not observe it here.

The latitudinal coordinate, denoted by a, of an object in the horizon system is called the *altitude* and is defined as the angle from the horizon up to the object. Azimuth can range from 0 to 2π radians, and altitude can range from $-\pi/2$ to $\pi/2$ radians, with negative values indicating that the object is below the horizon and hence not visible.

4.3.2   The Equatorial System

In the equatorial system, the longitudinal coordinate is called *right ascension*, denoted by α. Right ascension is measured eastward from the vernal equinox in the plane of the celestial equator. Right ascension can range from 0 to 2π radians. The latitudinal coordinate is called *declination*, denoted by δ. Declination is the angular distance, north or south, of an object from the celestial equator and can range from $-\pi/2$ to $\pi/2$ radians. The x-axis points toward the *vernal equinox*. The y-axis points toward the point on the celestial sphere with a right ascension of 6^{h}, and the z-axis points toward the north celestial pole. The equatorial system is a right-handed coordinate system.

4.3.3   The Ecliptic System

The longitudinal coordinate in the ecliptic system, denoted by λ, is called *celestial* or *ecliptic longitude* and is the angular distance, measured eastward in the plane of the ecliptic, from the vernal equinox to the object in question. The latitudinal coordinate, denoted by β, is called *celestial* or *ecliptic latitude* and is the angular distance north or south of an object from the plane of the ecliptic. Ecliptic longitude can take on values from 0 to 2π radians, and ecliptic latitude can range from $-\pi/2$ to $\pi/2$ radians. Like the equatorial system, the ecliptic system is a right-handed coordinate system. The x-axis again points toward the vernal equinox. The y-axis points toward the point on the celestial sphere with a celestial longitude of $90°$, and the z-axis points toward the north celestial pole.

4.3.4   The Observer's Geocentric System

The problem of specifying the location of an observer on the surface of the oblate Earth is more complicated that one might expect. To make matters more complicated, there are two coordinate systems that can be used to specify the location of an observer on the surface of the Earth.

First, there is the *geodetic coordinate system*. This is a system in which the longitudinal coordinate is everyday terrestrial *longitude*, denoted by λ (not to be confused with ecliptic longitude). The strict definition of *geodetic longitude* is the angle between the local meridian and the prime meridian at Greenwich. Following the IAU convention, west longitudes are considered algebraically negative and east longitudes are algebraically positive. Longitude can take on values from $-\pi$ to π radians. The subtle feature of the geodetic system is the strict definition of the latitudinal coordinate, called the *geodetic latitude*. The geodetic latitude, denoted by ϕ, is the acute angle between the observer's zenith and the Earth's equator and can take on values from $-\pi/2$ to $\pi/2$ radians. The second system, called the *geocentric system*, proves to be more useful for our purposes.

The geocentric system is a right-handed system in which the observer's position is specified by a radial coordinate, a longitudinal coordinate, and a latitudinal coordinate. The origin for this system is the center of the oblate Earth. The longitudinal coordinate is called the *geocentric longitude* and is equivalent to the geodetic longitude defined above. The *geocentric latitude*, denoted by ϕ', is the acute angle between the geocentric radius vector to the observer and the Earth's equator. Geocentric latitude can assume the same range of values as geodetic latitude. Rigorously, the geodetic and geocentric longitudes are not equivalent, though the difference, termed the *angle of the vertical*, is small ($\leq 11'$). The geocentric x-axis points toward the intersection of the Greenwich meridian and the Earth's equator. The y-axis points toward the point along the Earth's equator with longitude $+90°$ (east longitude), and the z-axis coincides with the Earth's rotational axis and points north.

In the geocentric coordinate system, it is easy to take the oblateness of the Earth into account when computing the coordinates of an observer. The calculations are lengthy, and no derivations will be presented here. The reader is referred to [Mueller 1969], [Taff 1985], or any other textbook on spherical astronomy. We seek explicit expressions for the position and velocity vector components of a terrestrial observer in the geocentric system. This is best accomplished by first computing the observer's position and velocity components in an *Earth-fixed* coordinate system, which is just a coordinate frame tied to the Earth's crust [Kaplan 1989]. In such a system, the observer's positon vector has the components

$$\begin{bmatrix} (aC + h)\cos\phi\cos\lambda \\ (aC + h)\cos\phi\sin\lambda \\ (aS + h)\sin\phi \end{bmatrix} \quad (4.3.1)$$

and the observer's velocity vector components are all zero. In these expressions, a is the equatorial radius of the Earth, ϕ and λ are the observer's geodetic coordinates, h is the observer's elevation above sea level, and C and S are parameters that depend on the Earth's flattening factor. Following [Kaplan 1989], we can now perform a series of matrix rotations on this

state vector to arrive at the observer's state vector with respect to the geo-
center. The resulting components will also be referred to the mean equator
and equinox of the chosen reference epoch, usually J2000.0.

The following subprogram computes the geocentric state vector of an observer on the surface of the Earth. It is called `GeocenObs`, and here its source
code listing is as follows:

```
sub GeocenObs(jed as double, obsr_geo() as double) static

    '----- Subprogram to compute the geocentric equatorial
    '----- state vectors of an observer.  The vectors are
    '----- referred to the J2000.0 frame.
    '----- Input:  jed         Julian day number on TDB scale
    '----- Output: obsr_geo()  observer's geocentric state vector
    '-----                     in the celestial reference frame.
    '------------------------------------------------------------------

    dim gast     as double
    dim h        as double
    dim coslat   as double
    dim sinlat   as double
    dim cos2lat  as double
    dim sin2lat  as double
    dim coslon   as double
    dim sinlon   as double
    dim c        as double
    dim s        as double
    dim polmotx  as double
    dim polmoty  as double
    dim g(min,1) as double
    dim dpsi     as double
    dim deps     as double
    dim dpsidot  as double
    dim depsdot  as double
    dim zeta     as double
    dim z        as double
    dim theta    as double
    dim zetadot  as double
    dim zdot     as double
    dim thetadot as double
    dim MeanEps  as double
    dim TrueEps  as double
    dim MeanEpsDot as double
    dim TrueEpsDot as double

    redim g(1 to 6)

    '----- elevation is expected to be in meters
    h = (obsr_ele / 1000#) * KM2AU
    coslat  = cos(obsr_lat)
    cos2lat = coslat * coslat
    sinlat  = sin(obsr_lat)
    sin2lat = sinlat * sinlat
    coslon  = cos(obsr_lon)
    sinlon  = sin(obsr_lon)
    c = 1# / sqr(cos2lat + (1# - EFlat) * (1# - EFlat) * sin2lat)
    s = (1# - EFlat) * (1# - EFlat) * c

    '----- Compute the observer's state vector
    '----- in the Earth-fixed frame.
    g(1) = (EarthRadAU * c + h) * coslat * coslon
    g(2) = (EarthRadAU * c + h) * coslat * sinlon
    g(3) = (EarthRadAU * s + h) * sinlat
    g(4) = 0#
    g(5) = 0#
```

```
g(6) = 0#

'----- Compute the required angular quantities
'----- and their derivatives.
call GetPrecessParams(J2000.0, jed, zeta, z, theta, _
     zetadot, zdot, thetadot)
call GetDpsiDeps(jed, dpsi, deps, dpsidot, depsdot)
call GetGST(jed, 1, gast)
call Obliquity(J2000.0, jed, 0, MeanEps, MeanEpsDot)
call Obliquity(J2000.0, jed, 1, TrueEps, TrueEpsDot)

'----- Somehow get the quantities polmotx, polmoty
polmotx = 0#
polmoty = 0#

'----- Wobble
call QRotate(g(), 2, polmotx, 0, 1, g())
call QRotate(g(), 1, polmoty, 0, 1, g())

'----- Spin
call QRotate(g(), 3, -gast, -EarAngVelRD, 1, g())

'----- Nutation
call QRotate(g(), 1,  TrueEps,  TrueEpsDot, 1, g())
call QRotate(g(), 3,  dpsi,  dpsidot, 1, g())
call QRotate(g(), 1, -MeanEps, -MeanEpsDot, 1, g())

'----- Precession
call QRotate(g(), 3,  zeta, zetadot, 1, g())
call QRotate(g(), 2, -theta, -thetadot, 1, g())
call QRotate(g(), 3,  z, zdot, 1, obsr_geo())

end sub
```

Note that `GeocenObs` makes use of several matrix routines, along with the routines for computing precessional and nutational data. The resulting position vector is in AU (astronomical units), and the velocity vector is in AU/day. There is a specific reason these units are chosen over, say, units of Earth's radius or the like. When one is computing the *apparent place* of a celestial object (see Chapter 6), the most advantageous coordinate system to use is the *barycentric equatorial* system. The apparent place is referred to the Earth's center, and if we wish to compute the apparent place as seen by an observer on the Earth's surface, we need only add (vectorially) the observer's geocentric position and velocity vectors to the barycentric position and velocity vectors of the Earth at the beginning of the reduction procedure. The resulting apparent place will then be referred to the observer's specific location. Also note that, by default, this routine assumes that the observer's state vector will be referred to the mean equator and equinox of J2000.0, but the user may modify the code so that the observer's state vector with respect to any equator and equinox can be obtained. This is left to the reader as a programming exercise.

Now we can write a driver for `GEOBSLOC` that will compute the geocentric rectangular coordinates of an observer anywhere on Earth at any time. The program is called `GEOBS` and its source code listing is as follows:

```
'----- GEOBS.BAS

defdbl a-z

$include "\fecsoftb\astrolib.dec"
$include "\fecsoftb\constant.inc"
$include "\fecsoftb\amodulo.bas"
$include "\fecsoftb\deg.bas"
$include "\fecsoftb\funarg.bas"
$include "\fecsoftb\geocenobs.bas"
$include "\fecsoftb\getgst.bas"
$include "\fecsoftb\getqm.bas"
$include "\fecsoftb\matxvec.bas"
$include "\fecsoftb\nutation.bas"
$include "\fecsoftb\obliquty.bas"
$include "\fecsoftb\precess.bas"
$include "\fecsoftb\qrotate.bas"
$include "\fecsoftb\rotmat.bas"

dim jdate              as double
dim obsr_geo(1 to 6)   as double
dim longitude          as double
dim latitude           as double
dim elevation          as double

cls
print "EXAMPLE DRIVER FOR GeocenObs"
print
input "Enter Julian day number on TDB scale  ", jdate
input "Enter observer's geodetic longitude (-W, dd.mmss) ", longitude
input "Enter observer's geodetic latitude  (+N, dd.mmss) ", latitude
input "Enter observer's elevation in meters  ", elevation
longitude = deg(longitude) * D2R
latitude  = deg(latitude)  * D2R

obsr_lon = longitude
obsr_lat = latitude
obsr_ele = elevation

call GeocenObs(jdate, obsr_geo())

print "Observer's state vector"
print using "+#.############## +#.############## +#.############## AU"; _
      obsr_geo(1);obsr_geo(2);obsr_geo(3)
print using "+#.############## +#.############## +#.############## AU/day"; _
      obsr_geo(4);obsr_geo(5);obsr_geo(6)

print
print "OK"

end
```

Here is a sample output screen for this program.

```
EXAMPLE DRIVER FOR GeocenObs

Enter Julian date on TDB scale  2449950.5
Enter observer's geodetic longitude (-W, dd.mmss)  -81.2029
Enter observer's geodetic latitude  (+N, dd.mmss)  35.4359
Enter observer's elevation in meters  354
Observer's state vector
-0.000013236431413 -0.000032027803139 +0.000024755758491 AU
+0.000201781543897 -0.000083331405927 +0.000000078595927 AU/day

OK
```

Again, note that these coordinates and velocities are referred to the mean equator and equinox of J2000.0.

4.4 Transformation from One Coordinate System to Another

Having defined the coordinate systems dealt with in this book, we now state the rules for transforming from one coordinate system to another. We write the transformation formulae in matrix notation. The following formulae allow conversions between the equatorial system and the horizon system.

$$\begin{pmatrix} x \\ y \\ z \end{pmatrix}_{A,a} = \mathbf{R}_3(-180°)\mathbf{R}_2(90° - \phi) \begin{pmatrix} x \\ y \\ z \end{pmatrix}_{h,\delta} \tag{4.4.1}$$

$$\begin{pmatrix} x \\ y \\ z \end{pmatrix}_{h,\delta} = \mathbf{R}_2(\phi - 90°)\mathbf{R}_3(180°) \begin{pmatrix} x \\ y \\ z \end{pmatrix}_{A,a} \tag{4.4.2}$$

Note that this transformation involves the object's *hour angle*, which must be computed from the sidereal time and the object's right ascension. The subprogram that carries out these transformations is called Eq2Hor, and its source code listing is as follows:

```
sub Eq2Hor(a() as double, s as integer, b() as double) static

  '----- Subprogram to convert an equatorial state vector to a horizon
  '----- state vector or the reverse transformation
  '----- Input:  a()  input vector
  '-----         s    = 0 for eq  -> hor
  '-----              = 1 for hor -> eq
  '----- Output: b()  output vector
  '-----------------------------------------------------------------------

  dim r2(min,2)  as double
  dim r3(min,2)  as double
  dim r(min,2)   as double
  dim dr2(min,2) as double
  dim dr3(min,2) as double
  dim dr(min,2)  as double

  redim r2(1 to 3, 1 to 3)
  redim r3(1 to 3, 1 to 3)
  redim r(1 to 3, 1 to 3)
  redim dr2(1 to 3, 1 to 3)
  redim dr3(1 to 3, 1 to 3)
  redim dr(1 to 3, 1 to 3)

  if s = 0 then   '----- Equatorial to horizon
    call RotMat(2, PIDIV2 - obsr_lat, r2(), dr2())
    call RotMat(3, -PI, r3(), dr3())
    call MatXMat(r3(), r2(), r(), 3, 3, 3)
  else            '----- Horizon to equatorial
    call RotMat(3, PI, r3(), dr3())
    call RotMat(2, obsr_lat - PIDIV2, r2(), dr2())
    call MatXMat(r2(), r3(), r(), 3, 3, 3)
  end if
```

```
    call MatXVec(r(), a(), b(), 3, 3)
end sub
```

Subprogram Eq2Hor requires an input vector and a switch that indicates the
direction of the transformation; the same routine can be used for transformation to and from the horizon system. Note that extensive use is made of
utility routines Rotmat, MatXMat, and MatXVec. The source code listings for
these routines are given in Chapter 9. RotMat computes the elements of a
rotation matrix about a given axis when supplied with the appropriate angle.
MatXMat carries out the multiplication of two given matrices, and MatXVec
carries out the multiplication of a matrix and a vector.

    The following formulae allow conversion between the equatorial system
and the ecliptic system.

$$\begin{pmatrix} x \\ y \\ z \end{pmatrix}_{\lambda,\beta} = \mathbf{R}_1(\epsilon) \begin{pmatrix} x \\ y \\ z \end{pmatrix}_{\alpha,\delta} \tag{4.4.3}$$

$$\begin{pmatrix} x \\ y \\ z \end{pmatrix}_{\alpha,\delta} = \mathbf{R}_1(-\epsilon) \begin{pmatrix} x \\ y \\ z \end{pmatrix}_{\lambda,\beta} \tag{4.4.4}$$

The subprogram to carry out these transformations is called Eq2Ecl, and its
source code listing is as follows:

```
sub Eq2Ecl(a() as double, s as integer, eps as double, b() as double) static
    '----- Subprogram to convert an equatorial state
    '----- vector to an ecliptic state vector or the
    '----- reverse transformation.
    '----- Input:  a()    input vector
    '-----         s      = 0 for eq  -> ecl
    '-----                = 1 for ecl -> eq
    '-----         eps    mean or apparent obliquity
    '----- Output: b()    output vector
    '-------------------------------------------------------------------

    dim r(min,2)  as double
    dim dr(min,2) as double

    redim r(1 to 3, 1 to 3)
    redim dr(1 to 3, 1 to 3)

    if s = 0 then       '----- Equatorial to ecliptic
        call RotMat(1,  eps, r(), dr())
    else                '----- Ecliptic to equatorial
        call RotMat(1, -eps, r(), dr())
    end if

    call MatXVec(r(), a(), b(), 3, 3)

end sub
```

Subprogram Eq2Ecl takes an input vector and an input value of the obliquity of the ecliptic and computes the output vector according to the switch s. As with Eq2Hor, the same subprogram can transform to and from the ecliptic system. Again, use is made of the utility routines RotMat, MatXMat, and MatXVec.

PROGRAMMING EXERCISE: Modify Eq2Ecl **not** to require the obliquity as an input parameter. Instead, make the Julian day number a parameter along with a switch indicating whether the mean or true obliquity is needed. Have the routine then compute the obliquity.

When dealing with transformations to and from the horizon system one can bypass the intermediate step of computing the object's hour angle by the fact that the conversion from right ascension and declination to hour angle and declination can also be expressed in terms of a matrix operation. Specifically, this transformation is a rotation of the right ascension/declination system about the z-axis through an angle equivalent to the local sidereal time. But this is not the complete transformation. The problem is that while the horizon coordinate system is a left-handed system, the other systems are right-handed systems. Therefore, in addition to the rotation about the z-axis, we must apply an additional matrix to the initial coordinate vector that preserves the orientations of the x- and z-axes but performs a reflection of the y-axis. Therefore, we can write the complete transformation from the right ascension/declination system to the hour angle/declination system as follows:

$$\begin{pmatrix} x \\ y \\ z \end{pmatrix}_{h,\delta} = \begin{pmatrix} 1 & 0 & 0 \\ 0 & -1 & 0 \\ 0 & 0 & 1 \end{pmatrix} \mathbf{R}_3(\text{LST}) \begin{pmatrix} x \\ y \\ z \end{pmatrix}_{\alpha,\delta} . \qquad (4.4.5)$$

The inverse transformation is written as follows:

$$\begin{pmatrix} x \\ y \\ z \end{pmatrix}_{\alpha,\delta} = \mathbf{R}_3(-\text{LST}) \begin{pmatrix} 1 & 0 & 0 \\ 0 & -1 & 0 \\ 0 & 0 & 1 \end{pmatrix} \begin{pmatrix} x \\ y \\ x \end{pmatrix}_{h,\delta} . \qquad (4.4.6)$$

Another convenient feature of matrices is that they can be applied successively to an original coordinate vector to rotate it into any desired coordinate system. For example, if one needs to convert directly from the ecliptic system to the horizon system, first apply the matrix necessary to transform into the right ascension/declination system and then apply the matrices necessary to transform to the horizon system, bypassing the hour angle computation as explained above. Be careful to carry out the matrix multiplications in the correct order for the desired transformation.

There is one more extremely important caveat. When dealing with *apparent* coordinates (defined explicitly in Chapter 6), remember to use the *true obliquity of the ecliptic* (the mean obliquity corrected for nutation) and the local *apparent* sidereal time (again, corrected for nutation). Otherwise, you can safely use the mean obliquity and local mean sidereal time.

As an example of how to use the coordinate transformation routines presented above, here is a program called COORDS that will perform the following conversions:

1. equatorial coordinates to horizon coordinates,

2. horizon coordinates to equatorial coordinates,

3. equatorial coordiantes to ecliptic coordinates, and

4. ecliptic coordinates to equatorial coordinates.

These are the only transformations provided for in program COORDS, but the source code is easy to modify in order to incorporate other transformations. Note that the program does *not* bypass the computation of the hour angle as described above. The source code listing for program COORDS is as follows:

```
'----- COORDS.BAS

defdbl a-z

$include "\fecsoftb\astrolib.dec"
$include "\fecsoftb\constant.inc"
$include "\fecsoftb\amodulo.bas"
$include "\fecsoftb\atan2.bas"
$include "\fecsoftb\deg.bas"
$include "\fecsoftb\dms.bas"
$include "\fecsoftb\dround.bas"
$include "\fecsoftb\eq2hor.bas"
$include "\fecsoftb\eq2ecl.bas"
$include "\fecsoftb\fmtdms.bas"
$include "\fecsoftb\matxmat.bas"
$include "\fecsoftb\matxvec.bas"
$include "\fecsoftb\pol2rec.bas"
$include "\fecsoftb\rec2pol.bas"
$include "\fecsoftb\rotmat.bas"
$include "\fecsoftb\vecmag.bas"

dim Which as integer
dim Alpha as double
dim Delta as double
dim RA as string
dim Del as string
dim LAST as double
dim Altitude as double
dim Azimuth as double
dim Az as string
dim Alt as string
dim Lambda as double
dim Beta as double
dim Lam as string
dim Bet as string
dim TrueEps as double
dim HourAngle as double
dim r1(min,1) as double
dim r2(min,1) as double
```

```
redim r1(1 to 6)
redim r2(1 to 6)

cls
print "EXAMPLE DRIVER FOR Eq2Ecl and Eq2Hor"
print

print "[1] EQ TO HOR [2] HOR TO EQ"
print "[3] EQ TO ECL [4] ECL TO EQ"
do
  input "Select one ", Which
loop until (Which <= 4 and Which > 0)

print
select case Which
  case 1
    print "Enter equatorial coordinates (ra, dec) in dd.mmss format"
    input " ", Alpha, Delta
    input "Enter observer latitude in dd.mmss format   ", obsr_lat
    input "Enter LAST in hh.mmss format   ", LAST
    Alpha = deg(Alpha)*H2R
    Delta = deg(Delta)*D2R
    obsr_lat = deg(obsr_lat)*D2R
    LAST = deg(LAST)*H2R
    HourAngle = LAST - Alpha
    r1(1) = HourAngle
    r1(2) = Delta
    r1(3) = 1#
    r1(4) = 0#
    r1(5) = 0#
    r1(6) = 0#

    '----- change to rectangular variables
    call Pol2Rec(r1(),r2())
    '----- transform
    call Eq2Hor(r2(),0,r2())
    '----- change to polar variables
    call Rec2Pol(r2(),r2())

    Azimuth  = r2(1)*R2D
    Altitude = r2(2)*R2D

    Az = FmtDms(Azimuth,4,1)
    Alt = FmtDms(Altitude,4,1)

    Alpha = Alpha*R2H
    Delta = Delta*R2D
    RA = FmtDms(Alpha,4,2)
    Del = FmtDms(Delta,4,1)

    print
    print "EQUATORIAL COORDINATES"
    print "RA ";RA;" DELTA ";Del
    print "HORIZON COORDINATES"
    print "AZIMUTH ";Az;" ALTITUDE ";Alt

  case 2
    print "Enter horizon coordinates (alt, az) in dd.mmss format"
    input " ", Altitude, Azimuth
    input "Enter observer latitude in dd.mmss format   ", obsr_lat
    input "Enter LAST in hh.mmss format   ", LAST
    Altitude = deg(Altitude)*D2R
    Azimuth = deg(Azimuth)*D2R
    obsr_lat = deg(obsr_lat)*D2R
    LAST = deg(LAST)*H2R
    r1(1) = Azimuth
```

```
    r1(2) = Altitude
    r1(3) = 1#
    r1(4) = 0#
    r1(5) = 0#
    r1(6) = 0#

    '----- change to rectangular variables
    call Pol2Rec(r1(),r2())
    '----- transform
    call Eq2Hor(r2(),1,r2())
    '----- change to polar variables
    call Rec2Pol(r2(),r2())

    HourAngle = r2(1)
    Delta = r2(2)

    Azimuth  = Azimuth*R2D
    Altitude = Altitude*R2D

    Az = FmtDms(Azimuth,4,1)
    Alt = FmtDms(Altitude,4,1)

    Alpha = LAST - HourAngle
    Alpha = amodulo(Alpha,TWOPI)*R2H
    Delta = Delta*R2D
    RA = FmtDms(Alpha,4,2)
    Del = FmtDms(Delta,4,1)

    print
    print "HORIZON COORDINATES"
    print "AZIMUTH ";Az;" ALTITUDE ";Alt
    print "EQUATORIAL COORDINATES"
    print "RA ";RA;" DELTA ";Del

  case 3
    print "Enter equatorial coordinates (ra, dec) in dd.mmss format"
    input " ", Alpha, Delta
    input "Enter true obliquity in dd.mmss format  ", TrueEps
    Alpha = deg(Alpha)*H2R
    Delta = deg(Delta)*D2R
    TrueEps = deg(TrueEps)*D2R
    r1(1) = Alpha
    r1(2) = Delta
    r1(3) = 1#
    r1(4) = 0#
    r1(5) = 0#
    r1(6) = 0#

    '----- change to rectangular variables
    call Pol2Rec(r1(),r2())
    '----- transform
    call Eq2Ecl(r2(),0,TrueEps,r2())
    '----- change to polar variables
    call Rec2Pol(r2(),r2())

    Lambda = r2(1)*R2D
    Beta = r2(2)*R2D

    Lam = FmtDms(Lambda,4,1)
    Bet = FmtDms(Beta,4,1)

    Alpha = Alpha*R2H
    Delta = Delta*R2D
    RA = FmtDms(Alpha,4,2)
    Del = FmtDms(Delta,4,1)

    print
    print "EQUATORIAL COORDINATES"
```

```
    print "RA ";RA;" DELTA ";Del
    print "ECLIPTIC COORDINATES"
    print "LAMBDA ";Lam;" BETA "Bet

  case 4
    print "Enter ecliptic coordinates (lon, lat) in dd.mmss format"
    input " ", Lambda, Beta
    input "Enter true obliquity in dd.mmss format  ", TrueEps
    Lambda = deg(Lambda)*D2R
    Beta = deg(Beta)*D2R
    TrueEps = deg(TrueEps)*D2R
    r1(1) = Lambda
    r1(2) = Beta
    r1(3) = 1#
    r1(4) = 0#
    r1(5) = 0#
    r1(6) = 0#

    '----- change to rectangular variables
    call Pol2Rec(r1(),r2())
    '----- transform
    call Eq2Ecl(r2(),1,TrueEps,r2())
    '----- change to polar variables
    call Rec2Pol(r2(),r2())

    Alpha = r2(1)*R2H
    Delta = r2(2)*R2D

    Lambda = Lambda * R2D
    Beta = Beta * R2D
    Lam = FmtDms(Lambda,4,1)
    Bet = FmtDms(Beta,4,1)

    RA = FmtDms(Alpha,4,2)
    Del = FmtDms(Delta,4,1)

    print
    print "ECLIPTIC COORDINATES"
    print "LAMBDA ";Lam;" BETA "Bet
    print "EQUATORIAL COORDINATES"
    print "RA ";RA;" DELTA ";Del

end select

print
print "OK"

end
```

Below are sample screens from program **COORDS**.

```
EXAMPLE DRIVER FOR Eq2Ecl and Eq2Hor

[1] EQ TO HOR [2] HOR TO EQ
[3] EQ TO ECL [4] ECL TO EQ
Select one 1

Enter equatorial coordinates (ra, dec) in dd.mmss format
16.2629189,-21.133868
Enter observer latitude in dd.mmss format  35.4359
Enter LAST in hh.mmss format  1.14452959

EQUATORIAL COORDINATES
RA 16h26m29.19s DELTA -21d13'38.68"
HORIZON COORDINATES
AZIMUTH +275d50'38.9193" ALTITUDE -45d55'27.7358"
```

```
OK

EXAMPLE DRIVER FOR Eq2Ecl and Eq2Hor

[1] EQ TO HOR [2] HOR TO EQ
[3] EQ TO ECL [4] ECL TO EQ
Select one 2

Enter horizon coordinates (alt, az) in dd.mmss format
-45.552774,275.503892
Enter observer latitude in dd.mmss format   35.4359
Enter LAST in hh.mmss format  1.14452959

HORIZON COORDINATES
AZIMUTH +275d50'38.92" ALTITUDE -45d55'27.74"
EQUATORIAL COORDINATES
RA 16h26m29.19s DELTA -21d13'38.68"

OK

EXAMPLE DRIVER FOR Eq2Ecl and Eq2Hor

[1] EQ TO HOR [2] HOR TO EQ
[3] EQ TO ECL [4] ECL TO EQ
Select one 3

Enter equatorial coordinates (ra, dec) in dd.mmss format
16.2629399,-21.133839
Enter true obliquity in dd.mmss format   23.2615791

EQUATORIAL COORDINATES
RA 16h26m29.40s DELTA -21d13'38.39"
ECLIPTIC COORDINATES
LAMBDA +248d17'30.82" BETA +00d27'57.59"

OK

EXAMPLE DRIVER FOR Eq2Ecl and Eq2Hor

[1] EQ TO HOR [2] HOR TO EQ
[3] EQ TO ECL [4] ECL TO EQ
Select one 4

Enter ecliptic coordinates (lon, lat) in dd.mmss format
248.173082,0.275759
Enter true obliquity in dd.mmss format   23.2615791

ECLIPTIC COORDINATES
LAMBDA +248d17'30.82" BETA +00d27'57.59"
EQUATORIAL COORDINATES
RA 16h26m29.40s DELTA -21d13'38.39"

OK
```

Again, note that the d's in the sample screens will actually show up as degree symbols.

PROGRAMMING EXERCISE: Modify Eq2Hor to perform the transformation from equatorial to horizon coordinates without the need for the intermediate hour angle.

PROGRAMMING EXERCISE: Write a subprogram that precesses an *ecliptic* state vector using an *ecliptic precession matrix*. Basically, this matrix should rotate the vector into the equatorial coordinate system, perform the equatorial precession matrix from Chapter 3, then rotate the new vector back into the ecliptic coordinate system. Make sure the appropriate obliquity is used.

Chapter 5

Orbital Elements and Ephemerides

5.1 Introduction

This chapter deals with the elements of elliptical, parabolic, hyperbolic, and nearly-parabolic orbits and how to use the elements to compute precise ephemerides for any object. In the past, positions of the major planets in the solar system were computed from detailed mathematical *planetary theories*. Nowadays, ephemerides are computed from numerical integrations. Producing a numerically integrated ephemeris is also mathematically involved, but less so than producing an analytical ephemeris. The methods developed in this chapter are more directly applied to comets, asteroids, and artificial satellites. Therefore, we will not discuss the computation of the positions of the major planets in this chapter. Nor will we deal directly with artificial satellites, as the programs presented here are easily modified for such purposes. We shall restrict our methods and examples to comets and asteroids. Kepler's equation is also discussed along with a modern method for its solution. The relationship between orbital elements and the position and velocity vectors of an object at a given instant of time is also addressed. Finally, a subroutine that corrects orbital elements for the effects of precession is developed and presented.

5.2 General Orbital Elements

The orbit of any celestial object can be described by a set of six parameters called the *elements* of the orbit. These classical elements are defined as follows:

a = semi-major axis of the orbit

e = eccentricity of the orbit

i = inclination of the orbit with respect to some reference plane

Ω = longitude of the ascending node of the orbit

ω = argument of perihelion of the orbit

T = time of perihelion passage of the object.

Before we proceed, elaboration upon these definitions is in order. The elements e and a specify respectively the shape and size of the orbit. The semi-major axis can be thought of as the average value of the radial distance of the object in orbit from the attracting body, although this is not strictly true. The eccentricity of the orbit is a measure of how much the orbit deviates from a perfect circular shape. It can take on values from 0 to 1, inclusive, and can even be larger than 1 in certain instances. An orbit with $e = 0$ is a circle, while elliptical orbits have eccentricities that satisfy $0 < e < 1$. The larger the value of e, the more elongated the orbit becomes. Orbits in the shape of a hyperbola have $e > 1$. Natural hyperbolic orbits are relatively rare, and the largest eccentricity known to date is only 1.06. If $e = 1$ exactly, the orbit is parabolic. Like hyperbolic orbits, perfectly parabolic orbits are rare. However, most comet orbits can be fairly closely approximated by a parabola when the comet is near perihelion. If the eccentricity is very close to 1, but not exactly equal to 1, the orbit is said to be *nearly parabolic*, and this may cause computational problems when solving Kepler's equation. However, the method we will adopt for solving Kepler's equation does not pose any difficulties, and it handles all types of orbits.

The elements i, Ω, and ω serve to specify the orientation of the orbital plane in space. i is the inclination of the orbital plane with respect to some reference plane, which for comets and asteroids is the *ecliptic*. The inclination can take on values from 0 to π radians, inclusive. If i satisfies $0 \leq i < \pi/2$ radians, then the object is said to observe *direct motion*. This means that the object orbits counter-clockwise as seen from the north pole of the solar system. If i satisfies $\pi/2 \leq i \leq \pi$ radians, then the object is said to observe *retrograde motion*. In other words, it orbits clockwise as seen from the north pole of the solar system. The longitude of the ascending node, Ω, is the angle (measured in the plane of the ecliptic) from the vernal equinox to the *ascending node* of the orbit. This is the point in the orbit where the object crosses the ecliptic going north. The *descending node* is the point where the object crosses the ecliptic going south. Ω can take on any value from 0 to 2π radians. The argument of perihelion, ω, is the angle (measured in the plane of the orbit) from the ascending node to the perihelion point. Note that ω and Ω are measured in two different planes. Like Ω, ω can take on any value from 0 to 2π radians.

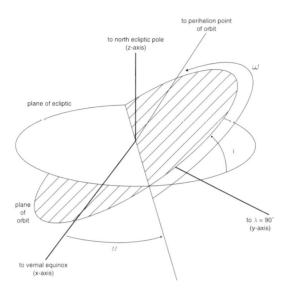

Figure 5.1. *Illustration of the orbital elements that determine the orbit's orientation in space. Note the location of the coordinate origin.*

Also, note that any quantity measured with respect to the vernal equinox is called a *longitude*. Any quantity measured with respect to the ascending node of the orbit is called an *argument*.

The final element, T, is the time at which the orbiting object passes through the perihelion point of the orbit. It may be specified as a Julian day number (with the correct time scale also specified) or as a year, month, and day with fractions (again, the correct time scale must also be specified). Either form is acceptable, but the use of the Julian day number makes the computations simpler.

For very precise computations, the mass of the orbiting object should also be specified, and some authors even go so far as to say that the object's mass constitutes a seventh orbital element. However, we prefer not to adopt this convention for two reasons.

1. The mass of any comet or asteroid is always very small when compared to the mass of the Sun. It is the sum of these two masses that is taken into account by the equations of planetary motion and the mass of the comet or asteroid can always be safely neglected.

2. The nonrelativistic motion of any object in the Sun's gravitational field is governed by three second-order linear differential equations, one for each Cartesian component (x, y, and z).

When the differential equation for each component is integrated twice

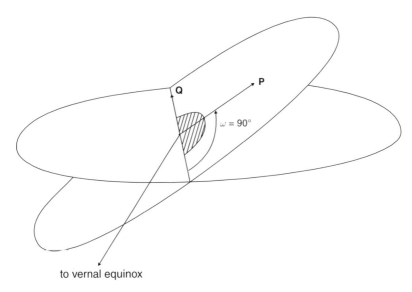

to vernal equinox

Figure 5.2.   *Vector* **P** *points toward the object's perihelion point. Vector* **Q** *points 90° from P in the sense of a right-handed coordinate system. Here, because ω = 90°,* **Q** *lies along the line of intersection between the orbital plane and the ecliptic plane.* **P** *and* **Q** *form an inertial reference frame.*

to calculate the object's position as a function of time, two constants of integration result. This gives a total of six constants of integration for all three components. Therefore, the problem can be solved with six constants, not seven, and one form for the constants of integration is the set of orbital elements described above. Rather than specifying the elements of the orbit at a given epoch, we can equivalently specify the initial components of the object's position and velocity vectors at a given epoch. As we shall see later in this chapter, the six components of the initial position and velocity vectors are another form of the six constants of integration that describe the object's orbital motion.

The element set a, e, i, Ω, ω, and T is only one possible set of elements that can be used. For example, the quantity $\tilde{\omega} = \omega + \Omega$ is called the *longitude of perihelion*, and it is sometimes specified instead of just ω. For retrograde orbits, the quantity $\tilde{\omega}_r = \omega - \Omega$ is useful when the inclination is near π radians. Sometimes the quantity q, called the *perihelion distance*, can be quoted instead of the element a. The use of this quantity is convenient because it is always positive and finite. The semi-major axis for hyperbolic orbits, as we shall see later in this chapter, is negative. A similar problem exists for parabolic orbits, for which the semi-major axis is infinite.

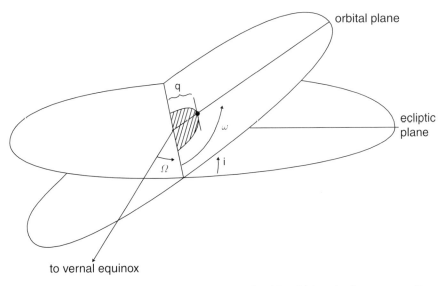

Figure 5.3. *Shaded portion indicates actual orbit. Object is shown at perihelion.* $\tilde{\omega} = \Omega + \omega$. *The element e serves only to specify the orbit's shape and is
not shown.*

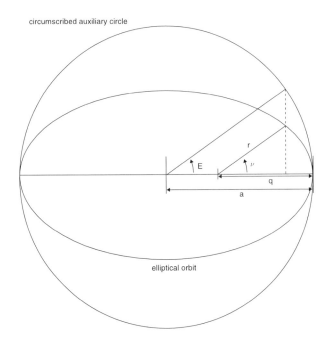

Figure 5.4. *Illustration of perihelion distance, true anomaly, semi-major axis,
and eccentric anomaly for an elliptic orbit.*

5.3 Elliptical Orbits

In this section, we will outline the details of the computation of heliocentric ephemerides for comets or asteroids in elliptical orbits. We assume the values for the element set q, e, i, Ω, ω, and T are given along with the equinox to which the angular elements are referred. We will assume that the mass of the comet or asteroid is negligible with respect to the Sun's mass, but our software will be written to take the mass into account if we wish to do so. In the following discussion, extensive use has been made of the exposition given in Chapter 3 of Herrick's textbook [Herrick 1974].

We begin by defining two vectors $\mathbf{P}$ and $\mathbf{Q}$. $\mathbf{P}$ is a unit vector in the direction of the perihelion point of the orbit. $\mathbf{Q}$ is the unit vector directed $90°$ from $\mathbf{P}$ in the direction of the body's motion. These two vectors are defined as follows:

$$\mathbf{P}_x = \cos\Omega\cos\omega - \sin\Omega\sin\omega\cos i \tag{5.3.1}$$

$$\mathbf{P}_y = \sin\Omega\cos\omega + \cos\Omega\sin\omega\cos i \tag{5.3.2}$$

$$\mathbf{P}_z = \sin\omega\sin i \tag{5.3.3}$$

$$\mathbf{Q}_x = -\cos\Omega\sin\omega - \sin\Omega\cos\omega\cos i \tag{5.3.4}$$

$$\mathbf{Q}_y = -\sin\Omega\sin\omega + \cos\Omega\cos\omega\cos i \tag{5.3.5}$$

$$\mathbf{Q}_z = \cos\omega\sin i. \tag{5.3.6}$$

These formulae work fine until the inclination approaches $0°$ or $180°$. In these cases, we make use of the elements $\tilde{\omega}$ and $\tilde{\omega}_r$, allowing us to put the expressions for $\mathbf{P}_x$, $\mathbf{P}_y$, $\mathbf{Q}_x$, and $\mathbf{Q}_y$ in the following form [Herrick 1974]:

$$\mathbf{P}_x = \frac{1}{2}(1+\cos i)\cos\tilde{\omega} + \frac{1}{2}(1-\cos i)\cos\tilde{\omega}_r \tag{5.3.7}$$

$$\mathbf{P}_y = \frac{1}{2}(1+\cos i)\sin\tilde{\omega} - \frac{1}{2}(1-\cos i)\sin\tilde{\omega}_r \tag{5.3.8}$$

$$\mathbf{Q}_x = -\frac{1}{2}(1+\cos i)\sin\tilde{\omega} - \frac{1}{2}(1-\cos i)\sin\tilde{\omega}_r \tag{5.3.9}$$

$$\mathbf{Q}_y = \frac{1}{2}(1+\cos i)\cos\tilde{\omega} - \frac{1}{2}(1-\cos i)\cos\tilde{\omega}_r \tag{5.3.10}$$

where $\tilde{\omega}$ is the *longitude of perihelion* and $\tilde{\omega}_r$ is called the *retrograde longitude of perihelion*. The expressions in equations (5.3.7)–(5.3.10) will be used in our development of a program for computing Keplerian ephemerides.

The next step in the process is to define a quantity called the *semilatus rectum* of the orbit. This quantity, denoted by p, is defined to be $q(1 + e)$, where q is the perihelion distance and e is the eccentricity. Note that p is always a positive, finite quantity and displays no singularities for any orbit. With p in hand, we are in a position to proceed to the next step, which is the solution of Kepler's equation.

The solution of Kepler's equation is, without a doubt, one of the most fascinating aspects of celestial mechanics. Literally hundreds of methods of solution exist, and the literature is filled with papers describing new methods, as well as variations on the old methods. The advent of the digital computer meant that high-speed solutions could be programmed, and the time required for iterative solutions was not prohibitively long. Nowadays, the object is not to find a method that works, but to find a method that exploits the speed of a fast desktop computer. Perhaps the best review of many popular methods for solving Kepler's equation can be found in a series of papers published in *Celestial Mechanics and Dynamical Astronomy* and co-authored by J. M. A. Danby and T. M. Burkhardt [Danby and Burkhardt 1983; Burkhardt and Danby 1983; and Danby 1987]. Danby also provides a clear exposition in the latest edition of his introductory textbook [Danby 1988]. Another wonderful account of the history behind Kepler's equation can be found in Colwell's recently published book [Colwell 1993]. Countless other papers provide sources of solutions to Kepler's equation.

For elliptical orbital motion, Kepler's equation is stated as

$$E = M + e \sin E \qquad (5.3.11)$$

where e is the eccentricity, E is the *eccentric anomaly* in radians, and M is the *mean anomaly* in radians. The mean anomaly is the angle measured in the plane of the orbit from the perihelion point to the body. The mean anomaly increases uniformly with time, and is the product of the time since perihelion passage and another quantity called the *mean motion*, denoted by n. We can calculate n from the elements q and e and the formula Gaussian constant of gravitation

$$n = \sqrt{\frac{\mu}{|a|^3}} \text{ radians/day} \qquad (5.3.12)$$

where

$\mu = k^2(1 + m)$
k = Gaussian constant of gravitation = 0.01720209895

m = mass of the body in solar masses
a = semi-major axis = $q/(1 - e)$.

For hyperbolic orbits, $e > 1$ and the semi-major axis will be negative. This is why the absolute value of a appears in equation (5.3.12). Also note that the calculation of μ is where the mass of the comet or asteroid is taken into account, if necessary. With this expression for n, we can now write the expression for the mean anomaly M as

$$M = (t - T)\sqrt{\frac{\mu}{|a|^3}} \text{ radians} \qquad (5.3.13)$$

where t is any arbitrary time and T is the time of perihelion passage. Note that we are using units of radians instead of degrees. Now, since we have M and e as functions of the orbital elements, we can proceed to solve Kepler's equation for the eccentric anomaly E.

There are many ways to approach Kepler's equation, and one simple method is to solve equation (5.3.11) by straightforward numerical iteration. That is, we pick an initial guess value for E and plug it into the right-hand side of Kepler's equation, and the result is an improved value of E on the left-hand side. We take this improved value of E and plug it back into the right-hand side and compute a better value. This scheme is continued until E is constant to the desired number of decimal places.

This process is straightforward and will work satisfactorily under most conditions. It is not perfect, however. When the eccentricity approaches 1, the process converges very slowly, and many more iterations are required to reach a given accuracy. There is also the problem of making an intelligent initial guess for E. The usual initial guess is to take $E \approx M$. We seek a method that requires as few iterations as possible, gives rapid convergence, and does not blow up as the eccentricity approaches 1. We would also like a method that can be used for hyperbolic orbits as well, but all known hyperbolic orbits have eccentricities only slightly greater than 1 (1.06, for example) and they can usually be treated as nearly-parabolic orbits. The Laguerre-Conway method is just such a method, and it is the one we will adopt for our purposes.

The Laguerre-Conway method of solving Kepler's equation [Conway 1986] had its origins as a method of finding the roots of an Nth degree polynomial. This method gives cubic convergence and works for all eccentricities, even those approaching unity. Danby gives an good review of the method [Danby 1987]. Most importantly, the Laguerre-Conway method almost always converges within ten iterations. A detailed derivation of the algorithm will not be given here; the reader is referred to Conway's original paper [Conway 1986]. The basic formulae for the method as applied to elliptical orbits are as follows:

$$f = E - e \sin E - M$$
$$f' = 1 - e \cos E$$
$$f'' = e \sin E$$

where the initial guess for E is given by

$$E = M + 0.85\, e\, \text{sign}(\sin M). \qquad (5.3.14)$$

The Laguerre-Conway iteration is defined by:

$$E_{n+1} = E_n + \frac{-5f}{f' + \text{sign}\,(f')\sqrt{|16(f')^2 - 20ff''|}} \qquad (5.3.15)$$

where e = eccentricity ($e < 1$ for elliptical orbits), M = mean anomaly, and primes denote partial derivatives of f with respect to E. Note that f is the function whose root we are attempting to find, and in this case, f is simply Kepler's equation. Equation (5.3.15) is used to compute an improved value of E, which is, in turn, used to compute improved values of f, f', and f''. Equation (5.3.15) is applied until $|f|$ is less than some specified value.

Once we have solved Kepler's equation for E, we can compute the *true anomaly*, which is the angle from the perihelion point of the orbit to the comet or asteroid. The true anomaly is denoted by ν, and for elliptical orbit, the required relationships between E and ν are:

$$r \sin \nu = a\sqrt{1 - e^2}\,\sin E \qquad (5.3.16)$$

$$r \cos \nu = a(\cos E - e) \qquad (5.3.17)$$

where r is the magnitude of the *radius vector*, which is the vector from the center of motion to the body and a is the semi-major axis. Fundamentally, $r \cos \nu$ and $r \sin \nu$ are, respectively, the x and y coordinates of the object in the orbital plane. It is the ultimate goal of any ephemeris program to obtain the quantities $r \sin \nu$ and $r \cos \nu$ for any orbit, because these two quantities can be used to compute the position and velocity vectors in a manner which is independent of the eccentricity of the orbit. This means that we can write a program that uses only two principal subroutines to compute an ephemeris: one that solves Kepler's equation and returns the quantities $r \sin \nu$ and $r \cos \nu$ for a given orbit, and a second that uses these two quantities to compute the body's position and velocity vectors.

With the values of $r \sin \nu$ and $r \cos \nu$ determined, the formulae for the position vector (denoted by $\mathbf{r}$) and the velocity vector (denoted by $\dot{\mathbf{r}}$) are:

$$\mathbf{r} = r\cos\nu\mathbf{P} + r\sin\nu\mathbf{Q} \text{ AU} \qquad (5.3.18)$$

$$\dot{\mathbf{r}} = \sqrt{\frac{\mu}{p}}\sin\nu\mathbf{P} + \sqrt{\frac{\mu}{p}}(e + \cos\nu)\mathbf{Q} \text{ AU/day} \qquad (5.3.19)$$

where $\mathbf{P}$ and $\mathbf{Q}$ are the vectors defined by equations (5.3.1)–(5.3.3), (5.3.4)–(5.3.6), and (5.3.7)–(5.3.9), $\mu = k^2(1 + m)$, and $p = q(1 + e)$. Note that equation (5.3.19) used the quantities $\sin\nu$ and $\cos\nu$; the quantity r was not needed. r can be computed from the relation

$$r = \sqrt{(r\sin\nu)^2 + (r\cos\nu)^2}. \qquad (5.3.20)$$

These position and velocity vectors are heliocentric ecliptic coordinates referred to the same ecliptic and equinox as the orbital elements.

The position and velocity vectors may now be converted to geocentric values by adding the geocentric ecliptic coordinates of the Sun to the heliocentric coordinates of the comet or asteroid. They may also be transformed to equatorial coordinates by the method explained in Chapter 4. If necessary, the position and velocity vectors may also be corrected for precession and nutation by the methods of Chapter 3.

5.4 Hyperbolic Orbits

For hyperbolic orbits, the eccentricity is greater than 1. For this reason, the only major difference between the methods of ephemeris computation for hyperbolic orbits and those for elliptical orbits is the appearance of hyperbolic functions in Kepler's equation. In addition, we must keep in mind that the semi-major axis for a hyperbolic orbit is negative, while the semilatus rectum and the perihelion distance are still positive.

We begin by computing the vectors $\mathbf{P}$ and $\mathbf{Q}$ as in the previous section. Then we compute the quantities n and M from equations (5.3.12) and (5.3.13). Next, as before, solve Kepler's equation by the Laguerre-Conway method as before, but for hyperbolic orbits, Kepler's equation takes the form

$$E = e\sinh E - M \qquad (5.4.1)$$

where E is the eccentric anomaly in radians, M is the mean anomaly in radians, and sinh denotes the hyperbolic sine function. To use the Laguerre-Conway algorithm to solve this equation for E, we make the following identifications:

$$f = e \sinh E - E - M$$
$$f' = e \cosh E - 1$$
$$f'' = e \sinh E$$

with the initial guess for E computed from:

$$E = \ln \left(\frac{2M}{e} + 1.85 \right) \tag{5.4.2}$$

where the primes denote differentiation of f with respect to E. The iteration method using equation (5.3.15) computes better approximations to E until the desired accuracy is reached. Once we have a value for E, the quantities $r \cos \nu$ and $r \sin \nu$ follow from the following formulae:

$$r \sin \nu = |a| \sqrt{e^2 - 1} \sinh E \tag{5.4.3}$$

$$r \cos \nu = |a| (e - \cosh E) \tag{5.4.4}$$

where we use the absolute value of a to take care of the fact that a is negative. Now we can use equations (5.3.18) and (5.3.19) to compute the position and velocity vectors.

5.5 Parabolic Orbits

Next we address the problem of computing $r \sin \nu$ and $r \cos \nu$ for bodies moving in parabolic orbits. Once again, we begin by computing the $\mathbf{P}$ and $\mathbf{Q}$ vectors as for elliptic or hyperbolic orbits. However, the procedure is a bit different. First, we compute the mean anomaly from the formula

$$M = (t - T) \sqrt{\frac{\mu}{2q^3}}. \tag{5.5.1}$$

Next, we compute the quantity $W = 1.5M$ and the quantities Y and ν from the formulae

$$Y = \left(W + \sqrt{W^2 + 1} \right)^{1/3} \tag{5.5.2}$$

and

$$\nu = 2 \tan^{-1} \left(\frac{Y - 1}{Y} \right). \tag{5.5.3}$$

This method of computing ν for parabolic orbits is a direct analytical solution of Barker's equation, which is the parabolic form of Kepler's equation and is stated as follows:

$$\frac{1}{3}\tan^3\left(\frac{\nu}{2}\right) + \tan\left(\frac{\nu}{2}\right) = M. \qquad (5.5.4)$$

Barker's equation differs from the other forms of Kepler's equation in that it has a straightforward analytical solution. After computing ν, we compute $r\sin\nu$ and $r\cos\nu$ from the equations

$$r\cos\nu = q\left(1 - \tan^2\left(\frac{\nu}{2}\right)\right) \qquad (5.5.5)$$

$$r\sin\nu = 2q\tan\left(\frac{\nu}{2}\right). \qquad (5.5.6)$$

Next we use equations (5.3.18) and (5.3.19) to compute the position and velocity vectors. Note that since $r\sin\nu$ and $r\cos\nu$ are functions of the quantity

$$\tan\left(\frac{\nu}{2}\right) \qquad (5.5.7)$$

we can actually bypass the computation of ν itself, because from equation (5.5.3) we can see that

$$\tan\left(\frac{\nu}{2}\right) = \frac{Y - 1}{Y}. \qquad (5.5.8)$$

5.6   Treatment with Universal Variables

The above methods are rigorous and constitute a powerful set of algorithms for the computation of Keplerian heliocentric ephemerides of comets or asteroids. However, we are faced with the problem of using a different form of Kepler's equation for each of the three types of orbits we may encounter. Would it not be nice to have an algorithm that uses only *one* form of Kepler's equation that can be solved for any eccentricity? Of course, the answer is "yes," and such a method can be derived from the theory of *universal variables*. There is one set of formulae that is valid for all conic sections and orbits, and computation time is reduced by the use of the *universal Kepler equation*. There is no need for program logic to "decide" which form of Kepler's equation to use in a given situation. Furthermore, we shall see that the universal Kepler equation can be solved nicely by the Laguerre-Conway method.

We will not present a detailed derivation of universal variable theory here. That would almost constitute an entire book by itself. The reader is referred to the textbook by Samuel Herrick [Herrick 1974] for details. Danby's treatment is also recommended [Danby 1988]. The specific algorithm we adopt here is that of Roger Mansfield [Mansfield 1986]. This algorithm is preferred since it makes use of the perihelion distance as an orbital element as opposed to the semi-major axis. Mansfield's algorithm provides a completely general method of computing the quantities $r \sin \nu$ and $r \cos \nu$, and, hence, the position and velocity vectors, for an object moving in any orbit. In addition, the algorithm can be inverted to allow the computation of the orbital element set given a state vector.

To derive the position and velocity vector from the orbital element set, we proceed as follows. First, compute the quantities α and p from

$$\alpha = \frac{\mu(1-e)}{q} \tag{5.6.1}$$

$$p = q(1+e) \tag{5.6.2}$$

where $\mu = k^2(1+m)$. Next we compute the components of the vectors $\mathbf{P}$ and $\mathbf{Q}$ from equations (5.3.1)–(5.3.6), using the modifications of equations (5.3.7)–(5.3.10) if necessary.

Kepler's equation in universal variables takes on the form

$$t - T = qs + \mu e s^3 c_3(\alpha s^2) \tag{5.6.3}$$

where t is an arbitrary time and s is a new quantity called the *universal anomaly*. s takes on the role of the eccentric anomaly in universal variables. The quantity $c_3(\alpha s^3)$ represents a new type of function called a *Stumpff function*, named for the famous German astronomer Karl Stumpff, who first developed the theory of universal variables. The general Stumpff function $c_n(x)$ is defined by the equation

$$c_n(x) = \sum_{k=0}^{\infty} \frac{(-1)^k x^k}{(2k+n)!} \qquad k = 0, 1, 2, \ldots \tag{5.6.4}$$

Note that equation (5.6.4) is an infinite series. For all real $x \neq 0$, it can be shown that the Stumpff functions obey the relationships

$$c_0\left(x^2\right) = \cos x \qquad c_0\left(-x^2\right) = \cosh x \tag{5.6.5}$$

$$c_1\left(x^2\right) = \frac{\sin x}{x} \qquad c_1\left(-x^2\right) = \frac{\sinh x}{x} \tag{5.6.6}$$

$$c_2\left(x^2\right) = \frac{1 - \cos x}{x^2} \qquad c_2\left(-x^2\right) = \frac{\cosh x - 1}{x^2} \tag{5.6.7}$$

$$c_3\left(x^2\right) = \frac{x - \sin x}{x^3} \qquad c_3\left(-x^2\right) = \frac{\sinh x - x}{x^3} \qquad (5.6.8)$$

and for $x = 0$, we have the relationship $c_n(x) = 1/n!$. We shall only make use of $c_0(x)$, $c_1(x)$, $c_2(x)$, and $c_3(x)$. We shall also make use of the property

$$\frac{d}{ds}s^n c_n(\alpha s^2) = s^{n-1} c_{n-1}(\alpha s^2) \qquad (5.6.9)$$

which can be derived straightforwardly by differentiating equation (5.6.4). These Stumpff functions can be evaluated for any argument through the use of a function called StumpffN. This routine is based on a similar one in Danby's book [Danby 1988]. Note that StumpffN makes use of the series definition for computing $c_2(x)$ and $c_3(x)$ and uses a *recursion relation* to compute $c_0(x)$ and $c_1(x)$. The source code listing for function StumpffN is as follows:

```
function StumpffN(x as double, norder as integer) local as double

   '----- Function to compute the nth order
   '----- Stumpff function for any argument x.
   '----- Input:    x          argument
   '-----           norder     order desired
   '----- Output:   nth order Stumpff function
   '----- Reference:  Danby.  FUN, pp. 172-174.
   '-----------------------------------------------------------------

   dim n  as integer
   dim a  as double
   dim b  as double
   dim c0 as double
   dim c1 as double
   dim c2 as double
   dim c3 as double

   n = 0
   while abs(x) > 0.1#
      incr n
      x = x / 4#
   wend

   a = (1# - x * (1# - x / 182#) / 132#)
   b = (1# - x * (1# - x * a / 90#) / 56#)
   c2 = (1# - x * (1# - x * b / 30#) / 12#) / 2#
   a = (1# - x * (1# - x / 210#) / 156#)
   b = (1# - x * (1# - x * a / 110#) / 72#)
   c3 = (1# - x * (1# - x * b / 42#) / 20#) / 6#

   c1 = 1# - x * c3
   c0 = 1# - x * c2
   while n > 0
      decr n
      c3 = (c2 + c0 * c3) / 4#
      c2 = c1 * c1 / 2#
      c1 = c0 * c1
      c0 = 2 * c0 * c0 - 1#
      x = x * 4#
   wend

   select case norder
      case 0
         StumpffN = c0
      case 1
```

```
      StumpffN = c1
   case 2
      StumpffN = c2
   case 3
      StumpffN = c3
 end select

end function
```

We can now solve the universal Kepler equation by the Laguerre-Conway method if we make the following definitions:

$$f = qs + \mu e s^3 c_3(\alpha s^2) - (t - T) \tag{5.6.10}$$

$$f' = q + \mu e s^2 c_2(\alpha s^2) \tag{5.6.11}$$

$$f'' = \mu e s c_1 (\alpha s^2) \tag{5.6.12}$$

and then apply equation (5.3.15). Note that the initial guess for s is $s = 0$. With the computed value of s, we obtain the quantities $r\cos\nu$ and $r\sin\nu$ from the formulae

$$r\cos\nu = q - \mu s^2 c_2(\alpha s^2) \tag{5.6.13}$$

$$r\sin\nu = \sqrt{\mu q(1 + e)} s c_1 (\alpha s^2) \tag{5.6.14}$$

which, of course, work for any orbit once s is known. We can now compute the components of the position and velocity vectors from the equations (5.3.18) and (5.3.19).

Our program for computing heliocentric ephemerides of comets or asteroids is called EPH, and it incorporates the method of universal variables in the solution of Kepler's equation. The program is built around three primary subprograms: Conway, which carries out the solution of the universal Kepler equation by the Laguerre-Conway method; HelEphemeris, which computes the body's position and velocity vectors at a single instant of time; and StumpffN, which is described above. The source code listings for EPH and its associated subprograms (except for StumpffN, whose listing is presented above) are as follows:

```
'----- EPH.BAS

defdbl a-z

$include "\fecsoftb\astrolib.dec"
$include "\fecsoftb\constant.inc"
$include "\fecsoftb\amodulo.bas"
$include "\fecsoftb\atan2.bas"
$include "\fecsoftb\conway.bas"
$include "\fecsoftb\helephem.bas"
```

```
$include "\fecsoftb\stumpff.bas"

dim Which            as integer
dim element(1 to 6) as double
dim mass            as double
dim StartingJD      as double
dim stepsize        as double
dim numsteps        as integer
dim mu              as double
dim posvec          as string
dim velvec          as string
dim i               as integer
dim jdate           as double
dim posvel(1 to 6)  as double

cls
print "EXAMPLE DRIVER FOR HelEphemeris"
print

print "[1] Input data from keyboard"
print "[2] Use default Comet Halley data"
input "Your choice  ", Which
print
select case Which
  case 1
    call GetUserData(element(), mass, StartingJD, stepsize, numsteps)
  case 2
    call UseThisData(element(), mass, StartingJD, stepsize, numsteps)
end select

'----- compute heliocentric gravitational constant for the body
mu = GaussK * GaussK * (1# + mass)

posvec = "position +##.############# +##.############# +##.############# AU"
velvec = "velocity +##.############# +##.############# +##.############# AU/DAY"

i = 0
jdate = StartingJD
do
  call HelEphemeris(element(), mu, jdate, posvel())
  print "date "; jdate
  print using posvec; posvel(1); posvel(2); posvel(3)
  print using velvec; posvel(4); posvel(5); posvel(6)
  i = i + 1
  jdate = jdate + stepsize
loop until i = numsteps

print
+print "OK"

end

sub GetUserData (element() as double, mass as double, StartingJD as _
    double, stepsize as double, numsteps as integer)

  '----- Subprogram to allow user to input desired data
  '----- from the keyboard.
  '-----------------------------------------------------------------------

  print
  input "Perihelion distance in AU    ", element(1)
  input "Eccentricity                 ", element(2)
  input "Inclination in degrees       ", element(3)
    element(3) = element(3) * D2R
  input "Long. of asc. node in degrees ", element(4)
    element(4) = element(4) * D2R
  input "Arg. of peri. in degrees     ", element(5)
    element(5) = element(5) * D2R
```

```
    input "Julian date of peri. passage  ", element(6)
    input "Body's mass in solar units    ", mass
    input "Starting Julian date          ", StartingJD
    input "Number of steps               ", numsteps
    if numsteps > 1 then
      input "Increment in days             ", stepsize
      print
    else
      stepsize = 0#
    end if

end sub

sub UseThisData (element() as double, mass as double, StartingJD as _
    double, stepsize as double, numsteps as integer)

    '----- Subprogram to supply default input data.  Data is taken
    '----- from the paper by Mansfield (AIAA Paper No. 86-2269-CP)
    '----- and is for Comet Halley.
    '----------------------------------------------------------------------

    '----- elements are referred to equinox/ecliptic of B1950

    '----- perihelion distance (AU)
    element(1) = 0.5871047#
    '----- eccentricity
    element(2) = 0.967276#
    '----- inclination (radians)
    element(3) = 162.23928# * D2R
    '----- longitude of ascending node (radians)
    element(4) = 58.14536# * D2R
    '----- argument of perihelion (radians)
    element(5) = 111.84809# * D2R
    '----- Julian date of perihelion passage (TDT)
    element(6) = 2446470.95175#
    '----- mass (solar masses)
    mass = 0#

    StartingJD = 2446446.5#
    stepsize   = 15#
    numsteps   = 5

end sub

sub conway(uelement() as double, mu as double, jed as double,_
                   r_cos_nu as double, r_sin_nu as double) static

    '----- Subprogram to solve Kepler's equation using the
    '----- method of Conway-Laguerre for universal variables.
    '----- Input:  uelement()  array of universal orbital elements
    '-----         mu          gravitational constant for the body
    '-----         jed         time for which computations are to
    '-----                     be performed
    '----- Output: r_cos_nu   r*cos(true anomaly)
    '-----         r_sin_nu   r*sin(true anomaly)
    '----------------------------------------------------------------------

    dim tspp  as double
    dim alpha as double
    dim s     as double
    dim niter as integer
    dim x     as double
    dim c1    as double
    dim c2    as double
    dim c3    as double
    dim f     as double
    dim fp    as double
    dim fpp   as double
```

```
dim term   as double
dim ds     as double

'----- compute time since perihelion passage in days
tspp = jed - uelement(6)

'----- compute alpha
alpha = mu * (1# - uelement(2)) / uelement(1)

'----- initial guess for s
s = 0#

'----- initialize iteration counter
niter = 0

do
   '----- compute stumpff functions
   x = alpha * s * s
   c1 = stumpffn(x, 1)
   c2 = stumpffn(x, 2)
   c3 = stumpffn(x, 3)

   f = uelement(1) * s + mu * uelement(2) * s * s * s * c3 - tspp
   fp = uelement(1) + mu * uelement(2) * s * s * c2
   fpp = mu * uelement(2) * s * c1

   '----- evaluate laguerre's method
   term = 16# * fp * fp - 20# * f * fpp
   ds = -5# * f / (fp + sgn(fp) * sqr(abs(term)))

   s = s + ds

   niter = niter + 1

   '----- check for convergence or more than ten iterations
   if niter > 10 then
     print "conway: more than ten iterations."
     exit do
   end if

   if (abs(f) < 1d-12) then exit do

loop

'----- now compute r_sin_nu and r_cos_nu
r_sin_nu = sqr(mu * uelement(1) * (1# + uelement(2))) * s * c1
r_cos_nu = uelement(1) - mu * s * s * c2

end sub
```

Note once more that the underscore character at the end of a line denotes the continuation of that line of code to the next line. When executed, EPH prompts the user to choose between entering data from the keyboard and using the default "hard-wired" data, which is for Halley's Comet and is taken from the paper by Roger Mansfield [Mansfield 1986]. This default data is stored in a subprogram called UseThisData. When the data is entered, the program computes the **P** and **Q** vectors in subprogram HelEphemeris. Kepler's equation is then solved using subprogram Conway. Next, the heliocentric position and velocity vectors are computed and returned in the array POSVEL(). We can think of POSVEL() as a six dimensional vector in which the first three elements are the body's position vector components and the last three elements are the body's velocity vector components. The vector constructed in this manner is called the *state vector* of the body. Therefore, the purpose of any ephemeris program is to compute an object's state vector for any instant of time.

The initial menu prompt of program EPH is shown below. In this example, the user has selected the option of using the default data.

```
EXAMPLE DRIVER FOR HelEphemeris

[1] Input data from keyboard
[2] Use default Comet Halley data
Your choice  2

DATE  2446446.5
POSITION  +0.7661010445554  +0.1412849664352  +0.1845468752430 AU
VELOCITY  -0.0101488586183  -0.0248531020570  +0.0014402002764 AU/DAY
DATE  2446461.5
POSITION  +0.5545853783727  -0.2315180562590  +0.1900220853194 AU
VELOCITY  -0.0186210061554  -0.0239728771526  -0.0010135920652 AU/DAY
DATE  2446476.5
POSITION  +0.2079075880834  -0.5382863144591  +0.1475610858581 AU
VELOCITY  -0.0266597162847  -0.0156586197919  -0.0046061695538 AU/DAY
DATE  2446491.5
POSITION  -0.2033521832732  -0.6916767159123  +0.0616012213407 AU
VELOCITY  -0.0270357463502  -0.0053792879580  -0.0064461766049 AU/DAY
DATE  2446506.5
POSITION  -0.5868244783278  -0.7234436555044  -0.0373588041138 AU
VELOCITY  -0.0239706312583  +0.0004510806971  -0.0065978726895 AU/DAY

OK
```

The user can specify the interval of the ephemeris computations as well as the number of steps in the ephemeris. There is nothing fancy about this program, and there are many ways in which it can be enhanced by the user. The program's greatest advantage is that it can handle orbits of all shapes. It can also handle low-inclination orbits well. There may be problems with orbits that have very small eccentricities, since in this case the orbit is nearly circular and the perihelion point becomes more and more ill-defined.

5.7 Conversion from State Vector to Orbital Elements

In section 5.2, we stated that the solution of the differential equations of motion for an object requires six independent constants of integration and one form for these constants is the orbital element set q, e, i, Ω, ω, and T. Another form for these six constants is the initial state vector. In other words, specifying the six components of the position and velocity vectors at some initial time t_o is completely equivalent to specifying the orbital elements. If the two specifications are equivalent, there must be some way of converting the initial state vector components to orbital elements. There is, and we present the algorithm below.

We assume we are given the initial position and velocity vectors $\mathbf{r}$ and $\dot{\mathbf{r}}$ and the time t. The first step is to compute the *angular momentum* vector (actually angular momentum per unit mass), and this is given by the vector cross-product of $\mathbf{r}$ and $\dot{\mathbf{r}}$.

$$\mathbf{L} = \mathbf{r} \times \dot{\mathbf{r}} \qquad (5.7.1)$$

Next, we compute the following quantities:

$$r = |\mathbf{r}| \qquad (5.7.2)$$

$$L = |\mathbf{L}| \qquad (5.7.3)$$

$$\mathbf{W} = \frac{\mathbf{L}}{L} \quad (\mathbf{W} \text{ is a } unit \ vector) \qquad (5.7.4)$$

$$\mathbf{U} = \frac{\mathbf{r}}{r} \quad (\mathbf{U} \text{ is a } unit \ vector) \qquad (5.7.5)$$

$$\mathbf{V} = \mathbf{W} \times \mathbf{U} \quad (\mathbf{V} \text{ is also a } unit \ vector) \qquad (5.7.6)$$

$$p = \frac{L^2}{\mu} \quad \left(\mu = k^2(1 + m) \text{ as before}\right) \qquad (5.7.7)$$

$$\alpha = \frac{2\mu}{r} - \dot{\mathbf{r}} \cdot \dot{\mathbf{r}}. \qquad (5.7.8)$$

Now we can obtain the elements from the following formulae:

$$e = \sqrt{1 - \alpha \frac{L^2}{\mu^2}} \qquad (5.7.9)$$

$$q = \frac{p}{1 + e} \qquad (5.7.10)$$

$$\chi = \frac{\sin i \sin \Omega}{1 + \cos i} = \frac{W_1}{1 + W_3} \qquad (5.7.11)$$

$$\psi = \frac{\sin i \cos \Omega}{1 + \cos i} = \frac{-W_2}{1 + W_3}. \qquad (5.7.12)$$

From χ and ψ we can compute i and Ω from

$$\sin i = \frac{2\sqrt{\chi^2 + \psi^2}}{1 + \chi^2 + \psi^2} \qquad (5.7.13)$$

$$\cos i = \frac{1 - \chi^2 - \psi^2}{1 + \chi^2 + \psi^2} \tag{5.7.14}$$

$$\sin \Omega = \frac{\chi}{\sqrt{\chi^2 + \psi^2}} \tag{5.7.15}$$

$$\cos \Omega = \frac{\psi}{\sqrt{\chi^2 + \psi^2}} \tag{5.7.16}$$

$$i = \texttt{atan2}(\sin i, \cos i) \tag{5.7.17}$$

$$\Omega = \texttt{atan2}(\sin \Omega, \cos \Omega). \tag{5.7.18}$$

Now we compute the quantities

$$\dot{r} = \dot{\mathbf{r}} \cdot \mathbf{U}, \quad r\dot{\nu} = \dot{\mathbf{r}} \cdot \mathbf{V} \tag{5.7.19}$$

from which we can form the following equations:

$$e \sin \nu = \dot{r} \sqrt{\frac{p}{\mu}} \tag{5.7.20}$$

$$e \cos \nu = r\dot{\nu} \sqrt{\frac{p}{\mu}} - 1. \tag{5.7.21}$$

These two equations allow us to compute ν from $\nu = \texttt{atan2}(e \sin \nu, e \cos \nu)$. However, we do not need the actual value of ν, so we can bypass its computation. If we define the quantity $z = e \sin \nu / (e + e \cos \nu)$, which is really $\tan(\nu/2)$, we can compute $\cos \nu$ and $\sin \nu$ from[1]

$$\cos \nu = \frac{1 - z^2}{1 + z^2} \tag{5.7.22}$$

$$\sin \nu = \frac{2z}{1 + z^2}. \tag{5.7.23}$$

Now we can compute $\mathbf{P}$ and $\mathbf{Q}$ from

$$\mathbf{P} = \mathbf{U} \cos \nu - \mathbf{V} \sin \nu \tag{5.7.24}$$

$$\mathbf{Q} = \mathbf{U} \sin \nu + \mathbf{V} \cos \nu \tag{5.7.25}$$

---

[1] In [Mansfield 1986], the left-hand sides—or equivalently, the right-hand sides—of these two equations are reversed.

and finally, we can compute ω from $\omega = \texttt{atan2}(\mathbf{P}_z, \mathbf{Q}_z)$. Now all that remains is to compute T, the time of perihelion passage. To get T, we compute the quantity w from

$$w = \sqrt{\frac{q}{\mu(1+e)}}\, z \tag{5.7.26}$$

and then compute the quantity s from the universal formula

$$s = 2\left(w - \frac{\alpha w^3}{3} + \frac{\alpha^2 w^5}{5} - \frac{\alpha^3 w^7}{7} + \frac{\alpha^4 w^9}{9} - \frac{\alpha^5 w^{11}}{11} + \cdots\right) \tag{5.7.27}$$

which is another infinite series. With s known, we can compute the time since perihelion passage from the equation

$$t - T = qs + \mu e s^3 c_3\left(\alpha s^2\right) \tag{5.7.28}$$

which is the universal Kepler equation. We have assumed that t is known, and therefore we can solve equation (5.7.28) for T to get

$$T = t - qs - \mu e s^3 c_3\left(\alpha s^2\right). \tag{5.7.29}$$

The program that implements this algorithm is called TSPP, and, like EPH, it is built around the key subprograms StumpffN and Stat2Eel. Subprogram Stat2Ele carries out the actual conversion of the state vector to the orbital element set. The program also provides the user with the option of entering data from the keyboard or using default data for Halley's comet, which should result in the default orbital elements used in program EPH. The source code listings for TSPP and its important subprograms are as follows:

```
'----- TSPP.BAS

defdbl a-z

$include "\fecsoftb\astrolib.dec"
$include "\fecsoftb\constant.inc"
$include "\fecsoftb\atan2.bas"
$include "\fecsoftb\stat2ele.bas"
$include "\fecsoftb\stumpff.bas"
$include "\fecsoftb\uvector.bas"
$include "\fecsoftb\vcross.bas"
$include "\fecsoftb\vdot.bas"
$include "\fecsoftb\vecmag.bas"

dim which as integer
dim state(1 to 6) as double
dim element(1 to 6) as double
dim mu             as double
dim jdate          as double
dim posvec         as string
dim velvec         as string

cls
```

```
print "EXAMPLE DRIVER FOR Stat2Ele"
print

print "[1] Input data from the keyboard"
print "[2] Use default data"
input "Your choice  ", which
select case which
  case 1
    call GetUserData(state(), mu, jdate)
  case 2
    call UseThisData(state(), mu, jdate)
end select

call Stat2Elem(state(), mu, jdate, element())

posvec = "+##.############## +##.############## +##.############## AU"
velvec = "+##.############## +##.############## +##.############## AU/DAY"

print
print "INITIAL STATE VECTOR"
print using posvec; state(1); state(2); state(3)
print using velvec; state(4); state(5); state(6)
print
print "ELEMENT SET"
print using "Perihelion distance (AU) ##.########"; element(1)
print using "Eccentricity             ##.#########"; element(2)
print using "Inclination      (deg) +###.########"; element(3) * R2D
print using "Long_. of node   (deg) +###.########"; element(4) * R2D
print using "Arg_. of peri_.  (deg) +###.########"; element(5) * R2D
print using "T (TDT)                ######.########"; element(6)

print
print "OK"

end

sub GetUserData(state() as double, mu as double, jdate as double)

  '----- Subprogram to allow user to input desired data.
  '----- from the keyboard.
  '-----------------------------------------------------------------------

  dim mass as double

  print
  print "Enter position vector"
  input "", state(1), state(2), state(3)
  print
  print "Enter velocity vector"
  input "", state(4), state(5), state(6)
  print
  input "Enter Julian Date  ", jdate
  print
  input "Enter mass in solar masses  ", mass
    mu = GaussK * GaussK * (1# + mass)

end sub

sub UseThisData(state() as double, mu as double, jdate as double)

  '----- Subprogram to supply default input data.
  '----- Data is taken from the paper by Mansfield
  '----- (AIAA Paper No. 86-2269-CP) and is for
  '----- Comet Halley.
  '-----------------------------------------------------------------------

  dim mass as double
```

```
'----- components referred to equinox/ecliptic of B1950

'----- position vector components
state(1) = 0.7661010445554045#
state(2) = 0.1412849664351819#
state(3) = 0.1845468752429582#

'----- velocity vector components
state(4) = -0.0101488586182795#
state(5) = -2.485310205695914D-02
state(6) = 1.440200276392141D-03

'----- mass
mass = 0#
mu = GaussK * GaussK * (1# + mass)

'----- julian day number (TDB)
jdate = 2446446.5#

end sub
```

The initial screen from program TSPP is shown below. As in the previous
example, the user has selected the option to use the default data.

```
EXAMPLE DRIVER FOR Stat2Ele

[1] Input data from the keyboard
[2] Use default data
Your choice  2

INITIAL STATE VECTOR
 +0.766101044555405   +0.141284966435182   +0.184546875242958 AU
 -0.010148858618280   -0.024853102056959   +0.001440200276392 AU/DAY

ELEMENT SET
Perihelion distance (AU)   0.58710470
Eccentricity               0.967276000
Inclination (deg)        +162.23928000
Long. of node (deg)       +58.14536000
Arg. of peri. (deg)      +111.84809000
T (TDT)              2446471.95175000

OK
```

In this example note that the time of perihelion passage is computed as a
Julian day number and that the initial orbital elements are fully recovered.

5.8   Precession and Orbital Elements

In this section, we present a program called ELEPREC that will transform
angular orbital elements referred to an initial equinox to elements referred to
another desired equinox.

We know that precession alters the coordinates of celestial objects. The
position of the equinox is constantly changing so any quantity that is measured relative to the equinox must necessarily change with time. Conse-
quently, the angular elements of an orbit change with time because of precession. When specifying the elements of any orbit, the equinox to which the

elements are referred must also be specified. For example, one may read that
the angular elements of a certain orbit are

$$i = 26°, \qquad \Omega = 123°, \qquad \omega = 90° \qquad (5.8.1)$$

where all angles are relative to the ecliptic and equinox of J2000. These are
the only orbital elements that depend on the position of the equinox; the
semi-major axis and eccentricity of the orbit are geometric in nature and
serve only to specify the size and shape of the orbit.

The formulae needed to transform elements from an initial equinox to another equinox can be derived using spherical trigonometry. We will not carry
out that derivation here but simply state the formulae. Let i_o, Ω_o, and ω_o
be the angular elements referred to the initial equinox and the unsubscripted
values be the elements referred to the final equinox. The rigorous transformation formulae, taken from the French almanac *Connaissance des Temps*,
are:

$$\cos i = \cos i_o \cos \pi_A + \sin i_o \sin \pi_A \cos(\Pi_A - \Omega_o) \qquad (5.8.2)$$

$$\sin i \sin(p_A + \Pi_A - \Omega) = \sin i_o \sin(\Pi_A - \Omega_o) \qquad (5.8.3)$$

$$\sin i \cos(p_A + \Pi_A - \Omega) = -\sin \pi_A \cos i_o + \cos \pi_A \sin i_o \cos(\Pi_A - \Omega_o) \qquad (5.8.4)$$

$$\sin \Delta\omega \sin i = \sin \pi_A \sin(\Pi_A - \Omega_A) \qquad (5.8.5)$$

$$\cos \Delta\omega \sin i = \sin i_o \cos \pi_A - \cos i_o \sin \pi_A \cos(\Pi_A - \Omega_o) \qquad (5.8.6)$$

$$\omega = \omega_o + \Delta\omega \qquad (5.8.7)$$

where the quantities π_A, Π_A, and p_A are fundamental precessional quantities that can be computed as explicit functions of time. The expressions
used in program ELEPREC are taken from [Lieske 1977]. These formulae are
completely rigorous and should suffice even in cases of low eccentricity. The
problem then is that the longitude of the node and the argument of perihelion become ill-defined. The source code listings for program ELEPREC and its
associated routines are as follows:

```
'----- ELEPREC.BAS

defdbl a-z

$include "\fecsoftb\astrolib.dec"
$include "\fecsoftb\constant.inc"
$include "\fecsoftb\amodulo.bas"
$include "\fecsoftb\atan2.bas"
$include "\fecsoftb\dms.bas"
$include "\fecsoftb\epoc2jed.bas"
$include "\fecsoftb\precelem.bas"

dim Eqnx1 as string
dim Eqnx2 as string
dim Inclination as double
dim Node as double
dim ArgPeri as double
dim element(1 to 3) as double

cls
print "EXAMPLE DRIVER FOR PrecessElements"
print

input "First equinox   ", Eqnx1
input "Final equinox   ", Eqnx2
input "Inclination    ", Inclination
input "Node           ", Node
input "Arg. peri.     ", ArgPeri

element(1) = Inclination * D2R
element(2) = Node * D2R
element(3) = ArgPeri * D2R

call PrecessElements(Eqnx1, element(), Eqnx2)

print
print "PRECESSED ELEMENTS"

Inclination = element(1) * R2D
Node = element(2) * R2D
ArgPeri = element(3) * R2D

print using "Inclination +###.#####"; Inclination
print using "Node        +###.#####"; Node
print using "Arg_. peri_.  +###.#####"; ArgPeri

print
print "OK"

end
```

Program **ELEPREC** begins by prompting the user for the initial equinox. This can be input either as a Julian day number (2447678.5, for example) or as a Julian or Besselian epoch (B1950, for example). The final equinox can also be input in either format. The program uses a subprogram called **Epoch2JED** to convert a Julian or Besselian epoch to its corresponding Julian day number. **ELEPREC** then prompts the user for the initial inclination, longitude of ascending node, and argument of perihelion and stores these values in an array called **ELEMENT()**. The main program then calls subprogram **PrecessElements**, passing the **ELEMENT()** array. In this routine, both the precessional parameters and the new elements are computed. The new inclination and longitude of ascending node are computed first, then the new argument of perihelion is computed. The new elements are stored in the *same* array in which they were passed to `PrecessElements`. This is *extremely* important. The array `ELEMENT()` is *not* preserved during program execution, so if anything is to be done to or with the initial elements it must be done *before* the transformation to the new equinox. The new elements are then displayed on the screen along with the initial ones. Below are two sample dialog screens from program `ELEPREC`.

```
EXAMPLE DRIVER FOR PrecessElements

First equinox  B1950
Final equinox  J2000
Inclination    12.1234
Node           102.495
Arg. peri.      24.9444

PRECESSED ELEMENTS
Inclination  +12.12136
Node        +103.16453
Arg. peri.   +24.97394

OK

EXAMPLE DRIVER FOR PrecessElements

First equinox  2451545
Final equinox  B1950
Inclination    12.12136
Node           103.16453
Arg. peri.      24.97394

PRECESSED ELEMENTS
Inclination  +12.12340
Node        +102.49500
Arg. peri.   +24.94440

OK
```

The programs and routines presented in this chapter make computing heliocentric ephemerides quick and easy. The user no longer has to worry about separate routines for orbits of different eccentricities. The code is easily modified to incorporate many useful options. For example, precession could be compensated for by allowing the user to input the desired reference equinox, and the orbital elements could be precessed to this equinox, if it differs from the equinox of the elements to begin with, via subprogram `PrecessElements`. By vectorially adding the geocentric coordinates of the Sun (or equivalently, the heliocentric coordinates of the Earth) to the heliocentric coordinates of the comet or asteroid, we obtain a geocentric ephemeris of the comet or asteroid. From here, we can obtain the object's *elongation* (angular distance from the Sun) and other useful data. Finally, notice that to modify the software for use with Earth-orbiting satellites, all we need do is change the value of the variable `GaussK` located in the file `constant.inc`. Its current value is that for heliocentric motion.

PROGRAMMING EXERCISE: Write a subprogram that uses an alternative algorithm for precessing orbital elements. Use the original element set to generate an equatorial position vector, which, for convenience, may be a unit vector. Then precess the position vector using the method in Chapter 3. Use the precessed state vector to generate a new set of orbital elements. See a paper by Lieske [Lieske 1994] for more information on precessing orbital elements from B1950 to J2000.

PROGRAMMING EXERCISE: Study the following program listing, and then write a brief description of the method it uses to precess orbital elements. Modify the program into a subprogram that may be included in another program. Test the subprogram with the sample data from the above example. Which method would you expect to be the more accurate and why?

```
'----- RIGOROUS.BAS

defdbl a-z

$include "\fecsoftb\astrolib.dec"
$include "\fecsoftb\constant.inc"
$include "\fecsoftb\acos.bas"
$include "\fecsoftb\amodulo.bas"
$include "\fecsoftb\atan2.bas"
$include "\fecsoftb\epoc2jed.bas"
$include "\fecsoftb\funarg.bas"
$include "\fecsoftb\mrotate.bas"
$include "\fecsoftb\nutation.bas"
$include "\fecsoftb\obliquty.bas"
$include "\fecsoftb\precess.bas"
$include "\fecsoftb\rotmat.bas"

dim epoch1     as string
dim epoch2     as string
dim I          as double
dim node       as double
dim arg        as double
dim p(1 to 3)  as double
dim q(1 to 3)  as double
dim w(1 to 3)  as double
dim p1(1 to 3) as double
dim q1(1 to 3) as double
dim w1(1 to 3) as double
dim newnode    as double
dim newi       as double
dim newarg     as double
dim eps1       as double
dim eps2       as double
dim epsdot     as double
dim jed1       as double
dim jed2       as double
dim zeta       as double
dim z          as double
dim theta      as double
dim zetadot    as double
dim zdot       as double
dim thetadot   as double

cls
print "EXAMPLE DRIVER FOR RIGOROUS ELEMENT PRECESSION"
print
```

```
input "Enter initial epoch or Julian date  ", epoch1
epoch1 = ucase$(epoch1)
input "Enter final epoch or Julian date   ", epoch2
epoch2 = ucase$(epoch2)

if left$(epoch1,1) = "J" or left$(epoch1,1) = "B" then
   call Epoch2JED(epoch1,jed1)
else
   jed1 = val(epoch1)
end if

if left$(epoch2,1) = "J" or left$(epoch2,1) = "B" then
   call Epoch2JED(epoch2,jed2)
else
   jed2 = val(epoch2)
end if

input "enter inclination   ", I
I = I * D2R
input "enter node  ", node
node = node * D2R
input "enter arg peri  ", arg
arg = arg * D2R

p(1) = cos(arg)*cos(node)-sin(arg)*sin(node)*cos(I)
p(2) = cos(arg)*sin(node)+sin(arg)*cos(node)*cos(I)
p(3) = sin(arg)*sin(I)

q(1) = -sin(arg)*cos(node)-cos(arg)*sin(node)*cos(I)
q(2) = -sin(arg)*sin(node)+cos(arg)*cos(node)*cos(I)
q(3) =  cos(arg)*sin(I)

w(1) =  sin(node)*sin(I)
w(2) = -cos(node)*sin(I)
w(3) =  cos(I)

'----- Compute the equatorial precessional angles
call GetPrecessParams(jed1,jed2,zeta,z,theta,zetadot,zdot,thetadot)

'----- precess p()
call Obliquity(J2000.0,jed1,0,eps1,epsdot)
call Obliquity(J2000.0,jed2,0,eps2,epsdot)
call MRotate (p(), 1, -eps1  , p())
call MRotate (p(), 3, -zeta  , p())
call MRotate (p(), 2,  theta , p())
call MRotate (p(), 3, -z     , p())
call MRotate (p(), 1,  eps2  , p())

'----- precess q()
call MRotate (q(), 1, -eps1  , q())
call MRotate (q(), 3, -zeta  , q())
call MRotate (q(), 2,  theta , q())
call MRotate (q(), 3, -z     , q())
call MRotate (q(), 1,  eps2  , q())

'----- precess w()
call MRotate (w(), 1, -eps1  , w())
call MRotate (w(), 3, -zeta  , w())
call MRotate (w(), 2,  theta , w())
call MRotate (w(), 3, -z     , w())
call MRotate (w(), 1,  eps2  , w())

'----- get new elements
newnode = atan2(w(1),-w(2))
newi    = atan2(sqr(p(3)^2+q(3)^2),w(3))
```

```
newarg  = atan2(p(3),q(3))

print "NEW ELEMENTS"
print newi * R2D
print newnode * R2D
print newarg * R2D

print
print "OK"

end
```

PROGRAMMING EXERCISE: The quantites $r \cos \nu$ and $r \sin \nu$, with their time derivatives, constitute the rectangular coordinates and velocities of an object in its orbit. Develop a routine that will convert these coordinates and velocities into ecliptic coordinates and velocities using rotation matrices. Compare this method to that using the **P** and **Q** vectors.

PROGRAMMING EXERCISE: The ephemeris routines developed in this chapter only model the Keplerian motion of a solar system object. There is no accounting for planetary perturbations, the finite velocity of light, or relativistic effects. These topics are presented in the next chapter. After completing that chapter, develop additional routines to go along with the ones already presented in the current chapter, which compensate for these additional effects. Try to make them modular so they can be used optionally at the discretion of the user.

Chapter 6

Position Reductions for Celestial Objects

6.1   Introduction

In this chapter, we present routines which are designed to perform rigorous positional reductions for solar system objects. The basic reduction procedure is for solar system objects for which a barycentric ephemeris is available and for stars. The effects of polar motion and atmospheric refraction are also considered, with appropriate software for implementing the corrections. Our reduction procedure is, strictly speaking, only for optical observations. We do not develop methods for the reduction of laser/radar ranging, Very Long Baseline Interferometry (VLBI), or other similar observatons. These more accurate observations, however, directly influence the accuracy of modern ephemerides.

6.2   Preliminary Explanations

The method described in this chapter has been fully documented in the *Astronomical Almanac* each year since 1984. In fact, the method is the exact same method used to prepare the data presented in the *Astronomical Almanac*. The procedure is rigorous and takes into account aberration, relativistic deflection of light due to the Sun's gravitational field, precession from J2000.0, nutation, and the fact that there is a finite light time from the Earth to the object. The user can even correct for the observer not actually being at the center of the Earth. With this correction, one can specify the position of a planet on the celestial sphere as seen from any location on the surface of the Earth.

6.2.1   Mean Place

Before we begin, we must first define the various ways we can specify an object's coordinates. We choose to employ the definitions assembled by Kaplan et al. [Kaplan 1989]. First, we have the *mean place*, which is defined by the object's barycentric (referred to the solar system *barycenter* or center of mass) equatorial rectangular coordinates. The mean place is referred to the mean equator and equinox of J2000.0. The mean place is also what one retrieves from an ephemeris data file to begin a reduction procedure.

6.2.2   Apparent Place

Of more practical importance is the *apparent place*, which is defined by the coordinates of the object with respect to the true equator and equinox of date as seen from the center of the Earth. Atmospheric refraction is not taken into account in the apparent place. The apparent place does, however, include the effects of precession, nutation, aberration, and relativistic light deflection due to the Sun's gravitational field. The aberrational correction arises from the fact that light takes a finite amount of time to travel from the object to the observer. Therefore, when the observer sees the object at time T, the object appears as it did not at time T, but at time $T - r/c$, where r is the object's geocentric distance and c is the speed of light. The aberrational correction also accounts for the simultaneous motions of the object and of the Earth at the time of observation. Our vantage point is constantly changing due to the Earth's orbital motion around the Sun (actually the solar system barycenter), and this is called the *annual aberration* for obvious reasons. Our vantage point also changes as the Earth rotates on its axis. This is called *diurnal aberration*, again, for obvious reasons.

6.2.3   Topocentric Place

One can take the apparent place and correct it for the fact that the observer is not really at the Earth's center, but on the surface of an oblate spheroid that is also rotating. These corrections are called, respectively, parallax and diurnal aberration, and their application to the apparent place yields the object's *topocentric place*. As with the apparent place, atmospheric refraction is ignored.

6.2.4   Virtual Place

An object's *virtual place* is merely its apparent place, but referred to the mean equator and equinox of J2000.0. The corrections for aberration and relativistic light deflection are still included however. Obviously, the virtual place is geocentric too.

6.2.5 Local Place

An object's *local place* is to its topocentric place as its virtual place is to its apparent place. That is, the local place is identical to the topocentric place, with the exception that the coordinates are referred to the mean equator and equinox of J2000.0. The virtual and local places are useful for reductions involving phenomena that do not depend on any specific coordinate system, such as planetary conjunctions.

6.2.6 Astrometric Place

Finally, if we start with an object's mean place and correct it only for light's finite travel time, we have the object's *astrometric place*. The underlying assumption is that for objects very close together (in the same telescopic field of view perhaps) in the sky, the effects of aberration, light deflection, precession, and nutation will be approximately the same for each object and these effects will essentially "cancel out of" the reduction procedure. The *relative* positions of the objects will not be influenced by these effects.

These terms, especially virtual place and local place, are not employed universally in astronomy. Instead, the perceived position of an object is often discussed in terms of the physical effects acting to alter its location in the sky.

6.3 Apparent Place of Major Planets

At the outset, one needs a *solar system barycentric ephemeris* of the desired planet. The "official" source for barycentric ephemerides used in the preparation of the *Astronomical Almanac* is the DE200 ephemeris produced by the Jet Propulsion Laboratory. DE200 was produced as the result of a large-scale numerical integration of the motions of the Sun, the nine major planets, and the Moon. DE200 directly gives the barycentric positions and velocities of these objects in an equatorial coordinate frame referred to the equinox of J2000.0. The time scale used for these ephemerides is the T_{eph} scale, so usually some time scale conversion is needed because astronomers usually refer Earth-based observations to the UTC time scale. Refer to Chapter 8 for more information on obtaining and preparing fundamental planetary ephemeris data files for use.

The procedure for obtaining a planet's apparent place can be summarized in five basic steps:

1. Convert the desired time for which the apparent place is to be computed from coordinated universal time (UTC) to barycentric dynamical time (TDB). We will use TDB as an approximation to T_{eph}.

2. Calculate the geocentric rectangular coordinates of the planet from a barycentric ephemeris of the planet and the Earth for the standard equator and equinox of J2000.0 and time argument TDB, allowing for light time calculated from heliocentric (actually solar system barycentric) coordinates. This step is called the *light time correction*.

3. Calculate the direction of the planet relative to the natural frame (the geocentric inertial frame that is instantaneously stationary in the space-time reference frame of the solar system), allowing for light deflection resulting from solar gravitation. This step can be referred to as the *light deflection correction*.

4. Calculate the direction of the planet relative to the geocentric proper frame by applying the correction for the Earth's orbital velocity about the barycenter (annual aberration). The resulting direction is for the standard equator and equinox of J2000.0. This is the *aberrational correction*.

5. Correct for precession and nutation to refer the coordinates to the true equator and equinox of date.

The computational details and the formulae used in the program are as follows:

Step 1: The apparent place is required for a time on the UTC scale, but the barycentric ephemerides use the TDB time scale. The following formulae are sufficient to convert TDT to TDB:

$$\mathrm{JD} = \mathrm{Julian\ day\ number} \qquad (6.3.1)$$

$$g = 357°53 + 0°9856003(\mathrm{JD} - 2451545.0) \qquad (6.3.2)$$

$$\mathrm{TDB} = \mathrm{TDT} + 0\overset{s}{.}001658 \sin g + 0\overset{s}{.}000014 \sin 2g \qquad (6.3.3)$$

where g is the mean anomaly of the Earth in its orbit. In many cases, the distinction between TDT and TDB can be neglected since the maximum difference is about $0\overset{s}{.}0017$ of time. Equation (6.3.3) is only good enough for optical observations. The routine described in Chapter 2 can be used to convert from the UTC time scale to the TDB time scale. For the remainder of this chapter, we will assume that all specified times are already on the TDB time scale and that no further conversion is necessary. The user is encouraged to add the time conversion routine to the drivers presented in this chapter.

Step 2: Let t = the TDB at which the apparent place is required. Using the barycentric ephemeris, extract the barycentric position and velocity of the Earth at time t. These vectors are denoted by $\mathbf{E}_B(t)$ and $\dot{\mathbf{E}}_B(t)$, respectively. Using the ephemeris again, compute the barycentric position vector $\mathbf{Q}_B$ of the planet at time $(t-\tau)$, where τ is the light time, so that light emitted by the planet at the event $\mathbf{Q}_B(t-\tau)$ arrives at the Earth at the event $\mathbf{E}_B(t)$. The problem with this is that the light time is not known in advance, so we must solve for it iteratively. We must first calculate the heliocentric position vector of the Earth ($\mathbf{E}$), the geocentric position vector of the planet ($\mathbf{P}$), and the the heliocentric position vector of the planet ($\mathbf{Q}$). To begin the iteration procedure, let $\tau = 0$ and calculate

$$\mathbf{P} = \mathbf{Q}_B(t - \tau) - \mathbf{E}_B(t) \qquad (6.3.4)$$

$$\mathbf{E} = \mathbf{E}_B(t) - \mathbf{S}_B(t) \qquad (6.3.5)$$

$$\mathbf{Q} = \mathbf{Q}_B(t - \tau) - \mathbf{S}_B(t - \tau). \qquad (6.3.6)$$

In these equations, $\mathbf{S}_B$ is the barycentric position vector of the Sun. This is also computed from the ephemeris. Now calculate an improved value of τ from

$$c\tau = P + \frac{2\mu}{c^2} \ln\left(\frac{E + P + Q}{E - P + Q}\right) \qquad (6.3.7)$$

where

$$\mu = \text{heliocentric gravitational constant} = GM_o$$
$$G = \text{gravitational constant}$$
$$M_o = \text{mass of the Sun}$$
$$c = \text{velocity of light in } AU/\text{day}$$
$$P = |\mathbf{P}|, \; Q = |\mathbf{Q}|, \; E = |\mathbf{E}|.$$

The symbol $||$ denotes the magnitude of a vector.

With this new value of τ, obtain the barycentric position of the planet at time $(t - \tau)$ from the ephemeris and get a more accurate value of τ. Repeat the process until two consecutive values of τ differ by the required tolerance. Note that the value of P calculated when $\tau = 0$ is the *geometric* distance from the Earth and the planet. The value of P calculated when τ has converged to its final value is the *relativistic light path distance* between the Earth and the planet. The two values will differ slightly, and the distinction may be important, depending on the specific application. A complete derivation of the light time equation used in this step is presented in [Murray 1983].

Step 3: Calculate the following unit vectors:

$$\mathbf{p} = \frac{\mathbf{P}}{P}, \qquad \mathbf{q} = \frac{\mathbf{Q}}{Q}, \qquad \mathbf{e} = \frac{\mathbf{E}}{E}. \tag{6.3.8}$$

Compute the geocentric position vector of the planet, corrected for light deflection, from the equation

$$\mathbf{p}_1 = \mathbf{p} + \frac{2\mu}{Ec^2} \cdot \frac{(\mathbf{p} \cdot \mathbf{q})\mathbf{e} - (\mathbf{e} \cdot \mathbf{p})\mathbf{q}}{1 + \mathbf{q} \cdot \mathbf{e}}. \tag{6.3.9}$$

To order μ/c^2, $\mathbf{p}_1$ is a unit vector.

Step 4: Now calculate the proper direction of the planet in the geocentric inertial frame that is moving with the instantaneous velocity $\mathbf{V}$ of the Earth relative to the natural frame from the equation

$$\mathbf{p}_2 = \frac{\beta^{-1}\mathbf{p}_1 + \dfrac{1 + (\mathbf{p}_1 \cdot \mathbf{V})}{1 + \beta^{-1}}\mathbf{V}}{1 + \mathbf{p}_1 \cdot \mathbf{V}} \tag{6.3.10}$$

where

$$\mathbf{V} = \frac{\dot{\mathbf{E}}_B}{c} \tag{6.3.11}$$

and

$$\beta = (1 - V^2)^{-1/2}. \tag{6.3.12}$$

The velocity $\mathbf{V}$ is expressed in units of the velocity of light and is equal to the Earth's velocity in the barycentric frame to order V^2.

Step 5: Finally, apply corrections for precession from J2000.0 to date and for nutation by multiplying $\mathbf{p}_2$ by the matrix $\mathbf{R}$, which is computed from the general precession matrix and the nutation matrix with the formula $\mathbf{R} = \mathbf{NP}$, where $\mathbf{N}$ is the nutation matrix and $\mathbf{P}$ is the precession matrix. $\mathbf{Q}$-matrices may be used if desired (see Chapter 9).

$$\mathbf{p}_3 = \mathbf{R}\mathbf{p}_2. \tag{6.3.13}$$

If necessary, the rectangular components of $\mathbf{p}_3$ can be converted to polar coordinates (right ascension and declination) using one of the utility routines described in Chapter 9. After all, we actually observe the polar coordinates (right ascension and declination) instead of the rectangular coordinates.

The subprogram that implements this reduction procedure is called `Reduce`, and its source code listing is as follows:

Flowchart for REDUCE.BAS

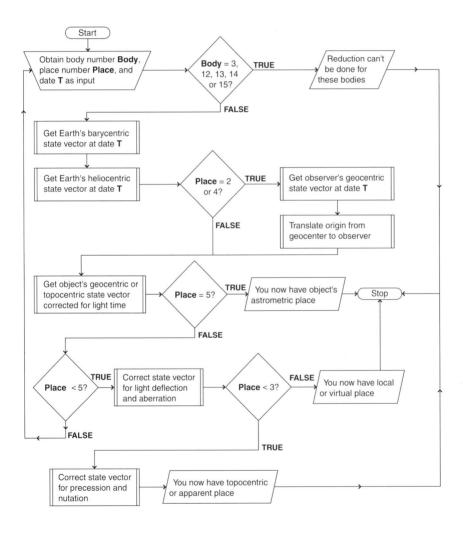

```
sub Reduce(jed as double, body as integer, place as integer, _
           stardata() as double, p3() as double) static

    '----- Subprogram for reducing source planetary or solar ephemerides
    '----- to apparent, topocentric, virtual, local, or astrometric
    '----- place. The processes are rigorous and include all  corrections.
    '----- This subprogram is intended for  use with  barycentric source
    '----- ephemerides such as DE200.
    '----- Input:  jed     desired time of reduction
    '-----         body    body number
    '-----                 = 99 for stellar reduction
    '-----         place   = 1 for apparent place
    '-----                 = 2 for topocentric place
    '-----                 = 3 for virtual place
    '-----                 = 4 for local place
    '-----                 = 5 for astrometric place
    '-----         stardata() array containing stellar data
    '----- Output: p3()    array containing the requested state vector
    '-------------------------------------------------------------------------

    dim Ltime           as double
    dim i               as integer
    dim first           as integer
    dim earth_ssb(min,1) as double
    dim earth_hel(min,1) as double
    dim  body_geo(min,1) as double
    dim  body_hel(min,1) as double
    dim  obsr_geo(min,1) as double
    dim       eb(min,1) as double
    dim    ebdot(min,1) as double
    dim       p1(min,1) as double
    dim       p2(min,1) as double
    dim zeta            as double
    dim z               as double
    dim theta           as double
    dim zetadot         as double
    dim zdot            as double
    dim thetadot        as double
    dim dpsi            as double
    dim deps            as double
    dim dpsidot         as double
    dim depsdot         as double
    dim TrueEps         as double
    dim MeanEps         as double
    dim TrueEpsDot      as double
    dim MeanEpsDot      as double

    if first = 0 then
      redim earth_ssb(1 to 6) as double
      redim earth_hel(1 to 6) as double
      redim  body_geo(1 to 6) as double
      redim  body_hel(1 to 6) as double
      redim  obsr_geo(1 to 6) as double
      redim        eb(1 to 3) as double
      redim     ebdot(1 to 3) as double
      redim        p1(1 to 6) as double
      redim        p2(1 to 6) as double

      first = 1
    end if

    if ((body = 3) or (body = 12) or (body = 13) or (body = 14) or _
       (body = 15)) then
         print "Reduce: CAN'T PERFORM REDUCTION FOR SPECIFIED BODY."
         stop
    end if

    '----- Earth's barycentric state vector
```

```
call GetStateVector(jed,3,12,1,StateVector())
for i = 1 to 6
  earth_ssb(i) = StateVector(3,12,1,i)
next i

'----- Earth's heliocentric state vector
call GetStateVector(jed,3,11,1,StateVector())
for i = 1 to 6
  earth_hel(i) = StateVector(3,11,1,i)
next i

if (place = 2) or (place = 4) then
  '----- Compute geocentric state vector of observer
  call GeocenObs(jed, obsr_geo())
  '----- Translate origin from geocenter to topocenter
  for i = 1 to 6
    earth_ssb(i) = earth_ssb(i) + obsr_geo(i)
  next i
end if

'----- Compute geo/topocentric state vector of object corrected
'----- for light time.
call LightTime(jed, body, earth_ssb(), earth_hel(), stardata(), _
               body_geo(), body_hel(), Ltime)

if place = 5 then
  '----- Compute the astrometric place
  for i = 1 to 6
    p3(i) = body_geo(i)
  next i
end if

if place < 5 then
  '----- Perform correction for relativistic light deflection
  call RayBend(earth_hel(), body_geo(), body_hel(), p1())

  '----- Perform correction for aberration
  call SplitStateVector(earth_ssb(), eb(), ebdot())
  call Aberrate(p1(), ebdot(), p2())

  if place < 3 then
    '----- Correction for precession and nutation from J2000.0
    call GetPrecessParams(J2000.0, jed, zeta, z, theta, _
         zetadot, zdot, thetadot)
    call GetDpsiDeps(jed, dpsi, deps, dpsidot, depsdot)
    call Obliquity(J2000.0, jed, 0, MeanEps, MeanEpsDot)
    call Obliquity(J2000.0, jed, 1, TrueEps, TrueEpsDot)

    '----- first correct for precession
    call QRotate(p2(), 3, -zeta, -zetadot, 1, p3())
    call QRotate(p3(), 2, theta, thetadot, 1, p3())
    call QRotate(p3(), 3, -z, -zdot, 1, p3())

    '----- Now correct for nutation
    call QRotate(p3(), 1, MeanEps, MeanEpsDot, 1, p3())
    call QRotate(p3(), 3, -dpsi, -dpsidot, 1, p3())
    call QRotate(p3(), 1, -TrueEps, -TrueEpsDot, 1, p3())
  else
    for i = 1 to 6
      p3(i) = p2(i)
    next i
  end if
end if

end sub
```

Flowchart for Light Time Correction
for Solar System Bodies Only

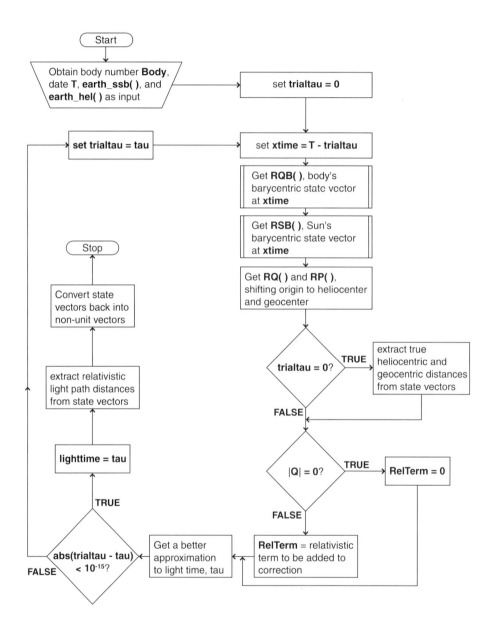

Remember that the underscore characters simply denote a continuation of the current line. There is a standard numbering sequence for specifying the Body input parameter, and this is described in Chapter 9. The first external routine called by Reduce is GetStateVector. This routine extracts a planet's barycentric state vector (position and velocity components) with respect to a given origin. In this instance, we need the position and velocity of Earth with respect to the solar system barycenter (SSB). On the next call, we need the Earth's state vector with respect to the Sun. GetStateVector is described in more detail in Chapter 9.

The routine GeocenObs performs the task of computing the observer's equatorial state vector in the J2000.0 reference frame. This routine is described in Chapter 4.

LightTime performs the correction for light travel time. RayBend corrects for relativistic light deflection, while Aberrate performs the aberration correction. The remaining routines are designed to compute precession and nutation quantites and apply the appropriate corrections to the body's state vector. Following are the source code listings for LightTime, RayBend, and Aberrate.

```
sub LightTime (jed as double, body as integer, earth_ssb() as double,_
        earth_hel() as double, stardata() as double, body_geo() as double, _
        body_hel() as double, Ltime as double) static

    '----- Subprogram to compute the vectors body_geo() and body_hel()
    '----- from a barycentric ephemeris of the object, Earth, and the Sun.
    '----- Input:   jed           desired time of reduction
    '-----          body          body number
    '-----                        = 99 for stellar reduction
    '-----          earth_ssb()   barycentric state vector of Earth at jed
    '-----          earth_hel()   heliocentric state vector of Earth
    '-----          stardata()    stellar data
    '----- Output: body_geo()     geometric geocentric state vector of object
    '-----          body_hel()    heliocentric state vector of object
    '-----          Ltime         light time in days to the object
    '----- ALL OUTPUT VECTORS ARE CORRECTED FOR LIGHT TIME.
    '--------------------------------------------------------------------

    dim inside                   as integer
    dim i                        as integer
    redim e(1 to 3)              as double
    redim edot(1 to 3)           as double
    redim rqb(1 to 6)            as double
    redim rsb(1 to 6)            as double
    redim  rq(1 to 6)            as double
    redim  rp(1 to 6)            as double
    redim   q(1 to 3)            as double
    redim qdot(1 to 3)           as double
    redim   p(1 to 3)            as double
    redim pdot(1 to 3)           as double
    redim unit_body_hel(1 to 6)  as double
    redim unit_body_geo(1 to 6)  as double
    dim mage                     as double
    dim magq                     as double
    dim magp                     as double
    dim trialtau                 as double
    dim tau                      as double
```

```
dim xtime                      as double
dim RelTerm                    as double
dim TrueHelDist                as double
dim TrueGeoDist                as double
dim AppHelDist                 as double
dim AppGeoDist                 as double
dim ra                         as double
dim de                         as double
dim sinra                      as double
dim cosra                      as double
dim sinde                      as double
dim cosde                      as double
dim plx                        as double
dim r                          as double
dim mura                       as double
dim mude                       as double
dim rdot                       as double
redim drda(1 to 3)               as double
redim drdd(1 to 3)               as double
dim dt                         as double
redim star(1 to 6)               as double

call SplitStateVector(earth_hel(), e(), edot())
call Vecmag(e(), mage)

if body <> 99 then

  trialtau = 0#
  do
    xtime = jed - trialtau

    '----- body's barycentric state vector
    call pleph(xtime, body, 12, rqb(), inside)

    '----- Sun's barycentric state vector
    call pleph(xtime,   11, 12, rsb(), inside)

    '----- body's heliocentric state vector
    for i = 1 to 6
      rq(i) = rqb(i) - rsb(i)
    '----- body's geocentric state vector
      rp(i) = rqb(i) - earth_ssb(i)
    next i

    '----- Calculate improved value of the light time
    call SplitStateVector(rq(), q(), qdot())
    call SplitStateVector(rp(), p(), pdot())
    call Vecmag(q(), magq)
    call Vecmag(p(), magp)

    if trialtau = 0# then
      TrueHelDist = magq
      TrueGeoDist = magp
    end if

    if magq = 0# then
      RelTerm = 0#
    else
      RelTerm = MUC * log((mage + magp + magq) / (mage - magp + magq))
    end if
    tau = (magp + RelTerm) / CAUD
    if abs(trialtau - tau) < 1d-15 then exit do
    trialtau = tau
  loop

else

  ra = stardata(1)
  de = stardata(2)
```

```
sinra = sin(ra)
cosra = cos(ra)
sinde = sin(de)
cosde = cos(de)
if stardata(3) = 0# then
  plx = 1d-7
else
  plx = stardata(3)
end if

'----- star's distance in AU
r = R2A / plx

'----- star's barycentric position vector
rqb(1) = r*cosra*cosde
rqb(2) = r*sinra*cosde
rqb(3) = r      *sinde

'----- Convert proper motions and radial velocity
'----- to units of AU/day
mura = stardata(4) * 15# * cosde / (JulCty * plx)
mude = stardata(5) / (JulCty * plx)
rdot = stardata(6) * 86400# * KM2AU

'----- Partial of unit vector wrt ra
drda(1) = - sinra * cosde
drda(2) =   cosra * cosde
drda(3) =   0#

'----- Partial of unit vector wrt de
drdd(1) = - cosra * sinde
drdd(2) = - sinra * sinde
drdd(3) =           cosde

'----- star's barycentric velocity vector
for i = 4 to 6
  rqb(i) = mura*drda(i-3) + mude*drdd(i-3) + rdot*rqb(i-3)/r
next i

'----- Correction for space motion
dt = jed - J2000.0
for i = 1 to 3
  rqb(i) = rqb(i) + rqb(i+3)*dt
next i

'----- Sun's barycentric state vector
call pleph(jed, 11, 12, rsb(), inside)

'----- star's heliocentric state vector
for i = 1 to 6
  rq(i) = rqb(i) - rsb(i)
next i

'----- star's geo/topocentric state vector
'----- This correction is annual parallax.
for i = 1 to 6
  rp(i) = rqb(i) - earth_ssb(i)
next i

call SplitStateVector(rq(), q(), qdot())
call SplitStateVector(rp(), p(), pdot())
call Vecmag(q(), magq)
call Vecmag(p(), magp)

TrueGeoDist = magp
TrueHelDist = magq

tau = r / CAUD
```

```
    end if

    Ltime = tau
    AppHelDist = magq
    AppGeoDist = magp

    for i = 1 to 6
      body_hel(i) = rq(i)
      body_geo(i) = rp(i)
    next i

    call Uvector(body_hel(), unit_body_hel())
    call Uvector(body_geo(), unit_body_geo())
    for i = 1 to 6
      body_geo(i) = unit_body_geo(i) * TrueGeoDist
      body_hel(i) = unit_body_hel(i) * TrueHelDist
    next i

end sub
sub RayBend(earth_hel() as double, body_geo() as double,_
            body_hel() as double, p1() as double) static

    '----- Subprogram to correct an input vector for relativistic
    '----- light deflection due to the Sun's gravity field.
    '----- Input:   earth_hel()  heliocentric state vector of Earth
    '-----          body_geo()   geocentric state vector of object
    '-----          body_hel()   heliocentric state vector of object
    '----- Output: p1()          geocentric state vector of object
    '-----                       corrected for light deflection
    '--------------------------------------------------------------------

    redim   ue(1 to 3) as double
    redim   up(1 to 3) as double
    redim   uq(1 to 3) as double
    redim    e(1 to 3) as double
    redim edot(1 to 3) as double
    redim    p(1 to 3) as double
    redim pdot(1 to 3) as double
    redim    q(1 to 3) as double
    redim qdot(1 to 3) as double
    dim mage        as double
    dim magp        as double
    dim pdotq       as double
    dim edotp       as double
    dim qdote       as double
    dim i           as integer

    '----- Extract the pos. portions of the state vectors
    call SplitStateVector(earth_hel(), e(), edot())
    call SplitStateVector( body_geo(), p(), pdot())
    call SplitStateVector( body_hel(), q(), qdot())

    '----- Form unit vectors
    call Uvector(e(), ue())
    call Uvector(p(), up())
    call Uvector(q(), uq())

    '----- Form dot products and other quantities
    call Vecmag(e(), mage)
    call Vecmag(p(), magp)
    call Vdot(3, up(), uq(), pdotq)
    call Vdot(3, ue(), up(), edotp)
    call Vdot(3, uq(), ue(), qdote)

    for i = 1 to 3
```

```
      p1(i) = up(i) + (MUC / mage) * (pdotq * ue(i) - edotp * uq(i))_
                                     / (1# + qdote)
      '----- Make p1() a non-unit vector
      p1(i) = magp * p1(i)
      p1(i+3) = body_geo(i+3)
   next i

end sub
sub Aberrate(p1() as double, ebdot() as double, p2() as double) static

   '----- Subprogram to correct an input vector for aberration.
   '----- Input:    p1()       geocentric state vector of object
   '-----           ebdot()    barycentric velocity of Earth
   '----- Output:   p2()       geocentric state vector of object
   '-----                      corrected for aberration
   '-----------------------------------------------------------------------

   dim v(min,1)    as double
   dim up(min,1)   as double
   dim p(min,1)    as double
   dim pdot(min,1) as double
   dim i           as integer
   dim first       as integer
   dim magp        as double
   dim magv        as double
   dim p1dotv      as double
   dim beta        as double

   if first = FALSE then
      redim v(1 to 3)
      redim up(1 to 3)
      redim p(1 to 3)
      redim pdot(1 to 3)

      first = TRUE
   end if

   '----- Extract the pos. portion of the state vector
   call SplitStateVector(p1(), p(), pdot())
   call Vecmag(p(), magp)

   '----- Need to make Ppos() a unit vector
   call Uvector(p(), up())

   for i = 1 to 3
      v(i) = ebdot(i) / CAUD
   next i

   call Vdot(3, up(), v(), p1dotv)
   call Vecmag(v(), magv)

   beta = 1# / sqr(1# - magv * magv)

   for i = 1 to 3
      p2(i) = ((up(i) / beta) + (1# + p1dotv / (1# + (1# / beta)))_
                               * v(i)) / (1# + p1dotv)
      '----- Make p2() a non-unit vector
      p2(i) = magp * p2(i)
      p2(i+3) = p1(i+3)
   next i

end sub
```

The convergence tolerance in **LightTime** is arbitrarily set to 10^{-15} days since

we normally get fifteen significant digits in a double precision number in
PowerBASIC. For faster program execution, this tolerance could be set to
10^{-8} days. This value will also ensure a computational precision of one milliarcsecond in the final coordinates [Kaplan 1989]. Keep in mind, though,
that 1 milliarcsecond is only good enough for optical observations.

No modifications to the main procedure are needed for the Moon. There
are only slight modifications to be made to the main procedure if one wants
to compute the apparent place of the Sun. In **Step 2** set $\mathbf{Q}_B = \mathbf{S}_B$, since the
"planet" under consideration is the Sun. Also, we must set $\mathbf{P} = \mathbf{S}_B(t - \tau) -$
$\mathbf{E}_B(t)$ for the same reason. The light time τ is calculated by iteration from
$\tau = P/c$ where $P = |\mathbf{P}|$. Finally, it is only necessary to calculate the unit
vector $\mathbf{p}$. In **STEP 3** we can set $\mathbf{p}_1 = \mathbf{p}$ since there is no light deflection from
the center of the Sun's disk. The rest of the computation remains unchanged,
and these modifications are easily handled by Reduce.

6.4   Apparent Place of Stellar Objects

The modifications necessary to use the primary algorithm for computing
the apparent places of stars or non-stellar objects such as galaxies are minor and easy enough to incorporate into the code. The main difference is
that the star's *Fundamental Katalog 5* equatorial coordinates, proper motion,
parallax, and radial velocity must be specified. From the parallax, the star's
distance may be obtained. If the parallax is not known or is subject to a large
uncertainty, then it may be set to some arbitrary value such as 10^{-7} seconds
of arc. This value for the parallax implies a distance of 10^7 parsecs (1 pc =
3.26 light years).

Given the star's equatorial coordinates and its distance, we can form its
position vector as

$$\mathbf{r} = \begin{bmatrix} r \cos \alpha \cos \delta \\ r \sin \alpha \cos \delta \\ r \sin \delta \end{bmatrix} \qquad (6.4.1)$$

where the unit is AU if r is expressed in AU, too. Next, we convert the given
proper motions and radial velocity to units of AU/day using the equations

$$\mu'_\alpha = \mu_\alpha 15 \cos \delta / (36525p) \qquad (6.4.2)$$

$$\mu'_\delta = \mu_\delta / (36525p) \qquad (6.4.3)$$

$$\dot{r}' = 86400\dot{r}/A \qquad (6.4.4)$$

where A is the number of km in 1 AU (1.4959787066×10^8) and p is the star's parallax. Now we must convert these velocity components to the space velocity components at the catalog epoch in the solar system barycentric frame of reference by using the following transformation:

$$\dot{\mathbf{r}} = \begin{bmatrix} -\sin\alpha & -\cos\alpha\,\sin\delta & \cos\alpha\cos\delta \\ \cos\alpha & -\sin\alpha\,\sin\delta & \sin\alpha\cos\delta \\ 0 & \cos\delta & \sin\delta \end{bmatrix} \begin{bmatrix} \mu'_\alpha \\ \mu'_\delta \\ \dot{r}' \end{bmatrix}. \qquad (6.4.5)$$

At this point, the reduction procedure can continue as in the planetary case. The remaining minor modifications needed for the stellar reduction are documented in the source code listing for `LightTime`.

6.5 Atmospheric Refraction

Once we have computed the apparent or topocentric place of a celestial object, the only remaining correction to be made to the coordinates is that caused by atmospheric refraction. There are almost as many methods of carrying out the atmospheric refraction correction as there are programmers. Everyone has his or her favorite algorithm. The algorithm adopted for this book is the one presented on pages 78–80 of [Taff 1981].

The correction for atmospheric refraction is most easily understood if we refer to the horizon coordinate system. Refraction simply increases the altitude of an object by a small amount that depends on the uncorrected altitude of the object, the air temperature, the air pressure, and even the humidity of the local atmosphere. Because temperature and pressure can change significantly over just seconds of time, it follows that the magnitude of the refraction correction can also vary rapidly as well. Therefore, atmospheric refraction can generally be ignored. One exception to this rule of thumb occurs when a real-time telescope-pointing algorithm is in use. For this application, the method of computing the refraction correction must be rapid enough to compensate for the potentially random variations in the local atmosphere. For general observational purposes, however, such compensation is rarely justified, and a general purpose algorithm for optional use is much more convenient. Also, observations are seldom made directly in the horizon coordinate system. Telescopes are usually pointed with coordinates specified in the equatorial system and so this system is the preferred one in which to develop a refraction algorithm. Taff's algorithm fills the need nicely.

The subprogram `Refract` performs the refraction correction to an input right ascension and declination. The source code listing is as follows:

```
sub Refract(ra1 as double, dec1 as double, lha as double, temp as double,_
        press as double, ra2 as double, dec2 as double) static
```

```
'----- Subprogram to correct right ascension and declination
'----- for atmospheric refraction
'----- Input:   ra1,dec1  uncorrected RA and DEC in radians
'-----          lha       local apparent hour angle in radians
'-----          temp      temperature in deg F
'-----          press     air pressure in inches of Hg
'----- Output:  ra2,dec2  corrected RA and DEC in radians
'----- Reference:  Taff. Computational Spherical Astronomy,
'-----             pp. 78-80.
'-----------------------------------------------------------------------

dim cosz    as double
dim z       as double
dim r1      as double
dim r2      as double
dim r       as double
dim tanzr   as double
dim rr      as double
dim diff    as double
dim rlocal  as double
dim denom   as double

cosz = sin(obsr_lat) * sin(dec1) + cos(obsr_lat) *_
       cos(dec1) * cos(lha)
z = acos(cosz)

r1 = 58.294# * A2R
r2 = -.0668# * A2R

r = 0#
do
   tanzr = tan(z - r)
   rr = r1 * tanzr + r2 * tanzr * tanzr * tanzr
   print rr * r2A
   diff = abs(rr - r)
   r = rr
loop until (diff <= 1d-15)

rlocal = (17# * press) * r / (460# + temp)

denom = 1# / (cos(dec1) * sin(z))
dec2 = dec1 + (rlocal * (sin(obsr_lat) - sin(dec1) * cos(z))) * denom
denom = 1# / (cos(dec2) * sin(z))
ra2 = ra1 + (rlocal * cos(obsr_lat) * sin(lha)) * denom

end sub
```

This simple algorithm evaluates rapidly and is easy to use. The user should
take care to express the temperature and air pressure in the proper units. Of
course, modifications to the subprogram can be made so that the temperature
can be input in degrees Celsius and the air pressure can be input in units of
millibars. Since the calling syntax for **Refract** is straightforward, no example
driver will be given.

This concludes our discussion of the various corrections to the coordinates
of a celestial object. This chapter contains an extensive toolbox of powerful
routines that can be incorporated into many types of programs. The reader
is encouraged to experiment.

Chapter 7

Rise, Transit, and Set Times

7.1 Introduction

The computation of the rise, transit, and set times for a celestial object is an often-needed process, but, unfortunately, one for which precise algorithms are seldom found in the literature. Until recently, the best source of rise/transit/set algorithms was the *Explanatory Supplement to the Astronomical Ephemeris*, now out of print. In his *Astronomical Algorithms*, Meeus gives the most practical algorithm for computing an object's times of rise, transit, and set for any location on Earth. In this chapter, we shall implement this algorithm as a powerful subprogram for the computation of these times for any object for any location on Earth.

7.2 Explanatory Notes

Before introducing the computational algorithm, we must first establish what we mean by the terms *rise time*, *set time*, and *transit time*. One normally thinks of a celestial object as *rising* when it just becomes visible over the observer's local horizon. However, atmospheric refraction plays an important role in the more precise astronomical definition of *rising*. Refraction tends to slightly increase an object's altitude above the horizon, so that when an observer thinks he or she sees the object rise, it is actually still below the horizon. Similarly, refraction can make an object appear to be setting when the object is actually already below the horizon. To make matters worse, the magnitude of the effect of refraction at the horizon is notoriously difficult to predict, and even the algorithm presented in Section 6.5 will not work in low altitude cases. Therefore, by convention, the magnitude of the effect of refraction at the horizon is taken to be 34 minutes of arc for the purposes of computing rise and set times.

Therefore, we now know that when we see a star just rising over the eastern horizon, the star is really still below the horizon and has an altitude of $-34'$. We can also think of the star as having a *zenith distance* of $90°34'$. Recall that altitude and zenith distance are complementary angles and are related by $h = 90° - z$, where h is the altitude and z is the zenith distance. When we see the star setting in the west, at the instant the star hits the horizon, it is already below the horizon and has an altitude of $-34'$, or equivalently, a zenith distance of $90°34'$ once again. We can now state the precise astronomical definitions of rise and set times for a star, or any point source, to be the instants when the star has the standard zenith distance of $90°34'$. Of course, we could also state this definition in terms of altitude. The definition of transit time is the instant when the star has its maximum altitude over the observer's horizon. Note that this is also the instant at which the star has a local apparent hour angle of 0^h.

Because the above definitions strictly apply only to point sources, we must modify the definitions to apply to extended sources such as the Sun and the Moon. In these instances, we define the times of rise and set to be the times when the upper limb of the extended disk of the Sun or Moon reaches the adopted standard zenith distance. Clearly, this more precise definition is nothing more than taking account of the semi-diameter of the object. The semi-diameters of the Sun and Moon change with time; in the case of the Sun, an average value of $16'$ is adopted. Therefore, the precise definition of the terms *sunrise* and *sunset* now becomes the instants when the upper limb of the Sun reaches a zenith distance of $90°34' + 16' = 90°50'$. The definitions are similar for the Moon, with the exception that the actual semi-diameter on the day in question is used in place of the average value of $16'$. In the case of the Moon, we must also take the lunar horizontal parallax into account because of the Moon's nearness to Earth. For the Moon, the adopted standard zenith distance is $90°34' + SD + \pi$, where SD is the lunar semi-diameter and π is the lunar parallax. Incidentally, for the purposes of this chapter, a *point source* is considered to be any celestial object other than the Sun and the Moon; planets are considered to be point sources.

From the above explanation, we now see that the computation of rise, transit, and set times is the computation of times when the object reaches a specific altitude or hour angle. Note that we are now dealing with the horizon coordinate system. In Chapter 4, we presented the method of converting equatorial coordinates into horizon coordinates. We begin with the expression

$$\sin h = \cos z = \sin \phi \sin \delta + \cos \phi \cos \delta \cos H \qquad (7.2.1)$$

where

h = apparent altitude,

z = apparent zenith distance,
ϕ = geodetic latitude,
δ = the object's apparent declination, and
H = the object's local apparent hour angle.

If we solve this equation for $\cos H$, we obtain

$$\cos H = \frac{\cos z - \sin \phi \sin \delta}{\cos \phi \cos \delta} \qquad (7.2.2)$$

which expresses H as a function of z, ϕ, and δ. To obtain the hour angle of an object at the instant of rise or set, we substitute for z the appropriate standard zenith distance for the object. Recall that hour angle is measured such that it increases eastward from the local meridian, so an object's hour angle at the time of rising will satisfy the relation $0^{\mathrm{h}} < H < 12^{\mathrm{h}}$, and the hour angle at setting will satisfy the relation $12^{\mathrm{h}} < H < 24^{\mathrm{h}}$. We must take care to place H in the correct quadrant according to whether we seek the rise time or the set time. Observe that if atmospheric refraction is neglected, $\cos z = 0$, and equation (7.2.2) reduces to

$$\cos H = -\tan \phi \tan \delta \qquad (7.2.3)$$

which is the expression often quoted in approximate rise/set algorithms.

If we now know H, we can obtain the local apparent sidereal time, LAST, because we assume we already know α, the object's apparent right ascension. Recall that H, α, and LAST are related through the expression

$$H = \mathrm{LAST} - \alpha \qquad (7.2.4)$$

which we can solve for LAST. Finally, we can convert this sidereal time to solar time to obtain the observed rise and set times which are usually specified on the UT (UT1 strictly) time scale. If we seek the transit time, we have $H = 0^{\mathrm{h}}$ and therefore LAST $= \alpha$, which is what we should expect since the apparent right ascension of *any* observer's local meridian is *always* the LAST.

In the preceding explanation, we have assumed that α and δ, the apparent coordinates of the object, are constant. In actuality, the apparent coordinates of celestial objects are not strictly constant because of the periodic effects of precession, nutation, aberration, etc. Therefore, it should come as no surprise that the coordinates of an object can change appreciably in the interval from rise to set, especially if we are dealing with the Moon. We also know that we can compute an object's apparent coordinates as a function of time. We now see the underlying complexity of the actual computation of precise rise, transit, and set times: to derive the times, we must know the object's coordinates at the times we wish to derive, but to know the times, we must know the object's coordinates. This is a seemingly infinite computational loop. However, we can adopt a procedure in which we begin with the coordinates at some known time, compute approximate rise/transit/set times, use these approximate times to compute new coordinates, and compute successively better times. This iterative procedure is continued until consecutive values of the rise/transit/set times are constant to the desired tolerance. Please keep in mind that because of the uncertain nature of refraction near the horizon and the nearly random meteorological processes at work in the atmosphere, the computation of rise/transit/set times to a precision of more than one minute of time is seldom justified. However, to illustrate the ease with which the algorithms may be used the software in this chapter will carry out the computations to one second of time, or better.

7.3   Subprogram for Computing Rise/Transit/Set Times

The subprogram for computing rise, transit, and set times is called RST and is based on Meeus' algorithm. The source code listing:

```
sub RST(jed as double, ra() as double, dec() as double, z0 as double, _
        deltat as double, ris as string, trn as string, set as string) static

'----- Subprogram to compute the times of rise, set, and transit for
'----- any object given the observer's location and arrays containing
'----- the APPARENT right ascension and declination of the object for
'----- three dates centered on the input JED.  The algorithm is
'----- completely rigorous,  and takes into account atmospheric
'----- refraction and the object's sidereal motion in the intervals
'----- between rising, setting, and transiting.  The algorithm is
'----- explained in Chapter 42 of Meeus' ASTRONOMICAL FORMULAE FOR
'----- CALCULATORS. With the appropriate values for z0, this routine
'----- can also be used to compute the times of civil, nautical, or
'----- astronomical twilight.
'----- Input:   jed   Julian day number at 0h UT1
'-----          ra()  array containing the object's apparent right
'-----                ascension at times jed-1, jed, and jed+1
'-----          dec() array containing the object's apparent
'-----                declination at times jed-1, jed, and jed+1
'-----          z0    the "standard" zenith distance for the object
'-----                at rise or set.  This quantity has different
'-----                values for different objects according to the
'-----                following table:
'-----                z0 = 90d 50'           Sun
'-----                z0 = 90d 34' + s - pi  Moon
'-----                z0 = 90d 34'           stars and planets
'-----                z0 = 108d              astronomical twilight
'-----                z0 = 102d              nautical twilight
'-----                z0 =  96d              civil twilight
'-----                z0 should be given by the program that calls RST
'-----                z0 is expressed in radians
'-----          deltat  TDT-UT1 in seconds of time
'----- Output:  ris   string containing rise time in
'-----                form hh.mm or an appropriate symbol
'-----          trn   string containing transit time
'-----                in form hh.mm or an appropriate symbol
'-----          set   string containing set time in
```

```
'-----                form hh.mm or an appropriate symbol
'----- Note that the times are on the UT1 scale!
'----- Reference:  Meeus.  ASTRONOMICAL FORMULAE FOR CALCULATORS,
'-----                4TH ED., Chapter 42.
'---------------------------------------------------------------------

dim rsflag as integer
dim h0     as double
dim cosh0  as double
dim c      as integer
dim newm   as double
dim oldm   as double
dim m      as double
dim m0     as double
dim m1     as double
dim m2     as double
dim ristime as double
dim settime as double
dim trntime as double
dim gast   as double
dim gast0  as double
dim d1     as double
dim d2     as double
dim d3     as double
dim r1     as double
dim r2     as double
dim r3     as double
dim alpha  as double
dim n      as double
dim delta  as double
dim h      as double
dim alt    as double
dim dm     as double

'----- Make sure the ra()'s are in continuous order
if (ra(2) < ra(1) and ra(3) > ra(2)) then
   ra(2) = ra(2) + TWOPI
   ra(3) = ra(3) + TWOPI
elseif (ra(2) > ra(1) and ra(3) < ra(2)) then
   ra(3) = ra(3) + TWOPI
end if

r1 = ra(2) - ra(1)
r2 = ra(3) - ra(2)
r3 = r2 - r1
d1 = dec(2) - dec(1)
d2 = dec(3) - dec(2)
d3 = d2 - d1

rsflag = -1

cosh0 = (cos(z0) - sin(obsr_lat) * sin(dec(2))) / (cos(obsr_lat) *_
        cos(dec(2)))

if cosh0 < -1# then      '----- object is circumpolar
   ris = "**********"
   if (z0*r2D >= 96#) then
      set = "**BRIGHT***"
   else
      set = "**NO set***"
   end if
   rsflag = 0
elseif cosh0 > 1# then '----- object never rises
   if (z0*r2D >= 96#) then
      ris = "---DARK----"
   else
      ris = "--NO RISE--"
   end if
   set = "-----------"
   rsflag = 0
```

```
    end if

    call GetGST(jed, 1, gast0)

    m0 = (ra(2) - obsr_lon - gast0) / TWOPI
      m0 = amodulo(m0, 1#)

    if rsflag then
      h0 = acos(cosh0)
        h0 = amodulo(h0, PI)
      m1 = m0 - h0 / TWOPI
        m1 = amodulo(m1, 1#)
      m2 = m0 + h0 / TWOPI
        m2 = amodulo(m2, 1#)

      '----- rising
      oldm = m1
      c = 1
      gosub Interpolate
      m = newm
      ristime = 24# * m
      if ristime > 24# then
        ristime = ristime - 24#
        '----- event occurs the following day
        ris = FmtDms$(ristime, 0, 2) + "(f)"
      elseif ristime < 0# then
        ristime = ristime + 24#
        '----- event occurs the previous day
        ris = FmtDms$(ristime, 0, 2) + "(p)"
      else
        ris = FmtDms$(ristime, 0, 2)
      end if

      '----- setting
      oldm = m2
      c = 1
      gosub Interpolate
      m = newm
      settime = 24# * M
      if settime > 24# then
        settime = settime - 24#
        set = FmtDms$(settime, 0, 2) + "(f)"
      elseif settime < 0# then
        settime = settime + 24#
        set = FmtDms$(settime, 0, 2) + "(p)"
      else
        set = FmtDms$(settime, 0, 2)
      end if
    end if

    '----- transiting
    oldm = m0
    c = 0
    gosub Interpolate
    m = newm
    trntime = 24# * m
    if trntime > 24# then
      trntime = trntime - 24#
      trn = FmtDms$(trntime, 0, 2) + "(f)"
    elseif trntime < 0# then
      trntime = trntime + 24#
      trn = FmtDms$(trntime, 0, 2) + "(p)"
    else
      trn = FmtDms$(trntime, 0, 2)
    end if

    exit sub

Interpolate:
```

```
 newm = oldm
 do
   gast = gast0 + 6.300388093# * newm
   gast = amodulo(gast, TWOPI)
   n = newm + deltat / 86400#
   alpha = ra(2) + 0.5# * n * (r1 + r2 + n * r3)
   alpha = amodulo(alpha, TWOPI)
   delta = dec(2) + 0.5# * n * (d1 + d2 + n * d3)
   h = gast + obsr_lon - alpha
   alt = asin(sin(delta) * sin(obsr_lat) + cos(delta) * _
         cos(obsr_lat) * cos(h))
   if c = 0 then
     dm = -h / TWOPI
   else
     dm = (alt - PIDIV2 + z0) / (TWOPI * cos(delta) * _
          cos(obsr_lat) * sin(h))
   end if
   newm = newm + dm
 loop until abs(dm) < 1d-15

return

end sub
```

There are some important facts to note about RST. The rise, transit, and set times are returned to the calling program in the form of strings. Note the use of the FmtDms function, which puts the decimal times into the string forms. The source code listing for FmtDms is presented in Chapter 9. Before calling this routine, the user must first compute and store a three-point apparent ephemeris of the object under consideration at 0^h TDT for three dates, centered on the date in question.

At any given instant in the computation of rise/transit/set times, the object's coordinates are obtained from the three-point ephemeris by an interpolation scheme. The code that performs this operation is hard-wired into RST instead of appearing in a separate routine.

RST contains logic that determines whether or not the object will be visible from the desired location. Be aware that some celestial objects never rise above the local horizon because they are too far south in declination (too far north for observers in the southern hemisphere). Some objects never set because they are close enough to the celestial pole (north or south, depending on the observer's location) so that they never go below the horizon; such objects are termed *circumpolar*. Further consideration, perhaps coupled with some mental geometric gymnastics, should make it obvious that even though an object may not rise over an observer's horizon, it will still transit the local meridian; the transit will simply take place below the horizon. For this reason, if RST determines that the object will not rise or is circumpolar, the software will still compute a transit time for the object. If an object is circumpolar, it will actually make two transits per day, one on the upper meridian and one on the lower meridian, but only the time of upper transit is computed by RST. Also, it is possible for the rise, transit, or set time of an object for a given date to fall on the previous or even the next day. This is a result of the change in the object's coordinates during the intervals between the events being computed. Whenever this situation occurs, RST takes this into account by appending an extra character enclosed in parentheses to the strings containing the times.

We now present a sample driver program called RISE, which illustrates the use of RST.

```
'----- RISE.BAS

defdbl a-z

$include "\fecsoftb\astrolib.dec"
$include "\fecsoftb\constant.inc"
$include "\fecsoftb\acos.bas"
$include "\fecsoftb\amodulo.bas"
$include "\fecsoftb\asin.bas"
$include "\fecsoftb\deg.bas"
$include "\fecsoftb\dms.bas"
$include "\fecsoftb\dround.bas"
$include "\fecsoftb\fmtdms.bas"
$include "\fecsoftb\funarg.bas"
$include "\fecsoftb\getgst.bas"
$include "\fecsoftb\nutation.bas"
$include "\fecsoftb\obliquty.bas"
$include "\fecsoftb\rst.bas"

dim jed          as double
dim deltat       as double
dim ra(1 to 3)   as double
dim dec(1 to 3)  as double
dim hp           as double
dim sd           as double
dim z0           as double
dim ris          as string
dim trn          as string
dim set          as string
dim fmt          as string

cls
print "EXAMPLE DRIVER FOR RST"
print

input "Enter deltat in seconds          ", deltat
input "Enter latitude (+N/-S, dd.mmss)  ", obsr_lat
   obsr_lat = D2R * deg(obsr_lat)
print "Enter longitude (-W/+E, dd.mmss)"
input "Enter '9999' for Ephemeris Meridian  ", obsr_lon
   if obsr_lon = 9999# then
     obsr_lon = 1.002738# * (deltat / 3600#) * H2R
   else
     obsr_lon = D2R * deg(obsr_lon)
   end if

'----- The following data is must be replaced for specific
'----- applications.
jed = 2450093.5#   '----- 1/11/1996
ra(1)  = H2R * deg(10.1917027#)
dec(1) = D2R * deg( 6.291308#)
ra(2)  = H2R * deg(11.0558576#)
dec(2) = D2R * deg( 2.383610#)
ra(3)  = H2R * deg(11.5311971#)
dec(3) = D2R * deg(-1.223363#)
```

```
hp = D2R * deg(0.444156#)
sd = asin(0.272493# * sin(hp))
z0 = D2R * deg(90.34#) + sd - hp

call RST(jed, ra(), dec(), z0, deltat, ris, trn, set)

print
print jed
fmt = "Rise \        \ Transit \        \ Set \        \"
print using fmt; ris, trn, set

print
print "OK"

end
```

Here is a sample output screen from program RISE.

```
EXAMPLE DRIVER FOR RST

Enter DeltaT in seconds                 60
Enter latitude (+N/-S, dd.mmss)         35.4359
Enter longitude (-W/+E, dd.mmss)
Enter '9999' for Ephemeris Meridian     -81.2029

 2450093.5
Rise 03h11m43s     Transit 09h29m14s     Set 15h40m38s

OK
```

The user must provide the subprogram presented in this chapter with accurate apparent coordinates of the object in question. These can be obtained from the current edition of the *Astronomical Almanac* or from any number of computer programs, such as the *Interactive Computer Ephemeris* or the *Floppy Almanac*. In all cases, the programs above will reproduce the results found in the *Astronomical Almanac*, from which the initial solar and lunar coordinates were taken.

PROGRAMMING EXERCISE: Modify RST to **not** perform an interpolation during the successive approximation procedure. Instead, have the routine extract the required positional data from an ephemeris data file and then reduce it to an apparent place. This will require material from Chapter 6 and Chapter 8. Note that this modified procedure will likely take longer to execute because the positional data must be reduced before it can be used.

Chapter 8

Sources of Fundamental Ephemerides

8.1 Introduction

In this chapter, we present information on how to obtain the fundamental ephemerides that form the basis of so many astronomical calculations. We describe in particular detail how to obtain and use the ephemerides produced at the Jet Propulsion Laboratory (JPL) because these ephemerides form the fundamental basis of many, if not all, national astronomical almanacs.

8.2 Origin of the Data Files

It is beyond the scope of this book to explain the theory behind the construction of the planetary ephemerides created at the JPL. To do so would involve considerable physics and mathematics. We will concentrate our efforts on getting the data files and putting them to use. The mathematical models used in the construction of the ephemerides have been well-documented in the literature. The reader is referred to the many papers by Myles Standish and to Chapter 5 in the *Explanatory Supplement* [Seidelmann 1992]. However, to provide a broad perspective, we will briefly outline the steps in the creation of the master ephemeris data files.

Each JPL ephemeris is the result of a large-scale numerical integration of the motions of the major solar system bodies over an extended period of time, the exact interval varying from ephemeris to ephemeris. The ephemeris represents a least squares fit to many years of observational data as well. These data were obtained from such diverse sources as lunar laser ranging, radar ranging, satellite astrometry, transit circle observations, and photographic astrometry. A detailed description of the sources for this observational data is given in [Standish 1990]. By first performing a least squares fit to the body of existing positional data and then using the resulting initial conditions to start

a numerical integration process, the astronomers at JPL create an ephemeris
that accurately describes the motions of solar system bodies over a period of
time.

Before we continue, the distinction between *accuracy* and *precision* should
be clarified. *Accuracy* refers to how well an ephemeris represents the true coordinates of solar system bodies. *Precision* refers to the number of significant
figures in the ephemeris' numerical representation. An accurate ephemeris
is one which predicts the future motions of celestial objects and reproduces
the past motions of the same objects in such a way as to agree with human
observations. At the time of this writing, the most accurate JPL planetary
ephemeris is DE405.

Once the existing positional data is sufficiently modeled by least squares
analysis, the actual numerical integration is performed. This consists of mod-
eling every force known to cause an observable effect in the analysis of a
body's motion. The particular effects included in this integration are outlined on page 280 of [Seidelmann 1992] and they are as follows:

- point-mass interactions among the Moon, planets, and the Sun,

- general relativistic effects,

- Newtonian perturbations of five prominent asteroids,

- Moon and Sun action upon the figure of the Earth, and

- Earth and Sun action upon the figure of the Moon.

The integrations also contain the nutational motion of the Earth and the librational motions of the Moon, but the final data files may not contain these data
because of practical file size limitations. The inclusion of general relativistic
effects is of special noteworthiness. It indicates a significant improvement in
observational accuracy, and this alone necessitates modified astrometric reduction algorithms. The five asteroids whose perturbations were included in
the integration are Ceres, Pallas, Vesta, Iris, and Bamberga, so chosen because they have the most profound effects on the Earth-Mars section of the
solar system over the period of time covered by the integration. Refer to page
281 of the *Explanatory Supplement* [Seidelmann 1992].

The output of one of these precise integrations essentially consists of a
very large table of numbers giving the state vectors (position and velocity
components) of the Sun, Moon, and the major planets at specified intervals
within the time span covered by the integration. Depending on the ephemeris,
nutational and librational data may also be included in the output. There
is, however, a problem with using the ephemeris in this form, and that is
the sheer size of the resulting data sets. There may well be a few hundred

thousand numbers in one ephemeris alone, and to extract the position and velocity of a body at a specific instant of time would require searching the data for two times that bracket the required time, and then performing an interpolation for each state vector component. Depending on the chosen interpolation scheme, one may also require knowledge of several more surrounding values to carry out the interpolation. To circumvent these problems, the ephemeris data for each body is fit with a set of Chebyshev coefficients which allows rapid evaluation and interpolation of the data for any given time covered by the initial integration. Again, a detailed description of this process is well beyond the scope of this book and the interested reader is referred to [Seidelmann 1992]. For a good discussion of Chebyshev polynomials, consult *Numerical Recipes* [Press 1992]. The end result is another large ASCII data file containing not the original ephemeris data, but the Chebyshev coefficients which reproduce the original data as accurately as possible. This data file is substantially smaller than the file containing the original data but compromises essentially nothing as far as the accuracy of the integration is concerned.

8.3 Obtaining the Ephemeris Data Files

There are two primary ways to obtain the JPL ephemeris data files: 1.) via the Internet or by purchasing the *JPL Planetary and Lunar Ephemerides* CD-ROM published by Willmann-Bell, Inc. The CD-ROM includes DE200, DE405 and DE406. At the time of this writing, JPL maintains copies of DE200, DE405 on its anonymous `ftp` server (which has the address `navigator.jpl.nasa.gov`). DE200 is the ephemeris used for the preparation of data presented in the *Astronomical Almanac*. DE405 is JPL's most up-to-date ephemeris and can be considered a successor to DE200. DE406 is the new "long ephemeris" replacing DE102. The most interesting aspect of DE406 is that it covers an extremely long time interval, making it useful for historical investigations and for long-term future predictions. Owing to its size, DE406 is not available via anonymous `ftp`. On the server, the DE200 and DE405 ASCII data files have been broken up into segments, each of which is approximately five to six megabytes in size and covers about twenty years. For each ephemeris, there is also a header file which contains information needed in the process of converting the ASCII files into binary format.

Upon logging in to the `ftp` server, the user should change to the `ephem` subdirectory and retrieve the file `READ.ME`, which contains detailed instructions on exactly what files are required for UNIX and non-UNIX computer systems. We assume that the reader is using a PC-compatible computer system, and because of the software included in this book, all that is required from the `ftp` site are the header file and one or more of the data files for the desired ephemeris. All of these files are standard ASCII files. The user should be aware of one very important caveat, and that is the difference between UNIX ASCII files and MS-DOS (or OS/2) ASCII files. In the UNIX world, each line of an ASCII file ends with a carriage return. In most non-UNIX environments (including MS-DOS and OS/2) each line of an ASCII file terminates with a carriage return and a line feed character. This difference is important because the files taken off the JPL server are UNIX ASCII files. A good Windows or OS/2 `ftp` client will correctly handle the translation to MS-DOS or OS/2 format.[1] Fortunately, MS-DOS and OS/2 share the same ASCII format conventions. There are many widely available text editors that let the user edit very large (multi-megabyte) files and also allow the user save them in either UNIX or non-UNIX ASCII format.

8.4   Processing the ASCII Data Files

The first step in processing one of the ASCII data files (after retrieving it, of course) is to convert it to binary format. We provide a slightly enhanced port of the FORTRAN program ASCEPH, which is in turn provided in the ephemeris software package on the JPL server. ASC2EPH does not actually compute ephemerides; it only puts the ASCII file into a binary format that other software can use. Following is the source code listing for ASC2EPH.

```
'-------------------------------------------------------------------------
'----- Program ASC2EPH.BAS
'----- This program converts a JPL ephemeris ASCII data file
'----- into a binary data file.
'-------------------------------------------------------------------------

$OPTIMIZE        SPEED
$CPU             8086
$COMPILE         EXE
$LIB IPRINT      ON
$STRING          32
$STACK           2048
$DIM             ALL
$HUGE
$OPTION CNTLBREAK ON
'-------------------------------------------------------------------------

defdbl a-z

option binary base 1

'----- integer variables
dim KSIZE as integer
dim I as integer, J as integer, K as integer, N as integer
dim NCON as integer, NROUT as integer, NCOEFF as integer
```

---

[1] Author's Note: My Windows `ftp` client would not correctly handle the conversion, so I had to convert the data files to the correct format manually using a text editor. If the user attempts to process the uncorrected files with the software described in the next section, the software will not work correctly. Therefore, the user must import these files into a text editor, one that allows files to be saved in either UNIX or MS-DOS format, and re-save them in the proper format.

```
dim NRW as integer, NUMDE as integer
dim InputFile as shared integer, OutputFile as shared integer
dim PromptForDates as shared integer
dim HeaderIncluded as shared integer
dim jrow as integer, jcol as integer
dim TRUE as shared integer, FALSE as shared integer, FIRST as integer
dim LPT( 1 to 3) as shared integer
dim IPT(1 to 3, 1 to 13) as shared integer
dim attribut as integer
dim ccount ac integer, nlines as integer, lin as integer
dim col as integer
dim row as integer
dim DeleteLogFile as shared integer
dim LeftOver as integer, NumZeros as integer
dim LengthOfHeader as integer, LengthOfRecord as integer
dim LengthOfFile as long

TRUE =  1
FALSE = 0
FIRST = TRUE

'----- double precision variables
dim AU as double, DB2Z as double, EMRAT as double
dim T1 as double, T2 as double
dim CVAL(1 to 400) as double
dim huge DB(1 to 10) as double
dim SS(1 to 3) as double
dim x1 as double

'----- string variables
dim CNAM(1 to 400) as string
dim TTL(1 to 3) as string * 65
dim L as string
dim InFile as shared string, OutFile as shared string
dim extension as string
dim HFile as string
dim HEADER as string
dim Version as string, f as string
dim Progress as string
dim Body(1 to 13) as string
Body(1) = "MER":Body(2) = "VEN":Body(3) = "EMB":Body(4) = "MAR"
Body(5) = "JUP":Body(6) = "SAT":Body(7) = "URA":Body(8) = "NEP"
Body(9) = "PLU":Body(10)= "MOO":Body(11)= "SUN":Body(12)= "NUT"
Body(13)= "LIB"

declare sub ParseCmdLine ()
declare sub NXTGRP (HEADER as string)
declare sub ERRPRT (I as integer, MSG as string)

'----- these lines maintain the current DOS colors
'----- of the character at location 2,2
attribut = screen(2,2,1)
color attribut mod 16, attribut\16, 0

'----- open a log file
open "asc2eph.log" for output as #3

'----- Write a fingerprint to the screen and
'----- to log file.
Version = "AC2EPH v1.100997b"
print
print "***Program ";Version;"  ";
print "                   Written by Joe Heafner "
print "***Converts JPL ASCII ephemeris data files to binary"
print "***The author can be reached via Internet:";
print "    heafnerj@mercury.interpath.com"
print
print #3,
```

```
print #3,"***Program ";Version;"  ";
print #3,"                       Written by Joe Heafner "
print #3,"***Converts JPL ASCII ephemeris data files to binary"
print #3,"***The author can be reached via Internet:";
print #3,"      heafnerj@mercury.interpath.com"
print #3,

call ParseCmdLine

'----- If you don't want all the data, set T1 and T2 to the begin
'----- and end times of the span you desire.  Units are JED.
if PromptForDates then
  input "Enter start JED ",T1
  do
    input "Enter final JED ",T2
  loop until (T2 > T1)
  if T1 = T2 then
    print "Start and final JED's cannot be the same. Using defaults."
    T1 = 0#
    T2 = 9999999#
  end if
else
  T1 = 0#
  T2 = 9999999#
end if

'----- Read the size and number of main ephemeris records.
'----- specify an ASCII data file
if InFile = "" then InputFile = FALSE
while InputFile = FALSE
  if isfalse(InputFile) then
    '----- prompt user for file name
    InFile = ""
    do
      input "File name to convert (XXXX to end): ",InFile
    loop until InFile <> ""
  end if
  InputFile = TRUE
wend

InFile = rtrim$(ltrim$(ucase$(InFile)))
if InFile = "XXXX" then
  kill "asc2eph.log"
  print
  print "OK"
  stop
elseif dir$(InFile) = "" then
  print "Requested input file does not exist."
  print "Specify another file or move to another directory."
  kill "asc2eph.log"
  print
  print "OK"
  stop
end if

print      "Input will be read from ";InFile
print #3, "Input will be read from ";InFile
print      "Output will be written to ";OutFile
print #3, "Output will be written to ";OutFile

'----- form the header file name
if isfalse(HeaderIncluded) then
  extension = right$(InFile,3)
  HFile = "HEADER."+extension
  if isfalse(len(dir$(HFile))) then
    print "Header file not present."
    kill "asc2eph.log"
    print
    print "OK"
    stop
```

```
   end if
end if

'----- open the header file for input
if HeaderIncluded then
  HFile = InFile
end if
if isfalse(len(dir$(InFile))) then
  print "Data file not present."
  kill "asc2eph.log"
  print
  print "OK"
  stop
else
  open HFile for input as #1
end if

'----- get KSIZE
line input #1, L
KSIZE = val(mid$(L, 7,6))
print "KSIZE = ";KSIZE
print #3, "KSIZE = ";KSIZE

'----- redim the coefficient array for this particular
'----- ephemeris file
redim DB(1 to KSIZE/2)

'----- Now for the alphameric heading records (GROUP 1010)
call NXTGRP(HEADER)
if HEADER <> "GROUP    1010" then
  call ERRPRT (1010, "NOT HEADER")
end if

'----- read in the values of TTL() and
for I = 1 to 3
  line input #1, L
  TTL(I) = rtrim$(ltrim$(L))
  print TTL(I)
  print #3, TTL(I)
next I

'----- Read start, end and record span  (GROUP 1030)
call NXTGRP(HEADER)
if HEADER <> "GROUP    1030" then
  call ERRPRT(1030, "NOT HEADER")
end if

'----- read in values of SS(1-3)
input #1, SS(1),SS(2),SS(3)

'----- read number of constants and names of constants (GROUP 1040/4).
call NXTGRP(HEADER)
if HEADER <> "GROUP    1040" then
  call ERRPRT(1040, "NOT HEADER")
end if

input #1, N

'----- now parse the constant names from each line of input
ccount = 1
nlines = N \ 10
for lin = 1 to nlines step 1
  line input #1, L
  L = ltrim$(L)
  for col = 1 to 73 step 8
    CNAM(ccount) = (mid$(L,col,6))
    '----- check needed in case last constant on a line
    '----- doesn't have 6 characters
    if len(CNAM(ccount)) < 6 then
```

```
      CNAM(ccount) = CNAM(ccount)+space$(6-len(CNAM(ccount)))
    end if
    incr ccount
  next col
next lin

'----- get the line with remaining constants
line input #1, L
L = ltrim$(L)
for col = 1 to 73 step 8
  CNAM(ccount) = (mid$(L,col,6))
    '----- check needed in case last constant on a line
    '----- doesn't have 6 characters
    if len(CNAM(ccount)) < 6 then
      CNAM(ccount) = CNAM(ccount)+space$(6-len(CNAM(ccount)))
    end if
  incr ccount
next col

NCON = N

'----- Read number of values and values (GROUP 1041/4)
call NXTGRP(HEADER)
if HEADER <> "GROUP    1041" then
  call ERRPRT(1041, "NOT HEADER")
end if

input #1, N

print
print #3,
print      "Ephemeris Constants"
print      "-------------------"
print #3, "Ephemeris Constants"
print #3, "-------------------"
for I = 1 to N
  input #1, CVAL(I)
  if CNAM(I) = "AU    " then AU = CVAL(I)
  if CNAM(I) = "EMRAT " then EMRAT = CVAL(I)
  if CNAM(I) = "DENUM " then NUMDE = CVAL(I)
  print using      "\      \   +.###############^^^^       ";CNAM(I),CVAL(I);
  print #3, using "\      \   +.###############^^^^       ";CNAM(I),CVAL(I);
  if I mod 2 = 0 then print #3,
next I
LeftOver = N mod 3
select case LeftOver
  case = 0
    NumZeros = 0
  case = 1,2
    NumZeros = 3 - LeftOver
end select
for I = 1 to NumZeros
  input #1, x1
next I

'----- Read pointers needed by INTERP (GROUP 1050)
call NXTGRP(HEADER)
if HEADER <> "GROUP    1050" then
  call ERRPRT(1050, "NOT HEADER")
end if

'----- read pointers from file
for jrow = 1 to 3
  for jcol = 1 to 13
    input #1, IPT(jrow,jcol)
  next jcol
next jrow

LPT(1) = IPT(1,13)
```

```
LPT(2) = IPT(2,13)
LPT(3) = IPT(3,13)

print
print
print #3,
print #3,
print      " Body      1st coeff      coefs/component      sets of coefs "
print      "----------------------------------------------------------------"
print #3, " Body      1st coeff      coefs/component      sets of coefs "
print #3, "----------------------------------------------------------------"
f =   " ## \ \     ###             ###             ###"
for jcol = 1 to 13
   print      using f;jcol;Body(jcol);IPT(1,jcol);IPT(2,jcol);IPT(3,jcol)
   print #3, using f;jcol;Body(jcol);IPT(1,jcol);IPT(2,jcol);IPT(3,jcol)
next jcol
print

'----- Open direct-access output file ('JPLEPH' by default)
if isfalse(OutputFile) then
   if len(dir$("JPLEPH")) then kill "JPLEPH"
   open "JPLEPH" for binary as #12
else
   open OutFile for binary as #12
end if

'----- BEGINNING OF HEADER.
for K = 1 to 3
   put$ #12, TTL(K)              '----- (195 bytes)
next K
put #12, , NCON                  '----- (2 bytes)
for K = 1 to NCON
   put$ #12, CNAM(K)             '----- (NCON*6 bytes)
next K
for K = 1 to 3
   put #12, , SS(K)              '----- (24 bytes)
next K
put #12, , AU                    '----- (16 bytes)
put #12, , EMRAT
for jrow = 1 to 3
   for jcol = 1 to 12
      put #12, , IPT(jrow,jcol)  '----- (72 bytes)
   next jcol
next jrow
put #12, , NUMDE                 '----- (2 bytes)
put #12, , LPT(1)                '----- (6 bytes)
put #12, , LPT(2)
put #12, , LPT(3)
for K = 1 to NCON
   put #12, , CVAL(K)            '----- (NCON*8 bytes)
next K
'----- Length of header = 317+NCON*14 bytes
'----- END OF HEADER.

'----- Read and write the ephemeris data records (GROUP 1070).
call NXTGRP(HEADER)
if HEADER <> "GROUP   1070" then
   call ERRPRT(1070, "NOT HEADER")
end if

'----- close the header file and open the actual data file
'----- if the header is in a separate file
if isfalse(HeaderIncluded) then
   close #1
   open InFile for input as #1
end if

NROUT = 0
```

```
'----- read the very first record in
if isfalse(eof(1)) then
  input #1, NRW, NCOEFF
  for K = 1 to NCOEFF
    input #1, DB(K)
  next K
  LeftOver = NCOEFF mod 3
  select case LeftOver
    case = 0
      NumZeros = 0
    case = 1,2
      NumZeros = 3 - LeftOver
  end select
  for K = 1 to NumZeros
    input #1, x1
  next K
end if

f = "  #### EPHEMERIS RECORD(S) WRITTEN.  LAST JED = #######.#"
row = csrlin
col = pos(0)
Progress = "Searching for first requested record "

do while (isfalse(eof(1)) and (DB(2) < T2))

  if (2*NCOEFF <> KSIZE) then
    call ERRPRT(NCOEFF, " 2*NCOEFF not equal to KSIZE")
  end if

  '----- Skip this data block if the end of the interval is less
  '----- than the specified start time or if the it does not begin
  '----- where the previous block ended.

  if ((DB(2) > T1) and (DB(1) >= DB2Z)) then

    if (FIRST) then

      '----- Don't worry about the intervals overlapping
      '----- or abutting if this is the first applicable
      '----- interval.
      DB2Z = DB(1)
      FIRST = FALSE
    end if

    if (DB(1) <> DB2Z) then
      '----- Beginning of current interval is past the end
      '----- of the previous one.
      call ERRPRT(NRW, "Records do not overlap or abut.")
    end if

    DB2Z = DB(2)
    incr NROUT

    '----- write the numbers to binary file
    for K = 1 to NCOEFF
      put #12, , DB(K)
    next K

    '----- Save this block's starting date, its interval span,
    '----- and its end date.
    if (NROUT = 1) then
      SS(1) = DB(1)
      SS(3) = DB(2) - DB(1)
    end if
    SS(2) = DB(2)

    '----- Update the user as to our progress every 10th block.

    if ((NROUT mod 10) = 1) then
```

```
      if (DB(1) >= T1) then
        locate row, col
        print using f; NROUT; DB(2);
      end if
    end if
  else
    locate row, col
    print Progress;
    Progress = Progress + "."
    if len(Progress) = 47 then
      Progress = left$(Progress, 37)
      locate row,col
      print space$(47);
      locate row,col
      print Progress;
    end if
  end if

  '----- read next block of coefficients unless EOF has
  '----- been reached
  if isfalse(eof(1)) then
    input #1, NRW, NCOEFF
    for K = 1 to NCOEFF
      input #1, DB(K)
    next K
    LeftOver = NCOEFF mod 3
    select case LeftOver
      case = 0
        NumZeros = 0
      case = 1,2
        NumZeros = 3 - LeftOver
    end select
    for K = 1 to NumZeros
      input #1, x1
    next K
  end if

loop

'----- end-of-file, but no records yet written OR
'----- just no records yet written
if ((istrue(eof(1)) and NROUT = 0) or (NROUT = 0)) then
  incr NROUT
  SS(1) = DB(1)
  SS(2) = DB(2)
  for K = 1 to NCOEFF
    put #12, , DB(K)
  next K
'----- end-of-file but T2 lies within most recently read record
elseif (istrue(eof(1)) ) then
  incr NROUT
  SS(2) = DB(2)
  for K = 1 to NCOEFF
    put #12, , DB(K)
  next K
elseif DB(2) > T2 then
  incr NROUT
  SS(2) = DB(2)
  for K = 1 to NCOEFF
    put #12, , DB(K)
  next K
end if

'----- Now write start and final JED to header
seek #12, (197+NCON*6)+1
put #12, , SS(1)
put #12, , SS(2)

locate row, col
```

```
print;
print #3,
print       using f; NROUT; DB(2)
print #3, using f; NROUT; DB(2)
print
print #3,

print       "Start JED for this file is ";SS(1)
print #3, "Start JED for this file is ";SS(1)
print       "Final JED for this file is ";SS(2)
print #3, "Final JED for this file is ";SS(2)
print
print #3,

LengthOfHeader = 317+NCON*14
LengthOfRecord = 8*NCOEFF
LengthOfFile   = LengthOfHeader+LengthOfRecord*NROUT
print       "Header is";LengthOfHeader;"bytes"
print #3, "Header is";LengthOfHeader;"bytes"
print       "Record is";LengthOfRecord;"bytes"
print #3, "Record is";LengthOfRecord;"bytes"
print       LengthOfFile;"bytes written"
print #3, LengthOfFile;"bytes written"
print       lof(12);"bytes actual file size"
print #3, lof(12);"bytes actual file size"
print
print #3,

'----- We're through. Wrap it up.
print       "OK"
print #3, "OK"
close #1
close #3
close #12
if DeleteLogFile then kill "asc2eph.log"

end

sub ERRPRT (I as integer, MSG as string)

  print "ERROR #";I; MSG
  kill "asc2eph.log"
  stop

end sub

sub NXTGRP (HEADER as string)

  dim BLANK as string
  HEADER = ""

  '----- read in one line at a time, stopping at the first
  '----- non-blank line we encounter
  do while (HEADER = "")
    line input #1, HEADER
    '----- remove leading and trailing spaces
    HEADER = ltrim$(rtrim$(HEADER))
  loop

  '----- now we've found the header. read the blank line...
  line input #1, BLANK

end sub

sub ShowBanner

  print "Usage: ASC2EPH [-i:FILE][-o:FILE][-D][-H][-K][-h]"
  print "Valid command line options are:"
  print
```

```
print tab(5);"-i:FILE";spc(3);"Use FILE as input assuming separate header file"
print               tab(15);"Will prompt if this option is not used"
print tab(5);"-o:FILE";spc(3);"Use FILE as name of binary file"
print               tab(15);"Default binary file name is JPLEPH"
print tab(5);"-D";spc(8);"Program will prompt for initial and final dates"
print               tab(15);"Defaults are full range of data file"
print tab(5);"-H";spc(8);"Assume data file has header included"
print               tab(15);"Default is separate header in HEADER.XXX"
print tab(5);"-K";spc(8);"Delete log file ASC2EPH.LOG"
print               tab(15);"Log file kept by default"
print tab(5);"-h";spc(8);"Display this help screen"
print
print "Command line options may be in any order."
print

end sub

sub ParseCmdLine

  dim Cmd as string, opt as string, switch as string
  dim slsh as integer, slsh1 as integer

  '----- uncomment only one of the next two lines
  Cmd = command$   '----- case sensitive
  '----- Cmd = ucase$(command$)   '----- case insensitive

  '----- find first occurance of "/" or "-"
  slsh = instr(Cmd, any "/-")
  do while slsh
    '----- find next occurance of "/" or "-"
    slsh1 = instr(slsh + 1, Cmd, any "/-")
    if slsh1 then
      opt = mid$(Cmd, slsh, slsh1-slsh)
    else
      opt = mid$(Cmd, slsh)
    end if
    opt = ltrim$(rtrim$(opt))
    switch = mid$(opt,2,1)
    select case switch
      case " "
        print "Space not allowed between - and option."
        print "Type asc2eph -h for help."
        close #3
        stop
      case "I", "i"
        InFile = ltrim$(rtrim$(mid$(opt, 4)))
        InputFile = TRUE
      case "K"
        DeleteLogFile = TRUE
      case "O", "o"
        OutFile = ltrim$(rtrim$(mid$(opt, 4)))
        if OutFile <> "" then
          OutputFile = TRUE
        else
          OutputFile = FALSE
          OutFile = "JPLEPH"
        end if
      case "D"
        PromptForDates = TRUE
      case "H"
        print    "Assuming included header."
        print #3,"Assuming included header."
        HeaderIncluded = TRUE
      case "h", "?"
        call ShowBanner
        close #3
        kill "asc2eph.log"
        stop
```

```
    case "v"
      close #3
      kill "asc2eph.log"
      print "OK"
      stop
    case else
      print "Option not recognized."
      print "Type asc2eph -h for help."
      close #3
      kill "asc2eph.log"
      stop
  end select
  '----- remove most recent option from command line
  if slsh1 then
    Cmd = mid$(Cmd,slsh1)
  else
    Cmd = " "
  end if
  Cmd = ltrim$(rtrim$(Cmd))
  slsh = instr(Cmd, any "/-")
loop

if (len(Cmd) and isfalse(slsh)) then
  print "Option not recognized."
  print
  call ShowBanner
  close #3
  kill "asc2eph.log"
  stop
end if

end sub
```

Obviously, the scope of this program is rather extensive. It also offers
some convenient features not found in the FORTRAN version from which it
is derived. Entering asc2eph /? at the command line gives the following
help screen:

```
C:\EPHEM\BASIC>asc2eph /?

***Program AC2EPH v1.112395                    Written by Joe Heafner
***Converts JPL ASCII ephemeris data files to binary
***The author can be reached via Internet:    heafnerj@mercury.interpath.com

Usage: ASC2EPH [/I:FILE] [/O:FILE] [/D] [/H] [/K] [/?]
Valid command line options are:

    /I:FILE   Use FILE as input assuming separate header file
              Will prompt if this option is not used
    /O:FILE   Use FILE as name of binary file
              Default binary file name is JPLEPH
    /D        Program will prompt for initial and final dates
              Defaults are full range of data file
    /H        Assume data file has header included
              Default is separate header in HEADER.XXX
    /K        Delete log file ASC2EPH.LOG
              Log file kept by default
    /?        Display this help screen

Command line options may be in any order.

C:\EPHEM\BASIC>
```

The version number (1.112395 in this case) indicates that the program was compiled on 23 November 1995. The exact version supplied with this book may have a later date, but the functionality of the program will not have changed. Although the names of the ephemeris data files available from JPL follow a logical convention, there will be times when a user will want to rename the files. For example, the DE200 data file covering the time span from 1800 to 2000 is named ASC1800.200, but suppose the user renames the file to something like DE200.ASC. The /i command line option allows the user to specify the new name for the input file. Following the JPL convention, the default name of the processed binary output file is JPLEPH (note the lack of a three character extension). The /o command line option lets the user specify the name of the output binary data file. By default, the binary data file will cover the same span of time as the input ASCII data file, but the /d command line option will cause the program to prompt the user for the desired initial and final Julian day numbers (on the TDB time scale). The user must calculate the desired Julian day numbers beforehand.

PROGRAMMING EXERCISE: Modify ASC2EPH to accept regular calendar dates as input and to perform the conversion to Julian day numbers automatically.

When prompted for the initial and final dates, entering 0 for the initial date causes the program to use the first date in the ASCII data file. Entering 9999999 for the final date causes the program to use the remaining range of dates in the ASCII data file. By default, the program will look for the header information in a separate file named header.xxx, where xxx is the ephemeris number (200, for example). Sometimes the user will want to merge the header information into the ASCII data file, and the /h command line option tells the program not to look for the separate header file. Finally, by default the entire output of ASC2EPH is written both to the screen and to a log file named asc2eph.log. The /k command line option deletes this log file after the program has stopped executing.

The following is an example command line used to invoke ASC2EPH. It assumes the data and header files are present.

```
asc2eph /i asc1950.200 /o ephem.dat /k
```

This command line causes the program to look for an input file named asc1950.200 in the current directory. If it cannot find this file, the program will terminate with an appropriate error message. The program will look for a header file named header.200, again terminating gracefully if this file is not present in the current directory. The output binary data file will be named ephem.dat instead of the default jpleph, and the log file will be deleted upon program termination.

Although ASC2EPH is a versatile program, one thing it is **not** designed to do is create a binary data file containing only the Chebyshev coefficients for a single body, Jupiter for example. Any binary data file created by ASC2EPH will automatically contain coefficients for all of the bodies in the original ASCII data file. Only the time span of the binary data file may be altered from that of the ASCII data file.

PROGRAMMING EXERCISE: Modify ASC2EPH to create binary data files containing data for only one body in the original ASCII data file. All of the existing functionality of the program should remain intact. It is good practice to fully document alterations in the source code.

PROGRAMMING EXERCISE: Once a binary data file has been created, run the program EPHTEST to validate the data file. This program will open another ASCII file that contains pre-computed positions and velocities for a basically random number and ordering of bodies contained in the binary data file and compares the pre-computed data with the same quantities computed on the fly. The results of the comparison are written to an ASCII log file for inspection. You should expect to see a discrepancy of no more than one unit in the last decimal place for any computed quantity.

8.5   Identifying a Binary Data File

Once a binary data file has been created, there may be a need to view the contents of the file's header. The header contains much useful information, such as the time span covered by the file, which bodies have data in the file, the length of each record in the file, and the names and values of all the constants used in producing the ephemeris at JPL. There is a program named EPHINFO that is designed to open an existing binary data file and print out the contents of the file's header to the screen. It is important to realize that EPHINFO does **not** create data files, but only analyzes existing data files. Following is the source code listing for EPHINFO.

```
'---------------------------------------------------------------------------
'----- Program EPHINFO.BAS
'----- Description: Opens a binary ephemeris file and prints the
'----- header information.
'---------------------------------------------------------------------------

'----- put compiler metastatements here
$OPTIMIZE    SPEED
$CPU         8086
$COMPILE     EXE
$LIB IPRINT ON
$STRING      32
$STACK       2048
```

```
$DIM         ALL
$HUGE
$OPTION CNTLBREAK ON
'-----------------------------------------------------------------------------

defdbl a-z

option binary base 1
option array  base 1

'----- this includes all ephemeris-related declarations
$include "\fecsoftb\ephdec.bas"

'----- put declarations unique to this program here
dim InFile    as shared string
dim InputFile as shared integer

dim Version as string

'----- these lines maintain the current DOS colors
'----- of the character at location 2,2
dim attribut as integer
attribut = screen(2,2,1)
color attribut mod 16, attribut\16, 0

'----- Write a fingerprint to the screen.
Version = "EPHINFO v1.100997b"
print
print "***Program ";Version;" ";
print "                    Written by Joe Heafner"
print "***Opens a binary ephemeris file and prints the header"
print "***The author can be reached via Internet:";
print "     heafnerj@mercury.interpath.com"
print

call ParseCmdLine

'----- begin main program
if InFile = "" then InputFile = FALSE
while InputFile = FALSE
  if isfalse(InputFile) then
    '----- prompt user for file name
    InFile = ""
    do
      input "File name to examine (XXXX to end): ",InFile
    loop until InFile <> ""
  end if
  InputFile = TRUE
wend

InFile = rtrim$(ltrim$(ucase$(InFile)))
if InFile = "XXXX" then
  print
  print "OK"
  stop
elseif dir$(InFile) = "" then
  print "Requested input file does not exist."
  print "Specify another file or move to another directory."
  print
  print "OK"
  stop
end if

call const(InFile)

print
print "OK"

end
```

```
'----- end main program

sub ParseCmdLine

   '----- Subroutine to parse the command line and set any global
   '----- flags that need to be set. This subroutine will need to
   '----- be modified for each and every program in which it is
   '----- included.
   '-------------------------------------------------------------------------

   dim Cmd as string, opt as string, switch as string
   dim slsh as integer, slsh1 as integer

   '----- uncomment only one of the next two lines
   Cmd = command$   '----- case sensitive
   '----- Cmd = ucase$(command$)   '----- case insensitive
   '----- find first occurance of "/" or "-"
   slsh = instr(Cmd, any "/-")
   do while slsh
      '----- find next occurance of "/" or "-"
      slsh1 = instr(slsh + 1, Cmd, any "/-")
      if slsh1 then
         opt = mid$(Cmd, slsh, slsh1-slsh)
      else
         opt = mid$(Cmd, slsh)
      end if
      opt = ltrim$(rtrim$(opt))
      switch = mid$(opt,2,1)
      select case switch
        case " "
          print "Space not allowed between - and option."
          print "Type ephinfo -h for help."
          stop
        case "h", "?"
          call ShowBanner
          stop
        case "I", "i"
          InFile = rtrim$(ltrim$(mid$(opt, 4)))
          InputFile = TRUE
        case "v"
          print "OK"
          stop
        case else
          print "Option not recognized."
          print "Type ephinfo -h for help."
          stop
      end select
      '----- remove most recent option from command line
      if slsh1 then
         Cmd = mid$(Cmd,slsh1)
      else
         Cmd = " "
      end if
      Cmd = ltrim$(rtrim$(Cmd))
      slsh = instr(Cmd, any "/-")
   loop

   if (len(Cmd) and isfalse(slsh)) then
      print "Option not recognized."
      print
      call ShowBanner
      stop
   end if

end sub

sub ShowBanner

   '----- Subroutine to display the help banner. This
   '----- routine will have to be modified for each
```

```
'----- program in which it is used.
'-------------------------------------------------------------------------
print "Usage: EPHINFO [-i:FILE][-h]"
print "Valid command line options are:"
print
print tab(5);"-i:FILE";spc(3);"Use FILE as input"
print                 tab(15);"Default input file is JPLEPH"
print tab(5);"-h";spc(8);"Display this help screen"
print
print "Command line options may be in any order."
print

end sub

'----- put any other subs/functions here
$include "\fecsoftb\ephopn.bas"
$include "\fecsoftb\const.bas"
```

As with ASC2EPH, invoking EPHINFO with no command line options starts the program in an interactive mode, prompting the user for a file name. The file name can also be specified on the command line through the /i option. Following is a typical screen from a sample run of EPHINFO.

```
C:\EPHEM\BASIC>ephinfo /i 1996bin.200

***Program EPHINFO v1.112395                    Written by Joe Heafner
***Opens a binary ephemeris file and prints the header
***The author can be reached via Internet:    heafnerj@mercury.interpath.com

JPL Planetary Ephemeris DE200/DE200
Start Epoch: JED=  2305424.5 1599 DEC 09 00:00:00
Final Epoch: JED=  2524624.5 2200 FEB 01 00:00:00
First valid JED in file  2450064.5
Final valid JED in file  2450480.5
Block interval  32 days
Length of file              89,021 bytes
Length of header             3,117 bytes
Coeffs per block               826
Length of each block         6,608 bytes
Blocks in file                  13
Bodies present in data file:
MER VEN EAR MAR JUP SAT URA NEP PLU MOO SUN
This ephemeris contains nutations.
This ephemeris does not contain librations.
This ephemeris has 200 ephemeris constants.
Display constant names and values (Y/N)? n

OK

C:\EPHEM\BASIC>
```

In this example, the user wants to read the header for the file 1996bin.200, which is a binary file containing DE200 ephemeris data for the year 1996. The program first identifies the ephemeris, in this case DE200. Then the program prints the start and final epochs for the *entire ephemeris, and not just for this particular data file*. Next, the program prints the first and final Julian day numbers for this particular file, followed by the interval covered by each block of coefficients in the data file. Next are the lengths of the entire file and of the header, followed by the total number of coefficients in each block, the length of each block, and the number of blocks in the file. The program then identifies which bodies are present in the ephemeris. The abbreviations should be obvious. DE200 contains nutations but no librations, and this is also indicated. Finally, the program tells how many ephemeris constants there are and offers the user the option of printing (to the screen, not to a printer) out their names and values. This need not be done in every situation, but it is a potentially useful option. Note that EPHINFO does not write its output to a file.

PROGRAMMING EXERCISE: Modify EPHINFO to write its output to an ASCII log file named EPHINFO.LOG. Notice that using the DOS redirection operator will not work with a PowerBASIC program unless output is directed to the screen, which must be opened as a DOS device from within the program. Consult the PowerBASIC documentation for details.

8.6   Using the Binary Data Files

Now we are in a position to actually use the data files to generate ephemerides. We eventually want to use an interactive program that will produce apparent, topocentric, virtual, local, and astrometric positions of the planets, Sun, and Moon. The primary benefit of this program is that it will use **any** binary data file created with the procedure outlined above. For the user who has access to the ASCII ephemeris data files via the Internet, this program can serve as a "front end" to any ephemeris that JPL produces. Of course, this assumes that JPL does not change the format of the ASCII data files. However, this is not likely to happen.

As mentioned above, JPL supplies a suite of FORTRAN subroutines that serves as an interface to the binary data files. These routines have changed only slightly over the last several years, and the changes that have occurred have been minor. The author has ported these routines, as they were at the beginning of the summer of 1995, to PowerBASIC, and these ports will be described here. Great care has been taken to ensure that these versions of these routines function identically to their FORTRAN counterparts.

8.6.1   EPHOPN

The subroutine EPHOPN is the routine that actually opens an existing binary ephemeris data file, reads the information in the file's header and stores it in memory. This routine **must** be called before anything is done to the

data in the file. However, it may be called as part of another subroutine.
Here is the source code listing for **EPHOPN**.

```
sub ephopn(FileName as string) static
   '----- Subroutine to open a binary ephemeris data file for access,
   '----- read the header information, and store it in memory for
   '----- later use.
   '-----------                ----------------------------------------------------

   dim i      as local integer
   dim j      as local integer
   dim efirst as static integer
   '----- make sure all variables read from the data file
   '----- are shared

   if (efirst = FALSE) then

      '----- default file name is jpleph
      if FileName = "" then FileName = "jpleph"

      '----- The existence of the data file MUST be confirmed
      '----- in the calling program. It is NOT checked here!
      open FileName for binary as #12

      '----- beginning of header.
      for j = 1 to 3
         get$ #12, 65, ttl(j)    '----- (195 bytes)
      next j
      get #12, , ncon            '----- (2 bytes)

      redim cnam(1 to ncon)
      for j = 1 to ncon
         get$ #12, 6, cnam(j)    '----- (ncon*6 bytes)
      next j
      for j = 1 to 3
         get #12, , ss(j)        '----- (24 bytes)
      next j
      get #12, , au              '----- (16 bytes)
      get #12, , emrat
      for i = 1 to 3
         for j = 1 to 12
            get #12, , ipt(i,j)  '----- (72 bytes)
         next j
      next i
      get #12, , numde           '----- (2 bytes)
      get #12, , lpt(1)          '----- (6 bytes)
      get #12, , lpt(2)
      get #12, , lpt(3)

      redim cval(1 to ncon) as shared double
      for j = 1 to ncon
         get #12, , cval(j)      '----- (ncon*8 bytes)
      next j
      '----- end of header.

      LengthOfFile = lof(12)

      LengthOfHeader = 317+14*ncon

      '----- Length of block of coeffs = 8*ncoeff bytes
      '----- calculate number of coeffs per block
      ncoeff = 0
      for j = 1 to 12
         if j = 12 then
            ncoeff = ncoeff+ipt(2,j)*ipt(3,j)*2
         else
```

```
          ncoeff = ncoeff+ipt(2,j)*ipt(3,j)*3
        end if
      next j
      ncoeff = ncoeff + lpt(2)*lpt(3)*3+2

      BlockLength = ncoeff*8

      NumBlocks = (LengthOfFile-LengthOfHeader)/BlockLength

      efirst = TRUE

    end if

  end if

end sub
```

EPHOPN takes a string variable as an input argument. If this input string
is null, then the routine assumes a default file name of JPLEPH, which is the
JPL default for binary ephemeris file names. Also note that this routine uses
a flag to indicate whether or not a file has already been opened on subsequent
calls. This prevents the header information from being loaded every time the
file is accessed. The most important thing to remember is that EPHOPN does
not verify the existence of the data file. It is incumbent upon the user to
ensure that the desired data file exists. Otherwise, the progam will terminate
with a nasty error message.

8.6.2   CONST

Subroutine CONST is a self-contained routine that is designed to print out
the contents of a data file's header. This routine forms the main part of the
EPHINFO program described earlier. It is not required for another program or
subroutine presented in this chapter. Following is the source code listing for
subroutine CONST.

```
sub const (FileName as string) static

    '----- Subroutine to display the constants from the ephemeris file.
    '----- Also prints other useful information about the file.
    '-------------------------------------------------------------------

    dim i as local integer
    dim j as local integer
    dim f as local string
    dim y as local string

    '----- open the file and read the header data
    call ephopn(FileName)

    for i = 1 to 3
      print ttl(i)
    next i

    print "First valid JED in file ";ss(1)
    print "Final valid JED in file ";ss(2)
    print "Block interval ";ss(3);"days"

    f = using$("########",LengthOfFile)
    print "Length of file              ";f;" bytes"
```

```
f = using$("########",LengthOfHeader)
print "Length of header              ";f;" bytes"

f = using$("########",BlockLength)
print "Length of each block          ";f;" bytes"

f = using$("########",ncoeff)
print "Coeffs per block              ";f

f = using$("########",NumBlocks)
print "Blocks in file                ";f

print "Bodies present in data file:  ";
if ipt(1, 1)<>0 then print "MER";" ";
if ipt(1, 2)<>0 then print "VEN";" ";
if ipt(1, 3)<>0 then print "EMB";" ";
if ipt(1, 4)<>0 then print "MAR";" ";
if ipt(1, 5)<>0 then print "JUP";" ";
if ipt(1, 6)<>0 then print "SAT";" ";
if ipt(1, 7)<>0 then print "URA";" ";
if ipt(1, 8)<>0 then print "NEP";" ";
if ipt(1, 9)<>0 then print "PLU";" ";
if ipt(1,10)<>0 then print "MOO";" ";
if ipt(1,11)<>0 then print "SUN";" "

if (ipt(1,12)=0 or ipt(2,12)=0 or ipt(3,12)=0) then
  print "This ephemeris does not contain nutations."
else
  print "This ephemeris contains nutations."
end if

if (lpt(1)=0 or lpt(2)=0 or lpt(3)=0) then
  print "This ephemeris does not contain librations."
else
  print "This ephemeris contains librations."
end if

print "This ephemeris has";ncon;"ephemeris constants."
do
  input "Display constant names and values (Y/N)"; Y
  y = ucase$(rtrim$(ltrim$(Y)))
loop until (y="Y" or y="N")
if y = "Y" then
  for i = 1 to ncon
    print using "\        \    +.###############^^^^       ";cnam(i),cval(i);
    if i mod 2 = 0 then print
  next i
  if ((i-1) mod 2 <> 0) then print
end if

end sub
```

8.6.3 PLEPH

The subroutine PLEPH is the main routine that the user will use to extract state vectors from the ephemeris data file. Basically, the user supplies the date (in the form of a Julian day number on the TDB time scale), a *target* number (identifies the desired body), a *center* number (identifies the coordinate origin), and the routine gives back the state vector of the desired body with respect to the desired coordinate origin, and a flag which indicates whether or not the specfied data lies within the range of dates covered by the ephemeris data file. Other FORTRAN incarnations of this routine did not supply this flag, and the user had to keep the specifed date within the range covered by the data file. Providing this flag gives some degree of protection in that the calling routine can simply check the value of this flag to see if the target date is contained in the data file. The user can also provide custom error messages in the calling program for cases where the date does not fall inside the data file's range. Following is the source code listing for PLEPH. Users must also remember that the state vectors returned by PLEPH are only geometric in nature. They are **not** corrected for light time, aberration, gravitational light deflection, precession, or nutation.

```
sub pleph(jd as double, targ as integer, cent as integer, rrd() as double,_
          inside as integer) static
   '------ Subroutine that reads the JPL planetary ephemeris and gives the
   '------ position and velocity of the point targ with respect to cent.
   '------
   '------ Input: jd    JED at which interpolation is wanted
   '------        targ  number of target point
   '------        cent  number of center point
   '------     The numbering convention for targ and cent is:
   '------
   '------     1 = Mercury         8 = Neptune
   '------     2 = Venus           9 = Pluto
   '------     3 = Earth          10 = Moon
   '------     4 = Mars           11 = Sun
   '---*-      5 = Jupiter        12 = SSB
   '------     6 = Saturn         13 = EMB
   '------     7 = Uranus         14 = Nutations (longitude and obliq)
   '------     15 = Librations, if on eph file
   '------
   '------     If nutations are wanted, set targ = 14. For librations,
   '------     set targ = 15. cent will be ignored on either call.
   '------
   '------ Output: rrd()   6 element array containing the state vector of targ
   '------                 relative to cent. The units are AU and AU/DAY. For
   '------                 librations the units are RAD and RAD/DAY. For
   '------                 nutations the first 4 elements of rrd() are set to
   '------                 nutations and rates, in RAD and RAD/DAY.
   '------         inside  TRUE if jd is within the ephemeris time span.
   '------                 If not, inside is set to FALSE.
   '------ -------------------------------------------------------------------

   dim i              as local integer
   dim j              as local integer
   dim fac            as double
   dim nemb           as integer
   dim ipv            as integer
   dim ncmp           as integer
   dim bary           as shared integer
   dim bsav           as shared integer
   dim pfirst         as integer
   dim jdtot          as double
   dim lme            as integer
   dim embf(min,1)    as double
   dim ve(min,1)      as double
   dim llist(min,1)   as integer
   dim L(min,1)       as integer
   dim tc(min,1)      as integer
   dim llst(min,1)    as integer
   dim jd2(min,1)     as double
   dim jed(min,1)     as double
```

```
'----- pv() is a 6 x 13 matrix. The column number (1-13) specifies
'-----   a body number. The row number (1 to 6) specifies a
'-----   component of the body's state vector x,y,z,xdot,ydot,zdot
'-----   in that order.
dim pv(min,2)        as double

dim pvsun(min,1)     as shared double

'----- 1st time in, be sure ephemeris is initialized
if pfirst = FALSE then
  redim  embf(1 to 2)
  redim    ve(1 to 2)
  redim llist(1 to 12)
  redim     L(1 to 2)
  redim    tc(1 to 2)
  redim  llst(1 to 13)
  redim   jd2(1 to 2)
  redim   jed(1 to 2)
  redim    pv(1 to 6, 1 to 13)
  redim pvsun(1 to 6)
  ipv = 2
  pfirst = TRUE
  call ephopn("")
  ve(1) = 1#/(1#+emrat)
  ve(2) = emrat*ve(1)

  jed(1) = 0#
  jed(2) = 0#
  for i = 1 to 6
    for j = 1 to 13
      pv(i,j) = 0
    next j
  next i
  embf(1) = -1#
  embf(2) =  1#
  for i = 1 to 12
    llist(i) = 0
  next i
  L(1) = 0
  L(2) = 0
  tc(1) = 0
  tc(2) = 0
  for i = 1 to 13
    llst(i) = i
    if i =  3 then llst(i) = 10
    if i = 12 then llst(i) = 11
    if i = 13 then llst(i) = 3
  next i
  fac = 0#
  nemb = 1
end if

'----- Initialize jed() for state and set up component count
jed(1) = jd
jed(2) = 0#

jdtot = jed(1) + jed(2)

if ((jdtot >= ss(1)) and (jdtot <= ss(2))) then
  inside = TRUE
else
  inside = FALSE
  exit sub
end if

ncmp = 3*ipv
```

```
'----- Check for nutation call
if (targ = 14) then
  if (ipt(2,12) > 0) then
    llist(11) = ipv
    call state(jed(),llist(),pv(),rrd())
    llist(11) = 0
    exit sub
  else
    print "pleph: NO NUTATIONS ON THE EPHEMERIS FILE."
    stop
  end if
end if

'----- Check for librations
if (targ = 15) then
  if (lpt(2) > 0) then
    llist(12) = ipv
    call state(jed(),llist(),pv(),rrd())
    llist(12) = 0
    for i = 1 to ncmp
      rrd(i) = pv(i,11)
    next i
    exit sub
  else
    print "pleph: NO LIBRATIONS ON THE EPHEMERIS FILE."
    stop
  end if
end if

'----- Check for targ = cent
if (targ = cent) then
  for i = 1 to ncmp
    rrd(i) = 0#
  next i
  exit sub
end if

'----- Force barycentric output by state
bsav = bary
bary = TRUE

'----- Set up proper entries in llist() array for state call
tc(1) = targ
tc(2) = cent
lme = 0

for i = 1 to 2
  L(i) = llst(tc(i))
  if (L(i) < 11) then llist(L(i)) = ipv
  if (tc(i) = 3) then
    lme = 3
    fac = -ve(1)
  elseif (tc(i) = 10) then
    lme = 10
    fac = ve(2)
  elseif (tc(i) = 13) then
    nemb = i
  end if
next i

if (llist(10) = ipv and L(1) <> L(2)) then llist(3) = ipv - llist(3)

'----- Make call to state
call state(jed(),llist(),pv(),rrd())

'----- Case: Earth-to-Moon
if (targ = 10 and cent = 3) then
  for i = 1 to ncmp
```

```
      rrd(i) = pv(i,10)
   next i

'----- Case: Moon-to-Earth
elseif (targ = 3 and cent = 10) then
   for i = 1 to ncmp
      rrd(i) = -pv(i,10)
   next i

'----- Case: EMB-to-Moon or -Earth
elseif ((targ = 13 or cent = 13) and llist(10) = ipv) then
   for i = 1 to ncmp
      rrd(i) = pv(i,10)*fac*embf(nemb)
   next i

'----- Otherwise, get Earth or Moon vector and then get output vector
else
   for i = 1 to ncmp
      pv(i,11) = pvsun(i)
      pv(i,13) = pv(i,3)
      if (lme > 0) then pv(i,lme) = pv(i,3)+fac*pv(i,10)
      rrd(i) = pv(i,targ) - pv(i,cent)
   next i
end if

'----- Clear state body array and restore barycenter flag
llist(3) = 0
llist(L(1)) = 0
llist(L(2)) = 0
bary = bsav

end sub
```

8.6.4 STATE

The subroutine STATE directly accesses the binary data file and extracts the Chebyshev coefficients for the desired body. This routine also handles the logic to determine the location of the correct block of coefficients within the file. STATE used to be the main routine through which the user interfaced with the data file, but PLEPH is much easier to use. One can think of PLEPH as a *wrapper* for STATE. Following is the source code listing for STATE.

```
sub state(jed() as double, LList() as integer, pv() as double, nut()_
   as double) static

'----- This subroutine reads and interpolates the JPL planetary
'----- ephemeris file.
'-----
'----- Input: jed() 2 element array containing the epoch at which
'-----                interpolation is wanted. Any combination of
'-----                jed(1)+jed(2) which falls within the time span on
'-----                the file is a permissible epoch. For ease in
'-----                programming, the user may put the entire epoch in
'-----                jed(1) and set jed(2) = 0. For maximum accuracy,
'-----                set jed(1) = most recent midnight at or before
'-----                interpolation epoch and set jed(2) = fractional
'-----                part of a day elapsed between jed(1) and epoch.
'-----                As an alternative, it may prove convenient to set
'-----                jed(1) = some fixed epoch, such as start of
'-----                integration and jed(2) = elapsed interval between
'-----                interval between then and epoch.
'-----
```

```
'-----
'-----              LList()   12 element array specifying what interpolation
'-----                        is wanted for each of the bodies on the file.
'-----
'-----                        LList(i)  =0, no interpolation for body i
'-----                                  =1, position only
'-----                                  =2, position and velocity
'-----
'-----              The designation of the astronomical bodies by i is:
'-----
'-----                   i  = 1: Mercury
'-----                      = 2: Venus
'-----                      = 3: Emb
'-----                      = 4: Mars
'-----                      = 5: Jupiter
'-----                      = 6: Saturn
'-----                      = 7: Uranus
'-----                      = 8: Neptune
'-----                      = 9: Pluto
'-----                      =10: Moon (geocentric)
'-----                      =11: Nutations in longitude and obliquity
'-----                      =12: Lunar librations (if on file)
'-----
'----- Output: pv()  6 x 13 array that will contain requested interpolated
'-----                quantities. the body specified by List(i) will have its
'-----                state in the array starting at pv(1,i). (on any given
'-----                call, only those words in pv which are affected by the
'-----                first 10 List entries (and by List(12) if librations are
'-----                on the file) are set. The rest of the pv array
'-----                is untouched.) the order of components starting in
'-----                pv(1,i) is: x,y,z,dx,dy,dz.
'-----
'-----                All output vectors are referenced to the earth mean
'-----                equator and equinox of epoch. The Moon state is always
'-----                geocentric; the other nine states are either heliocentric
'-----                or solar-system barycentric, depending on the setting of
'-----                common flags (see below).
'-----
'-----                Lunar librations, if on #12, are put into pv(K,11) if
'-----                List(12) is 1 or 2.
'-----
'-----         nut()  4-word array that will contain nutations and rates,
'-----                depending on the setting of List(11). The order of
'-----                quantities in nut() is:
'-----
'-----                   dpsi     (nutation in longitude)
'-----                   depsilon (nutation in obliquity)
'-----                   dpsi dot
'-----                   depsilon dot
'-----
'-----
'----- Other important variables:
'-----
'-----    km    logical flag defining physical units of the output
'-----          states. km = TRUE,  km and km/sec
'-----                     = FALSE, au and au/day
'-----          default value = FALSE (km determines time unit
'-----          for nutations and librations. angle unit is always radians.)
'-----
'-----    bary  logical flag defining output center.
'-----          only the 9 planets are affected.
'-----                bary = TRUE  = center is SSB
'-----                     = FALSE = center is Sun
'-----          default value = FALSE
'-----
'-----    pvsun() 6-word array containing the barycentric position and
'-----            velocity of the Sun.
'-----------------------------------------------------------------------------
```

```
dim t(min,1)  as double
dim jd(min,1) as double
dim pvsun(min,1) as shared double
dim dumpv(min,2) as double
dim sfirst as integer
dim nrl    as long

dim buff  as integer
dim ncf   as integer
dim na    as integer
dim aufac as double
dim km    as integer
dim s     as double
dim ipart as double
dim fpart as double

dim i  as integer
dim j  as integer
dim k  as integer
dim m  as integer
dim nr as long

'----- 1st time in, get pointer data, etc., from ephemeris file
if (sfirst = FALSE) then
  sfirst = TRUE
  aufac = 1#
  nrl = 0
  call ephopn("")
  redim  t(1 to 2)
  redim jd(1 to 4)
  redim pvsun(1 to 6)
  redim dumpv(1 to 3, 1 to 2)
  if (km) then
    t(2) = ss(3)*86400#
  else
    t(2) = ss(3)
    aufac = 1# / AU
  end if
end if

'----- Main entry point -- check epoch and read right record
s = jed(1) - 0.5#
call split (S,ipart,fpart)
jd(1) = ipart
jd(2) = fpart
call split (jed(2),ipart,fpart)
jd(3) = ipart
jd(4) = fpart
jd(1) = jd(1) + jd(3) + .5#
jd(2) = jd(2) + jd(4)
call split (jd(2),ipart,fpart)
jd(3) = ipart
jd(4) = fpart
jd(1) = jd(1) + jd(3)

'----- Error return of epoch out of range
if ((jd(1) < ss(1)) or (jd(1)+jd(4)) > ss(2)) then
  print "state: EPOCH OUT OF RANGE."
  stop
end if

'----- nr is the byte index of the first coefficient
nr = clng(fix((jd(1)-ss(1))/ss(3)))
nr = LengthOfHeader + nr * BlockLength
'----- use previous block if necessary
if (jd(1) = ss(2)) then nr = nr - BlockLength
```

```
if nr < 1& then
  print "state: BLOCK NOT PRESENT."
  stop
end if
'----- calculate relative time in interval (0 <= t(1) <= 1)
t(1) = ((jd(1)-(cdbl((nr-LengthOfHeader)/BlockLength)*ss(3)+_
                  ss(1)))+jd(4))/ss(3)
if t(1) < 0# then t(1) = t(1)+ 1#

'----- Read correct record if not in core
if (nr <> nrl) then
  redim huge db(1 to ncoeff)
  nrl = nr
  seek #12, nr+1&
  k = 0
  do
    incr k
    if k <= ncoeff then get #12, , db(k)
  loop until(eof(12) or k > ncoeff)
end if

'----- Interpolate SSbary Sun
buff = ipt(1,11)   '----- location of first coeff
ncf  = ipt(2,11)   '----- number of coeffs per component
na   = ipt(3,11)   '----- number of sets of coeffs per 32day interval

call interp(buff,t(),ncf,3,na,2,dumpv())

k = 0
for j = 1 to 2
  for i = 1 to 3
    incr k
    pvsun(k)=dumpv(i,j)*aufac
  next i
next j

'----- Check and interpolate whichever bodies are requested
for i = 1 to 10
  if (LList(i) <= 0) then iterate for
  if (ipt(2,I) <= 0) then
    call errprt(i ,"th body requested - not on file.")
  end if
  buff = ipt(1,I)   '----- location of first coeff
  ncf  = ipt(2,I)   '----- number of coeffs per component
  na   = ipt(3,I)   '----- number of sets of coeffs per 32day interval

  call interp(buff,t(),ncf,3,na,LList(i),dumpv())

  '----- need to re-map dumpv(1:3,1:2) --> temp(1:6)
  redim temp(1 to 6) as double
  k = 0
  for j = 1 to 2
    for m = 1 to 3
      incr k
      temp(k) = dumpv(m,j)
    next m
  next j

  for j = 1 to LList(i) * 3
    if ((i <= 9) and isfalse(bary)) then
      pv(j,I) = temp(j)*aufac-pvsun(j)
    else
      pv(j,I) = temp(j)*aufac
    end if
  next j

next i
```

```
'----- Do nutations if requested and if on file
if ((LList(11) > 0) and (ipt(2,12) > 0)) then
  buff = ipt(1,12)   '----- location of first coeff
  ncf  = ipt(2,12)   '----- number of coeffs per component
  na   = ipt(3,12)   '----- number of sets of coeffs per 32day interval

  call interp(buff,t(),ncf,2,na,LList(11),dumpv())

  '----- need to re-map dumpv(1:3,1:2) --> temp(1:6)
  k = 0
  for j = 1 to 2
    for m = 1 to 2
      incr k
      nut(k) = dumpv(m,j)
    next m
  next j
  nut(5) = 0#
  nut(6) = 0#

end if

'----- Get librations if requested and if on file
if ((lpt(2) > 0) and (LList(12) > 0)) then
  buff = lpt(1)   '----- location of first coeff
  ncf  = lpt(2)   '----- number of coeffs per component
  na   = lpt(3)   '----- number of sets of coeffs per 32day interval

  call interp(buff,t(),ncf,3,na,LList(12),dumpv())

  pv(1,11) = dumpv(1,1)
  pv(2,11) = dumpv(2,1)
  pv(3,11) = dumpv(3,1)
  pv(4,11) = dumpv(1,2)
  pv(5,11) = dumpv(2,2)
  pv(6,11) = dumpv(3,2)
end if

exit sub

end sub
```

8.7 Header File Format

This chapter would not be complete without a discussion of the format of the ephemeris header files. The header file contains all of the information that other programs need to extract the ephemeris constant names, constant values, and Chebyshev coefficients for a particular body.

The first line of the header file, which must not be a blank line, contains a quantity called KSIZE. This number is exactly twice the number of coefficients which exist for each block of data for this particular ephemeris. Remember that the actual coefficients are kept in a separate file. There is also another number on this same line called NCOEFF, and this is always half of KSIZE. Only KSIZE is used in the programs described above. After the line with KSIZE, there is a blank line, and then a line with a GROUP 1010 label. Then there is another blank line. All of the lines with group labels are preceded and followed by a blank line. The data groups are also preceded and followed by blank lines. This structure must be strictly adhered to if the header file is to be properly processed.

The GROUP 1010 data consists of three text strings, each on its own line. These three lines specify, respectively, the ephemeris identification, the ephemeris' first valid epoch, and the ephemeris' last valid epoch. These strings are never used by any computational routine, and they serve simply to identify the ephemeris. Also, note that the first and last epochs denoted here will not necessarily match those reported for a particular binary data file. These values apply for the ephemeris as a whole and not for a specific portion of the ephemeris data. These text strings are never modified by any processing software.

The next group of data is labeled as GROUP 1030. This group consists of three numbers on a single line. The first two numbers are nominally the first and last Julian day numbers for which the ephemeris is valid. The third number is the interval, in days, spanned by each set of Chebyshev coefficients. During processing, the first two numbers will usually be replaced by the corresponding numbers for the particular block(s) of data being used. If more than one block of coefficients is being processed into a single binary file, the first number is replaced by the first valid date for the first block of data. The second number is replaced by the last valid date for the last block of coefficients. The third number is never changed by processing.

The third data group, GROUP 1040, consists of an integer on a line by itself, followed by the specified number of lines containing character strings that correspond to the names of the constants for this particular ephemeris. For example, the number 200 on the first line of this group indicates that there are 200 ephemeris constants. The names are always arranged in 10 columns, and the names are at most six characters long. These constants specify values such as, among other things, the speed of light, the number of kilometers in an astronomical unit, and initial planetary position and velocity components used in the numerical integration. These constants usually change from one ephemeris to another, so be careful when comparing them.

The next group, GROUP 1041, consists of a single integer alone on a line (the same integer as in the previous group) followed by a set of numbers arranged in three columns. These numbers are the values of the constants named in the previous group. The first number corresponds to the first constant, and so on. Zeros may be used to pad the columns in case the number of constants is not a multiple of three. The processing software takes this into account. These numbers are formatted as double precision FORTRAN numbers.

GROUP 1050 is the next, and perhaps most mysterious, group of data. This group consists of a thirteen column by three row array of numbers. Each column corresponds to a body for which data may be present in the ephemeris. The columns correspond to barycentric data for Mercury, Venus, EMB (Earth-Moon barycenter), Mars, Jupiter, Saturn, Uranus, Neptune, Pluto, the Moon (geocentric, not barycentric), the Sun, nutation (longitude and obliquity), and lunar librations. Now, remember that each block of data in the ephemeris contains KSIZE/2 coefficients. The number on the first row of each column tells the position of the first coefficient for the body to which that column corresponds. For example, a value of 3 in the first row of the first column indicates that the coefficients for Mercury begin at position three in the array of KSIZE/2 coefficients. In fact, the number in the first row of the first column of GROUP 1050 is **always** a 3 because the first two numbers in the array of coefficients are the first and last Julian day numbers for which that block of coefficients is valid.

The number on the second row of each column in GROUP 1050 specifies how many coefficients there are for each cartesian (x, y, z) position or velocity vector component. This number will be larger for the faster moving bodies (such as Mercury and the Moon) because more coefficients are needed to model their motion than are needed to model the motion of the slower moving bodies (such as Uranus). Remember that the nutations only have one positon component (it actually specifies an angle) and one velocity component, and that there are two nutations (in longitude and obliquity).

The number on the third row of each GROUP 1050 column specifies how many sub-intervals the basic interval (given by the third number in GROUP 1030, as you recall) is divided into. Usually, each block of coefficients is valid for a 32 day span. However, the faster-moving bodies require a shorter interval of time over which to adequately model their motions. For instance, in the DE405 ephemeris, the Moon requires a 4 day interval, so there must be 8 sub-intervals in the larger 32 day span. Therefore, an 8 appears in the third row of the tenth column of GROUP 1050 in the DE405 header file.

Not every ephemeris contains nutation and lunar libration data. In cases where it does not, the twelfth and thirteenth columns in GROUP 1050 contain zeros.

This structure allows one to perform several checks for errors after the header has been processed. Consult the source code for ASC2EPH for details.

The final group label in the header file indicates GROUP 1070, but there are no group data present. That is because this group corresponds to the actual array of Chebyshev coefficients, and these coefficients are broken up into separate ASCII data files. These are the separate data files that the user will find on the JPL ftp site and on the JPL CD-ROM. Note that in the header file, the GROUP 1070 label must be followed by a blank line. The data file containing the coefficients must **not** begin with a blank line. Following is the file HEADER.405, which contains the header information for the DE405 ephemeris.

```
KSIZE=   2036     NCOEFF=   1018

GROUP   1010

JPL Planetary Ephemeris DE405/DE405
Start Epoch: JED=   2305424.5 1599 DEC 09 00:00:00
Final Epoch: JED=   2525008.5 2201 FEB 20 00:00:00

GROUP   1030

   2305424.50   2525008.50          32.

GROUP   1040

   156
 DENUM     LENUM     TDATEF    TDATEB    CENTER    CLIGHT    AU        EMRAT     GM1       GM2
 GMB       GM4       GM5       GM6       GM7       GM8       GM9       GMS       RAD1      RAD2
 RAD4      JDEPOC    X1        Y1        Z1        XD1       YD1       ZD1       X2        Y2
 Z2        XD2       YD2       ZD2       XB        YB        ZB        XDB       YDB       ZDB
 X4        Y4        Z4        XD4       YD4       ZD4       X5        Y5        Z5        XD5
 YD5       ZD5       X6        Y6        Z6        XD6       YD6       ZD6       X7        Y7
 Z7        XD7       YD7       ZD7       X8        Y8        Z8        XD8       YD8       ZD8
 X9        Y9        Z9        XD9       YD9       ZD9       XM        YM        ZM        XDM
 YDM       ZDM       XS        YS        ZS        XDS       YDS       ZDS       BETA      GAMMA
 J2SUN     GDOT      MA0001    MA0002    MA0004    MAD1      MAD2      MAD3      RE        ASUN
 PHI       THT       PSI       OMEGAX    OMEGAY    OMEGAZ    AM        J2M       J3M       J4M
 C22M      C31M      C32M      C33M      S31M      S32M      S33M      C41M      C42M      C43M
 C44M      S41M      S42M      S43M      S44M      LBET      LGAM      K2M       TAUM      AE
 J2E       J3E       J4E       K2E0      K2E1      K2E2      TAUE0     TAUE1     TAUE2     DROTEX
 DROTEY    GMAST1    GMAST2    GMAST3    KVC       IFAC      PHIC      THTC      PSIC      OMGCX
 OMGCY     OMGCZ     PSIDOT    MGMIS     ROTEX     ROTEY

GROUP   1041

   156
 0.405000000000000000D+03    0.405000000000000000D+03    0.000000000000000000D+00
 0.119970525194723000D+17    0.000000000000000000D+00    0.299792457999999984D+06
 0.149597870691000015D+09    0.813005600000000044D+02    0.491254745145081187D-10
 0.724345248616270270D-09    0.899701134671249882D-09    0.954953510577925806D-10
 0.282534590952422643D-06    0.845971518568065874D-07    0.129202491678196939D-07
 0.152435890078427628D-07    0.218869976542596968D-11    0.295912208285591095D-03
 0.243976000000000022D+04    0.605230000000000018D+04    0.339751499999999987D+04
 0.244040050000000000D+07    0.361762714603509283D+00   -0.907819677295860494D-01
-0.857149831817633490D-01    0.336749391398414016D-02    0.248945204676488743D-01
 0.129463006886503581D-01    0.612751941341837969D+00   -0.348365368494968186D+00
-0.195278288980229919D+00    0.109520683616991937D-01    0.156176843652620547D-01
 0.633110555360105742D-02    0.120517417295400386D+00   -0.925838478939452814D+00
-0.401540220801811010D+00    0.168112683039926443D-01    0.174830931338161642D-02
 0.758202868990537761D-03   -0.110186074282858815D+00   -0.132759945613255570D+01
-0.605889132614203740D+00    0.144816530597351029D-01    0.242463117760296197D-03
-0.281520734248005334D-03   -0.537970689883591202D+01   -0.830480581460151468D+00
-0.224828700228372841D+00    0.109201154300885245D-02   -0.651811656579268268D-02
-0.282078316536504749D-02    0.789439244197905232D+01    0.459647780162694541D+01
 0.155869757353026683D+01   -0.321755523930330892D-02    0.433580985895527619D-02
 0.192864656565384452D-02   -0.182653983068220320D+02   -0.116194450551811457D+01
-0.250103483937377857D+00    0.221188417417765429D-03   -0.376247593284657683D-02
-0.165101470306800195D-02   -0.160550425837682305D+02   -0.239421812161785681D+02
-0.940015672354883058D+01    0.264277104336691632D-02   -0.149831445535920970D-02
-0.679041903017956112D-03   -0.304833196039993162D+02   -0.872478355495796887D+00
 0.891156304098993240D+01    0.322210447723588042D-03   -0.314357030201520246D-02
-0.107794882973930419D-02   -0.808177327911484191D-03   -0.199463000162039940D-02
-0.108726266083810177D-02    0.601084816659129854D-03   -0.167445460615151469D-03
-0.855621449739861630D-04    0.450250815623389356D-02    0.767074700932378838D-03
 0.266056805177027132D-03   -0.351748209645188673D-06    0.517762539958483020D-05
 0.222910185439166520D-05    0.100000000000000000D+01    0.100000000000000000D+01
 0.199999999999999991D-06    0.000000000000000000D+00    0.139078737894227800D-12
 0.295912208285591104D-13    0.384685870771268372D-13    0.180000000000004D+01
 0.239999999999999991D+01    0.500000000000000000D+01    0.637813699999999972D+04
 0.696000000000000000D+06    0.512995970515812451D-02    0.382390655876860108D+00
```

```
0.129414222411027868D+01   0.452470449902280032D-04  -0.223092763198743000D-05
0.229944858701366994D+00   0.173800000000000000D+04   0.204312006654652935D-03
0.878546950779311043D-05  -0.145383007071999995D-06   0.225178243916622500D-04
0.308038097834293747D-04   0.487980736275513038D-05   0.177017646243481353D-05
0.425932863003029405D-05   0.169551626800036872D-05  -0.270970096656691754D-06
-0.717780149805999984D-05  -0.143951838384999992D-05  -0.854788154819000041D-07
-0.154903893130000000D-06   0.294743374914000000D-05  -0.288437212719999980D-05
-0.788967312838999998D-06   0.564041555719999991D-07   0.631612134219473138D-03
0.227858313997755964D-03   0.299221166597053480D-01   0.166716555849284465D+00
0.637813699999999972D+04   0.108262599999999994D-02  -0.253300000000000014D-05
-0.161600000000000007D-05   0.340000000000000024D+00   0.299999999999999989D+00
0.299999999999999989D+00   0.000000000000000000D+00   0.129089593915602298D-01
0.694178558405230284D-02   0.243999999999999995D-03  -0.119300000000000005D-02
0.646682543384255465D-13   0.127748118910414607D-13   0.333405877296029502D-14
0.000000000000000000D+00   0.299999999999999974D-03  -0.425951830000000000D-02
0.408844299999999994D+00  -0.171450900000000006D+01   0.000000000000000000D+00
-0.158167070000000005D-05   0.229888000000000009D+00   0.000000000000000000D+00
0.100000000000000000D+01   0.000000000000000000D+00   0.000000000000000000D+00
```

GROUP   1050

```
    3    171    231    309    342    366    387    405    423    441    753    819    899
   14     10     13     11      8      7      6      6      6     13     11     10     10
    4      2      2      1      1      1      1      1      1      8      2      4      4
```

GROUP   1070

For comparison, here is the header file for DE200.

KSIZE= 1652   NCOEFF= 826

GROUP   1010

JPL Planetary Ephemeris DE200/LE200
Start Epoch: JED= 2305424.5 1599 DEC 09 00:00:00
Final Epoch: JED= 2513392.5 2169 MAY 02 00:00:00

GROUP   1030

   2305424.50   2513392.50   32.

GROUP   1040

```
   200
   DENUM    LENUM    TDATEF   TDATEB   CENTER   CLIGHT   AU       EMRAT    GM1      GM2
   GMB      GM4      GM5      GM6      GM7      GM8      GM9      GMS      RAD1     RAD2
   RE       RAD4     RAD5     RAD6     RAD7     RAD8     RAD9     RADS     RADM     JDEPOC
   X1       Y1       Z1       XD1      YD1      ZD1      X2       Y2       Z2       XD2
   YD2      ZD2      XB       YB       ZB       XDB      YDB      ZDB      X4       Y4
   Z4       XD4      YD4      ZD4      X5       Y5       Z5       XD5      YD5      ZD5
   X6       Y6       Z6       XD6      YD6      ZD6      X7       Y7       Z7       XD7
   YD7      ZD7      X8       Y8       Z8       XD8      YD8      ZD8      X9       Y9
   Z9       XD9      YD9      ZD9      XS       YS       ZS       XDS      YDS      ZDS
   XM       YM       ZM       XDM      YDM      ZDM      DELK     DELN     ADAY1    ADAY2
   DDAY1    DDAY2    PHC0     PHC1     PHC2     PHC3     PHL0     PHL1     PHL2     PHL3
   PHB4     PHB5     PHB6     PHB7     PHB8     BETA     GAMMA    J2SUN    A2J2     MA0001
   MA0002   MA0004   MA0007   MA0324   PHASE    LOVENO   JD1950   XL       YL       ZL
   XDL      YDL      ZDL      PSLP0    PSLP1    AM       J2M      C22M     LBET     LGAM
   J3M      C31M     C32M     C33M     S31M     S32M     S33M     K2M      J4M      C41M
   C42M     C43M     C44M     S41M     S42M     S43M     S44M     AE       J2E      J3E
   J4E      V4       V4D      INC4Q    INC4QD   NOD4Q    NOD4QD   INC4     INC4D    NODE4
   NODE4D   OBLIQ    OBLIQD   LCU1     LCV1     LLO1     LCU2     LCV2     LLO2     AW550
   AW450    AW350    AW250    AW150    AW25     AW10     AW20     AW40     AWCIR    DW550
   DW450    DW350    DW250    DW150    DW25     DW10     DW20     DW40     DWCIR    QQQQQQ
```

GROUP   1041

```
200
0.200000000000000000D+03    0.200000000000000000D+03    0.000000000000000000D+00
0.920725222006000000D+12    0.110000000000000000D+02    0.299792457999999984D+06
0.149597870659999996D+09    0.813005869999999931D+02    0.491254745145081187D-10
0.724345620963276551D-09    0.899701165855730777D-09    0.954952894222405808D-10
0.282534210344592645D-06    0.845946850483065864D-07    0.128881623813803495D-07
0.153211248128427619D-07    0.227624775186369935D-11    0.295912208285591095D-03
0.243998999999999978D+04    0.605181300000000010D+04    0.637814000000000033D+04
0.339751499999999987D+04    0.713980000000000000D+05    0.603300000000000000D+05
0.254000000000000000D+05    0.243000000000000000D+05    0.250000000000000000D+04
0.696000000000000000D+06    0.173800000000000000D+04    0.244040050000000000D+07
0.357260212546963718D+00   -0.915490552856159795D-01   -0.859810041345356602D-01
0.336784520455775437D-02    0.248893428375858497D-01    0.129440715971588811D-01
0.608249437766441137D+00   -0.349132444047697943D+00   -0.195544325580217393D+00
0.109524199354744198D-01    0.156125069115477019D-01    0.632887643692262979D-02
0.116014917044544780D+00   -0.926605558053098188D+00   -0.401806265117824468D+00
0.168116200395885922D-01    0.174313126183694230D-02    0.755975079765192374D-03
-0.114688565462040842D+00  -0.132836653338579214D+01   -0.606155187469280321D+00
0.144820048365775587D-01    0.237285174568728968D-03   -0.283748756861612128D-03
-0.538420864140637789D+01  -0.831249997353602499D+00   -0.225098029260032084D+00
0.109236745067075908D-02   -0.652329390316976673D-02   -0.282301211072311879D-02
0.788988942673227545D+01    0.459570992672261092D+01    0.155842916634453466D+01
-0.321720514122007719D-02   0.433063208949070137D-02    0.192641681926973259D-02
-0.182698911379855176D+02  -0.116273304991353243D+01   -0.250376504345852458D+00
0.221544461295878102D-03   -0.376765491663647338D-02   -0.165324389089726979D-02
-0.160595043341729173D+02  -0.239429413060151006D+02   -0.940042772957514572D+01
0.264312595263412574D-02   -0.150348686458462075D-02   -0.681268556592018199D-03
-0.304879969725404685D+02  -0.873216536230233320D+00    0.891135208725031980D+01
0.322541768798400999D-03   -0.314875996554192863D-02   -0.108018551253387168D-02
0.295355755704857642D-02    0.518690279127932436D-02    0.165768290239528453D-02
-0.118264378739622216D-02  -0.664113621276332926D-03    0.281956025718169329D-03
-0.808177235835125067D-03  -0.199463003744199596D-02   -0.108726272162086774D-02
0.601084831482911921D-03   -0.167445469150060604D-03   -0.855620810990486379D-04
-0.266000000000000014D+00   0.438325140000000002D+00    0.267881350000000018D+00
0.378010017799999987D+00    0.153311651999999993D+00   -0.113067597900000005D+01
-0.254786022620000011D-01  -0.305369097300000003D+00    0.466166519999999973D+00
-0.263258083899999995D+00  -0.147084645000000014D+00    0.281095309700000007D+01
-0.244894056000000004D+01   0.733134284999999997D+00    0.395124141599999978D+00
0.972661997000000004D+00    0.736066497000000042D+00    0.202131468000000009D+00
0.929340109999999942D+00    0.100000000000000000D+01    0.100000000000000000D+01
0.000000000000000000D+00    0.000000000000000000D+00    0.174600000000000008D-12
0.320000000000000025D-13    0.408000000000000003D-13    0.159999999999999997D-14
0.260000000000000004D-14    0.407000120000000007D-01    0.299999999999999989D+00
0.243328242299999995D+07    0.603343019729665753D-02    0.382393007236771942D+00
0.128120436555489170D+01    0.100015500951082778D-03    0.149039876740924137D-04
-0.119434270765326686D-03   0.000000000000000000D+00    0.229971502189818905D+00
0.116178124180819698D-04    0.201509078929999991D-03    0.223035130900000015D-04
0.631686773467999944D-03    0.228022183594000008D-03    0.121260448836999998D-04
0.307082741328000016D-04    0.488840471683000020D-05    0.143603108488999995D-05
0.561066891941000030D-05    0.168743052295000008D-05   -0.334354467700000022D-06
0.222160557154000016D-01   -0.145383007071999995D-06   -0.717780149805999984D-05
-0.143951838384999992D-05  -0.854788154819000041D-07   -0.154903893130000006D-06
0.294743374914000000D-05   -0.288437212719999980D-05   -0.788967312838999998D-06
0.564041555719999991D-07    0.426352325064817810D-04    0.108263000000000001D-02
-0.253999999999999948D-02  -0.161000000000000004D-05    0.328707423250999966D+03
0.350891990467370988D+03    0.251808414931000009D+02    0.821694209999999967D-06
0.353371555189999995D+02   -0.323168329999999989D-05    0.185000000000000009D+01
-0.224503799999999999D-06   0.491719299999999961D+02   -0.806844599999999969D-05
0.234457890000000013D+02   -0.356299999999999981D-06    0.313651510611389995D+04
0.128458704906999992D+04    0.311802706596999997D+03    0.227737435290390022D+04
0.250018417932000011D+04    0.134034305437000000D+03   -0.865544899999999978D-01
-0.106402380000000005D+00  -0.177458539999999984D-01   -0.102198390000000000D+00
-0.280547849999999988D-01   0.813209909999999953D-01    0.364536050000000000D+00
-0.937227069999999919D-02  -0.274276500000000013D-01   -0.231163339999999995D+00
-0.320863949999999967D-01  -0.108613159999999993D-02   -0.205154549999999984D-01
0.938418349999999984D-01    0.896490030000000049D-01    0.841415249999999948D-01
0.302824380000000004D+00   -0.326802399999999993D-01   -0.152173299999999994D-01
-0.198168690000000008D-01   0.000000000000000000D+00    0.000000000000000000D+00
```

3	147	183	273	303	330	354	378	396	414	702	747	0
12	12	15	10	9	8	8	6	6	12	15	10	0
4	1	2	1	1	1	1	1	1	8	1	4	0

GROUP   1070

Notice that the two header files are basically alike, only differing in the number of coefficients and in the names and values of the constants. Another difference between the two header files is that the DE405 header contains GROUP 1050 data for both nutations and lunar librations, whereas the DE200 header only contains nutation data. Note the zeros in the last column of the GROUP 1050 data. Finally, below is a portion of one record of the DE200 data file.

```
      1    826
 0.244420850000000000D+07   0.244424050000000000D+07  -0.399530545303628966D+08
-0.128233975505655818D+08   0.120336363436316373D+07   0.250943591848893593D+05
-0.531482348370829186D+04   0.249470412449305684D+03   0.560640113519316685D+01
-0.173195745886748376D+01   0.109235214555567423D+00   0.108485739690835324D-02
-0.763111456568789414D-03   0.585051330650969149D-04   0.230927938195711784D+08
-0.119311497685686313D+08  -0.696570893127546995D+06   0.793036326937256526D+05
-0.125890137522678265D+04  -0.214853572786104593D+03   0.219582689214584121D+02
-0.617166052781903618D+00  -0.717809024827873454D-01   0.959146824371728997D-02
-0.363643565668787013D-03  -0.289844509612972886D-04   0.165754153333236724D+08
-0.504233316789969429D+07  -0.496931135633640690D+06   0.397541379011114768D+05
-0.120892118125335131D+03  -0.140646617220088132D+03   0.111467186981034185D+02
-0.149919261986570684D+00  -0.496754502545204354D-01   0.501048277840357957D-02
-0.115043500513477048D-03  -0.215524518063189907D-04  -0.557939985719998255D+08
-0.306624094697528053D+07   0.115311966816712613D+07  -0.228569097167769796D+05
-0.114247648453856118D+04   0.124532342439420447D+03  -0.721438990401788605D+01
 0.196070227095417160D+00   0.839599718544432015D-02  -0.152614396007775643D-02
 0.109034269591304806D-03  -0.403365395024396926D-05  -0.369116002533710469D+07
```

The number 826 on the first line of the block of data indicates the number of coefficients in the block. The number 1 indicates that this is the first record in this particular data file and **not** for the entire DE200 ephemeris. Also, the first two numbers in the block of data are the first and last Julian day numbers for which the coefficients in this block are valid.

One final word about the ephemeris data files is needed. The author has taken great pains to ensure that the software presented here will work with the JPL data files in their current form. Furthermore, the descriptive information on the format of the data files is as accurate as possible. However, the author is by no means the final authority on the JPL ephemerides. The astronomers at JPL who produce the ephemerides naturally reserve the right to alter the format of the data files as they see fit, although this is not likely in the forseeable future.

PROGAMMING EXERCISE: Modify EPHINFO to write its output to an ASCII file named EPHHEAD.XXX where XXX is the ephemeris number. This file should essentially be identical to the header file originally retrieved from the JPL ftp site. Examine the original header file to determine its structure. You may also need to consult the PowerBASIC documentation to see how to format the double precision numbers.

Chapter 9

Numerical Methods

9.1   Introduction

This chapter presents and describes the source code listings for all the utility routines and functions used by the primary routines developed elsewhere in this book. These utility routines are not necessarily related to astronomy, but they can be considered a small toolbox for the development of programs that require elementary math functions and operations that are not built into every programming language.

9.2   Utility Functions

The functions in this section are not all mathematical in nature, but they provide convenient methods of formatting numerical and text data. amodulo is a function that normalizes a numerical value X such that the relation $0 \leq X < N$ is satisfied, where N is the maximum value that X can take. For example, time is usually quoted in the range 0^h to 24^h. If, for example, during the computation of local sidereal time, one obtains a final result of 26^h, then one must normalize this value by reducing it to the range 0^h to 24^h, the final result being 2^h. amodulo conveniently performs this normalization, provided we pass as parameters the value to be normalized and the maximum value of the normalized range. amodulo's source code listing is as follows:

```
function amodulo(a as double, b as double) local as double

    '----- Function to reduce a to the range 0 - b.
    '-------------------------------------------------------------------------

    amodulo = a - b * int(a / b)

end function
```

Two useful functions are deg and dms. These functions are usually present
on pocket scientific calculators or pocket computers, and their purpose is to
convert decimal degrees (hours) into degrees (hours), minutes, and seconds,
and vice versa. An advantage of these functions is that a number of the
form dd.dddddd will convert to a number of the form dd.mmssss where dd
represents the number of degrees, mm represents the number of minutes, and
ssss represents the number of seconds. Any seconds past the first two "s"
places are to be interpreted as decimal seconds. For example, 12.127 degrees
converts to 12.07372 (12 degrees, 7 minutes, 37.2 seconds). Also, dms and
deg correctly handle negative values, and the user must keep track of units.
Following are the source code listings for deg and dms:

```
function deg(x as double) local as double

    '----- Converts from sexigesimal to decimal.
    '-----------------------------------------------------------------------

    dim dd    as double
    dim d     as double
    dim fixdd as double

    dd = abs(x)
    fixdd = fix(dd)
    d = fixdd + fix(100# * (dd - fixdd)) / 60#
    d = d + (10000# * (dd - fixdd) - 100# * fix(100# *_
                    (dd - fixdd))) / 3600#
    deg = sgn(x) * d

end function

function dms(x as double) local as double

    '----- Converts from decimal to sexigesimal.
    '-----------------------------------------------------------------------

    dim dd   as double
    dim fdd  as double
    dim dmfd as double
    dim d    as double

    dd = abs(x)
    fdd = fix(dd)
    dmfd = dd - fdd
    d = fdd + fix(60# * dmfd) / 100# + 0.006# * (60# * dmfd - fix(60# * dmfd))
    dms = sgn(x) * d

end function
```

The function FmtDms has essentially the same purpose as dms, only the
result is a formatted string that includes symbols for the appropriate units.
Through the use of flags, the user can also control the number of characters
in the integer portion of the formatted string and even the number of decimal
places in the seconds value. Following is the source code listing for FmtDms:

```
function FmtDms (x as double, n as integer, m as integer) local as string

'----- Function to format angular and time quantities.
'----- Input: x decimal value
'-----        n number of seconds decimal digits
```

```
'-----          m = 1 convert decimal degrees to:
'-----             ddd mm ss      if n = 0
'-----             ddd mm ss.f    if n = 1
'-----             ddd mm ss.ff   if n = 2
'-----             ddd mm ss.fff  if n = 3
'-----             ddd mm ss.ffff if n = 4
'-----          m = 2 converts decimal hours to:
'-----             hh mm ss       if n = 0
'-----             hh mm ss.f     if n = 1
'-----             hh mm ss.ff    if n = 2
'-----             hh mm ss.fff   if n = 3
'-----             hh mm ss.ffff  if n = 4
'----- Modified from Rex Shudde's code by Joe Heafner
'------------------------------------------------------------------------

dim dh(1 to 2) as string
dim mm(1 to 2) as string
dim ss(1 to 2) as string
dim s          as string
dim degr as double
dim minn as double
dim sec  as double
dim fig  as double
dim absx as double

dh(1) = chr$(248)  '----- degree symbol
mm(1) = chr$(39)   '----- arc-min symbol
ss(1) = chr$(34)   '----- arc-sec symbol
dh(2) = "h"
mm(2) = "m"
ss(2) = "s"

absx = abs(x)

'----- determine how many digits before the decimal
if (absx < 100#) then
fig = 2
else
fig = 3
end if

degr = fix(absx)
absx = 60# * (absx - degr)
minn = fix(absx)
sec = 60# * (absx - minn)
sec = DRound(sec, n)

'----- fix seconds and minutes for rollover
if (sec >= 60#) then
sec = 0#
minn = minn + 1#
end if

'----- fix minutes and degrees/hours for rollover
if (minn >= 60#) then
minn = 0#
degr = degr + 1#
end if

if (((degr = 24#) and m = 1#) or (degr = 360#)) then
degr = 0#
end if

s = ""
if x < 0# then
s = "-"
elseif m = 1 then
s = "+"
end if
```

```
s = s + right$(str$(1000+degr), fig) + dh(m)
s = s + right$(str$(100+minn), 2) + mm(m)
if n = 0 then
s = s + mid$(ltrim$(str$(100+sec+0.00001#)),2,n+2) + ss(m)
else
s = s + mid$(ltrim$(str$(100+sec+0.00001#)),2,n+3) + ss(m)
end if

FmtDms = s

end function
```

9.3   Interpolation

In some applications, it is necessary to perform interpolation on a table of
functional values. There are many published algorithms for interpolation, but
the one given in [Meeus 1991] is the one presented here because it is compact
and allows the use of 3- or 5-point tables of values. The function is called
Interpol and has the following source code listing:

```
function Interpol(x() as double, y() as double,_
                  i as integer, arg as double) local as double

    '----- Function for 3 or 5 point interpolation
    '----- using Meeus' algorithm.
    '-----Input:    x()    array of function arguments
    '-----          y()    array of function values at
    '-----                 the three arguments
    '-----          i      switch indicating whether a
    '-----                 3 or 5 point interpolation
    '-----                 is performed (i=3 for 3 pt.,
    '-----                 i=5 for 5 pt.)
    '-----          arg    argument for which a function value
    '-----                 is needed
    '-----------------------------------------------------------------------

    dim d1  as double
    dim d2  as double
    dim d3  as double
    dim d4  as double
    dim d5  as double
    dim d6  as double
    dim d7  as double
    dim d8  as double
    dim d9  as double
    dim d10 as double
    dim n   as double

    if i = 3 then
        d1 = y(2) - y(1)
        d2 = y(3) - y(2)
        d3 = d2 - d1
        n = (arg - x(2)) / (x(2) - x(1))
        Interpol = y(2) + (n / 2#) * (d1 + d2 + n * d3)
    else
        d1 = y(2) - y(1)
        d2 = y(3) - y(2)
        d3 = y(4) - y(3)
        d4 = y(5) - y(4)
        d5 = d2 - d1
        d6 = d3 - d2
```

```
    d7 = d4 - d3
    d8 = d6 - d5
    d9 = d7 - d6
    d10 = d9 - d8
    n = (arg - x(3)) / (x(3) - x(2))
    Interpol = y(3) + n * ((d2 + d3) / 2# - (d8 + d9) / 12#) +_
    n * n * (d6 / 2# - d10 / 24#) + n * n * n * ((d8 + d9) / 12#) +_
    n * n * n * n * (d10 / 24#)
  end if

end function
```

Besides performing simple interpolation, it may be necessary to find the extreme value of a tabulated quantity or to find the zeros of a tabulated function. For example, one may need to know when Mercury crosses the celestial equator, and to do this one would merely examine a table showing Mercury's declination as a function of time and attempt to find the time when the tabulated declination becomes zero. The subprogram Interp1 allows the user to perform these operations, again using Meeus' algorithm. Following is the source code listing for Interp1:

```
sub Interp1(x() as double, y() as double, L as integer, m as integer,_
           arg as double, v as double) static

    '----- Subprogram to perform interpolation on a list
    '----- of tabular values to find maxima/minima or
    '----- to find the zero of a function within the limits
    '----- of the table.  The algorithms used are those of Meeus.
    '----- Input:    x()     array of function arguments
    '-----           y()     array of function values at the
    '-----                   corresponding arguments
    '-----           L       = 3 for 3-pt. interpolation
    '-----                   = 5 for 5-pt. interpolation
    '-----           m       = 0 for zero of function
    '-----                   = 1 for a extremum of the function
    '----- Output:   arg     argument corresponding to the
    '-----                   extremum or zero of the tabular
    '-----                   function
    '-----           v       the value of the function
    '-----                   corresponding to arg
    '-------------------------------------------------------------------

    dim a as double
    dim b as double
    dim c as double
    dim d as double
    dim e as double
    dim f as double
    dim g as double
    dim h as double
    dim i as double
    dim j as double
    dim k as double
    dim nm as double
    dim n0 as double
    dim n1 as double

    if L = 3 then       '----- Use a 3 pt. table
      a = y(2) - y(1)
      b = y(3) - y(2)
      c = b - a
      if m = 1 then     '----- Find extremum of the tabular function
        v = y(2) - (a + b) * (a + b) / (8# * c)
```

```
      nm = -(a + b) / (2# * c)
      arg = x(2) + nm * (x(2) - x(1))
   else
      n1 = 0#     '----- Find zero of the tabular function
      do
         n0 = -2# * y(2) / (a + b + c * n1)
         if abs(n0 - n1) < 0.000000000000001# then exit do
         n1 = n0
      loop
      v = y(2) + 0.5# * n0 * (x(2) - x(1)) * (a + b + n0 * c)
      arg = x(2) + n0 * (x(2) - x(1))
   end if
else        '----- Use a 5 pt. table
   a = y(2) - y(1)
   b = y(3) - y(2)
   c = y(4) - y(3)
   d = y(5) - y(4)
   e = b - a
   f = c - b
   g = d - c
   h = f - e
   j = g - f
   k = j - h
   if m = 0 then       '----- Find extremum of tabular function
      n1 = 0#
      do
         nm = (6# * b + 6# * c - h - j + 3# * n1 * n1 * (h + j) +_
               2# * n1 * n1 * n1 * k) / (k - 12# * f)
         if abs(nm - n1) < 0.000000000000001# then exit do
         n1 = nm
      loop
      nm = nm * (x(4) - x(3))
      arg = x(3) + nm
      v = y(3) + 0.5# * nm * (b + c) + 0.5# * nm * nm * f + nm *_
        (nm * nm - 1#) * (h + j) / 12# + nm * nm * (nm * nm - 1) * k / 24#
   else      '----- Find zero of the tabular function
      n1 = 0#
      do
         n0 = (-24# * y(3) + n1 * n1 * (k - 12# * f) - 2# * n1 * n1 *_
           n1 * (h + j) - n1 * n1 * n1 * n1 * k)_
           / (2# * (6# * b + 6# * c - h - j))
         if abs(n0 - n1) < 0.000000000000001# then exit do
         n1 = n0
      loop
      n0 = n0 * (x(4) - x(3))
      arg = x(3) + n0
      v = y(3) + 0.5# * n0 * (b + c) + 0.5# * n0 * n0 * f + n0 *_
        (n0 * n0 - 1#) * (h + j) / 12# + n0 * n0 * (n0 * n0 - 1#) * k / 24#
   end if
end if

end sub
```

The user should take special note of the switches and parameters that must be set in order to use these routines.

9.4   Trigonometry Routines

Trigonometric functions form a large portion of computational astronomy. However, PowerBASIC, like most other modern programming languages, lacks many of the inverse trig functions that must be employed in the conversion from rectangular coordinates to polar coordinates. Fortunately, all the trig functions can be derived from PowerBASIC's native `atn` function and the other built-in trig functions. `acos` is an inverse cosine function that returns the inverse cosine in radians of the argument. `asin` provides a similar result for the inverse sine function. `atan2` is a special four-quadrant inverse tangent function that returns the inverse tangent computed from two input arguments that are proportional to the resulting angle's sine and cosine. The angle is returned in the range $0 \leq \theta < 2\pi$ radians and is placed in the correct quadrant. Following are the source code listings for `acos`, `asin`, and `atan2`:

```
function acos(x as double) local as double

   '----- Inverse cosine function.
   '--------------------------------------------------------------------------

   dim eps    as double
   dim a      as double
   dim PIDIV2 as shared double

   eps = 1d-33
   a = atn(x / (sqr(1# - x * x) - eps * (abs(x) = 1#)))
   acos = PIDIV2 - x

end function
function asin(x as double) local as double

   '----- Inverse sine function.
   '--------------------------------------------------------------------------

   dim eps as double

   eps = 1d-33
   asin = atn(x / (sqr(1# - x * x) - eps * (abs(x) = 1#)))

end function
function atan2 (y as double, x as double) local as double

   '----- Returns angle in range 0 to TWOPI.
   '--------------------------------------------------------------------------

   dim eps    as double
   dim PI     as shared double
   dim TWOPI  as shared double

   eps = 1d-33
   atan2 = atn(y / (x - eps * (x = 0#))) - PI * (x < 0#) +_
           TWOPI * (x >= 0#) * (y < 0#)

end function
```

9.5 Matrix and Vector Methods

Matrix and vector methods are perhaps the most important mathematical operations in modern computational spherical astronomy and celestial mechanics, and their use comprises the very heart of this book. The routines in this section constitute a small but efficient arsenal for attacking most elementary computational problems. These routines perform tasks such as matrix/matrix multiplication, matrix/vector multiplication, computation of elementary rotation matrices for a given angle, transposing a matrix, obtaining a unit vector from a non-unit vector, computing vector cross and dot products, and computing the magnitude of a given vector. All of the rotation matrices we deal with in this book are orthogonal, and the inverse of an orthogonal matrix is merely its transpose. That is why a routine for general matrix inversion has not been included. Following are the source code listings for these routines:

```
sub MatXMat (a() as double, b() as double, c() as double, L as integer,_
 m as integer, n as integer) static

'----- Matrix multiplication subroutine.
'----- Input:   a()   matrix A (L rows by m columns)
'-----          b()   matrix b (m rows by n columns)
'----- Output: c()   matrix c x b (L rows by n columns)
'----- NOTE: If a() and c() have the same name in the
'----- calling program, the original a() matrix is overwritten.
'-----------------------------------------------------------------------

dim i           as integer
dim j           as integer
dim k           as integer
dim s           as double
dim temp(min,2) as double

redim temp(1 to L, 1 to n)

for i = 1 to L
for j = 1 to n
s = 0#
for k = 1 to m
s = s + a(i, k) * b(k, j)
next k
temp(i, j) = s
next j
next i

for i = 1 to L
for j = 1 to n
c(i, j) = temp(i, j)
next j
next i

end sub
sub MatXVec(a() as double, b() as double, c() as double,_
L as integer, m as integer) static

'----- Matrix/vector multiplication subroutine.
'----- Input:   a()   matrix A (L rows by m columns)
'-----          b()   vector B (m rows by 1 column)
'----- Output: c()   vector A x B (L rows by 1 column)
'----- NOTE: If b() and c() have the same name in the
'----- calling program, the original b() will be
'----- overwritten.
'-----------------------------------------------------------------------

dim i           as integer
dim j           as integer
dim s           as double
dim temp(min,1) as double

redim temp(1 to 6)

for i = 1 to L
```

```
s = 0#
for j = 1 to m
s = s + a(i, j) * b(j)
next j
temp(i) = s
next i

for i = 1 to L
c(i) = temp(i)
next i

end sub
```

These routines are well commented, and their uses should be self-explanatory.

9.6 Generalized Matrix Methods

We now turn our attention to introducing a generalized way of handling matrices. The method we will discuss was first introduced by Yallop et al. [Yallop 1989]. Rotation matrices are a particularly convenient way of making the various transformations needed in the reduction of positional data, and they are computationally efficient as well.

Recall the basic rotation matrices that describe rotations about the x- ,y- , and z-axes:

$$\mathbf{R}_1(\phi) = \begin{bmatrix} 1 & 0 & 0 \\ 0 & \cos\phi & \sin\phi \\ 0 & -\sin\phi & \cos\phi \end{bmatrix} \tag{9.6.1}$$

$$\mathbf{R}_2(\phi) = \begin{bmatrix} \cos\phi & 0 & -\sin\phi \\ 0 & 1 & 0 \\ \sin\phi & 0 & \cos\phi \end{bmatrix} \tag{9.6.2}$$

$$\mathbf{R}_3(\phi) = \begin{bmatrix} \cos\phi & \sin\phi & 0 \\ -\sin\phi & \cos\phi & 0 \\ 0 & 0 & 1 \end{bmatrix} \tag{9.6.3}$$

where subscript 1 denotes a rotation about the x-axis through an angle ϕ, subscript 2 denotes a rotation about the y-axis through an angle ϕ, and subscript 3 denotes a rotation about the z-axis through an angle ϕ. Recall also that these matrices are orthogonal, which means that their inverses are equal to their transposes. Mathematically, we can write

$$\mathbf{R}_i^{-1}(\phi) = \mathbf{R}_i^T(\phi) \tag{9.6.4}$$

$$\mathbf{R}_i^T(\phi)\mathbf{R}_i(\phi) = \mathbf{R}_i(\phi)\mathbf{R}_i^T(\phi) = \mathbf{I} \tag{9.6.5}$$

$$\mathbf{R}_i^T(\phi)\mathbf{R}_j(\phi) = \mathbf{O}, \ i \neq j \tag{9.6.6}$$

where $\mathbf{R}_i^T$ is the transpose of $\mathbf{R}_i$, $\mathbf{I}$ is the identity matrix, and $\mathbf{O}$ is the null matrix.

In general, the rotation angle ϕ will be a function of time. We can now write the derivative of the matrix $\mathbf{R}_i$ as

$$\dot{\mathbf{R}}_i(\phi) = \dot{\phi}\frac{\partial}{\partial\phi}\mathbf{R}_i(\phi), \ i = 1, 2, 3 \qquad (9.6.7)$$

and the partials of the matrices are defined as

$$\frac{\partial}{\partial\phi}\mathbf{R}_1(\phi) = \begin{bmatrix} 0 & 0 & 0 \\ 0 & -\sin\phi & \cos\phi \\ 0 & -\cos\phi & -\sin\phi \end{bmatrix} \qquad (9.6.8)$$

$$\frac{\partial}{\partial\phi}\mathbf{R}_2(\phi) = \begin{bmatrix} -\sin\phi & 0 & -\cos\phi \\ 0 & 0 & 0 \\ \cos\phi & 0 & -\sin\phi \end{bmatrix} \qquad (9.6.9)$$

$$\frac{\partial}{\partial\phi}\mathbf{R}_3(\phi) = \begin{bmatrix} -\sin\phi & \cos\phi & 0 \\ -\cos\phi & -\sin\phi & 0 \\ 0 & 0 & 0 \end{bmatrix}. \qquad (9.6.10)$$

At this point, we introduce a type of matrix called a $\mathbf{Q}$-matrix, which we can use to simultaneously manipulate a position vector and a velocity vector. In other words, a $\mathbf{Q}$-matrix will allow the manipulation of state vectors. The general $\mathbf{Q}$-matrix corresponding to a rotation about the ith axis is defined as

$$\mathbf{Q}_i(\phi, \dot{\phi}) = \begin{bmatrix} \mathbf{R}_i(\phi) & \mathbf{O} \\ s\dot{\mathbf{R}}_i(\phi) & \mathbf{R}_i(\phi) \end{bmatrix} \qquad (9.6.11)$$

where the parameter s is always either zero or one, depending on whether the transformation is from one inertial frame to another or from an inertial frame to a rotating frame. Most of the time s will be zero.

If we now write an object's six-dimensional state vector as a column vector whose first three elements are the position components and other three elements are the velocity components, then we can write a general transformation on this state vector in terms of a $\mathbf{Q}$-matrix as

$$\begin{bmatrix} x' \\ y' \\ z' \\ \dot{x}' \\ \dot{y}' \\ \dot{z}' \end{bmatrix} = \begin{bmatrix} \mathbf{R}_i(\phi) & \mathbf{O} \\ s\dot{\mathbf{R}}_i(\phi) & \mathbf{R}_i(\phi) \end{bmatrix} \begin{bmatrix} x \\ y \\ z \\ \dot{x} \\ \dot{y} \\ \dot{z} \end{bmatrix} \qquad (9.6.12)$$

where the usual rules for matrix multiplication apply. We can shorten this even more if we denote the position vector as $\mathbf{r}$ and the velocity vector as $\dot{\mathbf{r}}$. The previous equation can now be written as

$$\begin{bmatrix} \mathbf{r}' \\ \dot{\mathbf{r}}' \end{bmatrix} = \begin{bmatrix} \mathbf{R}_i(\phi) & \mathbf{O} \\ s\dot{\mathbf{R}}_i(\phi) & \mathbf{R}_i(\phi) \end{bmatrix} \begin{bmatrix} \mathbf{r} \\ \dot{\mathbf{r}} \end{bmatrix} = \mathbf{Q}_i(\phi, \dot{\phi}) \begin{bmatrix} \mathbf{r} \\ \dot{\mathbf{r}} \end{bmatrix} \tag{9.6.13}$$

which is an extremely compact notation.

Any matrix equation that uses 3×3 matrices operating on a position or velocity vector can be recast as an equation that uses $\mathbf{Q}$-matrices to conveniently transform a state vector. Simply replace the matrix $\mathbf{R}_i(\phi)$ with the corresponding matrix $\mathbf{Q}_i(\phi, \dot{\phi})$.

Following are three subprograms (GetQMatrix; GetInvQMatrix; and QRotate) designed to manipulate $\mathbf{Q}$-matrices.

The inverse of a $\mathbf{Q}$-matrix is a matrix whose submatrices are inverses of the original submatrices. Since the submatrices are orthogonal, their inverses are their transposes. Strictly speaking, it is not mathematically correct to say that the inverse of $\mathbf{Q}$-matrix is its transpose because of the way a $\mathbf{Q}$-matrix is defined.

```
sub GetQMatrix(phi as double, phidot as double, axis as integer,_
               s as integer, qmatrix() as double) static

'----- Subprogrm to compute the elements of the
'----- Q-matrix for a given angle and its time
'----- derivative.
'----- Input:  phi          angle in radians
'-----         phidot       time der. of phi
'-----         axis         = 1 for x-axis
'-----                      = 2 for y-axis
'-----                      = 3 for z-axis
'-----         s            = 0 for inertial
'-----                         to inertial
'-----                      = 1 for inertial
'-----                         to rotating
'----- Output: qmatrix()   6X6 Q-matrix
'-------------------------------------------------------------------

redim  r(1 to 3, 1 to 3) as double
redim dr(1 to 3, 1 to 3) as double
dim i                    as integer
dim j                    as integer

'----- Form the 3X3 r() and dr() matrices
call RotMat(axis, phi, r(), dr())

'----- Form the 6X6 Q-matrix
for i = 1 to 3
  for j = 1 to 3
    qmatrix(i, j) = r(i, j)
    qmatrix(i, J + 3) = 0#
    qmatrix(i + 3, j) = phidot * dr(i, j) * s
    qmatrix(i + 3, j + 3) = r(i, j)
  next j
next i

end sub
```

```
sub GetInvQMatrix(qmatrix() as double, invqmatrix() as double) static

   '----- Subprogrm to compute the elements of the
   '----- inverse of a given Q-matrix.
   '----- Input:  qmatrix()      6X6 Q-matrix
   '----- Output: invqmatrix()   inverse of qmatrix()
   '------------------------------------------------------------------

   dim i as integer
   dim j as integer

   for i = 1 to 3
     for j = 1 to 3
        invqmatrix(i, j) = qmatrix(j, i)
        invqmatrix(i, j + 3) = 0#
        invqmatrix(i + 3, j) = qmatrix(j + 3, i)
        invqmatrix(i + 3, j + 3) = qmatrix(j + 3, i + 3)
     next j
   next i

end sub

sub QRotate(vin() as double, axis as integer, phi as double,_
            phidot as double, s as integer, vout() as double) static

   '----- Subprogram to perform a matrix rotation of a state vector
   '----- through a given angle about a desired axis. A right-handed
   '----- orthogonal coordinate system is assumed, and a 6X6 Q-matrix
   '----- is used.
   '----- Input:  vin()      input state vector
   '-----         axis       = 1 for x-axis
   '-----                    = 2 for y-axis
   '-----                    = 3 for z-axis
   '-----         phi        rotation angle in radians
   '-----         phidot     derivative of phi
   '-----         s          = 0 for inertial to inertial
   '-----                    = 1 for inertial to rotating
   '----- Output: vout()     transformed state vector
   '----- NOTE: The vin() and vout() can have the same name in the
   '----- calling program.
   '------------------------------------------------------------------

   dim i                     as integer
   redim   temp(1 to 6)      as double
   redim qmatrix(1 to 6, 1 to 6) as double

   call GetQMatrix(phi, phidot, axis, s, qmatrix())

   for i = 1 to 6
     temp(i) = vin(i)
   next i

   call MatXVec(qmatrix(), temp(), vout(), 6, 6)

end sub
```

The routine GetQMatrix is used to compute the elements of the **Q**-matrix corresponding to a rotation about the given axis through the given angle. The angle's time derivative should be specified if one is performing a rotation from an inertial coordinate system to a rotating coordinate system. Also, this routine makes use of the RotMat routine. GetInvQMatrix computes the elements of the inverse of a given **Q**-matrix. Finally, the subprogram QRotate is designed to apply a given rotation to a six-dimensional state vector.

The position reduction software described in Chapter 6 relies heavily on the concept of a **Q**-matrix. As with conventional rotation matrices, these matrices may be multiplied together to obtain the **Q**-matrix for a combination of rotations. Alternatively, the user may employ successive applications of QRotate to carry out several rotations. This is the approach used in the apparent place reduction program described in Chapter 6.

The final two pieces of code presented in this chapter are not actually programs at all. Instead, they are two support files that must be used by any driver program. The first is ASTROLIB.DEC, a file which contains all of the declarations for the subprograms and functions developed in this book. Following is the listing for ASTROLIB.DEC.

```
'----- This file contains declarations for the ASTROLIB routines.
'----------------------------------------------------------------------------
declare sub Aberrate(p1() as double, ebdot() as double, p2() as double)
declare function acos(x as double) as double
declare function amodulo (a as double, b as double) as double
declare function asin(x as double) as double
declare function atan2(y as double, x as double) as double
declare sub Cal2JED(m as integer, d as integer, y as integer,_
          utc as double, s as integer, tai_utc as double,_
          ut1_utc as double, w as integer, jed as double)
declare sub conway(uelement() as double, mu as double, jed as double,_
          rcostanom as double, rsintanom as double)
declare function deg(x as double) as double
declare function dms(x as double) as double
declare sub Epoch2JED(epoch as string, jed as double)
declare sub Eq2Ecl(a() as double, s as integer, obl as double,_
          b()as double)
declare sub Eq2Hor(a() as double, s as integer, b() as double)
declare function FmtDms(x as double, n as integer, m as integer) as string
declare sub FunArgIAU(jed as double, funarg() as double)
declare sub GeocenObs(jed as double, obsr_geo() as double)
declare sub GetDpsiDeps(jed as double, dpsi as double, deps as double, _
          dpsidot as double, depsdot as double)
declare sub GetGST(jed as double, s as integer, gst as double)
declare sub GetInvQMatrix(qmatrix() as double, invqmatrix() as double)
declare sub GetPrecessParams(jed1 as double, jed2 as double, zeta as double,_
          z as double, theta as double, zetadot as double, zdot as double,_
          thetadot as double)
declare sub GetQMatrix(phi as double, phidot as double, axis as integer,_
          s as integer, qmatrix() as double)
declare sub GetRPNmat (jed1 as double, jed2 as double, rpn as integer,_
          d as integer, m3() as double, m6() as double)
declare sub GetStateVector(jd as double, targ as integer, cent as integer,_
          recpol as integer, StateVector() as double)
declare sub HelEphemeris(uelement() as double, mu as double, jed as double,_
          posvel() as double)
declare sub Interp1(x() as double, y() as double, L as integer,_
          m as integer, arg as double, v as double)
declare function interpol(x() as double, y() as double,_
          i as integer, arg as double) as double
declare sub JED2Cal(jed as double, yr as integer, mo as integer,_
          dy as integer, ti as double)
declare sub JED2Epoch(jed as double, s as string, epoch as string)
declare sub LightTime(jed as double, Body as integer, earth_ssb() as double,_
          earth_hel() as double, StarData() as double, body_geo() as double,_
```

```
                 body_hel() as double, Ltime as double)
declare sub MatXMat(a() as double, b() as double, c() as double,_
            L as integer, m as integer, n as integer)
declare sub MatXVec(a() as double, b() as double, c() as double,_
            L as integer, m as integer)
declare sub MRotate(vin() as double, axis as integer, phi as double,_
            vout() as double)
declare sub Obliquity (jed1 as double, jed2 as double, m as integer,_
            obl as double, obldot as double)
declare sub Pol2Rec(a() as double, b() as double)
declare sub QRotate(vin() as double, axis as integer, phi as double,_
            phidot as double, s as integer, vout() as double)
declare sub RayBend(earth_hel() as double, body_geo() as double,_
            body_hel() as double, p1() as double)
declare sub Rec2Pol(a() as double, b() as double)
declare sub ReduceB(jed as double, body as integer, place as integer,_
            p3() as double)
declare sub Reduce(jed as double, body as integer,_
            place as integer, stardata() as double, p3() as double)
declare sub RotMat(axis as integer, a as double, r() as double,_
            dr() as double)
declare sub SplitStateVector(pv() as double, p() as double, v() as double)
declare sub Stat2Elem(posvel() as double, mu as double, jed as double,_
            uelement() as double)
declare function StumpffN(x as double, norder as integer) as double
declare sub Transpose(a() as double, b() as double, m as integer,_
            n as integer)
declare sub Uvector(a() as double, unita() as double)
declare sub Vcross(a() as double, b() as double, acrossb() as double)
declare sub Vdot(n as integer, a() as double, b() as double,_
            adotb as double)
declare sub Vecmag(a() as double, maga as double)
```

The second of these special files is `CONSTANT.INC`, which contains ini-
tializations for various numerical constants. Following is the listing for
`CONSTANT.INC`.

```
'----- This file contains global numerical constants and declarations.
'-----------------------------------------------------------------------------

'----- Gaussian gravitational constant
'-----------------------------------
dim GaussK as shared double
GaussK = 0.01720209895#

'----- values related to PI
'-------------------------
dim PI     as shared double
dim TWOPI  as shared double
dim PIDIV2 as shared double
PI    = 139755218526789# / 44485467702853#
TWOPI = 2# * PI
PIDIV2 = 0.5# * PI

'----- degrees to radians and radians to degrees
'-----------------------------------------------
dim D2R as shared double
dim R2D as shared double
D2R = PI / 180#
R2D = 180# / PI

'----- hours to radians and radians to hours
'-------------------------------------------
dim H2R as shared double
```

```
dim R2H as shared double
H2R = PI / 12#
R2H = 12# / PI

'----- arcseconds to radians and radians to arcseconds
'--------------------------------------------------
dim A2R as shared double
dim R2A as shared double
A2R = PI / 648000#
R2A = 648000# / PI

'----- AU to km and km to AU
'---------------------------
dim AU2KM as shared double
dim KM2AU as shared double
AU2KM = 149597870.66#
KM2AU = 1# / 149597870.66#

'----- speed of light in km/s and AU/day
'---------------------------------------
dim CKMS as shared double
dim CAUD as shared double
CKMS = 299792.458#
CAUD = CKMS * 86400# * KM2AU

'----- Earth's angular velocity in rad/s
'---------------------------------------
dim EarAngVelRD as shared double
EarAngVelRD = 6.30038748685432#

'----- Earth's equatorial radius in km and AU
'--------------------------------------------
dim EarthRadKM as shared double
dim EarthRadAU as shared double
EarthRadKM = 6378.137#
EarthRadAU = EarthRadKM * KM2AU

'----- Observer's geodetic coordinates
'-------------------------------------
dim obsr_lon as shared double
dim obsr_lat as shared double
dim obsr_ele as shared double

'----- Earth's flattening factor
'-------------------------------
dim EFlat as shared double
EFlat = 1# / 298.257#

'----- JED of standard epoch
'---------------------------
dim J2000.0 as shared double
J2000.0 = 2451545#

'----- days in a Julian century
'------------------------------
dim JulCty as shared double
JulCty = 36525#

'----- Earth's gravitational constant
'------------------------------------
dim MUC as shared double
MUC = 2# * GaussK * GaussK / (CAUD * CAUD)

'----- global state vector variable
'----------------------------------
dim StateVector(1 to 15, 1 to 15, 1 to 2, 1 to 6) as shared double
```

Notice that the observer's geodetic coordinates are only declared and not
specifically initialized. Although it is not recommended, the user could possi-

bly initialize these variables here, and then they would maintain these values in any program. However, it would be better to let the user enter these values as needed.

Chapter 10

A Command Line Ephemeris Program

10.1 Introduction

In this chapter, we present an interactive, command line driven ephemeris program that may be used to generate precise geometric, geocentric, or topocentric ephemerides of the Sun, the Moon, the major planets in the solar system, and stars. The program is comprised of many of the routines described in previous chapters.

10.2 Bringing It All Together

The ultimate test of any collection of computer routines is whether or not it may easily be used to build working programs. As an example, we have provided a program called **SEPHEM**, which stands for *Small Ephemeris*. This program is a command line driven ephemeris generator for the Sun, the Moon, the major planets in the solar system, and stars; it may not, in its current form, be used for comets or asteroids. Many, but not all, of the routines previously described in this book are utilized. Potential features have purposely been left out in order to allow experimental programming by the user. **SEPHEM** requires binary data files to manipulate, so the **ASC2EPH** program must be run before **SEPHEM** is run. Following is the source code for **SEPHEM**:

```
'--------------------------------------------------------------------------
'----- Program SEPHEM.BAS
'----- Description: A small command line ephemeris program
'--------------------------------------------------------------------------

'----- put compiler metastatements here
$OPTIMIZE    SPEED
$CPU         8086
$COMPILE     EXE
$FLOAT       EMULATE
$LIB IPRINT ON
```

```
$STRING     32
$STACK      2048
$DIM        ALL
$HUGE
$OPTION CNTLBREAK ON
'------------------------------------------------------------------------------

defdbl a-z

option binary base 1
option array  base 1

'----- this includes all ephemeris-related declarations
$include "\fecsoftb\ephdec.bas"
$include "\fecsoftb\astrolib.dec"
$include "\fecsoftb\constant.inc"

'----- put declarations unique to this program here
dim TDB        as double
dim Targ       as integer
dim Cent       as integer
dim p3(1 to 6)       as double
dim StarData(1 to 6) as double
dim obsr_geo(1 to 6) as double
dim dist       as double
dim InFile     as shared string
dim InputFile  as shared integer
dim RedGeo     as integer
dim SolSysSum  as integer
dim Place      as integer
dim I          as integer
dim PL         as string
dim r          as double
dim RA_hours   as double
dim DEC_deg    as double
dim RA         as string
dim DEC        as string
dim DateInc    as double
dim NumSteps   as integer
dim counter    as integer
dim xx         as double
dim yy         as double
dim zz         as double
dim xxdot      as double
dim yydot      as double
dim zzdot      as double
dim F          as string
dim G          as string

dim Version as string

'----- these lines maintain the current DOS colors
'----- of the character at location 2,2
dim attribut as integer
attribut = screen(2,2,1)
color attribut mod 16, attribut\16, 0

'----- Write a fingerprint to the screen.

Version = "SEPHEM v1.100997b"
print
print "***Program ";Version;"   ";
print "                        Written by Joe Heafner "
print "***Small ephemeris program"
print "***The author can be reached via Internet:";
print "     heafnerj@mercury.interpath.com"
print

call ParseCmdLine
```

```
'----- begin main program
if InFile = "" then InputFile = FALSE
while InputFile = FALSE
  if isfalse(InputFile) then
     '----- prompt user for file name
     InFile = ""
     do
        input "File name to use (xxxx to end): ",InFile
     loop until InFile <> ""
  end if
  InputFile = TRUE
wend

InFile = rtrim$(ltrim$(ucase$(InFile)))
if InFile = "xxxx" then
  print
  print "OK"
  stop
elseif dir$(InFile) = "" then
  print "Requested input file does not exist."
  print "Specify another file or move to another directory."
  print
  print "OK"
  stop
end if

call EPHOPN (InFile)
print "Using ephemeris DE"+ltrim$(str$(NUMDE))+_
      " with dates from";SS(1);"to";SS(2)

input "Enter start JED on TDB time scale  ", TDB
do
   input "[1] REDUCED PLACE [2] GEOMETRIC PLACE  ", RedGeo
loop until RedGeo = 1 or RedGeo = 2

if RedGeo = 1 then
   do
      input "[1] SOLAR SYSTEM SUMMARY [2] SPECIFIC BODY  ", SolSysSum
   loop until SolSysSum = 1 or SolSysSum = 2

   input "[1] APPARENT [2] TOPOCENTRIC [3] VIRTUAL [4] LOCAL [5] ASTROMETRIC  ",
   Place if Place = 2 or Place = 4 then
      input "Enter latitude  (dd.mmss)  ", obsr_lat
         obsr_lat = deg(obsr_lat)*D2R
      input "Enter longitude (dd.mmss)  ", obsr_lon
         obsr_lon = deg(obsr_lon)*D2R
      input "Enter elevation (meters)   ", obsr_ele
   end if

   select case Place
      case 1
        PL = "APPARENT"
      case 2
        PL = "TOPOCENTRIC"
      case 3
        PL = "VIRTUAL"
      case 4
        PL = "LOCAL"
      case 5
        PL = "ASTROMETRIC"
   end select

   if SolSysSum = 1 then
      print PL + " COORDINATES OF SOLAR SYSTEM BODIES ON"; TDB
      for I = 1 to 11
         if I <> 3 then
            call Reduce (TDB,I,Place,StarData(),p3())
            r = sqr(p3(1)*p3(1)+p3(2)*p3(2)+p3(3)*p3(3))
```

```
          RA_hours = atan2(p3(2), p3(1)) * R2H
          RA   = FmtDms(RA_hours,3,2)
          DEC_deg = asin(p3(3)/r) * R2D
          DEC = FmtDms(DEC_deg,2,1)

          print using "BODY ##"; I;
          print " ALPHA " + RA; " DELTA " + DEC;
          print using " DIST ##.#########"; r
        end if
      next I
  else
    Targ = 12
    do until (Targ < 12 or Targ = 99)
      input "Enter body number (1-11,99) ", Targ
    loop

    if Targ = 99 then
      '----- Read in star's FK5 catalog data
      'call GetStarData(FileName, StarData())
      '----- The previous line MUST be modified by the user to
      '----- indicate the correct name of the data file that
      '----- contains the stellar positional data. Don't forget
      '----- to declare FileName as a string variable.

      '----- FK5 data for Betelgeuse
      '----- Un-comment these lines for default data
      'StarData(1) = 5.9195297222# * H2R
      'StarData(2) = 7.4070416667# * D2R
      'StarData(3) = 0.005#     '----- arcsec
      'StarData(4) = 0.1730#    '----- s/cty
      'StarData(5) = 0.8700#    '----- "/cty
      'StarData(6) = 21#        '----- km/s
      input "Enter FK5 right ascension (hh.mmss) ", StarData(1)
        StarData(1) = deg(StarData(1)) * H2R
      input "Enter FK5 declination (dd.mmss) ", StarData(2)
        StarData(2) = deg(StarData(2)) * D2R
      input "Enter parallax (arcsec) ", StarData(3)
      input "Enter mu alpha (sec/cty) ", StarData(4)
      input "Enter mu delta (arcsec/cty) ", StarData(5)
      input "Enter radial velocity (km/s) ", StarData(6)
    end if

    input "Enter increment in days     ", DateInc
    input "Enter number of steps       ", NumSteps
    print PL " EPHEMERIS OF BODY"; Targ
    counter = 0
    do
      call Reduce (TDB,Targ,Place,StarData(),p3())
      r = sqr(p3(1)*p3(1)+p3(2)*p3(2)+p3(3)*p3(3))
      RA_hours = atan2(p3(2), p3(1)) * R2H
      RA   = FmtDms(RA_hours,3,2)
      DEC_deg = asin(p3(3)/r) * R2D
      DEC = FmtDms(DEC_deg,2,1)

      print using "#######.### "; TDB;
      print " ALPHA " + RA;

      if Targ <> 99 then
        print " DELTA " + DEC;
        print using " DIST ##.#########"; r
      else
        print " DELTA " + DEC
      end if

      incr counter
      TDB = TDB + DateInc
    loop until counter = NumSteps
```

```
   end if
else
  Targ = 16
  Cent = 16
  do until Targ < 16
   input "Enter target number (1-15) ", Targ
  loop
  do until Cent < 16
   input "Enter center number (1-15) ", Cent
  loop
  input "Enter increment in days    ", DateInc
  input "Enter number of steps      ", NumSteps
  print "GEOMETRIC EPHEMERIS OF BODY"; Targ; "WRT BODY"; Cent
  counter = 0
  do
     call GetStateVector(TDB,Targ,Cent,1,StateVector())
     xx = StateVector(Targ,Cent,1,1)
     yy = StateVector(Targ,Cent,1,2)
     zz = StateVector(Targ,Cent,1,3)
     xxdot = StateVector(Targ,Cent,1,4)
     yydot = StateVector(Targ,Cent,1,5)
     zzdot = StateVector(Targ,Cent,1,6)
     F = "#######.##### +##.######### +##.######### +##.######### AU"
     G = "             +##.######### +##.######### +##.######### AU/DAY"
     PRINT USING F; TDB; xx; yy; zz
     PRINT USING G; xxdot; yydot; zzdot
     incr counter
     TDB = TDB + DateInc
  loop until counter = NumSteps
end if

print
print "OK"
end
'----- end main program

sub ParseCmdLine

   '----- Subroutine to parse the command line and set any global
   '----- flags that need to be set. This subroutine will need to
   '----- be modified for each and every program in which it is
   '----- included.
   '----------------------------------------------------------------------

   dim Cmd as string, opt as string, switch as string
   dim slsh as integer, slsh1 as integer

   '----- uncomment only one of the next two lines
   Cmd = command$ '----- case sensitive
   '----- Cmd = ucase$(command$) '----- case insensitive

   '----- find first occurance of "/" or "-"
   slsh = instr(Cmd, any "/-")
   do while slsh
      '----- find next occurance of "/" or "-"
      slsh1 = instr(slsh + 1, Cmd, any "/-")
      if slsh1 then
        opt = mid$(Cmd, slsh, slsh1-slsh)
      else
        opt = mid$(Cmd, slsh)
      end if
      opt = ltrim$(rtrim$(opt))
      switch = mid$(opt,2,1)
      select case switch
        case " "
           print "Space not allowed between - and option."
           print "Type sephem -h for help."
           stop
        case "h", "?"
```

```
          call ShowBanner
          stop
        case "I", "i"
          InFile = ltrim$(rtrim$(mid$(opt, 4)))
          InputFile = TRUE
        case "v"
          print "OK"
          stop
        case else
          print "Option not recognized."
          print "Type sephem -h for help."
          stop
      end select
      '----- remove most recent option from command line
      if slsh1 then
        Cmd = mid$(Cmd,slsh1)
      else
        Cmd = " "
      end if
      Cmd = ltrim$(rtrim$(Cmd))
      slsh = instr(Cmd, any "/-")
    loop

    if (len(Cmd) and isfalse(slsh)) then
      print "Option not recognized."
      print
      call ShowBanner
      stop
    end if

end sub

sub ShowBanner

    '----- Subroutine to display the help banner. This
    '----- routine will have to be modified for each
    '----- program in which it is used.
    '------------------------------------------------------------------------

    print "Usage: SEPHEM [-i:FILE][-h]"
    print "Valid command line options are:"
    print
    print tab(5);"-i:FILE";spc( 3);"Use FILE as input"
    print                 tab(15);"Default input file is JPLEPH"
    print tab(5);"-h";      spc( 8);"Display this help screen"
    print
    print "Command line options may be in any order."
    print

end sub

'----- put any other subs/functions here
$include "\fecsoftb\aberrate.bas"
$include "\fecsoftb\amodulo.bas"
$include "\fecsoftb\atan2.bas"
$include "\fecsoftb\asin.bas"
$include "\fecsoftb\deg.bas"
$include "\fecsoftb\dround.bas"
$include "\fecsoftb\ephopn.bas"
$include "\fecsoftb\errprt.bas"
$include "\fecsoftb\fmtdms.bas"
$include "\fecsoftb\funarg.bas"
$include "\fecsoftb\geocenobs.bas"
$include "\fecsoftb\getgst.bas"
$include "\fecsoftb\getqm.bas"
$include "\fecsoftb\getstvec.bas"
$include "\fecsoftb\interp.bas"
$include "\fecsoftb\lighttim.bas"
```

```
$include "\fecsoftb\matxvec.bas"
$include "\fecsoftb\nutation.bas"
$include "\fecsoftb\obliquty.bas"
$include "\fecsoftb\pleph.bas"
$include "\fecsoftb\precess.bas"
$include "\fecsoftb\qrotate.bas"
$include "\fecsoftb\raybend.bas"
$include "\fecsoftb\rec2pol.bas"
$include "\fecsoftb\reduce.bas"
$include "\fecsoftb\rotmat.bas"
$include "\fecsoftb\split.bas"
$include "\fecsoftb\splitsta.bas"
$include "\fecsoftb\state.bas"
$include "\fecsoftb\uvector.bas"
$include "\fecsoftb\vdot.bas"
$include "\fecsoftb\vecmag.bas"
```

The /i command line option allows the user to select a particular data file to use. Any binary data file created by ASC2EPH may be used, and in the examples illustrated below, the user specifies the data file 1996bin.200. This filename indicates that the data file contains binary data for the year 1996 and is based on the DE200 ephemeris. Because all binary data files created with ASC2EPH share the same internal format, data from any JPL ephemeris may be used with SEPHEM. Tremendous flexibility is achieved by this standardization. If no data file is specified on the command line, SEPHEM starts in interactive mode and prompts the user for a file name.

A *geometric place* is the position of an object extracted directly from the ephemeris data file without any corrections at all. A *reduced place* is the position of an object corrected for any of the various possible physical phenomena (light time, light deflection, etc.).

Here is a sample output screen in which the user computes an apparent ephemeris of the major bodies in the solar system. Notice how SEPHEM prints the first and last valid Julian day numbers for which the data file contains ephemeris data.

```
C:\ALRED\BIN>sephem /i ..\data\1996bin.200

***Program SEPHEM v1.122395                   Written by Joe Heafner
***Small ephemeris program
***The author can be reached via Internet:    heafnerj@mercury.interpath.com

Using ephemeris DE200 with dates from 2450064.5 to 2450480.5
Enter start JED on TDB time scale  2450100.5
(1) REDUCED PLACE (2) GEOMETRIC PLACE  1
(1) SOLAR SYSTEM SUMMARY (2) SPECIFIC BODY  1
(1) APPARENT (2) TOPOCENTRIC (3) VIRTUAL (4) LOCAL (5) ASTROMETRIC  1
APPARENT COORDINATES OF SOLAR SYSTEM BODIES ON 2450100.5
BODY  1 ALPHA 20h02m59.385s DELTA -17d22'41.52" DIST  0.670418656
BODY  2 ALPHA 22h23m38.967s DELTA -11d40'43.76" DIST  1.223997969
BODY  4 ALPHA 20h40m46.581s DELTA -19d27'05.43" DIST  2.345744893
BODY  5 ALPHA 18h14m14.579s DELTA -23d10'26.57" DIST  6.148002109
BODY  6 ALPHA 23h29m14.021s DELTA -05d34'36.59" DIST 10.123680407
BODY  7 ALPHA 20h10m36.177s DELTA -20d35'55.61" DIST 20.730811657
BODY  8 ALPHA 19h48m43.892s DELTA -20d35'37.47" DIST 31.148178810
BODY  9 ALPHA 16h11m43.785s DELTA -07d57'11.27" DIST 30.422218805
BODY 10 ALPHA 17h22m38.167s DELTA -18d48'56.72" DIST  0.002412280
```

```
BODY 11 ALPHA 19h56m51.445s DELTA -20d43'29.61" DIST  0.983781396

OK
```

The bodies are numbered in a standard fashion, and the numbers correspond, respectively, to Mercury, Venus, Mars, Jupiter, Saturn, Uranus, Neptune, Pluto, the Moon, and the Sun. Remember that the d's will actually appear as degree symbols, and the distances are in AU's.

In the next example, the user computes a ten day topocentric ephemeris of Jupiter.

```
C:\ALRED\BIN>sephem /i ..\data\1996bin.200

***Program SEPHEM v1.122395                    Written by Joe Heafner
***Small ephemeris program
***The author can be reached via Internet:    heafnerj@mercury.interpath.com

Using ephemeris DE200 with dates from 2450064.5 to 2450480.5
Enter start JED on TDB time scale  2450064.5
(1) REDUCED PLACE (2) GEOMETRIC PLACE  1
(1) SOLAR SYSTEM SUMMARY (2) SPECIFIC BODY  2
(1) APPARENT (2) TOPOCENTRIC (3) VIRTUAL (4) LOCAL (5) ASTROMETRIC  2
Enter latitude  (dd.mmss)  35.4359
Enter longitude (dd.mmss)  -81.2029
Enter elevation (meters)   351
Enter body number (1-11,99) 5
Enter increment in days     1
Enter number of steps      10
TOPOCENTRIC EPHEMERIS OF BODY 5
2450064.500  ALPHA 17h38m54.977s DELTA -23d04'30.14" DIST  6.256678803
2450065.500  ALPHA 17h39m53.664s DELTA -23d05'04.45" DIST  6.257431625
2450066.500  ALPHA 17h40m53.038s DELTA -23d05'37.85" DIST  6.257968396
2450067.500  ALPHA 17h41m52.456s DELTA -23d06'09.81" DIST  6.258288612
2450068.500  ALPHA 17h42m51.915s DELTA -23d06'40.31" DIST  6.258391777
2450069.500  ALPHA 17h43m51.418s DELTA -23d07'09.26" DIST  6.258277406
2450070.500  ALPHA 17h44m51.510s DELTA -23d07'36.08" DIST  6.257945047
2450071.500  ALPHA 17h45m50.398s DELTA -23d08'03.13" DIST  6.257394302
2450072.500  ALPHA 17h46m49.960s DELTA -23d08'28.01" DIST  6.256624868
2450073.500  ALPHA 17h47m49.520s DELTA -23d08'51.39" DIST  6.255636575

OK
```

The observer's latitude and longitude are entered in a convenient format. A latitude of 35.4359 corresponds to 35 degrees, 43 minutes, and 59 seconds. The longitude is negative, indicating a west longitude.

SEPHEM may also be used to extract data directly from the ephemeris data file as the following example illustrates:

```
C:\ALRED\BIN>sephem /i ..\data\1996bin.200

***Program SEPHEM v1.122395                    Written by Joe Heafner
***Small ephemeris program
***The author can be reached via Internet:    heafnerj@mercury.interpath.com

Using ephemeris DE200 with dates from 2450064.5 to 2450480.5
Enter start JED on TDB time scale  2450200.5
(1) REDUCED PLACE (2) GEOMETRIC PLACE  2
```

```
Enter target number (1-15) 13
Enter center number (1-15) 12
Enter increment in days    1
Enter number of steps      5
GEOMETRIC EPHEMERIS OF BODY 13 WRT BODY 12
2450200.50000  -0.8076380335  -0.5502286993  -0.2384563937 AU
               +0.0100831362  -0.0126559714  -0.0054869251 AU/DAY
2450201.50000  -0.7974389140  -0.5628033298  -0.2439080519 AU
               +0.0103145795  -0.0124927032  -0.0054161371 AU/DAY
2450202.50000  -0.7870099314  -0.5752129415  -0.2492881632 AU
               +0.0105428523  -0.0123259425  -0.0053438350 AU/DAY
2450203.50000  -0.7763542862  -0.5874540682  -0.2545952249 AU
               +0.0107678947  -0.0121557421  -0.0052700416 AU/DAY
2450204.50000  -0.7654752383  -0.5995232970  -0.2598277571 AU
               +0.0109896480  -0.0119821556  -0.0051947801 AU/DAY

OK
```

In this particular case, the user computes the state vector of the Earth-Moon barycenter (body 13) with respect to the solar system barycenter (body 12). These position and velocity components are obtained directly from the data file; no reductions are performed.

10.3   Enhancing SEPHEM

As it stands, SEPHEM is a powerful program. There are, however, numerous enhancements that could be made. These are left as programming exercises for the user.

PROGRAMMING EXERCISE: Modify SEPHEM to write its output to a file specified by the user.

PROGRAMMING EXERCISE: Modify SEPHEM so the user can select either rectangular or polar coordinates for output.

PROGRAMMING EXERCISE: Modify SEPHEM to accept calendar dates instead of Julian day numbers.

PROGRAMMING EXERCISE: Modify SEPHEM to read default input information from an ASCII configuration file. The file should be named SEPHEM.IN, and should contain the input information organized line by line exactly as entered when prompted by the program (the first line contains the starting JED, etc.). Do not forget to update the help screen.

PROGRAMMING EXERCISE: Modify SEPHEM to work for stars and other objects beyond the solar system. Refer to the source code listing for hints.

Appendix A

C Source Code

A.1 ASTROCON.H

```c
#ifndef _CONSTS_
#define _CONSTS_

/* Gaussian gravitational constant */
#define GAUSSK (0.01720209895)

/* values related to PI */
#ifndef PI
#define PI (139755218526789.0 / 44485467702853.0)
#endif

#define TWOPI  (2.0 * PI)
#define PIDIV2 (0.5 * PI)

/* degrees to radians and radians to degrees */
#define D2R (PI / 180.0)
#define R2D (180.0 / PI)

/* hours to radians and radians to hours */
#define H2R (PI / 12.0)
#define R2H (12.0 / PI)

/* arcseconds to radians and radians to arcseconds */
#define A2R (PI / 648000.0)
#define R2A (648000.0 / PI)

/* AU to km and km to AU */
#define AU2KM (149597870.66)
#define KM2AU (1.0 / 149597870.66)

/* speed of light in km/s and AU/day */
#define CKMS (299792.458)
#define CAUD (CKMS * 86400.0 * KM2AU)

/* Earth's angular velocity in rad/s */
#define EarAngVelRD (6.30038748685432)

/* Earth's equatorial radius in km and AU */
#define EarthRadKM (6378.137)
#define EarthRadAU (EarthRadKM * KM2AU)

/* Earth's flattening factor */
```

187

```
#define EFlat (1.0 / 298.257)

/* JED of standard epoch */
#define J2000 (2451545.0)

/* days in a Julian century */
#define JulCty (36525.0)

/* Earth's gravitational constant */
#define MUC (2.0 * GAUSSK * GAUSSK / (CAUD * CAUD))

/* global state vector variable */
extern double StateVector[15][15][2][6];

extern double obsr_lon;
extern double obsr_lat;
extern double obsr_ele;

#endif /* _CONSTS_ */
```

A.2   ASTROLIB.H

```
#ifndef _ASTROLIB_
#define _ASTROLIB_

/**********************************************************************
Project:   fecsoftc
Filename: astrolib.h
Author:    Joe Heafner
Purpose:   Library routines header file.
Thanks to Charles Gamble for extensive modifications.
**********************************************************************/

#include <stdio.h>
#include <math.h>
#include <string.h>
#include <ctype.h>
#include "support.h"
#include "astrocon.h"

#ifndef TRUE
 #define TRUE   (1)
 #define FALSE  (0)
#endif

#ifndef SEEK_SET
 #define SEEK_SET   (0)
 #define SEEK_CUR   (1)
 #define SEEK_END   (2)
#endif

/* double precision matrix data type */
typedef double** DMatrix;

/* function prototypes */
void Aberrate(double *p1, double *EBdot, double *p2);
double amodulo(double a, double b);
void Cal2JED(int m, int d, int y, double utc, int s, double tai_utc,
   double ut1_utc, int w, double *jed);
void constants(char *FileName);
void Conway(double uele[], double mu, double jed, double *r_cos_nu,
   double *r_sin_nu);
DMatrix createDMatrix(int n);
double deg(double x);
double dms(double x);
```

```
double DRound(double x, int n);
FILE *ephopn(char *FileName);
void Epoch2JED(char *epoch, double *jed);
void Eq2Ecl(double *a, int s, double eps, double *b);
void Eq2Hor(double *a, int s, double *b);
void errprt(int group, char *message);
void FmtDms(double x, int n, int m, char *s);
void free_matrix(double **m, int nr, int nc);
void freeDMatrix(DMatrix m, int n);
void FunArgIAU(double jed, double *funarg);
void GeocenObs(double jed, double *obsr_geo);
void GetGST(double jed, int s, double *gst);
void GetInvQMatrix(DMatrix QMatrix, DMatrix InvQMatrix);
int  GetNumde(void);
void GetPrecessParams(double jed1, double jed2, double *zeta,
   double *z, double *theta, double *zetadot,
   double *zdot, double *thetadot);
void GetQMatrix(double phi, double phidot, int axis, int s,
   DMatrix QMatrix);
void GetRPNmat(double jed1, double jed2, int rpn, int d,
   DMatrix m3, DMatrix m6);
void GetStateVector(double JD, int TARG, int CENT, int recpol,
   double StateVector[15][15][2][6]);
void HelEphemeris(double *uelement, double mu, double jed, double *posvel);
void interp(int buff, double *t, int ncf, int ncm, int na, int fl,
   double pv[3][2]);
void Interp1(double *x, double *y, int L, int m, double *arg, double *v);
double Interpol(double *x, double *y, int i, double arg);
void JED2Cal(double jed, int *yr, int *mo, int *dy, double *ti);
void JED2Epoch(double jed, char *s, char *epoch);
double **matrix(int nr, int nc);
void MatXMat(DMatrix a, DMatrix b, DMatrix c, int n);
void MatXVec(DMatrix a, double *b, double *c, int l, int m);
void MRotate(double *vin, int axis, double phi, double *vout);
void GetDpsiDeps(double jed, double *dpsi, double *deps,
   double *dpsidot, double *depsdot);
void Obliquity(double jed1, double jed2, int m, double *obl,
   double *obldot);
void pleph(double jd, int targ, int cent, double *rrd, int *inside);
void Pol2Rec(double *a, double *b);
void PrecessElements(char *eqnx1, double *element, char *eqnx2);
void QRotate(double *vin, int axis, double phi, double phidot,
   int s, double *vout);
void RayBend(double *earth_hel, double *body_geo, double *body_hel,
   double *p1);
void Rec2Pol(double *a, double *b);
void Reduce (double jed, int body, int place, double StarData[],
   double p3[]);
void Refract(double ra1, double dec1, double lha, double temp,
   double press, double *ra2, double *dec2);
void RotMat(int axis, double phi, DMatrix r, DMatrix dr);
void RST(double jed, double *ra, double *dec, double z0, double deltat,
   char *ris, char *trn, char *set);
void split(double tt, double *ipart, double *fpart);
void SplitStateVector(double *pv, double *p, double *v);
void state(double *jed, int LList[], double pv[6][13], double *nut);
void Stat2Elem(double *posvel, double mu, double jed, double *uelement);
double StumpffN(double x, int Norder);
void Transpose(DMatrix a, DMatrix b, int n);
void Uvector(double *a, double *unita);
void Vcross(double *a, double *b, double *acrossb);
void Vdot(int n, double *a, double *b, double *adotb);
double Vecmag(double *a);
```

```
#endif /* _ASTROLIB_ */
```

A.3   SUPPORT.H

```
#ifndef _SUPPORT_
#define _SUPPORT_

/**********************************************************************
Project:  fecsoftc
Filename: support.h
Author:   Joe Heafner
Purpose:  General support routines header file.
Thanks to Charles Gamble for extensive modifications.
**********************************************************************/

#include <sys/types.h>
#include <netinet/in.h>
#include <stdarg.h>
#include <sys/param.h>
/* #include <386/endian.h> */

#define MAX_NAME_SIZE        255
#define MAX_EXTENSION_SIZE   5
#define BIG_ENDIAN_TEST      (htonl(1) == 1)

#ifndef TRUE
 #define TRUE    (1)
 #define FALSE   (0)
#endif

/* Function prototypes */
void make_little_endian(char *ptr, int len);
void convert_little_endian(char *ptr, int len);
void reverse_bytes(char *ptr, int len);
void ucase(char str[]);
void left(char str[], int n, char dest[]);
void right(char str[], int n, char dest[]);
void Trim(char str[]);
void RightTrim(char str[]);
void LeftTrim(char str[]);
int  fexist(char *filename);
int  LogOpen(char *filename);
void LogClose(void);
void LogMsg(FILE *fptr, const char *format, ...);

#endif /* _SUPPORT_ */
```

A.4   ASC2EPH.C

```
/**********************************************************************
Project:  asc2eph
Filename: asc2eph.c
Author:   Ported to C by Joe Heafner and Varian Swieter.
Purpose:  This program converts a JPL ephemeris ASCII data file
          into a binary data file. Note that the binary data files
          created with this program are not identical to those
          created with the JPL ephemeris software.
Thanks to Charles Gamble for extensive modifications.
**********************************************************************/

/* Header Files ****************************************************/
#include <stdio.h>
#include <stdlib.h>
#include <string.h>
#include <math.h>
```

```c
#include <errno.h>
#include <sys/types.h>
#include <netinet/in.h>
#include <sys/param.h>
#include "astrolib.h"
#include "support.h"

/* Function Prototypes *********************************************/
void ParseCmdLine(int argc, char *argv[], char *InFile, char *OutFile);
void PrintBanner(void);
void PrintUsage(void);
void ERRPRT(int group, char *message);
void NXTGRP(FILE *fptr, char *outstr);

/* Globals *********************************************************/
char szVersion[] = "ASC2EPH v1.031898c";
char szLogFile[] = "asc2eph.log";

#define MAX_KSIZE       2048
#define MAX_TTL         66
#define MAX_CNAME       7
#define DEFAULT_OUTPUT  "JPLEPH"

int DeletefpLogFile = FALSE,
    PromptForDates  = FALSE,
    HeaderIncluded  = FALSE,
    FIRST           = TRUE,
    KSIZE, NCON, tmpInt;

FILE *fpInputFile, *fpOutputFile, *fpHFile;

short IPT[3][13], LPT[3], NUMDE, tmpShort;

char InFile[MAX_NAME_SIZE+1]  = "",
     OutFile[MAX_NAME_SIZE+1] = "",
     HFile[MAX_NAME_SIZE+1]   = "",
     HEADER[MAX_NAME_SIZE+1]  = "";

double T1, T2, tmpDouble;

char Body[13][4] = { "MER", "VEN", "EMB", "MAR",
                     "JUP", "SAT", "URA", "NEP",
                     "PLU", "MOO", "SUN", "NUT",
                     "LIB" };

/****************************************************************
Name:    main
Purpose: Main routine for asc2eph.
Inputs:  argc - Number of command-line arguments.
         argv - Pointer to array of command-line arguments.
Outputs: None.
Returns: 0 if execution successful.
Status:  Finished.
Errors:  None known.
****************************************************************/
int main(int argc, char *argv[]) {

  char Progress[50] = "Searching for first requested record ",
       TTL[3][MAX_TTL] = { "", "", "" },
       CNAM[400][MAX_CNAME], right_buffer[4], line[1024];

  double DB[MAX_KSIZE], SS[3], CVAL[400], AU, EMRAT, DB2Z = 0;

  int DB_size, i, k, jrow, jcol, N, NROUT, NRW, NCOEFF,
      exponent, LeftOver, NumZeros, LengthOfHeader,
      LengthOfRecord, loop;

  long int fpeof, LengthOfFile;
```

```
/* Open the log file */
if (LogOpen(szLogFile) == FALSE)
  {
    fprintf(stdout, "Could not open log file '%s': %s\n\n",
      szLogFile, strerror(errno));
    exit(1); /* Exit with an error code */
  }

/* Write a fingerprint to the screen and to log file */
PrintBanner();

ParseCmdLine(argc, argv, InFile, OutFile);

/*
    If you don't want all the data, set T1 and T2 to the begin
    and end times of the span you desire. Units are JED.
*/
if (PromptForDates) {
  do {
    do {
      fprintf(stdout, "Enter start JED: ");
      fflush(stdout);
      fgets(line, sizeof(line), stdin);
    } while (sscanf(line, "%lf", &T1) != 1);

    do {
      fprintf(stdout, "Enter final JED: ");
      fflush(stdout);
      fgets(line, sizeof(line), stdin);
    } while (sscanf(line, "%lf", &T2) != 1);

    if (T2 < T1) {
      fprintf(stdout, "Final JED must be later than start JED!\n");
    }
  } while (T2 < T1);

  if (T1 == T2) {
    fprintf(stdout,
      "Start and final JED's cannot be the same. Using Defaults.\n");
    T1 = 0.0;
    T2 = 9999999.0;
  }
} else {
  T1 = 0.0;
  T2 = 9999999.0;
}

if (strlen(InFile) == 0) {
  /* Prompt user for file name */
  do {
    fprintf(stdout, "File name to convert (XXXX to end): ");
    fflush(stdout);
    fgets(InFile, MAX_NAME_SIZE+1, stdin);

    /* Remove whitespace from either end */
    Trim(InFile);
  } while (strlen(InFile) == 0);
}

/* We have a filename now */
ucase(InFile);  /* May not be used for OS/2 and UNIX compiles */
                /* if you want mixed-case filenames.          */

/* Test for user exit request */
if (strcmp(InFile, "XXXX") == 0) {
  LogMsg(stdout, "\nOK\n");
  LogClose();
```

```
  remove(szLogFile);
  return (0);
}

/* Test to see if filename exists */
if (!fexist(InFile)) {
  LogMsg(stdout, "Requested input file does not exist.\n");
  LogMsg(stdout, "Specify another file or move to another directory.\n");
  LogMsg(stdout, "\nOK\n");
  LogClose();
  exit(1);
}

if (strlen(OutFile) == 0) strcpy(OutFile, DEFAULT_OUTPUT);

LogMsg(stdout, "Input will be read from %s\n", InFile);
LogMsg(stdout, "Output will be written to %s\n", OutFile);

/* Form the header file name */
if (!HeaderIncluded) {
  right(InFile, 3, right_buffer);
  strcpy(HFile, "HEADER.");
  strcat(HFile, right_buffer);

  if (!fexist(HFile)) {
    LogMsg(stdout, "Header file not present.\n");
    LogMsg(stdout, "\nOK\n");
    LogClose();
    exit(1);
  }
}

if (HeaderIncluded) strcpy(HFile, InFile);

/* Open the header file for input */
if ((fpHFile = fopen(HFile, "r")) == NULL) {
  LogMsg(stdout, "Header file not present.\n");
  LogMsg(stdout, "\nOK\n");
  LogClose();
  exit(1);
}

/*
    Get KSIZE, throwing away 'KSIZE=', 'NCOEFF=', and
    NCOEFF decimal constant.
*/
if (fscanf(fpHFile, " %*s %d %*s %*d", &KSIZE) != 1) {
  LogMsg(stderr, "Error reading KSIZE\n");
  LogClose();
  fclose(fpHFile);
  exit(1);
}
LogMsg(stdout, "KSIZE= %d\n", KSIZE);

/*
    Set max size of coeficient array for this particular
    ephemeris file. If KSIZE is an odd number, then
    DB_size = (KSIZE / 2) + (KSIZE % 2).
*/
DB_size = KSIZE / 2;

if (DB_size > MAX_KSIZE) {
  /* Array is not large enough */
  LogMsg(stdout,
    "Adjust #define MAX_KSIZE to larger value & recompile.\n");
  LogMsg(stdout, "\nOK\n");
```

```
  LogClose();
  exit(1);
}

/* Initialize DB through DB_size */
NXTGRP(fpHFile, HEADER);
if (strcmp(HEADER, "GROUP    1010") != 0) {
  ERRPRT(1010, "NOT HEADER");
}

for (i = 0; i < 3; i++) {
  fscanf(fpHFile, " %65[^\n]", TTL[i]);
  LogMsg(stdout, "%s\n",   TTL[i]);
}

/* Read start, end and record span (GROUP 1030) */
NXTGRP(fpHFile, HEADER);
if (strcmp(HEADER, "GROUP    1030") != 0) {
  ERRPRT(1030, "NOT HEADER");
}

/* Read in values of ss[0], ss[1], ss[2] */
for (i = 0; i < 3; i++) {
  if (fscanf(fpHFile, " %lf", &SS[i]) != 1) {
    LogMsg(stderr, "Error reading SS[%d].\n", i);
    LogClose();
    fclose(fpHFile);
    exit(1);
  }
}

/* Read number of constants and names of constants (GROUP 1040/4) */
NXTGRP(fpHFile, HEADER);
if (strcmp(HEADER, "GROUP    1040") != 0) {
  ERRPRT(1040, "NOT HEADER");
}

if (fscanf(fpHFile, " %d", &N) != 1) {
  LogMsg(stderr, "Error reading N.\n");
  LogClose();
  fclose(fpHFile);
  exit(1);
}

/* Now parse the constant names from each line of input */
for (i = 0; i < N; i++) {
  if (fscanf(fpHFile, " %s", CNAM[i]) != 1) {
    LogMsg(stderr, "Error reading CNAM[%d].\n", i);
    LogClose();
    fclose(fpHFile);
    exit(1);
  }
}

NCON = N;

/* Read number of values and values (GROUP 1041/4) */
NXTGRP(fpHFile, HEADER);
if (strcmp(HEADER, "GROUP    1041") != 0) {
  ERRPRT(1041, "NOT HEADER");
}

if (fscanf(fpHFile, " %d", &N) != 1) {
  LogMsg(stderr, "Error reading N.\n");
  LogClose();
```

```
    fclose(fpHFile);
    exit(1);
}

LogMsg(stdout, "\n"
  "Ephemeris Constants\n"
  "-------------------\n");

for (i = 0; i < N; i++) {
  /*
      Read cval mask out D and read exponent
      then convert cval to reflect exponent.
  */
  if (fscanf(fpHFile, " %lfD%d", &CVAL[i], &exponent) != 2) {
    LogMsg(stderr, "Error reading CVAL[%d] and exponent.\n", i);
    LogClose();
    fclose(fpHFile);
    exit(1);
  }

  CVAL[i] *= pow(10, exponent);
  if (strcmp(CNAM[i], "AU")    == 0) AU    = CVAL[i];
  if (strcmp(CNAM[i], "EMRAT") == 0) EMRAT = CVAL[i];
  if (strcmp(CNAM[i], "DENUM") == 0) NUMDE = (int) CVAL[i];

  LogMsg(stdout, "%-6s   %+.15E\t", CNAM[i], CVAL[i]);

  if (i % 2) {
    LogMsg(stdout, "\n");
  }
}

LeftOver = N % 3;
switch (LeftOver) {
  case 0:
          NumZeros = 0;
          break;
  case 1:
  case 2:
          NumZeros = 3 - LeftOver;
          break;
}

for (i = 0; i < LeftOver; i++) {
  /* Throw away padded values */
  fscanf(fpHFile, " %*fD%*d");
}

NXTGRP(fpHFile, HEADER);
if (strcmp(HEADER, "GROUP   1050") != 0) {
  ERRPRT (1050, "NOT HEADER");
}

/* Read pointers from file */
for (jrow = 0; jrow < 3; jrow++) {
  for (jcol = 0; jcol < 13; jcol++) {
    if (fscanf(fpHFile, " %hd", &IPT[jrow][jcol]) != 1) {
      LogMsg(stderr, "Error reading IPT[%d][%d].\n", jrow, jcol);
      LogClose();
      fclose(fpHFile);
      exit(1);
    }
  }
}

LPT[0] = IPT[0][12];
```

```
LPT[1] = IPT[1][12];
LPT[2] = IPT[2][12];

LogMsg(stdout,
  "\n\n"
  " Body     1st coeff     coefs/component      sets of coefs\n"
  "----------------------------------------------------------------\n");

for (jcol = 0; jcol < 13; jcol++) {
  LogMsg(stdout,
    " %2d %3s       %3d                %3d                    %3d\n",
  jcol+1, Body[jcol], IPT[0][jcol], IPT[1][jcol], IPT[2][jcol]);
}
LogMsg(stdout, "\n");

/* Open direct-access output file ('JPLEPH' by default) */
if (strlen(OutFile) == 0) {
  if (fexist(DEFAULT_OUTPUT)) remove(DEFAULT_OUTPUT);
    strcpy(OutFile, DEFAULT_OUTPUT);
  }

  if ((fpOutputFile = fopen(OutFile, "wb")) == NULL) {
    LogMsg(stdout, "Can't create binary data file.\n");
    LogMsg(stdout, "\nOK\n");
    LogClose();
    fclose(fpHFile);
    exit(1);
  }

  /****** BEGINNING OF HEADER *******/
  for (k = 0; k < 3; k++)
    fprintf (fpOutputFile, "%-65s", TTL[k]); /* 195 bytes */

  tmpShort = (short) NCON;
  make_little_endian((char *)&tmpShort, sizeof(short));
  fwrite(&tmpShort, sizeof(short), 1, fpOutputFile); /* 2 bytes */

  for (k = 0; k < NCON; k++)
    fprintf(fpOutputFile, "%-6s", CNAM[k]); /* NCON*6 bytes */

  for (loop = 0; loop < 3; loop++) {
    tmpDouble = (double) SS[loop];
    make_little_endian((char *)&tmpDouble, sizeof(double));
    fwrite(&tmpDouble, sizeof(double), 1, fpOutputFile);
  } /* 24 bytes */

  tmpDouble = (double) AU;
  make_little_endian((char *)&tmpDouble, sizeof(double));
  fwrite(&tmpDouble, sizeof(double), 1, fpOutputFile); /* 8 bytes */

  tmpDouble = (double) EMRAT;
  make_little_endian((char *)&tmpDouble, sizeof(double));
  fwrite(&tmpDouble, sizeof(double), 1, fpOutputFile); /* 8 bytes */

  for (k = 0; k < 3; k++) {
    for (loop = 0; loop < 12; loop++) {
      tmpShort = (short)IPT[k][loop];
      make_little_endian((char *)&tmpShort, sizeof(short));
      fwrite(&tmpShort, sizeof(short), 1, fpOutputFile);
    } /* 72 bytes */
  }

  tmpShort = (short) NUMDE;
  make_little_endian((char *)&tmpShort, sizeof(short));
  fwrite(&tmpShort, sizeof(short), 1, fpOutputFile); /* 2 bytes */
```

```c
for (loop = 0; loop < 3; loop++) {
  tmpShort = (short) LPT[loop];
  make_little_endian((char *)&tmpShort, sizeof(short));
  fwrite(&tmpShort, sizeof(short), 1, fpOutputFile);
} /* 6 bytes */

for (loop = 0; loop < NCON; loop++) {
  tmpDouble = (double) CVAL[loop];
  make_little_endian((char *)&tmpDouble, sizeof(double));
  fwrite(&tmpDouble, sizeof(double), 1, fpOutputFile);
} /* NCON*8 bytes */

/* Length of header = 317+NCON*14 bytes */
/******* END OF HEADER *******/

/* Read and write the ephemeris data records (GROUP 1070) */
NXTGRP(fpHFile, HEADER);
if (strcmp(HEADER, "GROUP   1070") != 0) {
  ERRPRT(1070, "NOT HEADER");
}

/*
   Close the header file and open the actual data file
   if the header is in a seperate file.
*/
if (!HeaderIncluded) {
  fclose(fpHFile);
  if ((fpInputFile = fopen(InFile, "rt")) == NULL) {
    LogMsg(stdout, "Can't open ascii data file '%s'.\n", InFile);
    LogMsg(stdout, "\nOK\n");
    LogClose();
    exit(1);
  }
}

NROUT = 0;

if (HeaderIncluded) fpInputFile = fpHFile;

/* Read the very first record in */
if (!feof(fpInputFile)) {
  if (fscanf(fpInputFile, " %d %d", &NRW, &NCOEFF) != 2) {
    LogMsg(stderr, "Error reading NRW and NCOEFF.\n");
    LogClose();
    fclose(fpInputFile);
    exit(1);
  }

  for (k = 0; k < NCOEFF; k++) {
    /* Read DB mask out D and read exponent */
    /* and convert DB to reflect exponent.  */
    if (fscanf(fpInputFile, " %lfD%d", &DB[k], &exponent) != 2) {
      LogMsg(stderr, "Error reading DB[%d] and exponent.\n", k);
      LogClose();
      fclose(fpInputFile);
      exit(1);
    }
    DB[k] *= pow(10, exponent);
  }

  LeftOver = NCOEFF % 3;
  switch (LeftOver) {
    case 0:
            NumZeros = 0;
```

```
                 break;
      case 1:
      case 2:
                 NumZeros = 3 - LeftOver;
                 break;
      }

    /* Read in padded values and discard them */
    for (k = 0; k < NumZeros; k++) {
      fscanf(fpInputFile, " %*fD%*d");
    }
}

while (!feof(fpInputFile) && (DB[1] < T2)) {
  if ((2 * NCOEFF) != KSIZE) {
    ERRPRT(NCOEFF, " 2*NCOEFF not equal to KSIZE");
  }

  /*
      Skip this data block if the end of the interval is less
      than the specified start time or if it does not begin
      where the previous block ended.
  */
  if ((DB[1] > T1) && (DB[0] >= DB2Z)) {
    if (FIRST) {
      /*
          Don't worry about the intervals overlapping or abutting
          if this is the first applicable interval.
      */
      DB2Z = DB[0];
      FIRST = FALSE;
    }
    if (DB[0] != DB2Z) {
      /*
          Beginning of current interval is past the end
          of the previous one.
      */
      ERRPRT(NRW, "Records do not overlap or abut.");
    }

    DB2Z = DB[1];
    NROUT++;

    /* Write the numbers to binary file */
    for (loop = 0; loop < NCOEFF; loop++) {
      tmpDouble = (double) DB[loop];
      make_little_endian((char *)&tmpDouble, sizeof(double));
      fwrite(&tmpDouble, sizeof(double), 1, fpOutputFile);
    }

    /*
        Save this block's starting date, it's interval span,
        and its end date.
    */
    if (NROUT == 1) {
      SS[0] = DB[0];
      SS[2] = DB[1] - DB[0];
    }
    SS[1] = DB[1];

    /* Update the user as to our progress every 10th block */
    if ((NROUT % 10) == 1) {
      if (DB[0] >= T1) {
        fprintf(stdout,
          " %4d EPHEMERIS RECORD(S) WRITTEN.  LAST JED = %9.1f\r",
          NROUT, DB[1]);
      }
    }
```

```
    } else {
      fprintf(stdout, "%s\r", Progress);
      strcat(Progress, ".");
      if (strlen(Progress) == 47) {
        strcpy(Progress, "Searching for first requested record ");
        fprintf(stdout,
          "Searching for first requested record          \r");
      }
    }
  }

  /*
      Read next block of coefficients unless EOF has
      been reached.
  */
  if (!feof(fpInputFile)) {
    if (fscanf(fpInputFile, " %d %d", &NRW, &NCOEFF) != 2) {
      LogMsg(stderr, "Error reading NRW and NCOEFF.\n");
      LogClose();
      fclose(fpInputFile);
      exit(1);
    }

    for (k = 0; k < NCOEFF; k++) {
      /*
          Read DB mask out D and read exponent
          and convert DB to reflect exponent.
      */
      if (fscanf(fpInputFile, " %lfD%d", &DB[k], &exponent) != 2) {
        LogMsg(stderr, "Error reading DB[%d] and exponent.\n", k);
        LogClose();
        fclose(fpInputFile);
        exit(1);
      }
      DB[k] *= pow(10, exponent);
    }
    LeftOver = NCOEFF % 3;
    switch (LeftOver) {
      case 0:
              NumZeros = 0;
              break;
      case 1:
      case 2:
              NumZeros = 3 - LeftOver;
              break;
    }

    /* Read in padded values and discard them */
    for (k = 0; k < NumZeros; k++) {
      fscanf(fpInputFile, " %*fD%*d "); /* Need trailing space */
    }                                   /* to test eof.        */
  }
}

/*
    End of file, but no records yet written OR
    just no records yet written.
*/
if ((feof(fpInputFile) && (NROUT == 0)) || (NROUT == 0)) {
  NROUT++;
  SS[0] = DB[0];
  SS[1] = DB[1];
  for (loop = 0; loop < NCOEFF; loop++) {
    tmpDouble = (double) DB[loop];
    make_little_endian((char *)&tmpDouble, sizeof(double));
    fwrite(&tmpDouble, sizeof(double), 1, fpOutputFile);
  }
```

```
    }
    /* End of file but T2 lies within most recently read record */
    else if (feof(fpInputFile)) {
      NROUT++;
      SS[1] = DB[1];
      for (loop = 0; loop < NCOEFF; loop++) {
        tmpDouble = (double) DB[loop];
        make_little_endian((char *)&tmpDouble, sizeof(double));
        fwrite(&tmpDouble, sizeof(double), 1, fpOutputFile);
      }
    }
    else if (DB[1] > T2) {
      NROUT++;
      SS[1] = DB[1];
      for (loop = 0; loop < NCOEFF; loop++) {
        tmpDouble = (double) DB[loop];
        make_little_endian((char *)&tmpDouble, sizeof(double));
        fwrite(&tmpDouble, sizeof(double), 1, fpOutputFile);
      }
    }

    /* Reset file pointer from beginning of file */
    /* and write start and final JED to header.  */
    fpeof = ftell(fpOutputFile);
    fseek(fpOutputFile, (197 + NCON * 6), SEEK_SET);

    for (loop = 0; loop < 2; loop++) {
      tmpDouble = (double) SS[loop];
      make_little_endian((char *)&tmpDouble, sizeof(double));
      fwrite(&tmpDouble, sizeof(double), 1, fpOutputFile);
    }

    LengthOfHeader = 317 + NCON * 14;
    LengthOfRecord =   8 * NCOEFF;
    LengthOfFile = (long)LengthOfHeader + (long)LengthOfRecord * (long)NROUT;
    /* LengthOfFile should equal fpeof */

    LogMsg(stdout,
      " %4d EPHEMERIS RECORD(S) WRITTEN.  LAST JED = %9.11f\n", NROUT, DB[1]);
    LogMsg(stdout, "\nStart JED for this file is %9.11f\n", SS[0]);
    LogMsg(stdout, "Final JED for this file is %9.11f\n\n", SS[1]);
    LogMsg(stdout, "Header is %d bytes\n", LengthOfHeader);
    LogMsg(stdout, "Record is %d bytes\n", LengthOfRecord);
    LogMsg(stdout, " %ld bytes written\n", LengthOfFile);
    LogMsg(stdout, " %ld bytes actual file size\n", fpeof);

    LogMsg(stdout, "\nOK\n");

    /* Close all files */
    LogClose();
    fclose(fpOutputFile);
    fclose(fpInputFile);

    if (DeletefpLogFile) {
      remove(szLogFile);
    }

    return(0);
}

/***********************************************************************
Name:    ParseCmdLine
Purpose: Routine to parse the command line.
Inputs:  argc - Number of command-line arguments.
         argv - Pointer to array of command-line arguments.
Outputs: InFile  - Filename given by user for input file.
```

```
            OutFile - Filename given by user for output file.
Returns: Nothing.
Status:  Finished.
Errors:  None known.
*************************************************************************/
void ParseCmdLine(int argc, char *argv[], char *InFile, char *OutFile) {
  /*
      Command line parser ported from Basic and optimized for C
       by Varian Swieter.
  */

  int i;

  for (i = 1; i < argc; i++) {
    /*
        Find next occurance of "/" or "-" by looking at
        the first character of each argument.
    */
    if (argv[i][0] != '-' && argv[i][0] != '/') {
      /* Found an argument that did not begin with "/" or "-" */
      LogMsg(stdout, "Command line arguments must begin with '-' or '/'.\n");
      PrintUsage();
      LogClose();
      remove(szLogFile);
      exit(1);
    }

    switch (argv[i][1]) {
      case '\0':
              LogMsg(stdout, "Space not allowed between - and option.\n");
              LogMsg(stdout, "Type asc2eph -h for help.\n");
              LogClose();
              remove(szLogFile);
              exit(1);
      case 'I':
      case 'i':
              if (strlen(argv[i]) == 2) {
                /* We were given nothing after the "-I"
                   so return empty string */
                strcpy(InFile, "");
              } else {
                if (argv[i][2] != ':') {
                  /* User missed out colon so return empty string */
                  strcpy(InFile, "");
                } else {
                  strcpy(InFile, &(argv[i][3]));
                }
              }
              break;
      case 'O':
      case 'o':
              if (strlen(argv[i]) == 2) {
                /* We were given nothing after the "-O"
                   so return empty string */
                strcpy(OutFile, "");
              } else {
                if (argv[i][2] != ':') {
                  /* User missed out colon so return empty string */
                  strcpy(OutFile, "");
                } else {
                  strcpy(OutFile, &(argv[i][3]));
                }
              }

              /* If OutFile is an empty string then return "JPLEPH"
```

```
                             as a default */
                     if (strlen(OutFile) == 0) {
                       strcpy(OutFile, DEFAULT_OUTPUT);
                     }
                     break;
           case '?':  /* Using this for help will cause problems under UNIX */
                     /* because it is used by the shell for substitution.  */
           case 'h':
                     PrintUsage();
                     LogClose();
                     remove(szLogFile);
                     exit(0);
           case 'H':
                     LogMsg(stdout ,   "Assuming included header.\n");
                     HeaderIncluded = TRUE;
                     break;
           case 'D':
                     PromptForDates = TRUE;
                     break;
           case 'K':
                     DeletefpLogFile = TRUE;
                     break;
           case 'v':  /* Undocumented command line option */
                     /* to print version information.   */
                     LogMsg(stdout, "OK\n");
                     LogClose();
                     remove(szLogFile);
                     exit(0);
           default:
                     LogMsg(stdout, "Option not recognized.\n");
                     LogMsg(stdout, "Type asc2eph -h for help.\n");
                     LogClose();
                     remove(szLogFile);
                     exit(1);
    }
  }
}

/**********************************************************************
Name:    NXTGRP
Purpose: Finds the next data group in an ephemeris file.
Inputs:  fptr - File pointer to read from.
Outputs: outstr - Destination for the output string.
Returns: Nothing.
Status:  Finished.
Errors:  None known.
**********************************************************************/
void NXTGRP(FILE *fptr, char *outstr) {

  char string[50];
  char str[6];
  char num[5];

  fscanf(fptr, " %s %s", str, num);
  strcpy(string, str);
  strcat(string, "   ");
  strcat(string, num);

  strcpy(outstr, string);
}

/**********************************************************************
Name:    ERRPRT
Purpose: Prints error messages to stdout and log file.
Inputs:  group   - Error number.
         message - Error message.
Outputs: None.
```

```
Returns: Nothing.
Status:  Finished.
Errors:  None known.
**********************************************************************/
void ERRPRT(int group, char *message) {

  LogMsg(stdout, "\nERROR #%d %s\n", group, message);
  LogClose();
  fclose(fpHFile);
  fclose(fpOutputFile);
  exit(1);
}

/*********************************************************************
Name:    PrintBanner
Purpose: Prints a banner to stdout and log file.
Inputs:  None.
Outputs: None.
Returns: Nothing.
Status:  Finished.
Errors:  None known.
**********************************************************************/
void PrintBanner() {

  LogMsg(stdout, "\n");
  LogMsg(stdout, "***Program %s  ", szVersion);
  LogMsg(stdout, "                       Written by Joe Heafner\n");
  LogMsg(stdout, "***Converts JPL ASCII ephemeris data files to binary\n");
  LogMsg(stdout, "***The author can be reached via Internet:");
  LogMsg(stdout, "    heafnerj@mercury.interpath.com\n");
  LogMsg(stdout, "\n");
}

/*********************************************************************
Name:    PrintUsage
Purpose: Prints usage information.
Inputs:  None.
Outputs: None.
Returns: Nothing.
Status:  Finished.
Errors:  None known.
**********************************************************************/
void PrintUsage() {

  printf("Usage: ASC2EPH [-i:FILE][-o:FILE][-D][-H][-K][-h]\n");
  printf("Valid command line options are:\n");
  printf("\n");
  printf("    -i:FILE   Use FILE as input assuming separate header file\n");
  printf("              Will prompt if this option is not used\n");
  printf("    -o:FILE   Use FILE as name of binary file\n");
  printf("              Default binary file name is %s\n", DEFAULT_OUTPUT);
  printf("    -D        Program will prompt for initial and final dates\n");
  printf("              Defaults are full range of data file\n");
  printf("    -H        Assume data file has header included\n");
  printf("              Default is separate header in HEADER.XXX\n");
  printf("    -K        Delete log file ASC2EPH.LOG\n");
  printf("              Log file kept by default\n");
  printf("    -h        Display this help screen\n");
  printf("\n");
  printf("Command line options may be in any order.\n");
}
/* End Of File - asc2eph.c *******************************************/
```

A.5   ASTROCON.C

```
#include "astrocon.h"

/* global state vector variable */
double StateVector[15][15][2][6];

/* observer's geodetic coordinates */
double obsr_lon;
double obsr_lat;
double obsr_ele;
```

A.6   ASTROLIB.C

```
/************************************************************************
Project:    fecsoftc
Filename:   astrolib.c
Author:     Joe Heafner
Purpose:    Astronomical ephemeris library.
Thanks to Charles Gamble for extensive modifications.
************************************************************************/

/* Header Files ******************************************************/
#include <math.h>
#include <stdio.h>
#include <stdlib.h>
#include <string.h>
#include <errno.h>
#include "astrolib.h"
#include "support.h"

#ifndef MAX_FILENAME
  #define MAX_FILENAME   255
#endif

/* Globals **********************************************************/
/* Ephemeris header information */
char ttl[3][65], cnam[400][7];
int  ncon;
double SS[3], cval[400], au, emrat;
short int NUMDE, ipt[3][12], lpt[3];

/* Other data file specs not in header */
long LengthOfFile, ncoeff, BlockLength;
int LengthOfHeader, NumBlocks, bary, bsav;
double db[1100], pvsun[6];

static FILE *fpBinaryFile = NULL;

/* Temporary data used when reading in binary file */
short tmpShort;
double tmpDouble;
int tmpInt;
long tmpLong;

/************************************************************************
Name:     Aberrate
Purpose:  Function to correct an input vector for aberration.
Inputs:   p1    - Zero-offset geocentric state vector of object.
          EBdot - Zero-offset barycentric velocity of Earth.
Outputs:  p2 - Zero-offset geocentric state vector of object corrected
               for aberration.
Returns:  Nothing.
Status:   Finished.
Errors:   None known.
************************************************************************/
void Aberrate(double p1[], double EBdot[], double p2[]) {
```

```
double v[3], up[3], p[3], pdot[3], magP, magV, p1dotv, beta;
int i;

/* Extract the pos. portion of the state vector */
SplitStateVector(p1, p, pdot);
magP = Vecmag(p);

/* Need to make Ppos() a unit vector */
Uvector(p, up);

for (i=0; i<3; i++) {
  v[i] = EBdot[i] / CAUD;
}

Vdot(3, up, v, &p1dotv);
magV = Vecmag(v);

beta = 1.0 / sqrt(1.0 - magV * magV);

for (i=0; i<3; i++) {
  p2[i] = ((up[i] / beta) +
    (1.0 + p1dotv / (1.0 + (1.0 / beta))) * v[i]) / (1.0 + p1dotv);
  /* Make p2[] a non-unit vector */
  p2[i] = magP * p2[i];
  p2[i+3] = p1[i+3];
}

return;
}

/****************************************************************
Name:    amodulo
Purpose: Function to reduce a to the range 0 <= a < b.
Inputs:  a - See above.
         b - See above.
Outputs: None.
Returns: See above.
Status:  Finished.
Errors:  None known.
****************************************************************/
double amodulo(double a, double b) {

  double x;

  x = a - b * floor(a/b);
  return (x);
}

/****************************************************************
Name:    Cal2JED
Purpose: Function to compute the Julian date on the specified time scale.
         The Julian day algorithm of Meeus is used, and the algorithm for
         converting to TDB is due to Hirayama et al. and can be found in
         REFERENCE FRAMES IN ASTRONOMY AND GEOPHYSICS ed. by Kovalevsky
         et al., 1989, pp. 439-442.
Inputs:  m        - Month.
         d        - Day.
         y        - Year.
         utc      - UTC as hh.mmssss.
         s        - 1 for UT1, 2 for UT2, 3 for TDT,
                    4 for TDB, 5 for UTC.
         tai_utc  - TAI-UTC in seconds.
         ut1_utc  - UT1-UTC in seconds.
         w        - 1 for MJD, 0 otherwise.
Outputs: jed - Appropriate JED.
Returns: Nothing.
Status:  Finished.
Errors:  None known.
****************************************************************/
```

```c
void Cal2JED(int m, int d, int y, double utc, int s,
  double tai_utc, double ut1_utc, int w, double *jed) {
  double time, datnum, a, b, term1, corr, T;

  /* Convert to decimal hours */
  time = deg(utc);

  if ((m == 1) || (m == 2)) {
    y = y - 1;
    m = m + 12;
  }

  /*
      Test to see if date is in Gregorian calendar.
      Converts date to a number of the form YYYY.MMDD.
  */
  datnum = (double) y + 0.01 * (double) m + 0.0001 * (double) d;

  if (datnum >= 1582.1015) {
    /* Gregorian calendar */
    a = floor(0.01 * (double) y);
    b = 2.0 - a + floor(0.25 * (double) a);
  } else {
    /* Julian calendar */
    a = 0.0;
    b = 0.0;
  }

  if (y < 0) {
    /* Handles negative years */
    term1 = floor(365.25 * (double) y - 0.75);
  } else {
    term1 = floor(365.25 * (double) y);
  }

  *jed = term1 + floor(30.6001 * ((double) m + 1.0)) +
    (double) d + time / 24.0 + 1720994.5 + (double) b;

  switch (s) {
    case (1):
      corr = ut1_utc / 86400.0;
      break;
    case (2):
      corr = ut1_utc / 86400.0;
      *jed = *jed + corr;
      /* Compute date in Besselian years */
      T = 2000.0 + (*jed - 2451544.5333981) / 365.242198781;
      corr = 0.022 * sin(TWOPI * T);
      /* Additional terms go here */
      corr = corr / 86400.0;
      break;
    case (3):
      corr = (tai_utc + 32.184) / 86400.0;
      break;
    case (4):
      /* First convert to TDT */
      corr = (tai_utc + 32.184) / 86400.0;
      *jed = *jed + corr;
      T = (*jed - J2000) / JulCty;
      /* Now compute the new correction in microseconds */
      corr = 1656.675 * sin((35999.3729 * T + 357.5387) * D2R);
      /* Additional terms go here */
      /* Convert from microseconds to seconds */
      corr = corr * 0.000001;
      /* Convert to days */
      corr = corr / 86400.0;
      break;
```

```
      case (5):
        corr = 0.0;
        break;
      default:
        corr = 0.0;
  }

  *jed += corr;

  /* Return modified JED if requested */
  if (w == 1) *jed -= 2400000.5;
}

/**********************************************************************
Name:    constants
Purpose: Function to display the constants from the ephemeris file.
         Also prints other useful information about the file.
Inputs:  FileName - Filename of file to be read in.
Outputs: None.
Returns: Nothing.
Status:  Finished.
Errors:  None known.
**********************************************************************/
void constants(char *FileName) {

  int i;
  char Y[1024] = "";

  /* Open the file and read the header data */
  if (ephopn(FileName) == NULL) {
    LogMsg(stderr, "An error occurred in ephopn().\n");
    LogClose();
    exit(1);
  }

  for (i=0; i<3; i++)
    LogMsg(stdout, "%s\n", ttl[i]);

  LogMsg(stdout, "First valid JED in file  %9.1lf\n", SS[0]);
  LogMsg(stdout, "Final valid JED in file  %9.1lf\n", SS[1]);
  LogMsg(stdout, "Block interval %2.0lf days\n",      SS[2]);
  LogMsg(stdout,
    "Length of file             % 8.0ld bytes\n", LengthOfFile);
  LogMsg(stdout,
    "Length of header           % 8.0d bytes\n" , LengthOfHeader);
  LogMsg(stdout,
    "Length of each block       % 8.0ld bytes\n", BlockLength);
  LogMsg(stdout,
    "Coeffs per block           % 8.0ld\n"       , ncoeff);
  LogMsg(stdout,
    "Blocks in file             % 8.0d\n"        , NumBlocks);

  LogMsg(stdout, "Bodies present in data file:  ");
  if (ipt[0][0]  != 0) LogMsg(stdout, "MER ");
  if (ipt[0][1]  != 0) LogMsg(stdout, "VEN ");
  if (ipt[0][2]  != 0) LogMsg(stdout, "EMB ");
  if (ipt[0][3]  != 0) LogMsg(stdout, "MAR ");
  if (ipt[0][4]  != 0) LogMsg(stdout, "JUP ");
  if (ipt[0][5]  != 0) LogMsg(stdout, "SAT ");
  if (ipt[0][6]  != 0) LogMsg(stdout, "URA ");
  if (ipt[0][7]  != 0) LogMsg(stdout, "NEP ");
  if (ipt[0][8]  != 0) LogMsg(stdout, "PLU ");
  if (ipt[0][9]  != 0) LogMsg(stdout, "MOO ");
  if (ipt[0][10] != 0) LogMsg(stdout, "SUN\n");
```

```c
if (ipt[0][11] == 0 || ipt[1][11] == 0 || ipt[2][11] == 0)
  LogMsg(stdout, "This ephemeris does not contain nutations.\n");
else
  LogMsg(stdout, "This ephemeris contains nutations.\n");

if (lpt[0] == 0 || lpt[1] == 0 || lpt[2] == 0)
  LogMsg(stdout, "This ephemeris does not contain librations.\n");
else
  LogMsg(stdout, "This ephemeris contains librations.\n");

LogMsg(stdout, "This ephemeris has %d ephemeris constants.\n", ncon);

do {
  fprintf(stdout, "Display constant names and values (Y/N)? ");
  fflush(stdout);
  fgets(Y, sizeof(Y), stdin);
  Trim(Y);
  ucase(Y);
} while ((strcmp(Y, "Y") != 0) && (strcmp(Y, "N") != 0));

if (strcmp(Y, "Y") == 0) {
  LogMsg(stdout, "\n");
  for (i=0; i<ncon; i++) {
    LogMsg(stdout, "%6s  %+16.15E      ", cnam[i], cval[i]);
    if ((i+1) % 2 == 0) {
      LogMsg(stdout, "\n");
    }
  }

  if ((i % 2) != 0) {
    LogMsg(stdout, "\n");
  }
}
}

/***********************************************************************
Name:    Conway
Purpose: Function to solve Kepler's equation using the method of
         Conway-Laguerre for universal variables.
Inputs:  uele - Array of universal orbital elements.
         mu   - Gravitational constant for the body.
         jed  - Time for which computations are to be performed.
Outputs: r_cos_nu - r*cos(true anomaly).
         r_sin_nu - r*sin(true anomaly).
Returns: Nothing.
Status:  Finished.
Errors:  None known.
***********************************************************************/
void Conway(double uele[], double mu, double jed, double *r_cos_nu,
  double *r_sin_nu) {

  double tspp, alpha, s, x, c1, c2, c3, f, fp, fpp, term, ds;
  int niter;

  /* Compute time since perihelion passage in days */
  tspp = jed - uele[5];

  /* Compute alpha */
  alpha = mu * (1.0 - uele[1]) / uele[0];

  /* Initial guess for s */
  s = 0.0;

  /* Initialize iteration counter */
  niter = 0;

  do {
    /* Compute Stumpff functions */
```

```
    x = alpha * s * s;
    c1 = StumpffN(x, 1);
    c2 = StumpffN(x, 2);
    c3 = StumpffN(x, 3);

    f = uele[0] * s + mu * uele[1] * s * s * s * c3 - tspp;
    fp = uele[0] + mu * uele[1] * s * s * c2;
    fpp = mu * uele[1] * s * c1;

    /* Evaluate Laguerre's method */
    term = 16.0 * fp * fp - 20.0 * f * fpp;
    ds = -5.0 * f / (fp + fp/fabs(fp) * sqrt(fabs(term)));

    s = s + ds;

    niter = niter + 1;

    /* Check for convergence or more than ten iterations */
    if (niter > 10)
    {
      LogMsg(stderr, "Conway: more than ten iterations.\n");
      exit(1);
    }

    if (fabs(f) < 1e-12) break;

  } while(1);

  /* Now compute r_sin_nu and r_cos_nu */
  *r_sin_nu = sqrt(mu * uele[0] * (1.0 + uele[1])) * s * c1;
  *r_cos_nu = uele[0] - mu * s * s * c2;
}

/**********************************************************************
Name:    createDMatrix
Purpose: Creates an n x n double matrix.
Inputs:  n - Dimension of matrix to create.
Outputs: None.
Returns: DMatrix.
Status:  Finished.
Errors:  None known.
**********************************************************************/
DMatrix createDMatrix(int n) {

  DMatrix m;
  int i;

  m = calloc(n, sizeof(double*));
  if (m == NULL) {
    return NULL;
  }

  for (i=0; i<n; i++) {
    m[i] = calloc(n, sizeof(double));
    if (m[i] == NULL) {
      freeDMatrix(m, i); /* Avoids garbage */
      return NULL;
    }
  }

  return m;
}

/**********************************************************************
Name:    deg
Purpose: Converts dd.mmssss to dd.dddddd.
         Converts hh.mmssss to hh.mmmmmm.
Inputs:  x - Value to convert.
```

```
Outputs: None.
Returns: Converted value.
Status:  Finished.
Errors:  None known.
*******************************************************************/
double deg(double x) {

    double dd, d, fixdd, ddfixdd;

    if (x == 0.0) return (0.0);

    dd = fabs(x);
    fixdd = floor(dd);
    ddfixdd = dd - fixdd + 5.0e-10;
    d = fixdd + floor(100.0 * ddfixdd) / 60.0;
    d = d + (10000.0 * ddfixdd - 100.0 * floor(100.0 * ddfixdd)) / 3600.0;

    return ((x / dd) * d);
}

/*******************************************************************
Name:    dms
Purpose: Converts dd.dddddd to dd.mmssss.
         Converts hh.hhhhhh to hh.mmssss.
Inputs:  x - Value to convert.
Outputs: None.
Returns: Converted value.
Status:  Finished.
Errors:  None known.
*******************************************************************/
double dms(double x) {

    double dd, fdd, dmfd, d;

    if (x == 0.0) return (0.0);

    dd = fabs(x);
    fdd = floor(dd);
    dmfd = dd - fdd;
    d = fdd + floor(60.0 * dmfd) / 100.0 + 0.006 *
      (60.0 * dmfd - floor(60.0 * dmfd));

    return ((x / dd) * d);
}

/*******************************************************************
Name:    DRound
Purpose: Function to round a number to a given number of decimal places.
Inputs:  x - Value to round.
         n - Number of decimal places.
Outputs: None.
Returns: Rounded number.
Status:  Finished.
Errors:  None known.
*******************************************************************/
double DRound(double x, int n) {

    double a, y;
    int sgn;

    if (x > 0) {
      sgn = 1;
    }
    else if (x < 0) {
      sgn = -1;
    } else {
      sgn = 0;
    }

    a = pow(10.0, (double) n);
```

```
  y = floor((a * x) + ((double) sgn) * 0.5) / a;

  return y;
}

/************************************************************************
Name:     ephopn
Purpose: Function to open a binary ephemeris data file for access,
         read the header information, and store it in memory for
         later use.
Inputs:  FileName - Filename of file to be read in.
Outputs: None.
Returns: NULL on error.
         Open file pointer otherwise.
Status:  Finished.
Errors:  None known.
************************************************************************/
FILE *ephopn(char *FileName) {

  /* Make sure all variables read from the data file are global */
  int i, j;
  static int efirst;
  long curpos;

  if (!efirst) {
    /* Default file name is JPLEPH */
    if (strlen(FileName) == 0) {
      strcpy(FileName, "JPLEPH");
    }

    /*
        The existence of the data file MUST be confirmed
        in the calling program. It is NOT checked here!
    */
    if ((fpBinaryFile = fopen(FileName, "rb")) == NULL) {
      LogMsg(stderr,
        "EPHOPN: Can't open binary data file: %s\n", strerror(errno));
      return (NULL);
    }

    /* BEGINNING OF HEADER */
    /* 195 bytes */
    for (i = 0; i < 3; i++) {
      /* char TTL[3][65] */
      if (fread(ttl[i], sizeof(char), 65, fpBinaryFile) != 65) {
        LogMsg(stderr,
          "EPHOPN: Error reading binary data file: %s\n", strerror(errno));
        return (NULL);
      }
      ttl[i][64] = '\0';
    }

    /* 2 bytes */
    if (fread(&tmpShort, sizeof(short), 1, fpBinaryFile) != 1) {
      LogMsg(stderr,
        "EPHOPN: Error reading binary data file: %s\n", strerror(errno));
      return (NULL);
    }

    convert_little_endian((char *) &tmpShort, sizeof(short));
    ncon = (int) tmpShort;

    /* ncon*6 bytes */
    for (j = 0; j < ncon; ++j) {
      /* char CNAM[NCON][7] */
      if (fread(&cnam[j], sizeof(char), 6, fpBinaryFile) != 6) {
        LogMsg(stderr,
```

```
            "EPHOPN: Error reading binary data file: %s\n", strerror(errno));
      return (NULL);
    }
    cnam[j][6] = '\0';
}

/* 24 bytes, 8 each */
for (j = 0; j < 3; j++) {
  /* double SS[3] */
  if (fread(&tmpDouble, sizeof(double), 1, fpBinaryFile) != 1) {
    LogMsg(stderr,
      "EPHOPN: Error reading binary data file: %s\n", strerror(errno));
    return (NULL);
  }
  convert_little_endian((char *) &tmpDouble, sizeof(double));
  SS[j] = (double) tmpDouble;
}

/* 16 bytes, 8 each */
if (fread(&tmpDouble,   sizeof(double), 1, fpBinaryFile) != 1) {
  LogMsg(stderr,
    "EPHOPN: Error reading binary data file: %s\n", strerror(errno));
  return (NULL);
}
convert_little_endian((char *) &tmpDouble, sizeof(double));
au = (double) tmpDouble;

if (fread(&tmpDouble, sizeof(double), 1, fpBinaryFile) != 1) {
  LogMsg(stderr,
    "EPHOPN: Error reading binary data file: %s\n", strerror(errno));
  return (NULL);
}
convert_little_endian((char *) &tmpDouble, sizeof(double));
emrat = (double) tmpDouble;

/* 72 bytes */
for (i = 0; i < 3; i++) {
  /* short IPT[3][12] */
  for (j = 0; j < 12; j++) {
    if (fread(&tmpShort, sizeof(short), 1, fpBinaryFile) != 1) {
      LogMsg(stderr,
        "EPHOPN: Error reading binary data file: %s\n", strerror(errno));
      return (NULL);
    }
    convert_little_endian((char *) &tmpShort, sizeof(short));
    ipt[i][j] = (short) tmpShort;
  }
}

/* 2 bytes */
if (fread(&tmpShort, sizeof(short), 1, fpBinaryFile) != 1) {
  LogMsg(stderr,
    "EPHOPN: Error reading binary data file: %s\n", strerror(errno));
  return (NULL);
}
convert_little_endian((char *) &tmpShort, sizeof(short));
NUMDE = (short) tmpShort;

/* 6 bytes, 2 each */
for (i = 0; i < 3; i++) {
  if (fread(&tmpShort, sizeof(short), 1, fpBinaryFile) != 1) {
    LogMsg(stderr,
      "EPHOPN: Error reading binary data file: %s\n", strerror(errno));
    return (NULL);
```

```
      }
      convert_little_endian((char *) &tmpShort, sizeof(short));
      lpt[i] = (short) tmpShort;
    }

    /* ncon*8 bytes */
    for (j = 0; j < ncon; j++) {
      if (fread(&tmpDouble, sizeof(double), 1, fpBinaryFile) != 1) {
        LogMsg(stderr,
          "EPHOPN: Error reading binary data file: %s\n", strerror(errno));
        return (NULL);
      }
      convert_little_endian((char *) &tmpDouble, sizeof(double));
      cval[j] = (double) tmpDouble;
    }
    /* END OF HEADER */

    /* This block used to be a separate function */
    /* but it didn't work correctly.            */
    if ((curpos = ftell(fpBinaryFile)) == -1L) {
      LogMsg(stderr, "EPHOPN: ftell() returned -1L.\n");
      return (NULL);
    }

    if (fseek(fpBinaryFile, 0L, SEEK_END) != 0) {
      LogMsg(stderr, "EPHOPN: fseek() failed.\n");
      return (NULL);
    }

    LengthOfFile = ftell(fpBinaryFile);

    if (fseek(fpBinaryFile, curpos, SEEK_SET) != 0) {
      LogMsg(stderr, "EPHOPN: fseek() failed.\n");
      return (NULL);
    }
    /* end block */

    LengthOfHeader = 317L + 14L * (long) ncon;

    /* Length of block of coeffs = 8*NCOEFF bytes */
    /* calculate number of coeffs per block */
    ncoeff = 0L;

    for (j = 0; j < 12; j++) {
      if (j == 11)
        ncoeff = ncoeff + (long) ipt[1][j] * (long) ipt[2][j] * 2L;
      else
        ncoeff = ncoeff + (long) ipt[1][j] * (long) ipt[2][j] * 3L;
    }

    ncoeff = ncoeff + (long) lpt[1] * (long) lpt[2] * 3L + 2L;
    BlockLength = ncoeff * 8L;
    NumBlocks = (LengthOfFile - (long) LengthOfHeader) / BlockLength;
    efirst = TRUE;
  }

  return (fpBinaryFile);
}

/******************************************************************
Name:    Epoch2JED
Purpose: Function to convert an epoch to its corresponding JED.
Inputs:  epoch - J or B epoch (e.g. J2000).
Outputs: jed - Appropriate JED.
Returns: Nothing.
Status:  Finished.
```

```
Errors:   None known.
********************************************************************/
void Epoch2JED(char *epoch, double *jed) {

  double date;
  char buffer[80];

  strcpy(buffer, epoch);

  ucase(buffer);

  sscanf(buffer, "%*c %lf", &date);

  if (epoch[0] == 'J') {
    /* Julian epoch */
    *jed = (date - 2000.0) * 365.25 + 2451545.0;
  } else {
    /* Besselian epoch */
    *jed = (date - 1900.0) * 365.242198781731 + 2415020.31352;
  }

  return;
}

/********************************************************************
Name:     Eq2Ecl
Purpose: Subprogram to convert an equatorial state vector to an
         ecliptic state vector or the reverse transformation.
Inputs:  a   - Zero-offset input vector.
         s   - 0 for eq  -> ecl, 1 for ecl -> eq.
         eps - Mean or apparent obliquity.
Outputs: b - Zero-offset output vector.
Returns: Nothing.
Status:  Finished.
Errors:  None known.
********************************************************************/
void Eq2Ecl(double a[], int s, double eps, double b[]) {

  DMatrix r, dr;

  r  = createDMatrix(3);
  dr = createDMatrix(3);

  if (s == 0) {
    /* Equatorial to ecliptic */
    RotMat(1,  eps, r, dr);
  } else {
    /* Ecliptic to equatorial */
    RotMat(1, -eps, r, dr);
  }

  MatXVec(r, a, b, 3, 3);

  freeDMatrix(r, 3);
  freeDMatrix(dr,3);

  return;
}

/********************************************************************
Name:     Eq2Hor
Purpose: Function to convert an equatorial state vector to a
         horizon state vector or the reverse transformation.
Inputs:  a - Zero-offset input vector.
         s - 0 for eq -> hor, 1 for hor -> eq.
Outputs: b - Zero-offset output vector.
Returns: Nothing.
Status:  Finished.
Errors:  None known.
```

```
*****************************************************************/
void Eq2Hor(double a[], int s, double b[]) {

  DMatrix r2, r3, r, dr2, dr3, dr;

  r2 = createDMatrix(3);
  r3 = createDMatrix(3);
  r  = createDMatrix(3);
  dr2 = createDMatrix(3);
  dr3 = createDMatrix(3);
  dr = createDMatrix(3);

  if (s == 0) {
    /* Equatorial to horizon */
    RotMat(2, PIDIV2 - obsr_lat, r2, dr2);
    RotMat(3, -PI, r3, dr3);
    MatXMat(r3, r2, r, 3);
  } else {
    /* Horizon to equatorial */
    RotMat(3, PI, r3, dr3);
    RotMat(2, obsr_lat - PIDIV2, r2, dr2);
    MatXMat(r2, r3, r, 3);
  }

  MatXVec(r, a, b, 3, 3);

  freeDMatrix(r2, 3);
  freeDMatrix(r3, 3);
  freeDMatrix(r, 3);
  freeDMatrix(dr2, 3);
  freeDMatrix(dr3, 3);
  freeDMatrix(dr, 3);

  return;
}
/*****************************************************************
Name:     errprt
Purpose: Function to print error messages.
Inputs:   group   - Error code number.
          message - Error message.
Outputs: None.
Returns: Nothing.
Status:  Finished.
Errors:  None known.
*****************************************************************/
void errprt(int group, char *message) {

  LogMsg(stderr, "\nERROR #%d %s\n", group, message);
  exit(1);
}

/*****************************************************************
Name:     FmtDms
Purpose: Function to format angular and time quantities. Basically,
         this function is a pretty-print version of dms().
         Modified with permission from Rex Shudde's code by Joe Heafner.
Inputs:   x - Decimal value.
          n - Number of seconds decimal digits.
          m - 0 convert decimal degrees to:
                ddd mm ss       if n = 0
                ddd mm ss.f     if n = 1
                ddd mm ss.ff    if n = 2
                ddd mm ss.fff   if n = 3
                ddd mm ss.ffff  if n = 4
          m - 1 converts decimal hours to:
                hh mm ss        if n = 0
                hh mm ss.f      if n = 1
                hh mm ss.ff     if n = 2
```

```
                   hh mm ss.fff    if n = 3
                   hh mm ss.ffff   if n = 4
Outputs: s - Destination for output string.
Returns: Nothing.
Status:  Finished.
Errors:  None known.
********************************************************************/
void FmtDms(double x, int n, int m, char *s) {

    double absx, deg, min, sec;
    int nf;
    unsigned int fig;
    static int defd;
    static char dh[3];
    static char mm[3];
    static char ss[3];
    char buffer[16] = "               ";
    char right_buffer[16], left_buffer[16];

    strcpy(s, "              ");

    if (!defd) {
      defd++;
      dh[0] = '\xf8'; /* f8 is the hex code for degree symbol */
      dh[1] = 'h';
      dh[2] = '\0';
      mm[0] = '\x27'; /* 27 is the hex code for arcmin symbol */
      mm[1] = 'm';
      mm[2] = '\0';
      ss[0] = '\x22'; /* 22 is the hex code for arcsec symbol */
      ss[1] = 's';
      ss[2] = '\0';
    }

    absx = fabs(x);

    /* determine how many digits before the decimal */
    if (absx < 100) {
      fig = 2;
    } else {
      fig = 3;
    }

    deg = floor(absx);
    absx = 60.0 * (absx - deg);
    min = floor(absx);
    sec = 60.0 * (absx - min);
    sec = DRound(sec, n);

    if (sec >= 60.0) {
      sec = 0.0;
      min = min + 1.0;
    }

    if (min >= 60.0) {
      min = 0.0;
      deg = deg + 1.0;
    }

    if (((deg == 24.0) && m == 1) || (deg == 360.0)) {
      deg = 0.0;
    }

    strcpy(s, " ");
    if (x < 0) {
      strcpy(s, "-");
    }
    else if (m == 0) {
```

```
   strcpy(s, "+");
}

/* begin building up the return string in buffer */
sprintf(buffer, "%.0f", (1000.0+deg));
right(buffer, fig, right_buffer);
strcat(s, right_buffer);
left(dh, m+1, left_buffer);
right(left_buffer, 1, right_buffer);
strcat(s, right_buffer);

sprintf(buffer, "%.0f", (100.0+min));
right(buffer, 2, right_buffer);
strcat(s, right_buffer);
left(mm, m+1, left_buffer);
right(left_buffer, 1, right_buffer);
strcat(s, right_buffer);

switch (n) {
  case 0:
    sprintf(buffer, "%.0f", (100.0+sec+0.0000001));
    break;
  case 1:
    sprintf(buffer, "%.1f", (100.0+sec+0.0000001));
    break;
  case 2:
    sprintf(buffer, "%.2f", (100.0+sec+0.0000001));
    break;
  case 3:
    sprintf(buffer, "%.3f", (100.0+sec+0.0000001));
    break;
  case 4:
    sprintf(buffer, "%.4f", (100.0+sec+0.0000001));
}

if (n == 0) {
  nf = 2;
} else {
  nf = n + 3;
}

right(buffer, strlen(buffer)-1, right_buffer);
left(right_buffer, nf, left_buffer);
strcat(s, left_buffer);

left(ss, m+1, left_buffer);
right(left_buffer, 1, right_buffer);
strcat(s, right_buffer);
}

/*********************************************************************
Name:    free_matrix
Purpose: Free a double matrix allocated by matrix().
Inputs:  m    - Pointer to matrix.
         nrow - Number of rows.
         ncol - Number of columns.
Outputs: None.
Returns: Nothing.
Status:  Finished.
Errors:  None known.
*********************************************************************/
void free_matrix(double **m, int nrow, int ncol) {

  int i;

  for (i = 0;i < nrow;i++) {
    free(m[i]);
  }
```

```
   free(m);
}

/**********************************************************************
Name:    freeDMatrix
Purpose: Free all storage associated with matrix m.
Inputs:  m - Matrix to free.
         n - Dimension of matrix.
Outputs: None.
Returns: Nothing.
Status:  Finished.
Errors:  None known.
**********************************************************************/
void freeDMatrix(DMatrix m, int n)
{
   int i;

   for (i=0; i<n; i++)
   {
      free(m[i]); /* storage for doubles in row i */
   }
   free(m); /* storage for pointers to rows */

   return;
}

/**********************************************************************
Name:    FunArgIAU
Purpose: Function to compute the fundamental arguments using the IAU
         expressions.
Inputs:  jed - JED on TDB scale.
Outputs: funarg[0]   - Mean anomaly of Moon.
         funarg[1]   - Mean anomaly of Sun.
         funarg[2]   - Argument of lat. of Moon.
         funarg[3]   - Mean elongation of Moon.
         funarg[4]   - Mean longitude of Moon's ascending node.
         funarg[5]   - Mean longitude of Moon.
         funarg[i+6] - Derivative of ith fundamental argument.
         NOTE: All derivatives are in units of rad/day.
Returns: Nothing.
Status:  Finished.
Errors:  None known.
**********************************************************************/
void FunArgIAU(double jed, double *funarg) {

   static double jedz;
   double T, T2, T3, L, Ldot, lp, lpdot, F, Fdot, D, Ddot;
   double N, Ndot, LL, LLdot;

   if (jed == jedz) return;
   jedz = jed;

   T = (jed - J2000) / JulCty;
   T2 = T * T;
   T3 = T2 * T;

   /* Compute fundamental arguments */
   L = 485866.733 + (1325. * 1296000. + 715922.633) * T
      + 31.31 * T2 + 0.064 * T3;
   Ldot = (1325. * 1296000. + 715922.633) + 2. * 31.31 * T
      + 3. * 0.064 * T2;
   L = amodulo(L * A2R, TWOPI);
   Ldot = amodulo(Ldot * A2R / 36525., TWOPI);
   lp = 1287099.804 + (99. * 1296000. + 1292581.224) * T
      - 0.577 * T2 - 0.012 * T3;
   lpdot = (99. * 1296000. + 1292581.224) - 2. * 0.577 * T
      - 3. * 0.012 * T2;
```

```
    lp = amodulo(lp * A2R, TWOPI);
    lpdot = amodulo(lpdot * A2R / 36525., TWOPI);
 F = 335778.877 + (1342. * 1296000. + 295263.137) * T
    - 13.257 * T2 + 0.011 * T3;
 Fdot = (1342. * 1296000. + 295263.137) - 2. * 13.257 * T
    + 3. * 0.011 * T2;
    F = amodulo(F * A2R, TWOPI);
    Fdot = amodulo(Fdot * A2R / 36525., TWOPI);
 D = 1072261.307 + (1236. * 1296000. + 1105601.328) * T
    - 6.891 * T2 + 0.019 * T3;
 Ddot = (1236. * 1296000. + 1105601.328) - 2. * 6.891 * T
    + 3. * 0.019 * T2;
    D = amodulo(D * A2R, TWOPI);
    Ddot = amodulo(Ddot * A2R / 36525., TWOPI);
 N = 450160.28 - (5. * 1296000. + 482890.539) * T
    + 7.455 * T2 + 0.008 * T3;
 Ndot = (5. * 1296000. + 482890.539) + 2. * 7.455 * T
    + 3. * 0.008 * T2;
    N = amodulo(N * A2R, TWOPI);
    Ndot = amodulo(Ndot * A2R / 36525., TWOPI);
 LL = 785939.157 + (1336. * 1296000. + 1108372.598) * T
    - 5.802 * T2 + 0.019 * T3;
 LLdot = (1336. * 1296000. + 1108372.598) - 2. * 5.802 * T
    + 3. * 0.019 * T2;
    LL = amodulo(LL * A2R, TWOPI);
    LLdot = amodulo(LLdot * A2R / 36525., TWOPI);

    funarg[0]  = L;
    funarg[6]  = Ldot;
    funarg[1]  = lp;
    funarg[7]  = lpdot;
    funarg[2]  = F;
    funarg[8]  = Fdot;
    funarg[3]  = D;
    funarg[9]  = Ddot;
    funarg[4]  = N;
    funarg[10] = Ndot;
    funarg[5]  = LL;
    funarg[11] = LLdot;
}

/************************************************************************
Name:     GeocenObs
Purpose: Subprogram to compute the geocentric equatorial
         state vectors of an observer.  The vectors are
         referred to the J2000.0 frame.
Inputs:  JED - Julian Date on TDB scale.
Outputs: obsr_geo - Observer's geocentric state vector
                    in the celestial reference frame.
Returns: Nothing.
Status:  Finished.
Errors:  None known.
************************************************************************/
void GeocenObs(double jed, double obsr_geo[]) {

    double gast,h,CosLat,SinLat,Cos2Lat,Sin2Lat,CosLon,SinLon,C,S;
    double PolMotX,PolMotY,g[6],dpsi,deps,dpsidot,depsdot;
    double zeta,z,theta,zetadot,zdot,thetadot;
    double MeanEps,TrueEps,MeanEpsDot,TrueEpsDot;

    /* Elevation is expected to be in meters. */
    h = (obsr_ele / 1000.0) * KM2AU;
    CosLat  = cos(obsr_lat);
    Cos2Lat = CosLat * CosLat;
    SinLat  = sin(obsr_lat);
    Sin2Lat = SinLat * SinLat;
    CosLon  = cos(obsr_lon);
```

```
  SinLon = sin(obsr_lon);
  C = 1.0 / sqrt(Cos2Lat + (1.0 - EFlat) * (1.0 - EFlat) * Sin2Lat);
  S = (1.0 - EFlat) * (1.0 - EFlat) * C;

  /* Compute the observer's state vector in the Earth-fixed frame. */
  g[0] = (EarthRadAU * C + h) * CosLat * CosLon;
  g[1] = (EarthRadAU * C + h) * CosLat * SinLon;
  g[2] = (EarthRadAU * S + h) * SinLat;
  g[3] = 0.0;
  g[4] = 0.0;
  g[5] = 0.0;

  /* Compute the required angular quantities and their derivatives. */
  GetPrecessParams(J2000, jed, &zeta, &z, &theta,
    &zetadot, &zdot, &thetadot);
  GetDpsiDeps(jed, &dpsi, &deps, &dpsidot, &depsdot);
  GetGST(jed, 1, &gast);
  Obliquity(J2000, jed, 0, &MeanEps, &MeanEpsDot);
  Obliquity(J2000, jed, 1, &TrueEps, &TrueEpsDot);

  /* Somehow get the quantities PolMotX, PolMotY */
  PolMotX = 0.0;
  PolMotY = 0.0;

  /* Wobble */
  QRotate(g, 2, PolMotX, 0, 1, g);
  QRotate(g, 1, PolMotY, 0, 1, g);

  /* Spin */
  QRotate(g, 3, -gast, -EarAngVelRD, 1, g);

  /* Nutation */
  QRotate(g, 1,  TrueEps,  TrueEpsDot, 1, g);
  QRotate(g, 3,  dpsi,     dpsidot, 1, g);
  QRotate(g, 1, -MeanEps, -MeanEpsDot, 1, g);

  /* Precession */
  QRotate(g, 3,  zeta,    zetadot, 1, g);
  QRotate(g, 2, -theta,  -thetadot, 1, g);
  QRotate(g, 3,  z, zdot, 1, obsr_geo);
}

/**********************************************************************
Name:    GetGST
Purpose: Function to compute the Greenwich mean or Greenwich apparent
         sidereal time, depending on which is required.  Strictly speaking,
         the computed time is the DYNAMICAL SIDEREAL TIME, but for all
         practical purposes is the same as the observed sidereal time.
Inputs:  jed - JED on TDB scale.
         s   - 1 for apparent sidereal time, otherwise mean sidereal time.
Outputs: gst - GMST or GAST in radians.
Returns: Nothing.
Status:  Finished.
Errors:  None known.
**********************************************************************/
void GetGST(double jed, int s, double *gst) {

  static double jedz, sz;
  double T, dpsi, deps, dpsidot, depsdot;
  double meaneps, trueeps, meanepsdot, trueepsdot, eqeqnx, eqeqnxdot;

  if ((jed == jedz) && (s == sz)) return;
  jedz = jed;
  sz = s;

  T = (jed - J2000) / JulCty;
```

```
  /* compute GMST in seconds */
  *gst = 67310.54841 + T * ((876600.0 * 3600.0 + 8640184.812866)
    + T * (0.093104 + T * (-0.0000062)));

  /* convert to radians */
  *gst = amodulo(*gst / 3600.0, 24.0) * H2R;

  if (s == 1) {
    /* get nutation quantities */
    GetDpsiDeps(jed, &dpsi, &deps, &dpsidot, &depsdot);

    /* get mean obliquity */
    Obliquity(J2000, jed, 0, &meaneps, &meanepsdot);

    /* get true obliquity */
    Obliquity (J2000, jed, 1, &trueeps, &trueepsdot);

    /* get equation of the equinoxes */
    eqeqnx    = dpsi * cos(trueeps);
    eqeqnxdot = dpsidot * cos(trueeps) - dpsi * trueepsdot * sin(trueeps);
    *gst      += eqeqnx;
  }

  *gst = amodulo(*gst, TWOPI);
}

/**********************************************************************
Name:    GetInvQMatrix
Purpose: Function to compute the elements of the inverse of a
         given Q-matrix.
Inputs:  QMatrix - Zero-offset 6X6 Q-matrix.
Outputs: InvQMatrix - Zero-offset inverse of QMatrix.
Returns: Nothing.
Status:  Finished.
Errors:  None known.
**********************************************************************/
void GetInvQMatrix(DMatrix QMatrix, DMatrix InvQMatrix) {

  int i, j;

  for (i= 0; i<3; i++) {
    for (j=0; j<3; j++) {
      InvQMatrix[i][j] = QMatrix[j][i];
      InvQMatrix[i][j+3] = 0.0;
      InvQMatrix[i+3][j] = QMatrix[j+3][i];
      InvQMatrix[i+3][j+3] = QMatrix[j+3][i+3];
    }
  }
}

/**********************************************************************
Name:    GetPrecessParams
Purpose: Function that computes the general precession parameters and their
         derivatives for precessing equatorial rectangular coordinates and
         velocities from jed1 to jed2. Lieske's formulae are used.
Inputs:  jed1 - Initial Julian Date.
         jed2 - Final Julian Date.
Outputs: zeta     - equatorial precession parameter.
         z        - equatorial precession parameter.
         theta    - equatorial precession parameter.
         zetadot  - derivative in rad/day.
         zdot     - derivative in rad/day.
         thetadot - derivative in rad/day.
Returns: Nothing.
Status:  Finished.
Errors:  None known.
**********************************************************************/
```

```
void GetPrecessParams(double jed1, double jed2, double *zeta, double *z,
   double *theta, double *zetadot, double *zdot, double *thetadot) {

   double T1, T2, c1, c2, c3, c4, c5, c6, p1, p2, x, xdot;

   T1 = (jed1 - J2000) / JulCty;
   T2 = (jed2 - jed1) / JulCty;

   /* compute zeta, z, theta, zetadot, zdot, thetadot */
   c1 = 2306.2181;
   c2 =     1.39656;
   c3 =    -0.000139;
   c4 =     0.30188;
   c5 =    -0.000344;
   c6 =     0.017998;
   p1 = c1 + c2 * T1 + c3 * T1 * T1;
   p2 = c4 + c5 * T1;
   x = p1 * T2 + p2 * T2 * T2 + c6 * T2 * T2 * T2;
   xdot = p1 + 2.0 * p2 * T2 + 3.0 * c6 * T2 * T2;
   *zeta = x * A2R;
   *zetadot = xdot * A2R / JulCty;

   c1 = 2306.2181;
   c2 =     1.39656;
   c3 =    -0.000139;
   c4 =     1.09468;
   c5 =     0.000066;
   c6 =     0.018203;
   p1 = c1 + c2 * T1 + c3 * T1 * T1;
   p2 = c4 + c5 * T1;
   x = p1 * T2 + p2 * T2 * T2 + c6 * T2 * T2 * T2;
   xdot = p1 + 2.0 * p2 * T2 + 3.0 * c6 * T2 * T2;
   *z = x * A2R;
   *zdot = xdot * A2R / JulCty;

   c1 = 2004.3109;
   c2 =    -0.85330;
   c3 =    -0.000217;
   c4 =    -0.42665;
   c5 =    -0.000217;
   c6 =    -0.041833;
   p1 = c1 + c2 * T1 + c3 * T1 * T1;
   p2 = c4 + c5 * T1;
   x = p1 * T2 + p2 * T2 * T2 + c6 * T2 * T2 * T2;
   xdot = p1 + 2.0 * p2 * T2 + 3.0 * c6 * T2 * T2;
   *theta = x * A2R;
   *thetadot = xdot * A2R / JulCty;
}

/*******************************************************************
Name:    GetQMatrix
Purpose: Function to compute the elements of the Q-matrix for a
         given angle and its time derivative.
Inputs:  phi   - Angle in radians
         phidot - Time der. of phi.
         axis  - 1 for x-axis,
                 2 for y-axis,
                 3 for z-axis.
         s     - 0 for inertial to inertial,
                 1 for inertial to rotating.
Outputs: QMatrix - Zero-offset 6X6 Q-matrix.
Returns: Nothing.
Status:  Finished.
Errors:  None known.
*******************************************************************/
void GetQMatrix(double phi, double phidot, int axis,
   int s, DMatrix QMatrix) {

   DMatrix r, dr;
```

```
     int i, j;

     r  = createDMatrix(3);
     dr = createDMatrix(3);

     /* form the 3X3 r[] and dr[] matrices */
     RotMat(axis, phi, r, dr);

     /* form the 6X6 Q-matrix */
     for (i=0; i<3; i++) {
       for (j=0; j<3; j++) {
         QMatrix[i][j] = r[i][j];
         QMatrix[i][j+3] = 0.0;
         QMatrix[i+3][j] = phidot * dr[i][j] * s;
         QMatrix[i+3][j+3] = r[i][j];
       }
     }

     freeDMatrix(r, 3);
     freeDMatrix(dr, 3);
}

/**********************************************************************
Name:     GetRPNmat
Purpose:  Function to compute the precession matrix, the nutation
          matrix, or the combined R matrix for equatorial coordinates.
Inputs:   jed1 - Initial JED on TDB scale.
          jed2 - Final JED on TDB scale.
          rpn  - 1 for precession matrix,
                 2 for nutation matrix,
                 3 for R matrix.
          d    - 1 for zero-offset 3X3 matrix,
                 2 for zero-offset 6X6 Qmatrix.
Outputs:  m3 - Requested zero-offset 3X3 matrix.
          m6 - Requested zero-offset 6X6 matrix.
Returns:  Nothing.
Status:   Finished.
Errors:   None known.
**********************************************************************/
void GetRPNmat(double jed1, double jed2, int rpn, int d,
  DMatrix m3, DMatrix m6) {

     double dpsi, deps, dpsidot, depsdot, trueeps, trueepsdot,
       meaneps, meanepsdot, zeta, zetadot, z, zdot, theta, thetadot;
     DMatrix p1mat, p2mat, p3mat, pmat, n1mat, n2mat, n3mat,
       nmat, rmat, p, n;

     p1mat = createDMatrix(6);
     p2mat = createDMatrix(6);
     p3mat = createDMatrix(6);
     pmat  = createDMatrix(6);
     n1mat = createDMatrix(6);
     n2mat = createDMatrix(6);
     n3mat = createDMatrix(6);
     nmat  = createDMatrix(6);
     rmat  = createDMatrix(6);
     p     = createDMatrix(6);
     n     = createDMatrix(6);

     switch (rpn) {
       case 1:
         /* compute precession matrix */
         GetPrecessParams(jed1,jed2,&zeta,&z,&theta,&zetadot,&zdot,&thetadot);
         GetQMatrix(-zeta, -zetadot, 3, 0, p1mat);
         GetQMatrix(theta, thetadot, 2, 0, p2mat);
         GetQMatrix(-z, -zdot, 3, 0, p3mat);
         MatXMat(p2mat, p1mat, pmat, 6);
```

```
        MatXMat(p3mat, pmat, m3, 6);
        freeDMatrix(p3mat, 6);
        freeDMatrix(p2mat, 6);
        freeDMatrix(p1mat, 6);
        freeDMatrix(pmat, 6);
        break;
      case 2:
        /* compute nutation matrix */
        GetDpsiDeps(jed2, &dpsi, &deps, &dpsidot, &depsdot);
        Obliquity(jed1, jed2, 0, &meaneps, &meanepsdot);
        Obliquity(jed1, jed2, 1, &trueeps, &trueepsdot);
        GetQMatrix(meaneps, meanepsdot, 1, 0, n1mat);
        GetQMatrix(-dpsi, -dpsidot, 3, 0, n2mat);
        GetQMatrix(-trueeps, -trueepsdot, 1, 0, n3mat);
        MatXMat(n2mat, n1mat, nmat, 6);
        MatXMat(n3mat, nmat, m3, 6);
        freeDMatrix(n3mat, 6);
        freeDMatrix(n2mat, 6);
        freeDMatrix(n1mat, 6);
        freeDMatrix(nmat, 6);
        break;
      case 3:
        /* compute R matrix */
        GetPrecessParams(jed1,jed2,&zeta,&z,&theta,&zetadot,&zdot,&thetadot);
        GetQMatrix( -zeta, -zetadot, 3, 0, p1mat);
        GetQMatrix(theta, thetadot, 2, 0, p2mat);
        GetQMatrix(-z, -zdot, 3, 0, p3mat);
        MatXMat(p2mat, p1mat, pmat, 6);
        MatXMat(p3mat, pmat, p, 6);
        GetDpsiDeps(jed2, &dpsi, &deps, &dpsidot, &depsdot);
        Obliquity(jed1, jed2, 0, &meaneps, &meanepsdot);
        Obliquity(jed1, jed2, 1, &trueeps, &trueepsdot);
        GetQMatrix(meaneps, meanepsdot, 1, 0, n1mat);
        GetQMatrix(-dpsi, -dpsidot, 3, 0, n2mat);
        GetQMatrix(-trueeps, -trueepsdot, 1, 0, n3mat);
        MatXMat(n2mat, n1mat, nmat, 6);
        MatXMat(n3mat, nmat, n, 6);
        MatXMat(n, p, m3, 6);
        freeDMatrix(p3mat, 6);
        freeDMatrix(p2mat, 6);
        freeDMatrix(p1mat, 6);
        freeDMatrix(pmat, 6);
        freeDMatrix(p, 6);
        freeDMatrix(n3mat, 6);
        freeDMatrix(n2mat, 6);
        freeDMatrix(n1mat, 6);
        freeDMatrix(nmat, 6);
        freeDMatrix(n, 6);
        break;
   }
}

/************************************************************************
Name:    GetStateVector
Purpose: Function to retrieve the state vector of a given body
         w.r.t. a given origin at a given time. This routine is
         a wrapper for PLEPH.
Inputs:  jd    - Julian date on TDB time scale.
         targ  - Body identification number.
                 1=MER,   2=VEN,   3=EAR,   4=MAR
                 5=JUP,   6=SAT,   7=URA,   8=NEP
                 9=PLU,  10=MOO,  11=SUN,  12=SSB
                 13=EMB,  14=NUT,  15=LIB
         cent  - Origin identification number.
                 (Numbering as above).
```

```
              recpol - 1 for cartesian, 2 for orthogonal polar.
Outputs: StateVector - A 15x15x2x6 array containing the requested
                       state vector.
         NOTE: StateVector has the following form:
         StateVector[targ-1][cent-1][recpol-1][component]
Returns: Nothing.
Status:  Finished.
Errors:  None known.
**************************************************************/
void GetStateVector(double jd, int targ, int cent, int recpol,
  double StateVector[15][15][2][6]) {

  static double b[6] = {0.};
  static double rrd[6] = {0.};
  static double dpsi, deps, dpsidot, depsdot;
  int inside, i;

  /* Get the state vector from JPL ephemeris */
  pleph(jd, targ, cent, rrd, &inside);

  if (!inside) {
    LogMsg(stderr,
      "GetStateVector: requested date not covered by ephemeris file.\n");
    for (i=0; i<6; i++) {
      StateVector[targ-1][cent-1][recpol-1][i] = 999.;
    }
    exit (1);
  }

  /* Check for nutations */
  if (targ == 14) {
    dpsi    = rrd[0];
    deps    = rrd[1];
    dpsidot = rrd[2];
    depsdot = rrd[3];
    recpol  = 1;
  }

  if (recpol == 1) {
    for (i=0; i<6; i++) {
      StateVector[targ-1][cent-1][recpol-1][i] = rrd[i];
    }
  } else {
    /* Convert rectangular vector to polar vector */
    Rec2Pol(rrd, b);
    for (i=0; i<6; i++) {
      StateVector[targ-1][cent-1][recpol-1][i] = b[i];
    }
  }

  return;
}

/**********************************************************************
Name:    HelEphemeris
Purpose: Function to compute an orbiting body's heliocentric
         ecliptic state vector for a single instant of time
         given the universal orbital elements and the time.
         Reference: Mansfield. 1986. AIAA Paper 86-2269-CP.
Inputs:  uelement[] - Array of universal orbital elements:
         uelement[0] = q
         uelement[1] = e
         uelement[2] = i
         uelement[3] = node
         uelement[4] = arg. peri.
         uelement[5] = T
         mu          - Gravitational constant for the body.
```

```
        jed        - Time.
Outputs: posvel[] - State vector:
        posvel[0..2] = position vector.
        posvel[3..5] = velocity vector.
Returns: Nothing.
Status:  Finished.
Errors:  None known.
*********************************************************************/
void HelEphemeris(double *uelement, double mu, double jed, double *posvel) {

  int i;
  double LongPeri, RetLongPeri, cosi, sini, coslp, sinlp, cosrlp, sinrlp;
  double cosw, sinw, rcosnu, rsinnu, r, cosnu, sinnu, param, p[3], q[3];

  /* Compute longitude of perihelion */
  LongPeri = uelement[4] + uelement[3];
  /* Compute retrograde longitude of perihelion */
  RetLongPeri = uelement[4] - uelement[3];

  /* Compute the P vector */
  cosi   = cos(uelement[2]);
  sini   = sin(uelement[2]);
  coslp  = cos(LongPeri);
  sinlp  = sin(LongPeri);
  cosrlp = cos(RetLongPeri);
  sinrlp = sin(RetLongPeri);
  cosw   = cos(uelement[4]);
  sinw   = sin(uelement[4]);
  p[0] = 0.5 * (1.0 + cosi) * coslp + 0.5 * (1.0 - cosi) * cosrlp;
  p[1] = 0.5 * (1.0 + cosi) * sinlp - 0.5 * (1.0 - cosi) * sinrlp;
  p[2] = sinw * sini;

  /* Compute the Q vector */
  q[0] = -0.5 * (1.0 + cosi) * sinlp - 0.5 * (1.0 - cosi) * sinrlp;
  q[1] =  0.5 * (1.0 + cosi) * coslp - 0.5 * (1.0 - cosi) * cosrlp;
  q[2] = cosw * sini;

  /* Solve Kepler's equation */
  Conway(uelement, mu, jed, &rcosnu, &rsinnu);

  /* Compute magnitude of radius vector */
  r = sqrt(rcosnu * rcosnu + rsinnu * rsinnu);
  cosnu = rcosnu / r;
  sinnu = rsinnu / r;

  /* Compute heliocentric ecliptic position vector */
  for (i = 0; i < 3; i++) {
    posvel[i] = p[i] * rcosnu + q[i] * rsinnu;
  }

  /* Compute heliocentric ecliptic velocity vector */
  param = uelement[0] * (1.0 + uelement[1]);

  for (i = 3; i < 6; i++) {
    posvel[i]   = -p[i-3] * sqrt(mu / param) * sinnu;
    posvel[i] = posvel[i] + q[i-3] * sqrt(mu / param) *
      (uelement[1] + cosnu);
  }
}

/*********************************************************************
Name:    interp
Purpose: This subroutine differentiates and interpolates a set of
         Chebyshev coefficients to give position and velocity.
Inputs:  buff - 1st location of array of Chebyshev coefficients.
         t    - t[0] is fractional time in interval covered by
```

```
                    coefficients at which interpolation is wanted
                    (0 <= t[0] <= 1). t[1] is length of whole
                    interval in input time units.
          ncf    - Number of coefficients per component.
          ncm    - Number of components per set of coefficients.
          na     - Number of sets of coefficients in full array
                    (i.e., # of sub-intervals in full interval).
          fl     - Integer flag: =1 for positions only.
                                  =2 for pos and vel.
Outputs: dumpv - Interpolated quantities requested. Dimension
          expected is pv[ncm][fl].
Returns: Nothing.
Status:  Finished.
Errors:  None known.
************************************************************************/
void interp(int buff, double *t, int ncf, int ncm, int na,
  int fl, double dumpv[3][2]) {

  int i, j, l, n, m;
  static int bcoef, np, nv;
  static double pc[18], vc[18], cbody[1200];
  static double cbuf[15][3][8]={0.};
  static double twot, dna, dt1, temp, ll, tc, vfac;

  np = 2;
  nv = 3;
  twot = 0.0;
  pc[0] = 1.0;
  pc[1] = 0.0;
  vc[1] = 1.0;

  /*
      Entry point. Get correct sub-interval number for this set
      of coefficients and then get normalized chebyshev time
      within that subinterval.
  */

  dna = (double) na;
  dt1 = floor(t[0]);
  temp = dna*t[0];
  ll = floor((temp - dt1) + 1.0);

  /* 'tc' is the normalized chebyshev time (-1 <= tc <= 1) */
  tc = 2.0*(fmod(temp, 1.0) + dt1) - 1.0;

  /*
      Check to see whether chebyshev time has changed,
      and compute new polynomial values if it has.
      (The element pc[1] is the value of 'tc' and hence
      contains the value of 'tc' on the previous call.)
  */

  if (tc != pc[1]) {
    np = 2;
    nv = 3;
    pc[1] = tc;
    twot = tc + tc;
  }

  /*
      Be sure that at least 'ncf' polynomials have been evaluated
      and are stored in the array pc[].
  */

  if (np < ncf) {
    for (i=np; i<ncf; i++) {
      pc[i] = twot * pc[i-1] - pc[i-2];
```

```
    }
    np = ncf;
  }

  /* interpolate to get position for each component */

  /* number of coefficients for body */
  bcoef= ncf*na*ncm;

  /* stored body's coefficients in an array */
  n = buff;
  for (m=0; m<bcoef; m++) {
    cbody[m] = db[n];
    n++;
  }

  /* fill the cbuf[][][] array */
  n = 0;
  /* loop for each sub-interval */
  for (l=0; l<na; l++) {
    /* loop for each component */
    for (i=0; i<ncm; i++) {
      /* loop for each set of coeffs */
      for (j=0; j<ncf; j++) {
        cbuf[j][i][l] = cbody[n];
        n++;
      }
    }
  }

  for (i=0; i<ncm; i++) {
    dumpv[i][0] = 0.0;
    for (j=ncf-1; j>=0; j--) {
      dumpv[i][0] = dumpv[i][0] + pc[j] * cbuf[j][i][((int)ll)-1];
    }
  }
  if (fl <= 1) return;

  /*
      If velocity interpolation is wanted, be sure enough
      derivative polynomials have been generated and stored.
  */

  vfac = (dna+dna)/t[1];
  vc[2] = twot+twot;
  if (nv < ncf) {
    for (i=nv; i<ncf; i++) {
      vc[i]=twot * vc[i-1] + pc[i-1] + pc[i-1] - vc[i-2];
    }
    nv = ncf;
  }

  /* interpolate to get velocity for each component */

  for (i=0; i<ncm; i++) {
    dumpv[i][1] = 0.0;
    for (j=ncf-1; j>=1; j--) {
      dumpv[i][1] = dumpv[i][1] + vc[j] * cbuf[j][i][((int)ll)-1];
    }
    dumpv[i][1] = dumpv[i][1] * vfac;
  }
}

/***********************************************************************
Name:     Interp1
Purpose: Subprogram to perform interpolation on a list
         of tabular values to find maxima/minima or
         to find the zero of a function within the limits
```

```
                of the table.  The algorithms used are those of Meeus.
Inputs:   x[] - Array of function arguments.
          y[] - Array of function values at the
                corresponding arguments.
          L   - Equals 3 for 3-pt. interpolation.
                5 for 5-pt. interpolation.
          m   - Equals 0 for zero of function.
                1 for a extremum of the function.
Outputs:  arg - Argument corresponding to the
                extremum or zero of the tabular function.
          v   - The value of the function corresponding to arg.
Returns: Nothing.
Status:  Finished.
Errors:  None known.
*****************************************************************/
void Interp1(double *x, double *y, int L, int m, double *arg, double *v) {

    double a, b, c, d, e, f, g, h, j, k, nm, n0, n1;

    if (L == 3) {
      /* Use a 3 pt. table */
      a = y[1] - y[0];
      b = y[2] - y[1];
      c = b - a;
      if (m == 1) {
        /* Find extremum of the tabular function */
        *v = y[1] - (a + b) * (a + b) / (8.0 * c);
        nm = -(a + b) / (2.0 * c);
        *arg = x[1] + nm * (x[1] - x[0]);
      } else {
        n1 = 0.0; /* Find zero of the tabular function */
        do {
          n0 = -2.0 * y[1] / (a + b + c * n1);
          if (fabs(n0 - n1) < 0.000000000000001)
            break;
          n1 = n0;
        } while (1 == 1);
        *v = y[1] + 0.5 * n0 * (x[1] - x[0]) * (a + b + n0 * c);
        *arg = x[1] + n0 * (x[1] - x[0]);
      }
    } else {
      /* Use a 5 pt. table */
      a = y[1] - y[0];
      b = y[2] - y[1];
      c = y[3] - y[2];
      d = y[4] - y[3];
      e = b - a;
      f = c - b;
      g = d - c;
      h = f - e;
      j = g - f;
      k = j - h;
      if (m == 0) {
        /* Find extremum of tabular function */
        n1 = 0.0;
        do {
          nm = (6.0 * b + 6.0 * c - h - j + 3.0 * n1 * n1 *
            (h + j) + 2.0 * n1 * n1 * n1 * k) / (k - 12.0 * f);
          if (fabs(nm - n1) < 0.000000000000001)
            break;
          n1 = nm;
        } while (1 == 1);
        nm = nm * (x[3] - x[2]);
        *arg = x[2] + nm;
        *v = y[2] + 0.5 * nm * (b + c) + 0.5 * nm * nm * f + nm
          * (nm * nm - 1.0) * (h + j) / 12.0 + nm * nm * (nm * nm - 1.0)
          * k / 24.0;
```

```
    } else {
      /* Find zero of the tabular function */
      n1 = 0.0;
      do {
        n0 = (-24.0 * y[2] + n1 * n1 * (k - 12.0 * f) - 2.0 *
          n1 * n1 * n1 * (h + j) - n1 * n1 * n1 * n1 * k) / (2.0
          * (6.0 * b + 6.0 * c - h - j));
        if (fabs(n0 - n1) < 0.000000000000001)
          break;
        n1 = n0;
      } while (1 == 1);
      n0 = n0 * (x[3] - x[2]);
      *arg = x[2] + n0;
      *v = y[2] + 0.5 * n0 * (b + c) + 0.5 * n0 * n0 * f + n0
        * (n0 * n0 - 1.0) * (h + j) / 12.0 + n0 * n0 * (n0 * n0 - 1.0)
        * k / 24.0;
    }
  }
}

/************************************************************************
Name:     Interpol
Purpose: Function for 3 or 5 point interpolation
         using Meeus' algorithm.
Inputs:   x[] - Aarray of function arguments.
          y[] - Array of function values at
                the three arguments.
          i   - Switch indicating whether a
                3 or 5 point interpolation
                is performed (i=3 for 3 pt.,
                i=5 for 5 pt.).
          arg - Argument for which a function value
                is needed.
Outputs: None.
Returns: Interpolated value.
Status:  Finished.
Errors:  None known.
************************************************************************/
double Interpol(double *x, double *y, int i, double arg) {

  double d1, d2, d3, d4, d5, d6, d7, d8, d9, d10, n;

  if (i == 3) {
    d1 = y[1] - y[0];
    d2 = y[2] - y[1];
    d3 = d2 - d1;
    n = (arg - x[1]) / (x[1] - x[0]);
    return (y[1] + (n / 2.0) * (d1 + d2 + n * d3));
  } else {
    d1 = y[1] - y[0];
    d2 = y[2] - y[1];
    d3 = y[3] - y[2];
    d4 = y[4] - y[3];
    d5 = d2 - d1;
    d6 = d3 - d2;
    d7 = d4 - d3;
    d8 = d6 - d5;
    d9 = d7 - d6;
    d10 = d9 - d8;
    n = (arg - x[2]) / (x[2] - x[1]);
    return (y[2] + n * ((d2 + d3) / 2.0 - (d8 + d9) / 12.0) +
      n * n * (d6 / 2.0 - d10 / 24.0) + n * n * n *
      ((d8 + d9) / 12.0) + n * n * n * n * (d10 / 24.0));
  }
}

/************************************************************************
```

```
Name:    JED2Cal
Purpose: Function to convert a JED to an ordinary calendar date.
         The algorithm is that of Meeus.
Inputs:  jed - Julian Ephemeris Date.
Outputs: yr - Year.
         mo - Month.
         dy - Day.
         ti - Time of day in decimal hours.
Returns: Nothing.
Status:  Finished.
Errors:  None known.
**********************************************************************/
void JED2Cal(double jed, int *yr, int *mo, int *dy, double *ti) {

  static double jedz;
  double z, f, a, b, c, d, e, alpha, daywtime;

  if (jed == jedz) return;
  jedz = jed;

  z = floor(jed + 0.5);
  f = (jed + 0.5) - z;
  if (z < 2299161.0) {
    a = z;
  } else {
    alpha = floor((z - 1867216.25) / 36524.25);
    a = z + 1.0 + alpha - floor(0.25 * alpha);
  }

  b = a + 1524.0;
  c = floor((b - 122.1) / 365.25);
  d = floor(365.25 * c);
  e = floor((b - d) / 30.6001);
  daywtime = b - d - floor(30.6001 * e) + f;
  *dy = (int) floor(daywtime);
  *ti = 24.0 * (daywtime - (double) *dy);

  if (e  < 13.5) *mo = (int) floor(e - 1.0);
  if (e  > 13.5) *mo = (int) floor(e - 13.0);
  if (*mo > 2.5) *yr = (int) floor(c - 4716.0);
  if (*mo < 2.5) *yr = (int) floor(c - 4715.0);
}

/**********************************************************************
Name:    JED2Epoch
Purpose: Function to convert a given JED to its corresponding Julian
         or Besselian epoch. For example, 2451545.0 becomes J2000.
Inputs:  jed - Input jed.
         s   - J or B, whichever is desired.
Outputs: epoch - J or B epoch as a string.
Returns: Nothing.
Status:  Finished.
Errors:  None known.
**********************************************************************/
void JED2Epoch(double jed, char *s, char *epoch) {

  char d[80];
  double date;

  if (strcmp(s,"J") == 0) {
    date = 2000.0 + (jed - 2451545.0) / 365.25;
    sprintf(d, "%f", date);
  } else {
    date = 1900.0 + (jed - (double) 2415020.31352) /
      (double) 365.242198781731;
    sprintf(d, "%f", date);
  }
```

```
  strcpy(epoch, s);
  strcat(epoch, d);
}

/************************************************************************
Name:     LightTime
Purpose:  Subprogram to compute the vectors body_geo() and body_hel()
          from a barycentric ephemeris of the object, Earth, and the Sun.
Inputs:   JED       - Desired time of reduction.
          Body      - Body number, 99 for stellar reduction.
          earth_ssb - Barycentric state vector of Earth at JED.
          earth_hel - Heliocentric state vector of Earth.
          StarData  - Stellar data.
Outputs:  body_geo - Geometric geocentric state vector of object.
          body_hel - Heliocentric state vector of object.
          Ltime    - Light time in days to the object.
Returns:  Nothing.
Status:   Finished.
Errors:   None known.
************************************************************************/
void LightTime(double jed, int body, double earth_ssb[],
  double earth_hel[], double StarData[], double body_geo[],
  double body_hel[], double *Ltime) {

  int inside, i;
  double E[3],Edot[3],RQB[6],RSB[6],RQ[6],RP[6],Q[3],Qdot[3],P[3],Pdot[3];
  double unit_body_hel[6], unit_body_geo[6];
  double magE,magQ,magP,trialtau,tau,xtime,RelTerm,
         TrueHelDist=0,TrueGeoDist=0;
  double AppHelDist,AppGeoDist,RA,DE,sinRA,cosRA,sinDE,cosDE;
  double plx,r,muRA,muDE,rdot,drda[3],drdd[3],DT;

  SplitStateVector(earth_hel, E, Edot);
  magE = Vecmag(E);

  if (body != 99) {
    trialtau = 0.0;
    do {
      xtime = jed - trialtau;

      /* body's barycentric state vector */
      pleph(xtime, body, 12, RQB, &inside);

      /* Sun's barycentric state vector */
      pleph(xtime, 11, 12, RSB, &inside);

      /* body's heliocentric state vector */
      for (i=0; i<6; i++) {
        RQ[i] = RQB[i] - RSB[i];
        /* body's geocentric state vector */
        RP[i] = RQB[i] - earth_ssb[i];
      }

      /* Calculate improved value of the light time */
      SplitStateVector(RQ, Q, Qdot);
      SplitStateVector(RP, P, Pdot);
      magQ = Vecmag(Q);
      magP = Vecmag(P);

      if (trialtau == 0) {
        TrueHelDist = magQ;
        TrueGeoDist = magP;
      }

      if (magQ == 0) {
        RelTerm = 0.0;
      } else {
```

```
        RelTerm = MUC * log((magE + magP + magQ) / (magE - magP + magQ));
      }
      tau = (magP + RelTerm) / CAUD;
      if (fabs(trialtau - tau) < 1e-9) {
        break;
      }
      trialtau = tau;
    } while(1);
  } else {
    RA = StarData[0];
    DE = StarData[1];
    sinRA = sin(RA);
    cosRA = cos(RA);
    sinDE = sin(DE);
    cosDE = cos(DE);
    if (StarData[2] == 0) {
      plx = 1e-7;
    } else {
      plx = StarData[2];
    }

    /* Star's distance in AU */
    r = R2A / plx;

    /* Star's barycentric position vector */
    RQB[0] = r*cosRA*cosDE;
    RQB[1] = r*sinRA*cosDE;
    RQB[2] = r      *sinDE;

    /* Convert proper motions and radial velocity */
    /* to units of AU/day */
    muRA = StarData[3] * 15.0 * cosDE / (JulCty * plx);
    muDE = StarData[4] / (JulCty * plx);
    rdot = StarData[5] * 86400.0 * KM2AU;

    /* Partial of unit vector wrt RA */
    drda[0] = - sinRA * cosDE;
    drda[1] =   cosRA * cosDE;
    drda[2] =   0.0;

    /* Partial of unit vector wrt DE */
    drdd[0] = - cosRA * sinDE;
    drdd[1] = - sinRA * sinDE;
    drdd[2] =           cosDE;

    /* Star's barycentric velocity vector */
    for (i=3; i<6; i++) {
      RQB[i] = muRA*drda[i-3] + muDE*drdd[i-3] + rdot*RQB[i-3]/r;
    }

    /* Correction for space motion */
    DT = jed - J2000;
    for (i=0; i<3; i++) {
      RQB[i] = RQB[i] + RQB[i+3]*DT;
    }

    /* Sun's barycentric state vector */
    pleph(jed, 11, 12, RSB, &inside);

    /* Star's heliocentric state vector */
    for (i=0; i<6; i++) {
      RQ[i] = RQB[i] - RSB[i];
    }

    /* Star's geo/topocentric state vector */
    /* This correction is annual parallax. */
    for (i=0; i<6; i++) {
      RP[i] = RQB[i] - earth_ssb[i];
    }
```

```
  }

  SplitStateVector(RQ, Q, Qdot);
  SplitStateVector(RP, P, Pdot);
  magQ = Vecmag(Q);
  magP = Vecmag(P);

  TrueGeoDist = magP;
  TrueHelDist = magQ;

  tau = r / CAUD;
  }

  *Ltime = tau;
  AppHelDist = magQ;
  AppGeoDist = magP;

  for (i=0; i<6; i++) {
    body_hel[i] = RQ[i];
    body_geo[i] = RP[i];
  }

  Uvector(body_hel, unit_body_hel);
  Uvector(body_geo, unit_body_geo);

  /* I don't understand why this next loop is needed, but it is. */
  for (i=3; i<6; i++) {
   unit_body_hel[i] = RQ[i];
   unit_body_geo[i] = RP[i];
  }

  for (i=0; i<6; i++) {
    body_geo[i] = unit_body_geo[i] * TrueGeoDist;
    body_hel[i] = unit_body_hel[i] * TrueHelDist;
  }
}

/**********************************************************************
Name:    matrix
Purpose: Function that allocates a double matrix with dimensions
         m[nrow][ncol].
Inputs:  nrow - Number of rows.
         ncol - Number of columns.
Outputs: None.
Returns: Pointer to 2-D matrix of doubles.
Status:  Finished.
Errors:  None known.
**********************************************************************/
double **matrix(int nrow, int ncol) {

  long i;
  double **m;

  /* Allocate pointer to rows */
  m = (double **) malloc(nrow * sizeof(double *));
  if (!m) {
    LogMsg(stderr, "matrix(): allocation failure 1\n");
    exit(1);
  }

  /* Allocate rows and set pointers to them */
  for (i = 0;i < nrow;i++) {
    m[i] = (double *) malloc(ncol * sizeof(double));
    if (!m[i]) {
      LogMsg(stderr, "matrix(): allocation failure 2\n");
      exit(1);
    }
```

```
    }
    /* return pointer to array of pointers to rows */
    return m;
}

/************************************************************************
Name:    MatXMat
Purpose: Square matrix multiplication subroutine.
         NOTE: If a[][] and c[][] have the same name in the
         calling program, the original a[][] matrix is overwritten.
Inputs:  a[][] - Zero-offset matrix a.
         b[][] - Zero-offset matrix b.
         n     - Dimension of matrix.
Outputs: c[][] - Zero-offset matrix a x b.
Returns: Nothing.
Status:  Finished.
Errors:  None known.
************************************************************************/
void MatXMat(DMatrix a, DMatrix b, DMatrix c, int n) {

    int i, j, k;

    for (i=0; i<n; i++) {
      for (j=0; j<n; j++) {
        c[i][j] = 0.0;
        for (k=0; k<n; k++) {
          c[i][j] += a[i][k] * b[k][j];
        }
      }
    }
}

/************************************************************************
Name:    MatXVec
Purpose: Matrix/vector multiplication subroutine.
Inputs:  a[][] - Zero-offset matrix a (l rows by m columns).
         b[]   - Zero-offset vector b (m rows by 1 column).
         l     - Dimension of vector (i.e. lx1).
         m     - Dimension of matrix (i.e. mxl).
Outputs: c[]   - Zero-offset vector a x b (l rows by 1 column).
Returns: Nothing.
Status:  Finished.
Errors:  None known.
************************************************************************/
void MatXVec (DMatrix a, double b[], double c[], int l, int m) {

    int i, j;
    double s, temp[6];

    for (i=0; i<l; i++) {
      s = 0.0;
      for (j=0; j<m; j++) {
        s += a[i][j] * b[j];
      }
      temp[i] = s;
    }

    for (i=0; i<l; i++) {
      c[i] = temp[i];
    }
}

/************************************************************************
Name:    MRotate
Purpose: Function to perform a matrix rotation of an input vector
         through a given angle about a desired axis. A right-handed
         orthogonal coordinate system is assumed, and a 3X3
         rotation matrix is used, not a Q-matrix.
```

```
          NOTE: The vin[] and vout[] can have the same name in the
          calling program.
Inputs:   vin[]  - Zero-offset input vector.
          axis   - 1 for rot. about x-axis,
                   2 for rot. about y-axis,
                   3 for rot. about z-axis.
          phi    - Rotation angle in radians.
Outputs: vout[] - Zero-offset transformed vector.
Returns: Nothing.
Status:  Finished.
Errors:  None known.
*******************************************************************/
void MRotate(double vin[], int axis, double phi, double vout[]) {

  double cosphi, sinphi, T;

  cosphi = cos(phi);
  sinphi = sin(phi);

  switch (axis) {
    case 1:  /* rotate about x-axis */
      T = cosphi * vin[1] + sinphi * vin[2];
      vout[2] = -sinphi * vin[1] + cosphi * vin[2];
      vout[1] = T;
      vout[0] = vin[0];
      break;
    case 2:  /* rotate about y-axis */
      T = cosphi * vin[0] - sinphi * vin[2];
      vout[2] = sinphi * vin[0] + cosphi * vin[2];
      vout[0] = T;
      vout[1] = vin[1];
      break;
    case 3:  /* rotate about z-axis */
      T = cosphi * vin[0] + sinphi * vin[1];
      vout[1] = -sinphi * vin[0] + cosphi * vin[1];
      vout[0] = T;
      vout[2] = vin[2];
      break;
    default:
      LogMsg(stderr,"MRotate: axis not valid.\n");
      exit(1);
  }
}


/************************************************************************
Name:     GetDpsiDeps
Purpose: Function to compute dpsi, deps, dpsidot, and depsdot.
Inputs:  jed - JED on TDB scale.
Outputs: dpsi    - Nutation in longitude.
         deps    - Nutation in obliquity.
         dpsidot - Derivative of dpsi in radians/day.
         depsdot - Derivative of deps in radians/day.
Returns: Nothing.
Status:  Finished.
Errors:  None known.
*******************************************************************/
void GetDpsiDeps(double jed, double *dpsi, double *deps,
  double *dpsidot, double *depsdot) {

  double L, Ldot, LP, LPdot, F, Fdot, D, Ddot, N, Ndot, LL, LLdot;
  double T, c1, c2, c3, c4, c5, lamp, oamp, ls, os, arg, argdot;
  double funarg[12];
  int j;
  static double dpsiz, depsz, dpsidotz, depsdotz, jedz;

  /* 1980 IAU nutation coefficients */
  static double nc[106][9] = {
    {-171996., -174.2, 92025., 8.9,  0.,  0.,  0.,  0.,  1.},
```

```
{   2062.,    0.2,   -895., 0.5,   0.,   0.,   0.,   0.,   2.},
{     46.,    0.,    -24.,   0.,  -2.,   0.,   2.,   0.,   1.},
{     11.,    0.,      0.,   0.,   2.,   0.,  -2.,   0.,   0.},
{     -3.,    0.,      1.,   0.,  -2.,   0.,   2.,   0.,   2.},
{     -3.,    0.,      0.,   0.,   1.,  -1.,   0.,  -1.,   0.},
{     -2.,    0.,      1.,   0.,   0.,  -2.,   2.,  -2.,   1.},
{      1.,    0.,      0.,   0.,   2.,   0.,  -2.,   0.,   1.},
{ -13187.,   -1.6,  5736.,  -3.1,  0.,   0.,   2.,  -2.,   2.},
{   1426.,   -3.4,    54.,  -0.1,  0.,   1.,   0.,   0.,   0.},
{   -517.,    1.2,   224.,  -0.6,  0.,   1.,   2.,  -2.,   2.},
{    217.,   -0.5,   -95.,   0.3,  0.,  -1.,   2.,  -2.,   2.},
{    129.,    0.1,   -70.,   0.,   0.,   0.,   2.,  -2.,   1.},
{     48.,    0.,      1.,   0.,   2.,   0.,   0.,  -2.,   0.},
{    -22.,    0.,      0.,   0.,   0.,   0.,   2.,  -2.,   0.},
{     17.,   -0.1,     0.,   0.,   0.,   2.,   0.,   0.,   0.},
{    -15.,    0.,      9.,   0.,   0.,   1.,   0.,   0.,   1.},
{    -16.,    0.1,     7.,   0.,   0.,   2.,   2.,  -2.,   2.},
{    -12.,    0.,      6.,   0.,   0.,  -1.,   0.,   0.,   1.},
{     -6.,    0.,      3.,   0.,  -2.,   0.,   0.,   2.,   1.},
{     -5.,    0.,      3.,   0.,   0.,  -1.,   2.,  -2.,   1.},
{      4.,    0.,     -2.,   0.,   2.,   0.,   0.,  -2.,   1.},
{      4.,    0.,     -2.,   0.,   0.,   1.,   2.,  -2.,   1.},
{     -4.,    0.,      0.,   0.,   1.,   0.,   0.,  -1.,   0.},
{      1.,    0.,      0.,   0.,   2.,   1.,   0.,  -2.,   0.},
{      1.,    0.,      0.,   0.,   0.,   0.,  -2.,   2.,   1.},
{     -1.,    0.,      0.,   0.,   0.,   1.,  -2.,   2.,   0.},
{      1.,    0.,      0.,   0.,   0.,   1.,   0.,   0.,   2.},
{      1.,    0.,      0.,   0.,  -1.,   0.,   0.,   1.,   1.},
{     -1.,    0.,      0.,   0.,   0.,   1.,   2.,  -2.,   0.},
{  -2274.,   -0.2,   977.,  -0.5,  0.,   0.,   2.,   0.,   2.},
{    712.,    0.1,    -7.,   0.,   1.,   0.,   0.,   0.,   0.},
{   -386.,   -0.4,   200.,   0.,   0.,   0.,   2.,   0.,   1.},
{   -301.,    0.,    129.,  -0.1,  1.,   0.,   2.,   0.,   2.},
{   -158.,    0.,     -1.,   0.,   1.,   0.,   0.,  -2.,   0.},
{    123.,    0.,    -53.,   0.,  -1.,   0.,   2.,   0.,   2.},
{     63.,    0.,     -2.,   0.,   0.,   0.,   2.,   0.,   0.},
{     63.,    0.1,   -33.,   0.,   1.,   0.,   0.,   0.,   1.},
{    -58.,   -0.1,    32.,   0.,  -1.,   0.,   0.,   0.,   1.},
{    -59.,    0.,     26.,   0.,  -1.,   0.,   2.,   2.,   2.},
{    -51.,    0.,     27.,   0.,   1.,   0.,   2.,   0.,   1.},
{    -38.,    0.,     16.,   0.,   0.,   0.,   2.,   2.,   2.},
{     29.,    0.,     -1.,   0.,   2.,   0.,   0.,   0.,   0.},
{     29.,    0.,    -12.,   0.,   1.,   0.,   2.,  -2.,   2.},
{    -31.,    0.,     13.,   0.,   2.,   0.,   2.,   0.,   2.},
{     26.,    0.,     -1.,   0.,   0.,   0.,   2.,   0.,   0.},
{     21.,    0.,    -10.,   0.,  -1.,   0.,   2.,   0.,   1.},
{     16.,    0.,     -8.,   0.,  -1.,   0.,   0.,   2.,   1.},
{    -13.,    0.,      7.,   0.,   1.,   0.,   0.,  -2.,   1.},
{    -10.,    0.,      5.,   0.,  -1.,   0.,   2.,   2.,   1.},
{     -7.,    0.,      0.,   0.,   1.,   1.,   0.,  -2.,   0.},
{      7.,    0.,     -3.,   0.,   0.,   1.,   2.,   0.,   2.},
{     -7.,    0.,      3.,   0.,   0.,  -1.,   2.,   0.,   2.},
{     -8.,    0.,      3.,   0.,   1.,   0.,   2.,   2.,   2.},
{      6.,    0.,      0.,   0.,   1.,   0.,   0.,   2.,   0.},
{      6.,    0.,     -3.,   0.,   2.,   0.,   2.,  -2.,   2.},
{     -6.,    0.,      3.,   0.,   0.,   0.,   0.,   2.,   1.},
{     -7.,    0.,      3.,   0.,   0.,   0.,   2.,   2.,   1.},
{      6.,    0.,     -3.,   0.,   1.,   0.,   2.,  -2.,   1.},
{     -5.,    0.,      3.,   0.,   0.,   0.,   0.,  -2.,   1.},
{      5.,    0.,      0.,   0.,   1.,  -1.,   0.,   0.,   0.},
{     -5.,    0.,      3.,   0.,   2.,   0.,   2.,   0.,   1.},
{     -4.,    0.,      0.,   0.,   0.,   1.,   0.,  -2.,   0.},
{      4.,    0.,      0.,   0.,   1.,   0.,  -2.,   0.,   0.},
{     -4.,    0.,      0.,   0.,   0.,   0.,   0.,   1.,   0.},
{     -3.,    0.,      0.,   0.,   1.,   1.,   0.,   0.,   0.},
{      3.,    0.,      0.,   0.,   1.,   0.,   2.,   0.,   0.},
{     -3.,    0.,      1.,   0.,   1.,  -1.,   2.,   0.,   2.},
{     -3.,    0.,      1.,   0.,  -1.,  -1.,   2.,   2.,   2.},
{     -2.,    0.,      1.,   0.,  -2.,   0.,   0.,   0.,   1.},
{     -3.,    0.,      1.,   0.,   3.,   0.,   2.,   0.,   2.},
```

```c
	{	-3.,	0.,	1.,	0., 0.,-1., 2., 2., 2.},
	{	2.,	0.,	-1.,	0., 1., 1., 2., 0., 2.},
	{	-2.,	0.,	1.,	0.,-1., 0., 2.,-2., 1.},
	{	2.,	0.,	-1.,	0., 2., 0., 0., 0., 1.},
	{	-2.,	0.,	1.,	0., 1., 0., 0., 0., 2.},
	{	2.,	0.,	0.,	0., 3., 0., 0., 0., 0.},
	{	2.,	0.,	-1.,	0., 0., 0., 2., 1., 2.},
	{	1.,	0.,	-1.,	0.,-1., 0., 0., 0., 2.},
	{	-1.,	0.,	0.,	0., 1., 0., 0.,-4., 0.},
	{	1.,	0.,	-1.,	0.,-2., 0., 2., 2., 2.},
	{	-2.,	0.,	1.,	0.,-1., 0., 2., 4., 2.},
	{	-1.,	0.,	0.,	0., 2., 0., 0.,-4., 0.},
	{	1.,	0.,	-1.,	0., 1., 1., 2.,-2., 2.},
	{	-1.,	0.,	1.,	0., 1., 0., 2., 2., 1.},
	{	-1.,	0.,	1.,	0.,-2., 0., 2., 4., 2.},
	{	1.,	0.,	0.,	0.,-1., 0., 4., 0., 2.},
	{	1.,	0.,	0.,	0., 1.,-1., 0.,-2., 0.},
	{	1.,	0.,	-1.,	0., 2., 0., 2.,-2., 1.},
	{	-1.,	0.,	0.,	0., 2., 0., 2., 2., 2.},
	{	-1.,	0.,	0.,	0., 1., 0., 0., 2., 1.},
	{	1.,	0.,	0.,	0., 0., 0., 4.,-2., 2.},
	{	1.,	0.,	0.,	0., 3., 0., 2.,-2., 2.},
	{	-1.,	0.,	0.,	0., 1., 0., 2.,-2., 0.},
	{	1.,	0.,	0.,	0., 0., 1., 2., 0., 1.},
	{	1.,	0.,	0.,	0.,-1.,-1., 0., 2., 1.},
	{	-1.,	0.,	0.,	0., 0., 0.,-2., 0., 1.},
	{	-1.,	0.,	0.,	0., 0., 0., 2.,-1., 2.},
	{	-1.,	0.,	0.,	0., 0., 1., 0., 2., 0.},
	{	-1.,	0.,	0.,	0., 1., 0.,-2.,-2., 0.},
	{	-1.,	0.,	0.,	0., 0.,-1., 2., 0., 1.},
	{	-1.,	0.,	0.,	0., 1., 1., 0.,-2., 1.},
	{	-1.,	0.,	0.,	0., 1., 0.,-2., 2., 0.},
	{	1.,	0.,	0.,	0., 2., 0., 2., 2., 0.},
	{	-1.,	0.,	0.,	0., 0., 0., 2., 4., 2.},
	{	1.,	0.,	0.,	0., 0., 1., 0., 1., 0.}
};

if (jedz != jed) {
  jedz = jed;

  T = (jed - J2000) / JulCty;

  FunArgIAU(jed, funarg);
  L = funarg[0];
  Ldot = funarg[6];
  LP = funarg[1];
  LPdot = funarg[7];
  F   = funarg[2];
  Fdot  = funarg[8];
  D   = funarg[3];
  Ddot  = funarg[9];
  N   = funarg[4];
  Ndot  = funarg[10];
  LL = funarg[5];
  LLdot = funarg[11];

  /* evaluate the series */
  dpsiz = 0.;   /* initialize to zero */
  depsz = 0.;
  dpsidotz = 0.;
  depsdotz = 0.;
  for (j=0; j<106; j++) {
    lamp = nc[j][0];
    oamp = nc[j][2];
    ls   = nc[j][1];
    os   = nc[j][3];
    c1   = nc[j][4];
```

```
    c2    = nc[j][5];
    c3    = nc[j][6];
    c4    = nc[j][7];
    c5    = nc[j][8];
    arg   = c1 * L + c2 * LP + c3 * F + c4 * D + c5 * N;
    arg   = amodulo(arg, TWOPI);
    dpsiz += (lamp + ls * T) * sin(arg);
    depsz += (oamp + os * T) * cos(arg);
    argdot = c1 * Ldot + c2 * LPdot + c3 * Fdot + c4 * Ddot + c5 * Ndot;
    argdot = amodulo(argdot, TWOPI);
    dpsidotz += (lamp + ls * T) * argdot * cos(arg) +
      ls * sin(arg) / JulCty;
    depsdotz -= (oamp + os * T) * argdot * sin(arg) +
      os * cos(arg) / JulCty;
  }

  /* normalize and convert units */
  dpsiz *= 0.0001 * A2R;
  depsz *= 0.0001 * A2R;
  dpsidotz *= 0.0001 * A2R;
  depsdotz *= 0.0001 * A2R;
  }

  *dpsi = dpsiz;
  *deps = depsz;
  *dpsidot = dpsidotz;
  *depsdot = depsdotz;
}

/************************************************************************
Name:     Obliquity
Purpose:  Function to compute the mean obliquity of the ecliptic
          and its derivative using Lieske's formula.
Inputs:   jed1 - Initial JED on the TDB scale.
          jed2 - Final JED on the TDB scale.
          m    - 0 for mean obliquity,
                 1 for true obliquity.
Outputs:  obl    - Obliquity of the ecliptic in radians.
          obldot - Derivative in radians/day.
Returns:  Nothing.
Status:   Finished.
Errors:   None known.
*************************************************************************/
void Obliquity(double jed1, double jed2, int m, double *obl,
  double *obldot) {

  double t1, t2, e0, e1, e2, e3, e4, e5, e6, epsbar;
  double dpsi, deps, dpsidot, depsdot;

  t1 = (jed1 - J2000) / JulCty;
  t2 = (jed2 - jed1) / JulCty;

  e0 = 84381.448;
  e1 =    -46.815;
  e2 =     -0.00059;
  e3 =      0.001813;
  epsbar = e0 + e1 * t1 + e2 * t1 * t1 + e3 * t1 * t1 * t1;
  e1 = -46.815;
  e2 =   -0.00117;
  e3 =    0.005439;
  e4 =   -0.00059;
  e5 =    0.005439;
  e6 =    0.001813;
  *obl = epsbar + (e1 + t1 * (e2 + t1 * e3)) * t2
    + (e4 + e5 * t1) * t2 * t2
    + e6 * t2 * t2 * t2;
  *obldot = e1 + t1 * (e2 + t1 * e3)
```

```
      + 2.0 * (e4 + e5 * t1) * t2
      + 3.0 * e6 * t2 * t2;

   if (m == 1) {
      /* need true obliquity */
      GetDpsiDeps(jed2, &dpsi, &deps, &dpsidot, &depsdot);
      /* Unit conversion is needed because obl is  */
      /* in arc seconds, nutations are in radians. */
      *obl = *obl + deps * R2A;
      *obldot = *obldot + depsdot * R2A;
   }

   /* convert to radians and radians/day */
   *obl = *obl * A2R;
   *obldot = *obldot * A2R / JulCty;
}

/**********************************************************************
Name:    pleph
Purpose: Function that reads the JPL planetary ephemeris and gives the
         position and velocity of the point 'targ' with respect to 'cent'.
Inputs:  jd   - JED at which interpolation is wanted.
         targ - Number of target point.
         cent - Number of center point.
         The numbering convention for 'targ' and 'cent' is:
         1 = Mercury              8 = Neptune
         2 = Venus                9 = Pluto
         3 = Earth               10 = Moon
         4 = Mars                11 = Sun
         5 = Jupiter             12 = SSB
         6 = Saturn              13 = EMB
         7 = Uranus              14 = Nutations  (if present)
         15 = Librations (if present)
         If nutations are wanted, set targ = 14. For librations,
         set targ = 15. 'cent' will be ignored on either call.
Outputs: rrd[]  - 6 element array containing the state vector of 'targ'
                  relative to 'cent'. The units are AU and AU/DAY. For
                  librations the units are RAD and RAD/DAY. For
                  nutations the first 4 elements of RRD[] are set to
                  nutations and rates, in RAD and RAD/DAY.
         inside - TRUE if 'jd' is within the ephemeris time span.
                  If not, 'inside' is set to FALSE.
Returns: Nothing.
Status:  Finished.
Errors:  None known.
**********************************************************************/
void pleph(double jd, int targ, int cent, double *rrd, int *inside) {

   int i;
   static double fac;
   static int nemb, ipv, ncmp, lme;
   static int pfirst;
   static double jdtot;
   static double pv[6][13]={0.};
   static double embf[2], ve[2], jed[2];
   static int LList[12], LLst[13];
   static int L[2], tc[2];

   /*
       pv[] is a zero-offset 6x13 matrix. The column number (0-12) specifies
       a body number. The row number (0-5) specifies a component of the
       body's state vector x,y,z,xdot,ydot,zdot in that order.
   */

   /* necessary for zero-offset arrays */
   targ = targ - 1;
   cent = cent - 1;
   /*
```

```
       From here on, 'targ' and 'cent' are one less than their
       calling values.
*/

/* 1st time in, be sure ephemeris is initialized */
if (!pfirst) {
  pfirst = TRUE;
  ipv = 2; /* we want pos and vel */
  ephopn("");
  ve[0] = 1.0/(1.0+emrat);
  ve[1] = emrat*ve[0];

  jed[0] = 0.0;
  jed[1] = 0.0;

  embf[0] = -1.0;
  embf[1] =  1.0;
  for (i=0; i<12; i++) {
    LList[i] = 0;
  }
  L[0] = 0;
  L[1] = 0;
  tc[0] = 0;
  tc[1] = 0;
  for (i=0; i<13; i++) {
    LLst[i] = i;
    if (i ==  2) LLst[i] = 9;
    if (i == 11) LLst[i] = 10;
    if (i == 12) LLst[i] = 2;
  }
  fac = 0.0;
  nemb = 1;
}

/* Initialize jed[] for state() and set up component count */
jed[0] = jd;
jed[1] = 0.0;

jdtot = jed[0] + jed[1];

if ((jdtot >= SS[0]) && (jdtot <= SS[1])) {
  *inside = TRUE;
} else {
  *inside = FALSE;
  return;
}

ncmp = 3*ipv; /* total number of components */

/* check for nutation call */
if (targ == 13) {
  if (ipt[1][11] > 0) {
    LList[10] = ipv;
    state(jed, LList, pv, rrd);
    LList[10] = 0;
    return;
  } else {
    LogMsg(stderr, "pleph: no nutations on the ephemeris file.");
    exit(1);
  }
}

/* check for librations */
if (targ == 14) {
  if (lpt[1] > 0) {
    LList[11] = ipv;
    state(jed, LList, pv, rrd);
```

```
      LList[11] = 0;
      for (i=0; i<ncmp; i++) {
        rrd[i] = pv[i][10];
      }
      return;
    } else {
      LogMsg(stderr, "pleph: no librations on the ephemeris file.");
      exit(1);
    }
  }

  /* check for targ = cent */
  if (targ == cent) {
    for (i=0; i<ncmp; i++) {
      rrd[i] = 0.0;
    }
    return;
  }

  /* force barycentric output by state() */
  bsav = bary;
  bary = TRUE;

  /* set up proper entries in LList[] array for state() call */
  tc[0] = targ;
  tc[1] = cent;
  lme = 0;

  for (i=0; i<2; i++) {
    L[i] = LLst[tc[i]];
    if (L[i] < 10) LList[L[i]] = ipv;
    if (tc[i] == 2) {
      lme = 2;
      fac = -ve[0];
    }
    else if (tc[i] == 9) {
      lme = 9;
      fac = ve[1];
    }
    else if (tc[i] == 12) {
      nemb = i;
    }
  }

  if ((LList[9] == ipv) && (L[0] != L[1])) LList[2] = ipv - LList[2];

  /* make call to state() */
  state(jed, LList, pv, rrd);

  /* case: Earth-to-Moon */
  if ((targ == 9) && (cent == 2)) {
    for (i=0; i<ncmp; i++) {
      rrd[i] = pv[i][9];
    }

  /* case: Moon-to-Earth */
  }
  else if ((targ == 2) && (cent == 9)) {
    for (i=0; i<ncmp; i++) {
      rrd[i] = -pv[i][9];
    }

  /* case: EMB-to-Moon or -Earth */
  }
  else if ((targ == 12 || cent == 12) && LList[9] == ipv) {
    for (i=0; i<ncmp; i++) {
      rrd[i] = pv[i][9]*fac*embf[nemb];
```

```
    }

    /* otherwise, get Earth or Moon vector and then get output vector */
  } else {
    for (i=0; i<ncmp; i++) {
      pv[i][10] = pvsun[i];
      pv[i][12] = pv[i][2];
      if (lme > 0) pv[i][lme] = pv[i][2]+fac*pv[i][9];
      rrd[i] = pv[i][targ] - pv[i][cent];
    }
  }

  /* clear state() body array and restore barycenter flag */
  LList[2] = 0;
  LList[L[0]] = 0;
  LList[L[1]] = 0;
  bary = bsav;
}

/**************************************************************************
Name:     Pol2Rec
Purpose: Function to convert a polar state vector into a cartesian
         state vector.
         NOTE:  THIS ROUTINE EXPECTS THE POLAR VELOCITY VECTOR TO BE
         THE TOTAL VELOCITY CORRECTED FOR THE EFFECT OF LATITUDE.
Inputs:   a[] - Zero-offset polar state vector.
Outputs:  b[] - Zero-offset cartesian state vector.
Returns:  Nothing.
Status:   Finished.
Errors:   None known.
**************************************************************************/
void Pol2Rec(double a[], double b[]) {

  double lambda, beta, R, v_lambda, v_beta, v_r;
  double lambda_dot, beta_dot, r_dot, CosL, SinL, CosB, SinB;

  lambda   = a[0];
  beta     = a[1];
  R        = a[2];
  v_lambda = a[3];
  v_beta   = a[4];
  v_r      = a[5];

  /* separate the angluar derivatives from the total velocity components */
  CosL = cos(lambda);
  SinL = sin(lambda);
  CosB = cos(beta);
  SinB = sin(beta);

  lambda_dot = v_lambda / (R * CosB);
  beta_dot = v_beta / R;
  r_dot = v_r;

  /* position vector components */
  b[0] = R * CosL * CosB;
  b[1] = R * SinL * CosB;
  b[2] = R * SinB;

  /* velocity vector components */
  b[3] = r_dot * CosL * CosB - R * lambda_dot * SinL * CosB -
    R * beta_dot * CosL * SinB;
  b[4] = r_dot * SinL * CosB + R * lambda_dot * CosL * CosB -
    R * beta_dot * SinL * SinB;
  b[5] = r_dot * SinB + R * beta_dot * CosB;
}

/**************************************************************************
Name:     PrecessElements
```

```
Purpose: Subprogram to transform angular orbital elements
         from equinox eqnx1 to equinox eqnx2.
Inputs:  eqnx1   - String containing initial
                   eqninox.  e.g. B1950 or 2415020.5.
         element - Array containing elements
                   referred to eqnx1 as follows:
                   element[0] = inclination.
                   element[1] = long. of asc. node.
                   element[2] = arg. of peri.
         eqnx2   - String containing final
                   eqninox.  e.g. J2000 or 2451545.
Outputs: element[] - Array containing elements referred to eqnx2.
Returns: Nothing.
Status:  Finished.
Errors:  None known.
*********************************************************************/
void PrecessElements(char *eqnx1, double *element, char *eqnx2) {

   double   jd1, jd2, tt, t, tt2, t2, t3, tmp;
   double   SmallPI, LargePI, pa, cosi, sini, sinisinn, sinicosn;
   double   newi, newnode, sindwsini, cosdwsini, dw, newargp;

   ucase(eqnx1);
   ucase(eqnx2);
   if ((eqnx1[0] == 'B') || (eqnx1[0] == 'J')) {
      Epoch2JED(eqnx1, &jd1);
   } else {
      jd1 = atof(eqnx1);
   }

   if ((eqnx2[0] == 'B') || (eqnx2[0] == 'J')) {
      Epoch2JED(eqnx2, &jd2);
   } else {
      jd2 = atof(eqnx2);
   }

   tt = (jd1 - 2451545.0) / 365250.0;
   t = (jd2 - jd1) / 365250.0;
   tt2 = tt * tt;
   t2 = t * t;
   t3 = t2 * t;

   /* Compute precessional quantities */
   SmallPI = (470.029 - 6.603 * tt + 0.598 * tt2) * t +
      (-3.302 + 0.598 * tt) * t2 + 0.06 * t3;
   LargePI = 174.8763838888889 + (32894.789 * tt) / 3600.0 +
      (60.622 * tt2) / 3600.0 + ((-8698.089 - 50.491 * tt) * t) /
      3600.0 + (3.536 * t2) / 3600.0;
   pa = (50290.966 + 222.226 * tt - 0.042 * tt2) * t +
      (111.113 - 0.042 * tt) * t2 - 0.006 * t3;
   SmallPI = SmallPI * A2R;
   LargePI = LargePI * D2R;
   pa = pa * A2R;

   /* Compute new inclination and node */
   cosi = cos(element[0]) * cos(SmallPI) + sin(element[0]) *
      sin(SmallPI) * cos(LargePI - element[1]);

   sinisinn = sin(element[0]) * sin(LargePI - element[1]);
   sinicosn = -sin(SmallPI) * cos(element[0]) + cos(SmallPI) *
      sin(element[0]) * cos(LargePI - element[1]);

   sini = sqrt(sinisinn * sinisinn + sinicosn * sinicosn);
   newi = atan2(sini, cosi);
   if (newi < 0.0)
      newi += TWOPI;
```

```
  tmp = atan2(sinisinn, sinicosn);
  if (tmp < 0.0)
    tmp += TWOPI;
  newnode = pa + LargePI - tmp;
  newnode = amodulo(newnode, TWOPI);

  /* Compute new argument of perihelion */
  sindwsini = sin(SmallPI) * sin(LargePI - element[1]);
  cosdwsini = sin(element[0]) * cos(SmallPI) - cos(element[0]) *
    sin(SmallPI) * cos(LargePI - element[1]);
  dw = atan2(sindwsini, cosdwsini);
  if (dw < 0.0)
    dw += TWOPI;

  newargp = element[2] + dw;
  newargp = amodulo(newargp, TWOPI);

  /* Put new elements in element[] array */
  element[0] = newi;
  element[1] = newnode;
  element[2] = newargp;
}

/******************************************************************
Name:    QRotate
Purpose: Function to perform a matrix rotation of a state vector through
         a given angle about a desired axis.  A right-handed orthogonal
         coordinate system is assumed, and a 6X6 Q-matrix is used.
         NOTE: The vin[] and vout[] can have the same name in
         the calling program.
Inputs:  vin    - Zero-offset input state vector.
         axis   - 1 for x-axis,
                  2 for y-axis,
                  3 for z-axis.
         phi    - Rotation angle in radians.
         phidot - Derivative of phi.
         s      - 0 for inertial to inertial,
                  1 for inertial to rotating.
Outputs: vout[] - Zero-offset transformed state vector.
Returns: Nothing.
Status:  Finished.
Errors:  None known.
******************************************************************/
void QRotate(double vin[], int axis, double phi, double phidot,
  int s, double vout[]) {

  int i;
  double temp[6];
  DMatrix QMatrix;

  QMatrix = createDMatrix(6);

  GetQMatrix(phi, phidot, axis, s, QMatrix);

  for (i=0; i<6; i++) {
    temp[i] = vin[i];
  }

  MatXVec(QMatrix, temp, vout, 6, 6);

  freeDMatrix(QMatrix, 6);
}

/******************************************************************
Name:    RayBend
Purpose: Function to correct an input vector for relativistic light
         deflection due to the Sun's gravity field.
Inputs:  earth_hel[] - Zero-offset heliocentric state vector of Earth.
```

```
             body_geo[]  - Zero-offset geocentric state vector of object.
             body_hel[]  - Zero-offset heliocentric state vector of object.
Outputs: p1[] - Zero-offset geocentric state vector of object
               corrected for light deflection.
Returns: Nothing.
Status:  Finished.
Errors:  None known.
*********************************************************************/
void RayBend(double earth_hel[], double body_geo[], double body_hel[],
  double p1[6]) {

    double ue[3], up[3], uq[3], E[3], Edot[3], P[3], Pdot[3], Q[3], Qdot[3];
    double magE, magP, pdotq, edotp, qdote;
    int i;

    /* extract the pos. portions of the state vectors */
    SplitStateVector(earth_hel, E, Edot);
    SplitStateVector( body_geo, P, Pdot);
    SplitStateVector( body_hel, Q, Qdot);

    /* form unit vectors */
    Uvector(E, ue);
    Uvector(P, up);
    Uvector(Q, uq);

    /* form dot products and other quantities */
    magE = Vecmag(E);
    magP = Vecmag(P);
    Vdot(3, up, uq, &pdotq);
    Vdot(3, ue, up, &edotp);
    Vdot(3, uq, ue, &qdote);

    for (i=0; i<3; i++) {
      p1[i] = up[i] + (MUC / magE) * (pdotq * ue[i] - edotp * uq[i])
        / (1.0 + qdote);
      /* make p1[] a non-unit vector */
      p1[i] = magP * p1[i];
      p1[i+3] = body_geo[i+3];
    }
}


/*********************************************************************
Name:    Rec2Pol
Purpose: Subprogram to convert a cartesian state vector into a
         polar state vector. NOTE: THE POLAR VELOCITY VECTOR IS
         THE TOTAL VELOCITY, CORRECTED FOR THE EFFECT OF LATITUDE.
Inputs:  a[] - Zero-offset cartesian state vector.
Outputs: b[] - Zero-offset polar state vector.
Returns: Nothing.
Status:  Finished.
Errors:  None known.
*********************************************************************/
void Rec2Pol(double a[], double b[]) {

    double x, y, z, x_dot, y_dot, z_dot,
      rho, r, lambda, beta, lambda_dot,
      beta_dot, r_dot;

    x = a[0];
    y = a[1];
    z = a[2];
    x_dot = a[3];
    y_dot = a[4];
    z_dot = a[5];

    rho = sqrt(x * x + y * y);
      r = sqrt(rho * rho + z * z);
```

```
lambda = atan2(y, x);
if (lambda < 0.0)
  lambda += TWOPI;

beta    = atan2(z, rho);
if (beta < 0.0)
  beta += TWOPI;

if (z < 0) {
  beta = beta - TWOPI;
}

if (rho == 0) {
  lambda_dot = 0.0;
  beta_dot = 0.0;
} else {
  lambda_dot = (x*y_dot-y*x_dot) / (rho*rho);
  beta_dot = (z_dot*rho*rho-z*(x*x_dot+y*y_dot))/(r*r*rho);
}

r_dot = (x * x_dot + y * y_dot + z * z_dot) / r;

/* position vector components */
b[0] = lambda;
if (b[0] >= TWOPI)
  b[0] = b[0] - TWOPI;

b[1] = beta;
b[2] = r;
/* total velocity vector components */
b[3] = r * lambda_dot * cos(beta);
b[4] = r * beta_dot;
b[5] = r_dot;
}

/**********************************************************************
Name:     Reduce
Purpose:  Function for reducing source planetary or solar ephemerides
          to apparent, topocentric, virtual, local, or astrometric
          place. The processes are rigorous and include all corrections.
          This function is intended for use with barycentric source
          ephemerides such as DE200.
Inputs:   jed          - Desired time of reduction.
          body         - Body number (99 for stellar reduction).
          place        - 1 for apparent place, 2 for topocentric place,
                         3 for virtual place, 4 for local place,
                         5 for astrometric place.
          StarData[]   - Array containing stellar data.
Outputs:  p3[] - Array containing the requested state vector.
Returns:  Nothing.
Status:   Finished.
Errors:   None known.
**********************************************************************/
void Reduce(double jed, int body, int place, double StarData[],
  double p3[]) {

  int i;
  double Ltime;
  double earth_ssb[6], earth_hel[6], body_geo[6];
  double body_hel[6], obsr_geo[6];
  double eb[6], ebdot[6], p1[6], p2[6];
  double zeta,z,theta,zetadot,zdot,thetadot;
  double dpsi,deps,dpsidot,depsdot;
  double TrueEps,MeanEps,TrueEpsDot,MeanEpsDot;

  if ((body == 3) || (body == 12) || (body == 13) ||
    (body == 14) || (body == 15)) {
```

```
  LogMsg(stderr,
    "Reduce: can't perform reduction for specified body.\n");
  exit(1);
}

/* Earth's barycentric state vector */
GetStateVector(jed, 3, 12, 1, StateVector);
for (i=0; i<6; i++) {
  earth_ssb[i] = StateVector[3-1][12-1][1-1][i];
}

/* Earth's heliocentric state vector */
GetStateVector(jed, 3, 11, 1, StateVector);
for (i=0; i<6; i++) {
  earth_hel[i] = StateVector[3-1][11-1][1-1][i];
}

if ((place == 2) || (place == 4)) {
  /* Compute geocentric state vector of observer */
  GeocenObs(jed, obsr_geo);
  /* Translate origin from geocenter to topocenter */
  for (i=0; i<6; i++) {
    earth_ssb[i] = earth_ssb[i] + obsr_geo[i];
  }
}

/* Compute geo/topocentric state vector of object corrected
for light time. */
LightTime(jed, body, earth_ssb, earth_hel, StarData, body_geo,
  body_hel, &Ltime);

if (place == 5) {
  /* Compute the astrometric place */
  for (i=0; i<6; i++) {
    p3[i] = body_geo[i];
  }
}

if (place < 5) {
  /* Perform correction for relativistic light deflection */
  RayBend(earth_hel, body_geo, body_hel, p1);

  /* Perform correction for aberration */
  SplitStateVector(earth_ssb, eb, ebdot);
  Aberrate(p1, ebdot, p2);

  if (place < 3) {
    /* Correction for precession and nutation from J2000.0 */
    GetPrecessParams(J2000, jed, &zeta, &z, &theta, &zetadot,
      &zdot, &thetadot);
    GetDpsiDeps(jed, &dpsi, &deps, &dpsidot, &depsdot);
    Obliquity(J2000, jed, 0, &MeanEps, &MeanEpsDot);
    Obliquity(J2000, jed, 1, &TrueEps, &TrueEpsDot);

    /* First correct for precession */
    QRotate(p2, 3, -zeta, -zetadot, 1, p3);
    QRotate(p3, 2, theta, thetadot, 1, p3);
    QRotate(p3, 3, -z, -zdot, 1, p3);

    /* Now correct for nutation */
    QRotate(p3, 1, MeanEps, MeanEpsDot, 1, p3);
    QRotate(p3, 3, -dpsi, -dpsidot, 1, p3);
    QRotate(p3, 1, -TrueEps, -TrueEpsDot, 1, p3);
  } else {
    for (i=0; i<6; i++) {
```

```
      p3[i] = p2[i];
    }
  }
}

  return;
}

/*************************************************************************
Name:    Refract
Purpose: Subprogram to correct right ascension and declination
         for atmospheric refraction.
         Reference:  Taff. Computational Spherical Astronomy, pp. 78-80.
Inputs:  ra1   - Uncorrected RA and DEC in radians.
         dec1  - Uncorrected RA and DEC in radians.
         lha   - Local apparent hour angle in radians.
         temp  - Temperature in deg F.
         press - Air pressure in inches of Hg.
Outputs: ra2   - Corrected RA and DEC in radians.
         dec2  - Corrected RA and DEC in radians.
Returns: Nothing.
Status:  Finished.
Errors:  None known.
*************************************************************************/
void Refract(double ra1, double dec1, double lha, double temp,
  double press, double *ra2, double *dec2) {

  double cosz, z, r1, r2, r, tanzr, rr, diff, rlocal, denom;

  cosz = sin(obsr_lat) * sin(dec1) + cos(obsr_lat) * cos(dec1) * cos(lha);
  z = acos(cosz);

  r1 = 58.294 * A2R;
  r2 = -0.0668 * A2R;

  r = 0.0;
  do {
    tanzr = tan(z - r);
    rr = r1 * tanzr + r2 * tanzr * tanzr * tanzr;
    printf("%f\n", rr * R2A);
    diff = fabs(rr - r);
    r = rr;
  } while (diff > 1e-15);

  rlocal = (17.0 * press) * r / (460.0 + temp);

  denom = 1.0 / (cos(dec1) * sin(z));
  *dec2 = dec1 + (rlocal * (sin(obsr_lat) - sin(dec1) * cos(z))) * denom;
  denom = 1.0 / (cos(*dec2) * sin(z));
  *ra2 = ra1 + (rlocal * cos(obsr_lat) * sin(lha)) * denom;
}

/*************************************************************************
Name:    RotMat
Purpose: Function to compute the 3X3 rotation matrix and its partial
         derivative for a rotation about the Ith coordinate axis
         through an angle phi.
Inputs:  axis - 1 for x-axis,
                2 for y-axis,
                3 for z-axis.
         phi  - Rotation angle in radians.
Outputs: r[]  - Zero-offset 3X3 rotation matrix.
         dr[] - Zero-offset 3X3 partial derivative of the matrix r[].
Returns: Nothing.
Status:  Finished.
Errors:  None known.
*************************************************************************/
void RotMat(int axis, double phi, DMatrix r, DMatrix dr) {
```

```
double cosphi, sinphi;

cosphi = cos(phi);
sinphi = sin(phi);

switch (axis) {
  case 1:  /* rotate about x-axis */
    r[0][0] = 1.0;
    r[0][1] = 0.0;
    r[0][2] = 0.0;
    r[1][0] = 0.0;
    r[1][1] =  cosphi;
    r[1][2] =  sinphi;
    r[2][0] = 0.0;
    r[2][1] = -sinphi;
    r[2][2] =  cosphi;
    dr[0][0] = 0.0;
    dr[0][1] = 0.0;
    dr[0][2] = 0.0;
    dr[1][0] = 0.0;
    dr[1][1] = -sinphi;
    dr[1][2] =  cosphi;
    dr[2][0] = 0.0;
    dr[2][1] = -cosphi;
    dr[2][2] = -sinphi;
    break;
  case 2:  /* rotate about y-axis */
    r[0][0] =  cosphi;
    r[0][1] = 0.0;
    r[0][2] = -sinphi;
    r[1][0] = 0.0;
    r[1][1] = 1.0;
    r[1][2] = 0.0;
    r[2][0] =  sinphi;
    r[2][1] = 0.0;
    r[2][2] =  cosphi;
    dr[0][0] = -sinphi;
    dr[0][1] = 0.0;
    dr[0][2] = -cosphi;
    dr[1][0] = 0.0;
    dr[1][1] = 0.0;
    dr[1][2] = 0.0;
    dr[2][0] =  cosphi;
    dr[2][1] = 0.0;
    dr[2][2] = -sinphi;
    break;
  case 3:  /* rotate about z-axis */
    r[0][0] =  cosphi;
    r[0][1] =  sinphi;
    r[0][2] = 0.0;
    r[1][0] = -sinphi;
    r[1][1] =  cosphi;
    r[1][2] = 0.0;
    r[2][0] = 0.0;
    r[2][1] = 0.0;
    r[2][2] = 1.0;
    dr[0][0] = -sinphi;
    dr[0][1] =  cosphi;
    dr[0][2] = 0.0;
    dr[1][0] = -cosphi;
    dr[1][1] = -sinphi;
    dr[1][2] = 0.0;
    dr[2][0] = 0.0;
    dr[2][1] = 0.0;
    dr[2][2] = 0.0;
    break;
```

```
    default:
      LogMsg(stderr,"RotMat: axis not valid.\n");
      exit(1);
  }
}

/***********************************************************************
Name:     RST_Interpolate
Purpose:  Interpolation routine used by RST.
Inputs:   c       - flag
          z0      - The "standard" zenith distance for the object
                    at rise or set.  This quantity has different
                    values for different objects according to the
                    following table:
                    z0 = 90d 50'          Sun.
                    z0 = 90d 34' + s - pi Moon.
                    z0 = 90d 34'          stars and planets.
                    z0 = 108d             astronomical twilight.
                    z0 = 102d       nautical twilight.
                    z0 =  96d            civil twilight.
                    z0 should be given by the program that calls RST.
                    z0 is expressed in radians.
          oldm    - intermediate value
          gast0   - GAST at 0h
          deltat  - TDT-UT1 in seconds of time.
          ra[]    - Array containing the object's apparent right
                    ascension at times jed-1, jed, and jed+1.
          dec[]   - Array containing the object's apparent
                    declination at times jed-1, jed, and jed+1.
          rx, dx  - RA and DEC of object on day x
Outputs:  newm    - intermediate value
Returns:  Nothing.
Status:   Finished.
Errors:   None known.
***********************************************************************/
static void RST_Interpolate(int c, double z0, double oldm, double gast0,
  double deltat, double *ra, double *dec, double r1, double r2, double r3,
  double d1, double d2, double d3, double *newm) {

  double alpha, dm, h, gast, delta, alt, n;

  *newm = oldm;
  do {
    gast = gast0 + 6.300388093 * (*newm);
    gast = amodulo(gast, TWOPI);
    n = *newm + deltat / 86400.0;
    alpha = ra[1] + 0.5 * n * (r1 + r2 + n * r3);
    alpha = amodulo(alpha, TWOPI);
    delta = dec[1] + 0.5 * n * (d1 + d2 + n * d3);
    h = gast + obsr_lon - alpha;
    alt = asin(sin(delta) * sin(obsr_lat) + cos(delta) * cos(obsr_lat) * cos(h));
    if (c == 0) {
      dm = -h / TWOPI;
    } else {
      dm = (alt - PIDIV2 + z0) / (TWOPI * cos(delta) * cos(obsr_lat) * sin(h));
    }
    *newm = (*newm) + dm;
  } while (fabs(dm) >= 1e-15);
}

/***********************************************************************
Name:     RST
Purpose:  Subprogram to compute the times of rise, set, and transit for
          any object given the observer's location and arrays containing
          the APPARENT right ascension and declination of the object for
          three dates centered on the input JED.  The algorithm is
          completely rigorous,  and takes into account atmospheric
          refraction and the object's sidereal motion in the intervals
          between rising, setting, and transiting.  The algorithm is
```

```
      explained in Chapter 42 of Meeus' ASTRONOMICAL FORMULAE FOR
      CALCULATORS. With the appropriate values for z0, this routine
      can also be used to compute the times of civil, nautical, or
      astronomical twilight. Note that the times are on the UT1 scale!
      Reference: Meeus. ASTRONOMICAL FORMULAE FOR CALCULATORS,
      4TH ED., Chapter 42.
Inputs:  jed     - Julian day number at 0h UT1
         ra[]    - Array containing the object's apparent right
                   ascension at times jed-1, jed, and jed+1.
         dec[]   - Array containing the object's apparent
                   declination at times jed-1, jed, and jed+1.
         z0      - The "standard" zenith distance for the object
                   at rise or set. This quantity has different
                   values for different objects according to the
                   following table:
                   z0 = 90d 50'        Sun.
                   z0 = 90d 34' + s - pi Moon.
                   z0 = 90d 34'        stars and planets.
                   z0 = 108d           astronomical twilight.
                   z0 = 102d         nautical twilight.
                   z0 =  96d            civil twilight.
                   z0 should be given by the program that calls RST.
                   z0 is expressed in radians.
         deltat - TDT-UT1 in seconds of time.
Outputs: ris[] - String containing rise time in
                   form hh.mm or an appropriate symbol.
         trn[] - String containing transit time
                   in form hh.mm or an appropriate symbol.
         set[] - String containing set time in
                   form hh.mm or an appropriate symbol.
Returns: Nothing.
Status:  Finished.
Errors:  None known.
*********************************************************************/
void RST(double jed, double *ra, double *dec, double z0, double deltat,
  char *ris, char *trn, char *set) {

  int rsflag, c;
  double h0, cosh0, newm, oldm, m, m0, m1, m2;
  double ristime, settime, trntime, gast0;
  double d1, d2, d3, r1, r2, r3;

  /* Make sure the ra[]'s are in continuous order */
  if ((ra[1] < ra[0]) && (ra[2] > ra[1])) {
    ra[1] = ra[1] + TWOPI;
    ra[2] = ra[2] + TWOPI;
  }
  else if ((ra[1] > ra[0]) && (ra[2] < ra[1])) {
    ra[2] = ra[2] + TWOPI;
  }

  r1 = ra[1] - ra[0];
  r2 = ra[2] - ra[1];
  r3 = r2 - r1;
  d1 = dec[1] - dec[0];
  d2 = dec[2] - dec[1];
  d3 = d2 - d1;

  rsflag = -1;

  cosh0 = (cos(z0) - sin(obsr_lat) * sin(dec[1])) / (cos(obsr_lat) * cos(dec[1]));

  if (cosh0 < -1.0) {
    /* Object is circumpolar */
    strcpy(ris, "***********");
    if ((z0 * R2D) >= 96.0) {
      strcpy(set, "**BRIGHT***");
    } else {
      strcpy(set, "**NO set***");
```

```
      }
      rsflag = 0;
   }
   else if (cosh0 > 1.0) {
      /* Object never rises */
      if ((z0 * R2D) >= 96.0) {
         strcpy(ris, "---DARK----");
      } else {
         strcpy(ris, "--NO RISE--");
      }
      strcpy(set, "-----------");
      rsflag = 0;
   }

   GetGST(jed, 1, &gast0);

   m0 = (ra[1] - obsr_lon - gast0) / TWOPI;
   m0 = amodulo(m0, 1.0);

   if (rsflag) {
      h0 = acos(cosh0);
      h0 = amodulo(h0, PI);
      m1 = m0 - h0 / TWOPI;
      m1 = amodulo(m1, 1.0);
      m2 = m0 + h0 / TWOPI;
      m2 = amodulo(m2, 1.0);

      /* Rising */
      oldm = m1;
      c = 1;
      RST_Interpolate(c, z0, oldm, gast0, deltat, ra, dec, r1,
         r2, r3, d1, d2, d3, &newm);
      m = newm;
      ristime = 24.0 * m;
      if (ristime > 24.0) {
         ristime = ristime - 24.0;
         /* Event occurs the following day */
         FmtDms(ristime, 0, 1, ris);
         strcat(ris, "(f)");
      }
      else if (ristime < 0.0) {
         ristime = ristime + 24.0;
         /* Event occurs the previous day */
         FmtDms(ristime, 0, 1, ris);
         strcat(ris, "(p)");
      } else {
         FmtDms(ristime, 0, 1, ris);
      }

      /* Setting */
      oldm = m2;
      c = 1;
      RST_Interpolate(c, z0, oldm, gast0, deltat, ra, dec, r1,
         r2, r3, d1, d2, d3, &newm);
      m = newm;
      settime = 24.0 * m;
      if (settime > 24.0) {
         settime = settime - 24.0;
         FmtDms(settime, 0, 1, set);
         strcat(set, "(f)");
      }
      else if (settime < 0.0) {
         settime = settime + 24.0;
         FmtDms(settime, 0, 1, set);
         strcat(set, "(p)");
      } else {
         FmtDms(settime, 0, 1, set);
      }
```

```
    }

    /* Transiting */
    oldm = m0;
    c = 0;
    RST_Interpolate(c, z0, oldm, gast0, deltat, ra, dec, r1,
        r2, r3, d1, d2, d3, &newm);
    m = newm;
    trntime = 24.0 * m;
    if (trntime > 24.0) {
      trntime = trntime - 24.0;
      FmtDms(trntime, 0, 1, trn);
      strcat(trn, "(f)");
    }
    else if (trntime < 0.0) {
      trntime = trntime + 24.0;
      FmtDms(trntime, 0, 1, trn);
      strcat(trn, "(p)");
    } else {
      FmtDms(trntime, 0, 1, trn);
    }
}

/*****************************************************************
Name:     split
Purpose:  Function to break a number into an integer part and a
          fractional part. For negative input numbers, 'ipart'
          contains the next more negative number and 'fpart' contains
          a positive fraction.
Inputs:   tt - Number to be split.
Outputs:  ipart - Integer part.
          fpart - Fractional part.
Returns:  Nothing.
Status:   Finished.
Errors:   None known.
*****************************************************************/
void split(double tt, double *ipart, double *fpart) {

    *ipart = floor(tt);
    *fpart = tt - *ipart;

    if ((tt < 0) && (*fpart != 0)) {
      *ipart = *ipart - 1.0;
      *fpart = *fpart + 1.0;
    }
}

/*****************************************************************
Name:     SplitStateVector
Purpose:  Subprogram to split a state vector into its position
          and velocity components.
Inputs:   pv[] - Zero-offset 6-d state vector.
Outputs:  p[] - Zero-offset 3-d position vector.
          v[] - Zero-offset 3-d velocity vector.
Returns:  Nothing.
Status:   Finished.
Errors:   None known.
*****************************************************************/
void SplitStateVector(double pv[], double p[], double v[]) {

    int i;

    for (i=0; i<3; i++) {
      p[i] = pv[i];
      v[i] = pv[i+3];
    }
}

/*****************************************************************
```

```
Name:     state
Purpose:  This subroutine reads and interpolates the JPL planetary
          ephemeris file.
Inputs:   jed[]    - 2 element array containing the JED epoch at which
                     interpolation is wanted. Any combination of
                     jed[0]+jed[1] which falls within the time span on
                     the file is a permissible epoch. For ease in
                     programming, the user may put the entire epoch in
                     jed[0] and set jed[1] = 0. For maximum accuracy,
                     set jed[0] = most recent midnight at or before
                     interpolation epoch and set jed[1] = fractional
                     part of a day elapsed between jed[0] and epoch.
                     As an alternative, it may prove convenient to set
                     jed[0] = some fixed epoch, such as start of
                     integration and jed[1] = elapsed interval between
                     interval between then and epoch.
          LList[] - 12 element array specifying what interpolation
                     is wanted for each of the bodies on the file.
                     LList[i] =0, no interpolation for body i,
                              =1, position only,
                              =2, position and velocity.
                     The designation of the astronomical bodies by i is:
                     i = 0: Mercury,
                       = 1: Venus,
                       = 2: Emb,
                       = 3: Mars,
                       = 4: Jupiter,
                       = 5: Saturn,
                       = 6: Uranus,
                       = 7: Neptune,
                       = 8: Pluto,
                       = 9: Moon (geocentric),
                       =10: Nutations in longitude and obliquity (if present),
                       =11: Lunar librations (if present).
Outputs: pv[]     - 6 x 13 array that will contain requested interpolated
                     quantities. the body specified by LList[i] will have its
                     state in the array starting at pv[0][i]. (On any given
                     call, only those words in pv[] which are affected by the
                     first 10 LList[] entries (and by LList[12] if librations
                     are on the file) are set. The rest of the pv[] array
                     is untouched.) the order of components starting in
                     pv[0][i] is: x,y,z,dx,dy,dz.

                     All output vectors are referenced to the earth mean
                     equator and equinox of epoch. The Moon state is always
                     geocentric; the other nine states are either heliocentric
                     or solar-system barycentric, depending on the setting of
                     common flags (see below).

                     Lunar librations, if in the data file, are put into
                     pv[k][11] if LList[11] is 1 or 2.

          nut[]    - 4-word array that will contain nutations and rates,
                     depending on the setting of LList[10]. The order of
                     quantities in nut[] is:
                     dpsi      (nutation in longitude),
                     depsilon (nutation in obliquity),
                     dpsi dot,
                     depsilon dot.
Returns: Nothing.
Status:  Finished.
Errors:  None known.
*****************************************************************/
void state(double *jed, int LList[], double pv[][13], double *nut) {
/******************************************************************
* Other important variables:                                    *
```

```
*                                                                    *
* km    Logical flag defining physical units of the output          *
*       states. km = TRUE,   units are km and km/sec,               *
*                   = FALSE, units are au and au/day.               *
*       default value = FALSE (km determines time unit              *
*       for nutations and librations. Angle unit is always radians.) *
*                                                                    *
* bary Logical flag defining output center.                         *
*       only the 9 planets are affected.                            *
*                      bary = TRUE  = center is SSB,                 *
*                           = FALSE = center is Sun.                *
*             default value = FALSE.                                *
*                                                                    *
* pvsun[] 6-word array containing the barycentric position and      *
*             velocity of the Sun.                                  *
*********************************************************************/
    static double t[2], jd[4], temp[6];
    static double dumpv[3][2]={{0.,0.},{0.,0.},{0.,0.}};
    static int sfirst;
    static long int nrl;

    static int buff, ncf, na, km = 0;
    static double aufac, s, ipart, fpart;

    int i, j, k, m;
    static long int nr;

    /* 1st time in, get pointer data, etc., from ephemeris file */
    if (!sfirst) {
      sfirst = TRUE;
      aufac = 1.0;
      nrl = 0L;
      ephopn("");
      if (km) {
        t[1] = SS[2]*86400.0;
      } else {
        t[1] = SS[2];
        aufac = 1.0 / au;
      }
    }

    /* main entry point -- check epoch and read right record */
    s = jed[0] - 0.5;
    split(s, &ipart, &fpart);
    jd[0] = ipart;
    jd[1] = fpart;
    split(jed[1], &ipart, &fpart);
    jd[2] = ipart;
    jd[3] = fpart;
    jd[0] = jd[0] + jd[2] + 0.5;
    jd[1] = jd[1] + jd[3];
    split(jd[1], &ipart, &fpart);
    jd[2] = ipart;
    jd[3] = fpart;
    jd[0] = jd[0] + jd[2];

    /* error return of epoch out of range */
    if ((jd[0] < SS[0]) || (jd[0]+jd[3]) > SS[1]) {
      LogMsg(stderr, "state: epoch out of range.\n");
      exit(1);
    }

    /* 'nr' is the byte index of the first coefficient */
    nr = (long) (floor((jd[0]-SS[0])/SS[2]));
    nr = LengthOfHeader + nr * BlockLength;
```

```
/* use previous block if necessary */
if (jd[0] == SS[1])
  nr = nr - BlockLength;
if (nr < 1L) {
  LogMsg(stderr, "state: block not present.\n");
  exit(1);
}

/* calculate relative time in interval (0 <= t[0] <= 1) */
t[0] = ((jd[0]-(((double)nr - (double)(LengthOfHeader))/(double)BlockLength
  * SS[2] + SS[0])) + jd[3]) / SS[2];
if (t[0] < 0.0)
  t[0] = t[0]+ 1.0;

/* read correct record if not in core */
if (nr != nrl) {
  nrl = nr;
  if (fseek(fpBinaryFile, (long) (nr), 0) != 0) {
    LogMsg(stderr, "state: fseek() failed.\n");
    exit(1);
  }
  k = 0;
  do {
    if (k < ncoeff) {
      fread(&tmpDouble, sizeof(double), 1, fpBinaryFile);
      convert_little_endian((char *) &tmpDouble, sizeof(double));
      db[k] = (double) tmpDouble;
    }
    k++;
  } while (!feof(fpBinaryFile) && k <= ncoeff);
}

/* interpolate SSBARY Sun */
buff = ipt[0][10]-1; /* location of first coeff */
ncf  = ipt[1][10]; /* number of coeffs per component */
na   = ipt[2][10]; /* number of sets of coeffs per 32day interval */

interp(buff, t, ncf, 3, na, 2, dumpv);

k = 0;
for (j=0; j<2; j++) {
  for (i=0; i<3; i++) {
    pvsun[k] = dumpv[i][j]*aufac;
    k++;
  }
}

/* check and interpolate whichever bodies are requested */
for (i=0; i<10; i++) {
  if (LList[i] <= 0)
    continue;
  if (ipt[1][i] <= 0) {
    errprt(i ,"th body requested - not on file.\n");
  }
  buff = ipt[0][i]-1; /* location of first coeff */
  ncf  = ipt[1][i]; /* number of coeffs per component */
  na   = ipt[2][i]; /* number of sets of coeffs per 32day interval */

  interp(buff, t, ncf, 3, na, LList[i], dumpv);

  /* need to re-map dumpv[1..3][1..2] --> temp[1..6] */
  k = 0;
  for (j=0; j<2; j++) {
    for (m=0; m<3; m++) {
      temp[k] = dumpv[m][j];
      k++;
    }
```

```
    }

    for (j=0; j<(LList[i]*3); j++) {
      if ((i <= 8) && (!bary)) {
        pv[j][i] = temp[j]*aufac-pvsun[j];
      } else {
        pv[j][i] = temp[j]*aufac;
      }
    }
  }

  /* do nutations if requested and if on file */
  if ((LList[10] > 0) && (ipt[1][11] > 0)) {
    buff = ipt[0][11]-1; /* location of first coeff */
    ncf  = ipt[1][11]; /* number of coeffs per component */
    na   = ipt[2][11]; /* number of sets of coeffs per 32day interval */

    interp(buff, t, ncf, 2, na, LList[10], dumpv);

    /* need to re-map dumpv(1:3,1:2) --> temp(1:6) */
    k = 0;
    for (j=0; j<2; j++) {
      for (m=0; m<2; m++) {
        nut[k] = dumpv[m][j];
        k++;
      }
    }
    nut[4] = 0.0;
    nut[5] = 0.0;
  }

  /* get librations if requested and if on file */
  if ((lpt[1] > 0) && (LList[11] > 0)) {
    buff = lpt[0]-1; /* location of first coeff */
    ncf  = lpt[1]; /* number of coeffs per component */
    na   = lpt[2]; /* number of sets of coeffs per 32day interval */

    interp(buff, t, ncf, 3, na, LList[11], dumpv);

    pv[0][10] = dumpv[0][0];
    pv[1][10] = dumpv[1][0];
    pv[2][10] = dumpv[2][0];
    pv[3][10] = dumpv[0][1];
    pv[4][10] = dumpv[1][1];
    pv[5][10] = dumpv[2][1];
  }
}

/**********************************************************************
Name:     Stat2Elem
Purpose:  Subprogram to transform the components of a state vector into
          the universal orbital element set at a given time.
          Reference: Mansfield. 1986. AIAA Paper 86-2269-CP.
Inputs:   posvel[] - State vector.
          mu       - Gravitational const.
          jed      - Time.
Outputs:  uelement[] - Array of universal elements:
                       uelement[0] = q.
                       uelement[1] = e.
                       uelement[2] = i.
                       uelement[3] = node.
                       uelement[4] = arg.peri.
                       uelement[5] = T.
Returns:  Nothing.
Status:   Finished.
Errors:   None known.
```

```
*********************************************************************/
void Stat2Elem(double *posvel, double mu, double jed, double *uelement) {

    int i;
    double r[3], rdot[3], L[3], wvec[3], u[3], v[3], pvec[3], qvec[3];
    double magr, magL, p, vsquared, alpha, chi, psi, sini, cosi, sinn, cosn;
    double rnudot, rrdot, magrdot, esinnu, ecosnu, sinnu, cosnu;
    double z, w, h, s, x, c3, tspp;

    /* Get pos. and vel. vectors from state vector */
    r[0] = posvel[0];
    r[1] = posvel[1];
    r[2] = posvel[2];
    rdot[0] = posvel[3];
    rdot[1] = posvel[4];
    rdot[2] = posvel[5];

    /* Compute magr */
    magr = Vecmag(r);

    /* Compute angular momentum vector */
    Vcross(r, rdot, L);

    /* Compute magL */
    magL = Vecmag(L);

    /* Compute wvec[] */
    Uvector(L, wvec);

    /* Compute u[] */
    Uvector(r, u);

    /* Compute v[] */
    Vcross(wvec, u, v);

    /* Compute semilatus rectum */
    p = magL * magL / mu;

    /* Compute square of velocity */
    Vdot(3, rdot, rdot, &vsquared);

    /* Compute alpha */
    alpha = 2.0 * mu / magr - vsquared;

    /* Compute eccentricity */
    uelement[1] = sqrt(1.0 - alpha * magL * magL / (mu * mu));

    /* Compute perihelion distance */
    uelement[0] = p / (1.0 + uelement[1]);

    /* Compute node and inclination */
    /* First compute chi and psi */
    chi = wvec[0] / (1.0 + wvec[2]);
    psi = -wvec[1] / (1.0 + wvec[2]);
    /* Now get inclination */
    sini = 2.0 * sqrt(chi * chi + psi * psi) / (1.0 + chi * chi + psi * psi);
    cosi = (1.0 - chi * chi - psi * psi) / (1.0 + chi * chi + psi * psi);
    uelement[2] = atan2(sini, cosi);
    if (uelement[2] < 0.0)
        uelement[2] += TWOPI;

    /* Now get node */
    sinn = chi / sqrt(chi * chi + psi * psi);
    cosn = psi / sqrt(chi * chi + psi * psi);
    uelement[3] = atan2(sinn, cosn);
    if (uelement[3] < 0.0)
```

```
      uelement[3] += TWOPI;

   /* Compute arg. peri. */
   /* Compute rnudot */
   Vdot(3, rdot, v, &rnudot);
   /* Compute magrdot */
   Vdot(3, r, rdot, &rrdot);
   magrdot = rrdot / magr;
   esinnu = magrdot * sqrt(p / mu);
   ecosnu = rnudot * sqrt(p / mu) - 1.0;
   /* Proceed to compute arg. peri. */
   z = esinnu / (uelement[1] + ecosnu);
   sinnu = 2.0 * z / (1.0 + z * z);
   cosnu = (1.0 - z * z) / (1.0 + z * z);
   /* Get the pvec[] and qvec[] vectors */
   for (i = 0; i < 3; i++) {
     pvec[i] = u[i] * cosnu - v[i] * sinnu;
     qvec[i] = u[i] * sinnu + v[i] * cosnu;
   }

   /* Finally compute arg. peri. */
   uelement[4] = atan2(pvec[2], qvec[2]);
   if (uelement[4] < 0.0)
     uelement[4] += TWOPI;

   /* Compute time of peri. passage */
   w = sqrt(uelement[0] / (mu * (1.0 + uelement[1]))) * z;
   h = alpha * w * w;
   s = 2.0 * ((((((h / 13.0 - 1.0 / 11.0) * h + 1.0 / 9.0) * h - 1.0 / 7.0)
       * h + 1.0 / 5.0) * h - 1.0 / 3.0) * h + 1.0) * w;
   /* Compute Stumpff functions */
   x = alpha * s * s;
   c3 = StumpffN(x, 3);
   tspp = uelement[0] * s + mu * uelement[1] * s * s * s * c3;
   uelement[5] = jed - tspp;
}
/*************************************************************************
Name:     StumpffN
Purpose:  Function to compute the nth order Stumpff function for any x.
          Reference: Danby. FUN, pp. 172-174.
Inputs:   x        - Argument.
          Norder - Order desired.
Outputs: None.
Returns: nth order Stumpff function.
Status:  Finished.
Errors:  None known.
*************************************************************************/
double StumpffN(double x, int Norder) {

   int n = 0;
   double a, b, c0, c1, c2, c3;

   do {
     n++;
     x = x / 4.0;
   } while (fabs(x) > 0.1);

   a = (1.0 - x * (1.0 - x / 182.0) / 132.0);
   b = (1.0 - x * (1.0 - x * a / 90.0) / 56.0);
   c2 = (1.0 - x * (1.0 - x * b / 30.0) / 12.0) / 2.0;
   a = (1.0 - x * (1.0 - x / 210.0) / 156.0);
   b = (1.0 - x * (1.0 - x * a / 110.0) / 72.0);
   c3 = (1.0 - x * (1.0 - x * b / 42.0)/ 20.0) / 6.0;

   c1 = 1.0 - x * c3;
   c0 = 1.0 - x * c2;
```

```
  do {
    n--;
    c3 = (c2 + c0 * c3) / 4.0;
    c2 = c1 * c1 / 2.0;
    c1 = c0 * c1;
    c0 = 2.0 * c0 * c0 - 1.0;
    x = x * 4.0;
  } while (n > 0);

  switch (Norder) {
    case 0:
      return (c0);
      case 1:
      return (c1);
    case 2:
      return (c2);
      case 3:
      return (c3);
    default:
      LogMsg(stderr, "StumpffN: Norder not 1, 2, or 3\n");
      exit(1);
  }

  return(-999);
}

/*************************************************************************
Name:     Transpose
Purpose: Function to compute the transpose of a matrix.
Inputs:  a[][] - Zero-offset matrix a (n rows by n columns).
Outputs: b[][] - Zero-offset matrix transpose (n rows by n columns).
Returns: Nothing.
Status:  Finished.
Errors:  None known.
*************************************************************************/
void Transpose(DMatrix a, DMatrix b, int n) {

  int i, j;

  for (i=0; i<n; i++) {
    for (j=0; j<n; j++) {
      b[i][j] = a[j][i];
    }
  }
}

/*************************************************************************
Name:     Uvector
Purpose: Unit vector subroutine.
Inputs:  a[] - Zero-offset column vector (3 rows by 1 column).
Outputs: unita[] - Zero-offset unit vector (3 rows by 1 column).
Returns: Nothing.
Status:  Finished.
Errors:  None known.
*************************************************************************/
void Uvector(double a[], double unita[]) {

  double maga;
  int i;

  maga = sqrt(a[0]*a[0] + a[1]*a[1] + a[2]*a[2]);
  for (i=0; i<3; i++) {
    if (maga != 0) {
      unita[i] = a[i]/maga;
    } else {
      unita[i] = 0.0;
    }
  }
```

```
}

/*********************************************************************
Name:     Vcross
Purpose: Vector cross product subroutine.
Inputs:  a - Zero-offset vector a (3 rows by 1 column).
         b - Zero-offset vector b (3 rows by 1 column).
Outputs: acrossb - a X b (3 rows by 1 column).
Returns: Nothing.
Status:  Finished.
Errors:  None known.
*********************************************************************/
void Vcross(double a[], double b[], double acrossb[]) {

    acrossb[0] = a[1] * b[2] - a[2] * b[1];
    acrossb[1] = a[2] * b[0] - a[0] * b[2];
    acrossb[2] = a[0] * b[1] - a[1] * b[0];
}

/*********************************************************************
Name:     Vdot
Purpose: Vector dot product function.
Inputs:  n  - Number of rows.
         a[] - Zero-offset column vector with N rows.
         b[] - Zero-offset column vector with N rows.
Outputs: adotb - Dot product of a and b.
Returns: Nothing.
Status:  Finished.
Errors:  None known.
*********************************************************************/
void Vdot(int n, double a[], double b[], double *adotb) {

    int i;

    *adotb = 0.0;
    for (i = 0; i<n; i++) {
        *adotb += a[i] * b[i];
    }
}

/*********************************************************************
Name:     Vecmag
Purpose: Vector magnitude function.
Inputs:  a[] - Zero-offset column vector (3 rows by 1 column).
Outputs: None.
Returns: Magnitude of vector.
Status:  Finished.
Errors:  None known.
*********************************************************************/
double Vecmag (double a[]) {

    double x;

    x = sqrt(a[0] * a[0] + a[1] * a[1] + a[2] * a[2]);

    return (x);
}

/* End Of File - astrolib.c ********************************/
```

A.7 COORDS.C

```
/*********************************************************************
Project:  coords
Filename: coords.c
Author:   Joe Heafner.
Purpose:  Example driver for Eq2Ecl and Eq2Hor.
*********************************************************************/
```

```c
/* Header Files ***************************************************/
#include <stdio.h>
#include <stdlib.h>
#include <math.h>
#include "astrolib.h"

/****************************************************************
Name:    main
Purpose: Main routine for coords.
Inputs:  None.
Outputs: None.
Returns: 0 if execution successful.
Status:  Finished.
Errors:  None known.
****************************************************************/
int main(void) {

  char line[1024];
  int   Which;
  double  Alpha, Delta, LAST, Altitude, Azimuth;
  double  Lambda, Beta, TrueEps, HourAngle, r1[6], r2[6];
  char  RA[40], Del[40], Az[40], Alt[40], Lam[40], Bet[40];

  printf("EXAMPLE DRIVER FOR Eq2Ecl and Eq2Hor\n\n");

  do {
    do {
      fprintf(stdout, "[1] EQ TO HOR [2] HOR TO EQ\n");
      fprintf(stdout, "[3] EQ TO ECL [4] ECL TO EQ\n");
      fprintf(stdout, "Select option (1-4): ");
      fflush(stdout);
      fgets(line, sizeof(line), stdin);
    } while (sscanf(line, "%d", &Which) != 1);
  } while ((Which < 1) || (Which > 4));

  switch (Which) {
  case 1:
    do {
      fprintf(stdout,
        "Enter equatorial coordinates (ra, dec) in dd.mmss format: ");
      fflush(stdout);
      fgets(line, sizeof(line), stdin);
    } while (sscanf(line, "%lf, %lf", &Alpha, &Delta) != 2);

    do {
      fprintf(stdout, "Enter observer latitude in dd.mmss format: ");
      fflush(stdout);
      fgets(line, sizeof(line), stdin);
    } while (sscanf(line, "%lf", &obsr_lat) != 1);

    do {
      fprintf(stdout, "Enter LAST in hh.mmss format: ");
      fflush(stdout);
      fgets(line, sizeof(line), stdin);
    } while (sscanf(line, "%lf", &LAST) != 1);

    Alpha = deg(Alpha) * H2R;
    Delta = deg(Delta) * D2R;
    obsr_lat = deg(obsr_lat) * D2R;
    LAST = deg(LAST) * H2R;
    HourAngle = LAST - Alpha;
    r1[0] = HourAngle;
    r1[1] = Delta;
    r1[2] = 1.0;
    r1[3] = 0.0;
    r1[4] = 0.0;
```

```
      r1[5] = 0.0;

      /* Change to rectangular variables */
      Pol2Rec(r1, r2);
      /* Transform */
      Eq2Hor(r2, 0, r2);
      /* Change to polar variables */
      Rec2Pol(r2, r2);

      Azimuth  = r2[0] * R2D;
      Altitude = r2[1] * R2D;

      FmtDms(Azimuth, 4, 0, Az);
      FmtDms(Altitude, 4, 0, Alt);
      Alpha = Alpha * R2H;
      Delta = Delta * R2D;
      FmtDms(Alpha, 4, 1, RA);
      FmtDms(Delta, 4, 0, Del);

      printf("\n");
      printf("EQUATORIAL COORDINATES\n");
      printf("RA %s DELTA %s\n", RA, Del);
      printf("HORIZON COORDINATES\n");
      printf("AZIMUTH %s ALTITUDE %s\n", Az, Alt);
      break;
    case 2:
      do {
        fprintf(stdout,
          "Enter horizon coordinates (alt, az) in dd.mmss format: ");
        fflush(stdout);
        fgets(line, sizeof(line), stdin);
      } while (sscanf(line, "%lf, %lf", &Altitude, &Azimuth) != 2);

      do {
        fprintf(stdout, "Enter observer latitude in dd.mmss format: ");
        fflush(stdout);
        fgets(line, sizeof(line), stdin);
      } while (sscanf(line, "%lf", &obsr_lat) != 1);

      do {
        fprintf(stdout, "Enter LAST in hh.mmss format: ");
        fflush(stdout);
        fgets(line, sizeof(line), stdin);
      } while (sscanf(line, "%lf", &LAST) != 1);

      Altitude = deg(Altitude) * D2R;
      Azimuth = deg(Azimuth) * D2R;
      obsr_lat = deg(obsr_lat) * D2R;
      LAST = deg(LAST) * H2R;
      r1[0] = Azimuth;
      r1[1] = Altitude;
      r1[2] = 1.0;
      r1[3] = 0.0;
      r1[4] = 0.0;
      r1[5] = 0.0;

      /* Change to rectangular variables */
      Pol2Rec(r1, r2);
      /* Transform */
      Eq2Hor(r2, 1, r2);
      /* Change to polar variables */
      Rec2Pol(r2, r2);

      HourAngle = r2[0];
      Delta = r2[1];
```

```
Azimuth  = Azimuth * R2D;
Altitude = Altitude * R2D;

FmtDms(Azimuth, 4, 0, Az);
FmtDms(Altitude, 4, 0, Alt);

Alpha = LAST - HourAngle;
Alpha = amodulo(Alpha,TWOPI) * R2H;
Delta = Delta * R2D;
FmtDms(Alpha, 4, 1, RA);
FmtDms(Delta, 4, 0, Del);

printf("\n");
printf("HORIZON COORDINATES\n");
printf("AZIMUTH %s ALTITUDE %s\n", Az, Alt);
printf("EQUATORIAL COORDINATES\n");
printf("RA %s DELTA %s\n", RA, Del);
break;
case 3:
  do {
    fprintf(stdout,
      "Enter equatorial coordinates (ra, dec) in dd.mmss format: ");
    fflush(stdout);
    fgets(line, sizeof(line), stdin);
  } while (sscanf(line, "%lf, %lf", &Alpha, &Delta) != 2);

  do {
    fprintf(stdout, "Enter true obliquity in dd.mmss format: ");
    fflush(stdout);
    fgets(line, sizeof(line), stdin);
  } while (sscanf(line, "%lf", &TrueEps) != 1);

  Alpha = deg(Alpha) * H2R;
  Delta = deg(Delta) * D2R;
  TrueEps = deg(TrueEps) * D2R;
  r1[0] = Alpha;
  r1[1] = Delta;
  r1[2] = 1.0;
  r1[3] = 0.0;
  r1[4] = 0.0;
  r1[5] = 0.0;

  /* Change to rectangular variables */
  Pol2Rec(r1, r2);
  /* Transform */
  Eq2Ecl(r2, 0, TrueEps, r2);
  /* Change to polar variables */
  Rec2Pol(r2, r2);

  Lambda = r2[0] * R2D;
  Beta = r2[1] * R2D;

  FmtDms(Lambda, 4, 0, Lam);
  FmtDms(Beta, 4, 0, Bet);

  Alpha = Alpha * R2H;
  Delta = Delta * R2D;
  FmtDms(Alpha, 4, 1, RA);
  FmtDms(Delta, 4, 0, Del);

  printf("\n");
  printf("EQUATORIAL COORDINATES\n");
  printf("RA %s DELTA %s\n", RA, Del);
  printf("ECLIPTIC COORDINATES\n");
  printf("LAMBDA %s BETA %s\n", Lam, Bet);
  break;
```

```
case 4:
  do {
    fprintf(stdout,
      "Enter ecliptic coordinates (lon, lat) in dd.mmss format: ");
    fflush(stdout);
    fgets(line, sizeof(line), stdin);
  } while (sscanf(line, "%lf, %lf", &Lambda, &Beta) != 2);

  do {
    fprintf(stdout, "Enter true obliquity in dd.mmss format: ");
    fflush(stdout);
    fgets(line, sizeof(line), stdin);
  } while (sscanf(line, "%lf", &TrueEps) != 1);

  Lambda = deg(Lambda) * D2R;
  Beta = deg(Beta) * D2R;
  TrueEps = deg(TrueEps) * D2R;
  r1[0] = Lambda;
  r1[1] = Beta;
  r1[2] = 1.0;
  r1[3] = 0.0;
  r1[4] = 0.0;
  r1[5] = 0.0;

  /* Change to rectangular variables */
  Pol2Rec(r1, r2);
  /* Transform */
  Eq2Ecl(r2, 1, TrueEps, r2);
  /* Change to polar variables */
  Rec2Pol(r2, r2);

  Alpha = r2[0] * R2H;
  Delta = r2[1] * R2D;

  Lambda = Lambda * R2D;
  Beta = Beta * R2D;
  FmtDms(Lambda, 4, 0, Lam);
  FmtDms(Beta, 4, 0, Bet);

  FmtDms(Alpha, 4, 1, RA);
  FmtDms(Delta, 4, 0, Del);

  printf("\n");
  printf("ECLIPTIC COORDINATES\n");
  printf("LAMBDA %s BETA %s\n", Lam, Bet);
  printf("EQUATORIAL COORDINATES\n");
  printf("RA %s DELTA %s\n", RA, Del);
  break;
}

printf("\nOK\n");
return (0);
}

/* End Of File - coords.c *****************************************/
```

A.8   ELEPREC.C

```
/*********************************************************************
Project:  eleprec
Filename: eleprec.c
Author:   Joe Heafner.
Purpose:  Example driver for PrecessElements.
*********************************************************************/

/* Header Files ****************************************************/
```

```c
#include <stdio.h>
#include <stdlib.h>
#include <math.h>
#include "astrolib.h"

/************************************************************************
Name:    main
Purpose: Main routine for eleprec.
Inputs:  None.
Outputs: None.
Returns: 0 if execution successful.
Status:  Finished.
Errors:  None known.
************************************************************************/
int main(void) {

   char line[1024];
   char Eqnx1[50], Eqnx2[50];
   double Inclination, Node, ArgPeri, element[3];

   printf("EXAMPLE DRIVER FOR PrecessElements\n\n");

   fprintf(stdout, "First equinox: ");
   fflush(stdout);
   fgets(Eqnx1, sizeof(Eqnx1), stdin);
   Trim(Eqnx1);

   fprintf(stdout, "Final equinox: ");
   fflush(stdout);
   fgets(Eqnx2, sizeof(Eqnx2), stdin);
   Trim(Eqnx2);

   do {
      fprintf(stdout, "Inclination: ");
      fflush(stdout);
      fgets(line, sizeof(line), stdin);
   } while (sscanf(line, "%lf", &Inclination) != 1);

   do {
      fprintf(stdout, "Node: ");
      fflush(stdout);
      fgets(line, sizeof(line), stdin);
   } while (sscanf(line, "%lf", &Node) != 1);

   do {
      fprintf(stdout, "Arg. peri.: ");
      fflush(stdout);
      fgets(line, sizeof(line), stdin);
   } while (sscanf(line, "%lf", &ArgPeri) != 1);

   element[0] = Inclination * D2R;
   element[1] = Node * D2R;
   element[2] = ArgPeri * D2R;

   PrecessElements(Eqnx1, element, Eqnx2);

   printf("\nPRECESSED ELEMENTS\n");

   Inclination = element[0] * R2D;
   Node = element[1] * R2D;
   ArgPeri = element[2] * R2D;

   printf("Inclination %+10.5f\n", Inclination);
   printf("Node        %+10.5f\n", Node);
   printf("Arg. peri.  %+10.5f\n", ArgPeri);

   printf("\nOK\n");
   return (0);
```

```
}
/* End Of File - eleprec.c ****************************************/
```

A.9   EPH.C

```
/************************************************************************
Project:   eph
Filename:  eph.c
Author:    Joe Heafner.
Purpose:   Example driver for HelEphemeris.
************************************************************************/

/* Header Files ****************************************************/
#include <stdio.h>
#include <stdlib.h>
#include <math.h>
#include "astrolib.h"

void GetUserData(double *element, double *mass, double *StartingJD,
  double *stepsize, int *numsteps);
void UseThisData (double *element, double *mass, double *StartingJD,
  double *stepsize, int *numsteps);

/************************************************************************
Name:     main
Purpose:  Main routine for eph.
Inputs:   None.
Outputs:  None.
Returns:  0 if execution successful.
Status:   Finished.
Errors:   None known.
************************************************************************/
int main(void) {

  char line[1024];
  int Which, numsteps, i;
  double element[6], mass, StartingJD, stepsize;
  double mu, jdate, posvel[6];

  printf("EXAMPLE DRIVER FOR HelEphemeris\n\n");

  do {
    do {
      fprintf(stdout, "[1] Input data from keyboard\n");
      fprintf(stdout, "[2] Use default Comet Halley data\n");
      fprintf(stdout, "Your choice: ");
      fflush(stdout);
      fgets(line, sizeof(line), stdin);
    } while (sscanf(line, "%d", &Which) != 1);
  } while ((Which < 1) || (Which > 2));

  printf("\n");

  switch (Which) {
  case 1:
    GetUserData(element, &mass, &StartingJD, &stepsize, &numsteps);
    break;
  case 2:
    UseThisData(element, &mass, &StartingJD, &stepsize, &numsteps);
    break;
  }

  /* Compute heliocentric gravitational constant for the body */
  mu = GAUSSK * GAUSSK * (1.0 + mass);
```

```
    i = 0;
    jdate = StartingJD;
    do {
      HelEphemeris(element, mu, jdate, posvel);
      printf("date %f\n", jdate);
      printf("position %+17.13f %+17.13f %+17.13f AU\n",
        posvel[0], posvel[1], posvel[2]);
      printf("velocity %+17.13f %+17.13f %+17.13f AU/DAY\n",
        posvel[3], posvel[4], posvel[5]);
      i++;
      jdate += stepsize;
    } while (i < numsteps);

    printf("\nOK\n");
    return (0);
}

/************************************************************************
Name:     GetUserData
Purpose:  Routine to allow user to input desired data
          from the keyboard.
Inputs:   None.
Outputs:  element.
          mass.
          StartingJD.
          stepsize.
          numsteps.
Returns:  Nothing
Status:   Finished.
Errors:   None known.
*************************************************************************/
void GetUserData(double *element, double *mass, double *StartingJD,
  double *stepsize, int *numsteps) {

  char line[1024];

  printf("\n");
  do {
    fprintf(stdout, "Perihelion distance in AU: ");
    fflush(stdout);
    fgets(line, sizeof(line), stdin);
  } while (sscanf(line, "%lf", &element[0]) != 1);

  do {
    fprintf(stdout, "Eccentricity: ");
    fflush(stdout);
    fgets(line, sizeof(line), stdin);
  } while (sscanf(line, "%lf", &element[1]) != 1);

  do {
    fprintf(stdout, "Inclination in degrees: ");
    fflush(stdout);
    fgets(line, sizeof(line), stdin);
  } while (sscanf(line, "%lf", &element[2]) != 1);

  do {
    fprintf(stdout, "Long. of asc. node in degrees: ");
    fflush(stdout);
    fgets(line, sizeof(line), stdin);
  } while (sscanf(line, "%lf", &element[3]) != 1);

  do {
    fprintf(stdout, "Arg. of peri. in degrees: ");
    fflush(stdout);
    fgets(line, sizeof(line), stdin);
  } while (sscanf(line, "%lf", &element[4]) != 1);
```

```
  do {
    fprintf(stdout, "Julian date of peri. passage: ");
    fflush(stdout);
    fgets(line, sizeof(line), stdin);
  } while (sscanf(line, "%lf", &element[5]) != 1);

  element[2] = element[2] * D2R;
  element[3] = element[3] * D2R;
  element[4] = element[4] * D2R;

  do {
    fprintf(stdout, "Body's mass in solar units: ");
    fflush(stdout);
    fgets(line, sizeof(line), stdin);
  } while (sscanf(line, "%lf", mass) != 1);

  do {
    fprintf(stdout, "Starting Julian date: ");
    fflush(stdout);
    fgets(line, sizeof(line), stdin);
  } while (sscanf(line, "%lf", StartingJD) != 1);

  do {
    do {
      fprintf(stdout, "Number of steps: ");
      fflush(stdout);
      fgets(line, sizeof(line), stdin);
    } while (sscanf(line, "%d", numsteps) != 1);
  } while (*numsteps < 0);

  if (*numsteps > 1) {
    do {
      fprintf(stdout, "Increment in days: ");
      fflush(stdout);
      fgets(line, sizeof(line), stdin);
    } while (sscanf(line, "%lf", stepsize) != 1);
    printf("\n");
  } else {
    *stepsize = 0.0;
  }
}

/************************************************************************
Name:     UseThisData
Purpose:  Routine to supply default input data.  Data is taken
          from the paper by Mansfield (AIAA Paper No. 86-2269-CP)
          and is for Comet Halley. Elements are referred to equinox/ecliptic
          of B1950.
Inputs:   None.
Outputs:  element.
          mass.
          StartingJD.
          stepsize.
          numsteps.
Returns:  Nothing
Status:   Finished.
Errors:   None known.
*************************************************************************/
void UseThisData(double *element, double *mass, double *StartingJD,
  double *stepsize, int *numsteps) {

  /* Perihelion distance (AU) */
  element[0] = 0.5871047;
  /* Eccentricity */
  element[1] = 0.967276;
  /* Inclination (radians) */
  element[2] = 162.23928 * D2R;
```

```
    /* Longitude of ascending node (radians) */
    element[3] = 58.14536 * D2R;
    /* Argument of perihelion (radians) */
    element[4] = 111.84809 * D2R;
    /* Julian date of perihelion passage (TDT) */
    element[5] = 2446471.95175;
    /* Mass (solar masses) */
    *mass = (double)0.0;

    *StartingJD = (double)2446446.5;
    *stepsize   = (double)15.0;
    *numsteps   = (int)5;
}

/* End Of File - eph.c **********************************************/
```

A.10 EPHINFO.C

```
/***********************************************************************
Project: ephinfo
Filename: ephinfo.c
Author: Ported to C by Joe Heafner and Varian Swieter.
Purpose: Opens a binary ephemeris file and prints the header information.
Thanks to Charles Gamble for extensive modifications.
***********************************************************************/

/* Header Files ****************************************************/
#include <stdio.h>
#include <stdlib.h>
#include <string.h>
#include <errno.h>
#include "astrolib.h"
#include "support.h"

/* Function Prototypes ********************************************/
void ParseCmdLine(int argc, char *argv[], char *InFile);
void PrintBanner(void);
void PrintUsage(void);

/* Globals *******************************************************/
char szVersion[] = "EPHINFO v1.031898c";
char szLogFile[] = "ephinfo.log";

/***********************************************************************
Name:  main
Purpose: Main routine for ephinfo.
Inputs:  argc - Number of command-line arguments.
 argv - Pointer to array of command-line arguments.
Outputs: None.
Returns: 0 if execution successful.
Status:  Finished.
Errors:  None known.
***********************************************************************/
int main (int argc, char *argv[]) {

char InFile[MAX_NAME_SIZE+1] = "";

/* Open the log file */
if (LogOpen(szLogFile) == FALSE) {
fprintf(stderr,
"Could not open log file '%s': %s\n\n", szLogFile, strerror(errno));
exit(1); /* Exit with an error code */
}

PrintBanner();
ParseCmdLine(argc, argv, InFile);
```

```
if (strlen(InFile) == 0) {
/* Prompt user for file name */
do {
fprintf(stdout, "File name to use (XXXX to end): ");
fflush(stdout);
fgets(InFile, MAX_NAME_SIZE+1, stdin);

/* Remove whitespace from either end */
Trim(InFile);
} while (strlen(InFile) == 0);
}

/* We have a filename now. */
ucase(InFile); /* May not be used for OS/2 and UNIX compiles */
/* if you want mixed-case filenames. */

/* Test for user exit request */
if (strcmp(InFile, "XXXX") == 0) {
LogMsg(stdout, "\nOK\n");
LogClose();
remove(szLogFile);
return (0);
}

/* Test to see if filename exists */
if (!fexist(InFile)) {
LogMsg(stdout, "Requested input file does not exist.\n");
LogMsg(stdout, "Specify another file or move to another directory.\n");
LogMsg(stdout, "\nOK\n");
LogClose();
exit(1);
}

constants(InFile);

LogMsg(stdout, "\nOK\n");
LogClose(); /* Close the log file */
return(0);
}

/***************************************************************************
Name:    ParseCmdLine
Purpose: Routine to parse the command line.
Inputs:  argc - Number of command-line arguments.
 argv - Pointer to array of command-line arguments.
Outputs: InFile - Filename given by user for input file.
Returns: Nothing.
Status:  Finished.
Errors:  None known.
***************************************************************************/
void ParseCmdLine(int argc, char *argv[], char *InFile) {

/*
Command line parser ported from Basic and optimized for C
by Varian Swieter.
*/

int i;

for (i = 1; i < argc; i++) {
/*
Find next occurance of "/" or "-" by looking at
the first character of each argument.
*/
if (argv[i][0] != '-' && argv[i][0] != '/') {
/* Found an argument that did not begin with "/" or "-" */
LogMsg(stderr,
```

```
"Command line arguments must begin with '-' or '/'.\n");
PrintUsage();
LogClose();
remove(szLogFile);
exit(1);
}

switch (argv[i][1]) {
case '\0':
LogMsg(stderr, "Space not allowed between - and option.\n");
LogMsg(stderr, "Type ephinfo -h for help.\n");
LogClose();
remove(szLogFile);
exit(1);
case 'I':
case 'i':
if (strlen(argv[i]) == 2) {
/* We were given nothing after the "-I" so return empty string */
strcpy(InFile, "");
} else {
if (argv[i][2] != ':') {
/* User missed out colon so return empty string */
strcpy(InFile, "");
} else {
strcpy(InFile, &(argv[i][3]));
}
}
break;
case '?': /* Using this for help will cause problems under UNIX */
/* because it is used by the shell for substitution. */
case 'h':
PrintUsage();
LogMsg(stdout, "OK\n");
LogClose();
remove(szLogFile);
exit(0);
case 'v': /* Undocumented command line option */
/* to print version information. */
LogMsg(stdout, "OK\n");
LogClose();
remove(szLogFile);
exit(0);
default:
LogMsg(stderr, "Option not recognized.\n");
LogMsg(stderr, "Type ephinfo -h for help.\n");
LogClose();
remove(szLogFile);
exit(1);
}
}
}

/*******************************************************************
Name:    PrintBanner
Purpose: Prints a banner to stdout and log file.
Inputs:  None.
Outputs: None.
Returns: Nothing.
Status:  Finished.
Errors:  None known.
*******************************************************************/
void PrintBanner() {

LogMsg(stdout, "\n");
LogMsg(stdout, "***Program %s  ", szVersion);
```

```
LogMsg(stdout, "                        Written by Joe Heafner\n");
LogMsg(stdout, "***Opens a binary ephemeris file and prints the header\n");
LogMsg(stdout, "***The author can be reached via Internet:");
LogMsg(stdout, "     heafnerj@mercury.interpath.com\n");
LogMsg(stdout, "\n");
}

/**********************************************************************
Name:   PrintUsage
Purpose: Prints usage information.
Inputs:  None.
Outputs: None.
Returns: Nothing.
Status:  Finished.
Errors:  None known.
**********************************************************************/
void PrintUsage() {

printf("Usage: EPHINFO [-i:FILE][-h]\n");
printf("Valid command line options are:\n");
printf("\n");
printf("   -i:FILE   Use FILE as input\n");
printf("   -h        Display this help screen\n");
printf("\n");
printf("Command line options may be in any order.\n");
printf("\n");
}

/* End Of File - ephinfo.c ****************************************/
```

A.11   EPHTEST.C

```
/**********************************************************************
Project: ephtest
Filename: ephtest.c
Author: Joe Heafner
Purpose: Tests a binary ephemeris file against the correct test data
obtained from JPL.
Thanks to Charles Gamble for extensive modifications.
**********************************************************************/

/* Header Files ***************************************************/
#include <stdio.h>
#include <stdlib.h>
#include <string.h>
#include <errno.h>
#include "astrolib.h"
#include "support.h"

/* Function Prototypes ******************************************/
void ParseCmdLine(int argc, char *argv[], char *InFile);
void PrintBanner(void);
void PrintUsage(void);

/* Globals ******************************************************/
char szVersion[] = "EPHTEST v1.031898c";
char szLogFile[] = "ephtest.log";
extern short int NUMDE;

/**********************************************************************
Name:   main
Purpose: Main routine for ephtest.
Inputs:  argc - Number of command-line arguments.
 argv - Pointer to array of command-line arguments.
Outputs: None.
Returns: 0 if execution successful.
```

```
Status:  Finished.
Errors:  None known.
*******************************************************************/
int main(int argc, char *argv[]) {

char InFile[MAX_NAME_SIZE+1] = "";
char TestFile[MAX_NAME_SIZE+1] = "";
char line[1024] = "";
FILE *fpTestFile = NULL;
int  bFirst, bInside, i;
int  ENUM = 0;
int  Target = 0;
int  Center = 0;
int  Component = 0;
double JDate = 0.0;
double CValue = 0.0, MyValue = 0.0, Residual = 0.0;
double RRD[6];

/* Open the log file */
if (LogOpen(szLogFile) == FALSE) {
fprintf(stderr,
"Could not open log file '%s': %s\n\n", szLogFile, strerror(errno));
exit(1); /* Exit with an error code */
}

PrintBanner();
ParseCmdLine(argc, argv, InFile);

if (strlen(InFile) == 0) {
/* Prompt user for file name */
do {
fprintf(stdout, "File name to use (XXXX to end): ");
fflush(stdout);
fgets(InFile, sizeof(InFile), stdin);

/* Remove whitespace from either end */
Trim(InFile);
} while (strlen(InFile) == 0);
}

/* We have a filename now */
ucase(InFile); /* May not be used for OS/2 and UNIX compiles */
/* if you want mixed-case filenames. */

/* Test for user exit request */
if (strcmp(InFile, "XXXX") == 0) {
LogMsg(stdout, "\nOK\n");
LogClose();
remove(szLogFile);
return (0);
}

/* Test to see if filename exists */
if (!fexist(InFile)){
LogMsg(stdout, "Requested input file does not exist.\n");
LogMsg(stdout, "Specify another file or move to another directory.\n");
LogMsg(stdout, "\nOK\n");
LogClose();
exit(1);
}

/* Open the input file and read in the header info */
if (ephopn(InFile) == NULL) {
LogMsg(stderr, "An error occurred in ephopn().\n");
LogClose();
exit(1);
```

```
}

/* See if the test file exists */
sprintf(TestFile, "testpo.%d", NUMDE);
if (!fexist(TestFile)) {
LogMsg(stderr, "Test file '%s' not found.\n", TestFile);
LogMsg(stderr, "\nOK\n");
LogClose();
exit(1);
}

/* Open the test file */
if ((fpTestFile = fopen(TestFile, "r")) == NULL) {
LogMsg(stderr,
"Could not open test file '%s': %s.\n", TestFile, strerror(errno));
LogClose();
exit(1);
}

/* Read in the first six lines, which we don't need */
for (i = 1; i <= 6; i++) {
if (!fgets(line, sizeof(line), fpTestFile)) {
LogMsg(stderr,
"An error occurred reading line %d from '%s'\n", i, TestFile);
LogClose();
fclose(fpTestFile);
exit(1);
}
}

/* Setup some boolean values */
bInside = FALSE;
bFirst = TRUE;

/* Read in one line at a time, and parse the data */
do {
/* Read a line in */
fgets(line, sizeof(line), fpTestFile);
/* Force termination - just in case */
line[sizeof(line)-1] = '\0';
/* Strip off trailing whitespace */
RightTrim(line);

if (strlen(line) > 0) {
/* Extract the individual values */
if (sscanf(&line[0], "%d", &ENUM) != 1) {
LogMsg(stderr, "Invalid data found in '%s'\n", TestFile);
LogClose();
fclose(fpTestFile);
exit(1);
}

if (sscanf(&line[16], "%lf", &JDate) != 1) {
LogMsg(stderr, "Invalid data found in '%s'\n", TestFile);
LogClose();
fclose(fpTestFile);
exit(1);
}

if (sscanf(&line[26], "%d", &Target) != 1) {
LogMsg(stderr, "Invalid data found in '%s'\n", TestFile);
LogClose();
fclose(fpTestFile);
exit(1);
}
```

```
if (sscanf(&line[29], "%d", &Center) != 1) {
LogMsg(stderr, "Invalid data found in '%s'\n", TestFile);
LogClose();
fclose(fpTestFile);
exit(1);
}

if (Center == 0)
Center = 11;

if (sscanf(&line[33], "%d", &Component) != 1) {
LogMsg(stderr, "Invalid data found in '%s'\n", TestFile);
LogClose();
fclose(fpTestFile);
exit(1);
}


if (sscanf(&line[35], "%lf", &CValue) != 1) {
LogMsg(stderr, "Invalid data found in '%s'\n", TestFile);
LogClose();
fclose(fpTestFile);
exit(1);
}

if (ENUM != NUMDE) {
LogMsg(stderr, "Test file and binary file don't match.\n");
LogClose();
fclose(fpTestFile);
exit(1);
}

pleph(JDate, Target, Center, RRD, &bInside);

if (bInside) {
if (bFirst) {
LogMsg(stdout,
"---JED-----T--C-N--------JPL VALUE--"
                                "---------USER VALUE----------RESIDUAL----\n");
bFirst = FALSE;
}

MyValue = RRD[Component-1];
Residual = MyValue - CValue;
if (fabs(Residual) >= 0.000000000001) {
LogMsg(stdout, " *****WARNING: NEXT RESIDUAL >= 1D-12 ***** \n");
}

LogMsg(stdout,
"%8.1f %2d %2d %1d %+19.12f %+19.12f %+19.12f\n",
JDate, Target, Center, Component, CValue, MyValue, Residual);
}
}
} while (!feof(fpTestFile));

LogMsg(stdout, "\nOK\n");
LogClose(); /* Close the log file */
fclose(fpTestFile); /* Close the test file */
return (0);
}

/************************************************************************
Name:  ParseCmdLine
Purpose: Routine to parse the command line.
Inputs:  argc - Number of command-line arguments.
 argv - Pointer to array of command-line arguments.
```

```
Outputs: InFile - Filename given by user for input file.
Returns: Nothing.
Status:  Finished.
Errors:  None known.
*********************************************************************/
void ParseCmdLine(int argc, char *argv[], char *InFile) {

/*
Command line parser ported from Basic and optimized for C
by Varian Swieter.
*/

int i;

for (i = 1; i < argc; i++) {
/*
Find next occurance of "/" or "-" by looking at the
first character of each argument.
*/
if (argv[i][0] != '-' && argv[i][0] != '/') {
/* Found an argument that did not begin with "/" or "-" */
LogMsg(stderr, "Command line arguments must begin with '-' or '/'.\n");
PrintUsage();
LogClose();
remove(szLogFile);
exit(1);
}

switch (argv[i][1]) {
case '\0':
LogMsg(stderr, "Space not allowed between - and option.\n");
LogMsg(stderr, "Type ephtest -h for help.\n");
LogClose();
remove(szLogFile);
exit(1);
case 'I':
case 'i':
if (strlen(argv[i]) == 2) {
/* We were given nothing after the "-I" so return empty string */
strcpy(InFile, "");
} else {
if (argv[i][2] != ':') {
/* User missed out colon so return empty string */
strcpy(InFile, "");
} else {
strcpy(InFile, &(argv[i][3]));
}
}
break;
case '?': /* Using this for help will cause problems under UNIX */
/* because it is used by the shell for substitution. */
case 'h':
PrintUsage();
LogMsg(stdout, "OK\n");
LogClose();
remove(szLogFile);
exit(0);
case 'v': /* Undocumented command line option */
/* to print version information. */
LogMsg(stdout, "OK\n");
LogClose();
remove(szLogFile);
exit(0);
default:
LogMsg(stderr, "Option not recognized.\n");
```

```
LogMsg(stderr, "Type ephtest -h for help.\n");
LogClose();
remove(szLogFile);
exit(1);
}
}
}

/********************************************************************
Name:    PrintBanner
Purpose: Prints a banner to stdout and log file.
Inputs:  None.
Outputs: None.
Returns: Nothing.
Status:  Finished.
Errors:  None known.
********************************************************************/
void PrintBanner() {

LogMsg(stdout, "\n");
LogMsg(stdout, "***Program %s  ", szVersion);
LogMsg(stdout, "                      Written by Joe Heafner\n");
LogMsg(stdout, "***Tests a binary ephemeris file against JPL test data\n");
LogMsg(stdout, "***The author can be reached via Internet:");
LogMsg(stdout, "    heafnerj@mercury.interpath.com\n");
LogMsg(stdout, "\n");
}

/********************************************************************
Name:    PrintUsage
Purpose: Prints usage information.
Inputs:  None.
Outputs: None.
Returns: Nothing.
Status:  Finished.
Errors:  None known.
********************************************************************/
void PrintUsage() {

printf("Usage: EPHTEST [-i:FILE][-h]\n");
printf("Valid command line options are:\n");
printf("\n");
printf("   -i:FILE   Use FILE as input\n");
printf("   -h        Display this help screen\n");
printf("\n");
printf("Command line options may be in any order.\n");
printf("\n");
}

/* End Of File - ephtest.c *******************************/
```

A.12   GEOBS.C

```
/********************************************************************
Project:  geobs
Filename: geobs.c
Author:   Joe Heafner.
Purpose:  Example driver for GeocenObs.
********************************************************************/

/* Header Files ***************************************************/
#include <stdio.h>
#include <stdlib.h>
#include <math.h>
#include "astrolib.h"
```

```
/**********************************************************************
Name:     main
Purpose:  Main routine for geobs.
Inputs:   None.
Outputs:  None.
Returns:  0 if execution successful.
Status:   Finished.
Errors:   None known.
**********************************************************************/
int main(void) {

  double jdate=0.0, longitude=0.0, latitude=0.0, elevation=0.0, obsr_geo[6];
  char line[1024];

  printf("EXAMPLE DRIVER FOR GeocenObs\n\n");

  do {
    fprintf(stdout, "Enter Julian day number on TDB scale: ");
    fflush(stdout);
    fgets(line, sizeof(line), stdin);
  } while (sscanf(line, "%lf", &jdate) != 1);

  do {
    fprintf(stdout, "Enter observer's geodetic longitude (-W, dd.mmss): ");
    fflush(stdout);
    fgets(line, sizeof(line), stdin);
  } while (sscanf(line, "%lf", &longitude) != 1);

  do {
    fprintf(stdout, "Enter observer's geodetic latitude  (+N, dd.mmss): ");
    fflush(stdout);
    fgets(line, sizeof(line), stdin);
  } while (sscanf(line, "%lf", &latitude) != 1);

  do {
    fprintf(stdout, "Enter observer's elevation in meters: ");
    fflush(stdout);
    fgets(line, sizeof(line), stdin);
  } while (sscanf(line, "%lf", &elevation) != 1);

  longitude = deg(longitude) * D2R;
  latitude  = deg(latitude)  * D2R;

  obsr_lon = longitude;
  obsr_lat = latitude;
  obsr_ele = elevation;

  GeocenObs(jdate, obsr_geo);

  printf("Observer's state vector\n");
  printf("%+17.15f %+17.15f %+17.15f AU\n",
    obsr_geo[0], obsr_geo[1], obsr_geo[2]);
  printf("%+17.15f %+17.15f %+17.15f AU/day\n",
    obsr_geo[3], obsr_geo[4], obsr_geo[5]);

  printf("\nOK\n");
  return (0);
}

/* End Of File - geobs.c ***********************************/
```

A.13   JDTEST.C

```
/**********************************************************************
Project:  jdtest
```

```
Filename: jdtest.c
Author:   Joe Heafner.
Purpose:  Example driver for Cal2JED.
********************************************************************/

/* Header Files ****************************************************/
#include <stdio.h>
#include <stdlib.h>
#include <math.h>
#include "astrolib.h"

/********************************************************************
Name:    main
Purpose: Main routine for jdtest.
Inputs:  None.
Outputs: None.
Returns: 0 if execution successful.
Status:  Finished.
Errors:  None known.
********************************************************************/
int main(void) {

  int day, month, year, w, s;
  double utc, tai_utc, ut1_utc, jed, jd[5];
  char line[1024], m;

  printf("EXAMPLE DRIVER FOR Cal2JED\n\n");

  do {
    fprintf(stdout, "Enter Day: ");
    fflush(stdout);
    fgets(line, sizeof(line), stdin);
  } while (sscanf(line, "%d", &day) != 1);

  do {
    fprintf(stdout, "Enter Month: ");
    fflush(stdout);
    fgets(line, sizeof(line), stdin);
  } while (sscanf(line, "%d", &month) != 1);

  do {
    fprintf(stdout, "Enter Year: ");
    fflush(stdout);
    fgets(line, sizeof(line), stdin);
  } while (sscanf(line, "%d", &year) != 1);.

  do {
    fprintf(stdout, "Enter UTC as hh.mmssss: ");
    fflush(stdout);
    fgets(line, sizeof(line), stdin);
  } while (sscanf(line, "%lf", &utc) != 1);

  do {
    fprintf(stdout, "Enter TAI-UTC in seconds: ");
    fflush(stdout);
    fgets(line, sizeof(line), stdin);
  } while (sscanf(line, "%lf", &tai_utc) != 1);

  do {
    fprintf(stdout, "Enter UT1-UTC in seconds: ");
    fflush(stdout);
    fgets(line, sizeof(line), stdin);
  } while (sscanf(line, "%lf", &ut1_utc) != 1);

  do {
    do {
      fprintf(stdout, "Do you want MJD's (y/n)?: ");
```

```
      fflush(stdout);
      fgets(line, sizeof(line), stdin);
    } while (sscanf(line, "%c", &m) != 1);
  } while ((toupper(m) != 'Y') && (toupper(m) != 'N'));

  if (toupper(m) == 'Y') {
    w = 1;
  } else {
    w = 0;
  }

  for (s = 1; s <= 5; s++) {
    Cal2JED(month, day, year, utc, s, tai_utc, ut1_utc, w, &jed);
    jd[s-1] = jed;
  }

  if (toupper(m) == 'Y') {
    printf("\nMODIFIED JULIAN DATES ON ALL FIVE TIME SCALES:\n\n");
  } else {
    printf("\nJULIAN DATES FOR DIFFERENT TIME SCALES:\n\n");
  }

  printf("%16.8f UT1\n", jd[0]);
  printf("%16.8f UT2\n", jd[1]);
  printf("%16.8f TDT\n", jd[2]);
  printf("%16.8f TDB\n", jd[3]);
  printf("%16.8f UTC\n", jd[4]);

  printf("\nOK\n");
  return (0);
}

/* End Of File - jdtest.c *****************************************/
```

A.14 NUTTEST.C

```
/****************************************************************
Project:  nuttest
Filename: nuttest.c
Author:   Joe Heafner.
Purpose:  Example driver for GetDpsiDeps.
****************************************************************/

/* Header Files ************************************************/
#include <stdio.h>
#include <stdlib.h>
#include <math.h>
#include "astrolib.h"

/****************************************************************
Name:    main
Purpose: Main routine for nuttest.
Inputs:  None.
Outputs: None.
Returns: 0 if execution successful.
Status:  Finished.
Errors:  None known.
****************************************************************/
int main(void) {

  double jdate, dpsi, deps, dpsidot, depsdot, inc = 1.0;
  double MeanEps, MeanEpsDot, TrueEps, TrueEpsDot, TEps, MEps;
  int NumSteps = 0, i;
  char line[1024], temp[30], right_buffer[30];
  char m[30], t[30], dp[30], de[30];

  printf("EXAMPLE DRIVER FOR GetDpsiDeps\n\n");
```

```
do {
  fprintf(stdout, "Enter Julian date on TDB scale: ");
  fflush(stdout);
  fgets(line, sizeof(line), stdin);
} while (sscanf(line, "%lf", &jdate) != 1);

do {
  do {
    fprintf(stdout, "Enter number of steps (1 - 15): ");
    fflush(stdout);
    fgets(line, sizeof(line), stdin);
  } while (sscanf(line, "%d", &NumSteps) != 1);
} while ((NumSteps < 0) || (NumSteps > 15));

if (NumSteps >= 1) {
  do {
    do {
      fprintf(stdout, "Enter increment in days: ");
      fflush(stdout);
      fgets(line, sizeof(line), stdin);
    } while (sscanf(line, "%lf", &inc) != 1);
  } while (inc < 1.0);
} else {
  NumSteps = 0;
}

printf("    JED       Mean Obl.   True     dpsi     deps\n");
printf("-------------------------------------------------------\n");

i = 0;

do {
  /* Get nutation parameters */
  GetDpsiDeps(jdate, &dpsi, &deps, &dpsidot, &depsdot);
  /* Get mean obliquity */
  Obliquity(J2000, jdate, 0, &MeanEps, &MeanEpsDot);
  /* Get true obliquity */
  Obliquity(J2000, jdate, 1, &TrueEps, &TrueEpsDot);

  TEps = TrueEps * R2D;
  MEps = MeanEps * R2D;
  dpsi = dpsi * R2D;
  deps = deps * R2D;

  FmtDms(MEps, 3, 0, m);

  FmtDms(TEps, 3, 0, temp);
  right(temp, 7, t);

  FmtDms(dpsi, 4, 0, temp);
  left(temp, 1, dp);
  right(temp, 8, right_buffer);
  strcat(dp, right_buffer);

  FmtDms(deps, 4, 0, temp);
  left(temp, 1, de);
  right(temp, 8, right_buffer);
  strcat(de, right_buffer);

  printf("%9.1f  %s %s %s %s\n", jdate, m, t, dp, de);

  jdate += inc;
  i++;
} while (i < NumSteps);
```

```
   printf("\nOK\n");
   return (0);
}

/* End Of File - nuttest.c ****************************************/
```

A.15   PRETRAN.C

```
/***********************************************************************
Project:  pretran
Filename: pretran.c
Author:   Joe Heafner.
Purpose:  Example driver for GetPrecessParams.
***********************************************************************/

/* Header Files ****************************************************/
#include <stdio.h>
#include <stdlib.h>
#include <math.h>
#include "astrolib.h"

/***********************************************************************
Name:    main
Purpose: Main routine for pretran.
Inputs:  None.
Outputs: None.
Returns: 0 if execution successful.
Status:  Finished.
Errors:  None known.
***********************************************************************/
int main(void) {

  char line[1024];
  char epoch1[30], epoch2[30], *ptr;
  double jed1, jed2, r1[3], r2[3];
  double zeta=0.0, z=0.0, theta=0.0, zetadot=0.0, zdot=0.0, thetadot=0.0;

  printf("EXAMPLE DRIVER FOR GetPrecessParams\n\n");

  do {
    fprintf(stdout, "Enter initial epoch or Julian date: ");
    fflush(stdout);
    fgets(epoch1, sizeof(epoch1), stdin);
    if ((ptr = strrchr(epoch1, '\n')) != NULL)
      *ptr = '\0';
    ucase(epoch1);
    Trim(epoch1);
  } while (strlen(epoch1) < 1);

  do {
    fprintf(stdout, "Enter final epoch or Julian date: ");
    fflush(stdout);
    fgets(epoch2, sizeof(epoch2), stdin);
    if ((ptr = strrchr(epoch2, '\n')) != NULL)
      *ptr = '\0';
    ucase(epoch2);
    Trim(epoch2);
  } while (strlen(epoch2) < 1);

  if ((epoch1[0] == 'J') || (epoch1[0] == 'B'))
    Epoch2JED(epoch1, &jed1);
  else
    jed1 = atof(epoch1);

  if ((epoch2[0] == 'J') || (epoch2[0] == 'B'))
    Epoch2JED(epoch2, &jed2);
```

```
  else
    jed2 = atof(epoch2);

  do {
    fprintf(stdout, "Enter initial position vector X component: ");
    fflush(stdout);
    fgets(line, sizeof(line), stdin);
  } while (sscanf(line, "%lf", &r1[0]) != 1);

  do {
    fprintf(stdout, "Enter initial position vector Y component: ");
    fflush(stdout);
    fgets(line, sizeof(line), stdin);
  } while (sscanf(line, "%lf", &r1[1]) != 1);

  do {
    fprintf(stdout, "Enter initial position vector Z component: ");
    fflush(stdout);
    fgets(line, sizeof(line), stdin);
  } while (sscanf(line, "%lf", &r1[2]) != 1);

  printf("\nINITIAL POSITION VECTOR COMPONENTS\n");
  printf("%+13.10f %+13.10f %+13.10f\n\n", r1[0], r1[1], r1[2]);

  /* Compute the precessional angles */
  GetPrecessParams(jed1, jed2, &zeta, &z, &theta, &zetadot, &zdot, &thetadot);

  /* Perform the matrix rotations one at a time.      */
  /* Note the order of application of the matrices. */
  MRotate(r1, 3, -zeta, r1);
  MRotate(r1, 2, theta, r1);
  MRotate(r1, 3, -z, r2);

  printf("PRECESSED POSITION VECTOR COMPONENTS\n");
  printf("%+13.10f %+13.10f %+13.10f\n", r2[0], r2[1], r2[2]);

  printf("\nOK\n");
  return (0);
}

/* End Of File - pretran.c *****************************************/
```

A.16   RIGOROUS.C

```
/*********************************************************************
Project:   rigorous
Filename:  rigorous.c
Author:    Joe Heafner.
Purpose:   Example driver for rigorous element precession.
*********************************************************************/

/* Header Files ****************************************************/
#include <stdio.h>
#include <stdlib.h>
#include <math.h>
#include "astrolib.h"

/*********************************************************************
Name:     main
Purpose: Main routine for rigorous.
Inputs:   None.
Outputs:  None.
Returns:  0 if execution successful.
Status:   Finished.
Errors:   None known.
*********************************************************************/
int main(void) {
```

```
char line[1024], *ptr;
char epoch1[30], epoch2[30];
double jed1, jed2;
double I, node, arg, p[3], q[3], w[3];
double newi, newnode, newarg;
double zeta, z, theta, zetadot, zdot, thetadot;
double eps1, eps2, epsdot;

printf("EXAMPLE DRIVER FOR RIGOROUS ELEMENT PRECESSION\n\n");

do {
  fprintf(stdout, "Enter initial epoch or Julian date: ");
  fflush(stdout);
  fgets(epoch1, sizeof(epoch1), stdin);
  if ((ptr = strrchr(epoch1, '\n')) != NULL)
    *ptr = '\0';
  ucase(epoch1);
  Trim(epoch1);
} while (strlen(epoch1) < 1);

do {
  fprintf(stdout, "Enter final epoch or Julian date: ");
  fflush(stdout);
  fgets(epoch2, sizeof(epoch2), stdin);
  if ((ptr = strrchr(epoch2, '\n')) != NULL)
    *ptr = '\0';
  ucase(epoch2);
  Trim(epoch2);
} while (strlen(epoch2) < 1);

if ((epoch1[0] == 'J') || (epoch1[0] == 'B'))
  Epoch2JED(epoch1, &jed1);
else
  jed1 = atof(epoch1);

if ((epoch2[0] == 'J') || (epoch2[0] == 'B'))
  Epoch2JED(epoch2, &jed2);
else
  jed2 = atof(epoch2);

do {
  fprintf(stdout, "Enter inclination: ");
  fflush(stdout);
  fgets(line, sizeof(line), stdin);
} while (sscanf(line, "%lf", &I) != 1);
I = I * D2R;

do {
  fprintf(stdout, "Enter node: ");
  fflush(stdout);
  fgets(line, sizeof(line), stdin);
} while (sscanf(line, "%lf", &node) != 1);
node = node * D2R;

do {
  fprintf(stdout, "Enter arg peri: ");
  fflush(stdout);
  fgets(line, sizeof(line), stdin);
} while (sscanf(line, "%lf", &arg) != 1);
arg = arg * D2R;

p[0] = cos(arg) * cos(node) - sin(arg) * sin(node) * cos(I);
p[1] = cos(arg) * sin(node) + sin(arg) * cos(node) * cos(I);
p[2] = sin(arg) * sin(I);
```

```
q[0] = -sin(arg) * cos(node) - cos(arg) * sin(node) * cos(I);
q[1] = -sin(arg) * sin(node) + cos(arg) * cos(node) * cos(I);
q[2] =  cos(arg) * sin(I);

w[0] =  sin(node) * sin(I);
w[1] = -cos(node) * sin(I);
w[2] =  cos(I);

/* Compute the equatorial precessional angles */
GetPrecessParams(jed1, jed2, &zeta, &z, &theta, &zetadot, &zdot, &thetadot);

/* Precess p[] */
Obliquity(J2000, jed1, 0, &eps1, &epsdot);
Obliquity(J2000, jed2, 0, &eps2, &epsdot);
MRotate (p, 1, -eps1 , p);
MRotate (p, 3, -zeta , p);
MRotate (p, 2,  theta , p);
MRotate (p, 3, -z    , p);
MRotate (p, 1,  eps2 , p);

/* Precess q[] */
MRotate (q, 1, -eps1 , q);
MRotate (q, 3, -zeta , q);
MRotate (q, 2,  theta , q);
MRotate (q, 3, -z    , q);
MRotate (q, 1,  eps2 , q);

/* Precess w[] */
MRotate (w, 1, -eps1 , w);
MRotate (w, 3, -zeta , w);
MRotate (w, 2,  theta , w);
MRotate (w, 3, -z    , w);
MRotate (w, 1,  eps2 , w);

/* Get new elements */
newnode = atan2(w[0], -w[1]);
if (newnode < 0.0)
  newnode += TWOPI;

newi    = atan2(sqrt(p[2]*p[2] + q[2]*q[2]), w[2]);
if (newi < 0.0)
  newi += TWOPI;

newarg  = atan2(p[2], q[2]);
if (newarg < 0.0)
  newarg += TWOPI;

printf("NEW ELEMENTS\n");
printf(" %.13f\n", newi * R2D);
printf(" %.13f\n", newnode * R2D);
printf(" %.13f\n", newarg * R2D);

printf("\nOK\n");
return (0);
}

/* End Of File - rigorous.c ****************************************/
```

A.17   RISE.C

```
/*********************************************************************
Project:  rise
Filename: rise.c
Author:   Joe Heafner.
Purpose:  Example driver for RST.
```

```
*********************************************************************/
/* Header Files ****************************************************/
#include <stdio.h>
#include <stdlib.h>
#include <math.h>
#include "astrolib.h"

/********************************************************************
Name:    main
Purpose: Main routine for rise.
Inputs:  None.
Outputs: None.
Returns: 0 if execution successful.
Status:  Finished.
Errors:  None known.
*********************************************************************/
int main(void) {

  char line[1024];
  double jed, deltat, ra[3], dec[3], hp, sd, z0;
  char ris[100], trn[100], set[100];

  printf("EXAMPLE DRIVER FOR RST\n\n");

  do {
    fprintf(stdout, "Enter deltat in seconds: ");
    fflush(stdout);
    fgets(line, sizeof(line), stdin);
  } while (sscanf(line, "%lf", &deltat) != 1);

  do {
    fprintf(stdout, "Enter latitude (+N/-S, dd.mmss): ");
    fflush(stdout);
    fgets(line, sizeof(line), stdin);
  } while (sscanf(line, "%lf", &obsr_lat) != 1);
  obsr_lat = D2R * deg(obsr_lat);

  do {
    fprintf(stdout, "Enter longitude (-W/+E, dd.mmss)\n");
    fprintf(stdout, "Enter '9999' for Ephemeris Meridian: ");
    fflush(stdout);
    fgets(line, sizeof(line), stdin);
  } while (sscanf(line, "%lf", &obsr_lon) != 1);
  if (obsr_lon == 9999.0) {
    obsr_lon = 1.002738 * (deltat / 3600.0) * H2R;
  } else {
    obsr_lon = D2R * deg(obsr_lon);
  }

  /* The following data is must be replaced for specific */
  /* applications.                                       */
  jed = 2450093.5;   /* 1/11/1996 */
  ra[0]  = H2R * deg(10.1917027);
  dec[0] = D2R * deg( 6.291308);
  ra[1]  = H2R * deg(11.0558576);
  dec[1] = D2R * deg( 2.383610);
  ra[2]  = H2R * deg(11.5311971);
  dec[2] = D2R * deg(-1.223363);

  hp = D2R * deg(0.444156);
  sd = asin(0.272493 * sin(hp));
  z0 = D2R * deg(90.34) + sd - hp;

  RST(jed, ra, dec, z0, deltat, ris, trn, set);

  printf("\n");
```

```
    printf("%f\n", jed);
    printf("Rise %s Transit %s Set %s\n", ris, trn, set);

    printf("\nOK\n");
    return (0);
}

/* End Of File - rise.c ******************************************/
```

A.18 RPNMAT.C

```
/************************************************************************/
Project:   rpnmat
Filename:  rpnmat.c
Author:    Joe Heafner.
Purpose:   Example driver for GetRPNmat.
/************************************************************************/

/* Header Files ********************************************************/
#include <stdio.h>
#include <stdlib.h>
#include <math.h>
#include "astrolib.h"

/************************************************************************/
Name:      main
Purpose:   Main routine for rpnmat.
Inputs:    None.
Outputs:   None.
Returns:   0 if execution successful.
Status:    Finished.
Errors:    None known.
/************************************************************************/
int main(void) {

    int i, Which;
    char line[1024];
    double jed1, jed2;
    DMatrix m6, pmat;

    printf("EXAMPLE DRIVER FOR GetRPNmat\n\n");

    do {
        fprintf(stdout, "Enter JED1 on TDB scale: ");
        fflush(stdout);
        fgets(line, sizeof(line), stdin);
    } while (sscanf(line, "%lf", &jed1) != 1);

    do {
        fprintf(stdout, "Enter JED2 on TDB scale: ");
        fflush(stdout);
        fgets(line, sizeof(line), stdin);
    } while (sscanf(line, "%lf", &jed2) != 1);

    do {
        do {
            fprintf(stdout, "[1] Precession [2] Nutation [3] Combined: ");
            fflush(stdout);
            fgets(line, sizeof(line), stdin);
        } while (sscanf(line, "%d", &Which) != 1);
    } while ((Which < 1) || (Which > 3));

    printf("\n");

    pmat = createDMatrix(6);
    m6 = createDMatrix(6);
```

```
    GetRPNmat(jed1, jed2, Which, 1, pmat, m6);

    for (i = 0; i < 6; i++) {
      printf("%+11.8f %+11.8f %+11.8f %+11.8f %+11.8f %+11.8f\n",
        pmat[i][0], pmat[i][1], pmat[i][2], pmat[i][3], pmat[i][4], pmat[i][5]);
    }

    freeDMatrix(pmat, 6);
    freeDMatrix(m6, 6);

    printf("\nOK\n");
    return (0);
}

/* End Of File - rpnmat.c ****************************************/
```

A.19 SEPHEM.C

```
/**********************************************************************
Project: sephem
Filename: sephem.c
Author: Joe Heafner.
Purpose: A small command line ephemeris program.
Thanks to Charles Gamble for extensive modifications.
**********************************************************************/

/* Header Files ****************************************************/
#include <stdio.h>
#include <stdlib.h>
#include <string.h>
#include <errno.h>
#include "astrolib.h"
#include "support.h"

/* Function Prototypes *******************************************/
void ParseCmdLine(int argc, char *argv[], char *InFile);
void PrintBanner(void);
void PrintUsage(void);

/* Globals *****************************************************/
char szVersion[]  = "SEPHEM v1.031898c";
char szLogFile[]  = "sephem.log";
extern short int NUMDE;
extern double SS[];
extern double obsr_lon, obsr_lat, obsr_ele;

/**********************************************************************
Name:   main
Purpose: Main routine for sephem.
Inputs:  argc - Number of command-line arguments.
 argv - Pointer to array of command-line arguments.
Outputs: None.
Returns: 0 if execution successful.
Status:  Finished.
Errors:  None known.
**********************************************************************/
int main (int argc, char *argv[]) {

char InFile[MAX_NAME_SIZE+1] = "";
char RA[100], DEC[100];
char line[1024];
char PL[20];
int RedGeo = 0, SolSysSum = 0, Place = 0;
int i, Targ, Cent, NumSteps, counter;
double TDB = 0.0;
double xx, yy, zz;
double xxdot, yydot, zzdot;
double r, RA_hours, DEC_deg, DateInc;
```

```
double StarData[6], p3[6];

/* Open the log file */
if (LogOpen(szLogFile) == FALSE) {
fprintf(stderr,
"Could not open log file '%s': %s\n\n", szLogFile, strerror(errno));
exit(1); /* Exit with an error code */
}

PrintBanner();
ParseCmdLine(argc, argv, InFile);

if (strlen(InFile) == 0) {
/* Prompt user for file name */
do {
fprintf(stdout, "File name to use (XXXX to end): ");
fflush(stdout);
fgets(InFile, MAX_NAME_SIZE+1, stdin);

/* Remove whitespace from either end */
Trim(InFile);
} while (strlen(InFile) == 0);
}

/* We have a filename now */
ucase(InFile); /* May not be used for OS/2 and UNIX compiles */
/* if you want mixed-case filenames. */

/* Test for user exit request */
if (strcmp(InFile, "XXXX") == 0) {
LogMsg(stdout, "\nOK\n");
LogClose();
remove(szLogFile);
return (0);
}

/* Test to see if filename exists */
if (!fexist(InFile)) {
LogMsg(stdout, "Requested input file does not exist.\n");
LogMsg(stdout, "Specify another file or move to another directory.\n");
LogMsg(stdout, "\nOK\n");
LogClose();
exit(1);
}

/* Open the input file and read in the header info */
if (ephopn(InFile) == NULL) {
LogMsg(stderr, "An error occurred in ephopn().\n");
LogClose();
exit(1);
}

LogMsg(stdout,
"Using ephemeris DE%d with dates from %lf to %lf\n",
NUMDE, SS[0], SS[1]);

do {
fprintf(stdout, "Enter start JED on TDB time scale: ");
fflush(stdout);
fgets(line, sizeof(line), stdin);
} while (sscanf(line, "%lf", &TDB) != 1);

do {
do {
fprintf(stdout, "[1] REDUCED PLACE [2] GEOMETRIC PLACE: ");
fflush(stdout);
```

```
fgets(line, sizeof(line), stdin);
} while (sscanf(line, "%d", &RedGeo) != 1);
} while ((RedGeo != 1) && (RedGeo != 2));

if (RedGeo == 1) {
do {
do {
fprintf(stdout, "[1] SOLAR SYSTEM SUMMARY [2] SPECIFIC BODY: ");
fflush(stdout);
fgets(line, sizeof(line), stdin);
} while (sscanf(line, "%d", &SolSysSum) != 1);
} while ((SolSysSum != 1) && (SolSysSum != 2));

do {
do {
fprintf(stdout, "[1] APPARENT [2] TOPOCENTRIC [3] VIRTUAL "
                               "[4] LOCAL [5] ASTROMETRIC: ");
fflush(stdout);
fgets(line, sizeof(line), stdin);
} while (sscanf(line, "%d", &Place) != 1);
} while ((Place < 1) || (Place > 5));

if ((Place == 2) || (Place == 4)) {
do {
obsr_lat = 0.0;
fprintf(stdout, "Enter latitude (dd.mmss): ");
fflush(stdout);
fgets(line, sizeof(line), stdin);
} while (sscanf(line, "%lf", &obsr_lat) != 1);
obsr_lat = deg(obsr_lat) * D2R;

do {
obsr_lon = 0.0;
fprintf(stdout, "Enter longitude (dd.mmss): ");
fflush(stdout);
fgets(line, sizeof(line), stdin);
} while (sscanf(line, "%lf", &obsr_lon) != 1);
obsr_lon = deg(obsr_lon) * D2R;

do {
obsr_ele = 0.0;
fprintf(stdout, "Enter elevation (meters): ");
fflush(stdout);
fgets(line, sizeof(line), stdin);
} while (sscanf(line, "%lf", &obsr_ele) != 1);
}

switch (Place) {
case 1:
strcpy(PL, "APPARENT");
break;
case 2:
strcpy(PL, "TOPOCENTRIC");
break;
case 3:
strcpy(PL, "VIRTUAL");
break;
case 4:
strcpy(PL, "LOCAL");
break;
case 5:
strcpy(PL, "ASTROMETRIC");
break;
}

if (SolSysSum == 1) {
LogMsg(stdout,
"%s COORDINATES OF SOLAR SYSTEM BODIES ON %lf\n", PL, TDB);
```

```
for (i = 1; i <= 11; i++) {
if (i != 3) {
Reduce(TDB, i, Place, StarData, p3);
r = sqrt(p3[0]*p3[0]+p3[1]*p3[1]+p3[2]*p3[2]);
RA_hours = atan2(p3[1], p3[0]) * R2H;
/* adjust for C's atan2() function */
if (RA_hours < 0.0) {
RA_hours += 24.0;
}
FmtDms(RA_hours, 3, 1, RA);
DEC_deg = asin(p3[2] / r) * R2D;
FmtDms(DEC_deg, 2, 0, DEC);

LogMsg(stdout,
"BODY %2d ALPHA %s DELTA %s DIST %12.9lf\n", i, RA, DEC, r);
}
}
} else {
Targ = 12;
do {
do {
fprintf(stdout, "Enter body number (1-11,99): ");
fflush(stdout);
fgets(line, sizeof(line), stdin);
} while (sscanf(line, "%d", &Targ) != 1);
} while ((Targ < 1 || Targ > 11) && Targ != 99);

if (Targ == 99) {
/* Read in star's FK5 catalog data */
/* GetStarData(FileName, StarData[]); */
/*
The previous line MUST be modified by the user to
indicate the correct name of the data file that
contains the stellar positional data.
*/

/* FK5 data for Betelgeuse */
/*
Un-comment these lines for default data
StarData[0] = 5.9195297222 * H2R
StarData[1] = 7.4070416667 * D2R
StarData[2] = 0.005   (arcsec)
StarData[3] = 0.1730 (s/cty)
StarData[4] = 0.8700 ("/cty)
StarData[5] = 21   (km/s)
*/

do {
fprintf(stdout, "Enter FK5 right ascension (hh.mmss): ");
fflush(stdout);
fgets(line, sizeof(line), stdin);
} while (sscanf(line, "%lf", &StarData[0]) != 1);
StarData[0] = deg(StarData[0]) * H2R;

do {
fprintf(stdout, "Enter FK5 declination (dd.mmss): ");
fflush(stdout);
fgets(line, sizeof(line), stdin);
} while (sscanf(line, "%lf", &StarData[1]) != 1);
StarData[1] = deg(StarData[1]) * D2R;

do {
fprintf(stdout, "Enter parallax (arcsec): ");
fflush(stdout);
fgets(line, sizeof(line), stdin);
} while (sscanf(line, "%lf", &StarData[2]) != 1);
```

```
do {
fprintf(stdout, "Enter mu alpha (sec/cty): ");
fflush(stdout);
fgets(line, sizeof(line), stdin);
} while (sscanf(line, "%lf", &StarData[3]) != 1);

do {
fprintf(stdout, "Enter mu delta (arcsec/cty): ");
fflush(stdout);
fgets(line, sizeof(line), stdin);
} while (sscanf(line, "%lf", &StarData[4]) != 1);

do {
fprintf(stdout, "Enter radial velocity (km/s): ");
fflush(stdout);
fgets(line, sizeof(line), stdin);
} while (sscanf(line, "%lf", &StarData[5]) != 1);
}

do {
fprintf(stdout, "Enter increment in days: ");
fflush(stdout);
fgets(line, sizeof(line), stdin);
} while (sscanf(line, "%lf", &DateInc) != 1);

do {
do {
fprintf(stdout, "Enter number of steps: ");
fflush(stdout);
fgets(line, sizeof(line), stdin);
} while (sscanf(line, "%d", &NumSteps) != 1);
} while (NumSteps <= 0);

LogMsg(stdout, "%s EPHEMERIS OF BODY %d\n", PL, Targ);
counter = 0;

do {
Reduce(TDB, Targ, Place, StarData, p3);
r = sqrt(p3[0] * p3[0] + p3[1] * p3[1] + p3[2] * p3[2]);
RA_hours = atan2(p3[1], p3[0]) * R2H;
/* adjust for C's atan2() function */
if (RA_hours < 0.0) {
RA_hours += 24.0;
}
FmtDms(RA_hours, 3, 1, RA);
DEC_deg = asin(p3[2] / r) * R2D;
FmtDms(DEC_deg, 2, 0, DEC);

LogMsg(stdout, "%11.3lf ALPHA %s", TDB, RA);

if (Targ != 99) {
LogMsg(stdout, " DELTA %s", DEC);
LogMsg(stdout, " DIST %11.9lf\n", r);
} else {
LogMsg(stdout, " DELTA %s\n", DEC);
}

counter++;
TDB += DateInc;
} while (counter < NumSteps);
}
} else {
do {
do {
fprintf(stdout, "Enter target number (1-15): ");
```

```
fflush(stdout);
fgets(line, sizeof(line), stdin);
} while (sscanf(line, "%d", &Targ) != 1);
} while ((Targ < 1) || (Targ > 15));

do {
do {
fprintf(stdout, "Enter center number (1-15): ");
fflush(stdout);
fgets(line, sizeof(line), stdin);
} while (sscanf(line, "%d", &Cent) != 1);
} while ((Cent < 1) || (Cent > 15));

do {
fprintf(stdout, "Enter increment in days: ");
fflush(stdout);
fgets(line, sizeof(line), stdin);
} while (sscanf(line, "%lf", &DateInc) != 1);

do {
do {
fprintf(stdout, "Enter number of steps: ");
fflush(stdout);
fgets(line, sizeof(line), stdin);
} while (sscanf(line, "%d", &NumSteps) != 1);
} while (NumSteps <= 0);

LogMsg(stdout, "GEOMETRIC EPHEMERIS OF BODY %d WRT BODY %d\n", Targ, Cent);
counter = 0;
do {
GetStateVector(TDB, Targ, Cent, 1, StateVector);
xx = StateVector[Targ-1][Cent-1][0][0];
yy = StateVector[Targ-1][Cent-1][0][1];
zz = StateVector[Targ-1][Cent-1][0][2];
xxdot = StateVector[Targ-1][Cent-1][0][3];
yydot = StateVector[Targ-1][Cent-1][0][4];
zzdot = StateVector[Targ-1][Cent-1][0][5];
LogMsg(stdout, "%13.5lf %+14.10lf %+14.10lf %+14.10lf AU\n", TDB, xx, yy, zz);
LogMsg(stdout, "               %+14.10lf %+14.10lf %+14.10lf AU/DAY\n",
               xxdot, yydot, zzdot);
counter++;
TDB += DateInc;
} while (counter < NumSteps);
}

LogMsg(stdout, "\nOK\n");
LogClose(); /* Close the log file */
return(0);
}

/***********************************************************************
Name:    ParseCmdLine
Purpose: Routine to parse the command line.
Inputs:  argc - Number of command-line arguments.
 argv - Pointer to array of command-line arguments.
Outputs: InFile - Filename given by user for input file.
Returns: Nothing.
Status:  Finished.
Errors:  None known.
***********************************************************************/
void ParseCmdLine(int argc, char *argv[], char *InFile) {

/*
Command line parser ported from Basic and optimized for C
by Varian Swieter.
*/
```

```
int i;

for (i = 1; i < argc; i++) {
/*
Find next occurance of "/" or "-" by looking at
the first character of each argument.
*/
if (argv[i][0] != '-' && argv[i][0] != '/') {
/* Found an argument that did not begin with "/" or "-" */
LogMsg(stderr,
"Command line arguments must begin with '-' or '/'.\n");
PrintUsage();
LogClose();
remove(szLogFile);
exit(1);
}

switch (argv[i][1])  {
case '\0':
LogMsg(stderr, "Space not allowed between - and option.\n");
LogMsg(stderr, "Type SEPHEM -h for help.\n");
LogClose();
remove(szLogFile);
exit(1);
case 'I':
case 'i':
if (strlen(argv[i]) == 2) {
/* We were given nothing after the "-I" so return empty string */
strcpy(InFile, "");
} else {
if (argv[i][2] != ':') {
/* User missed out colon so return empty string */
strcpy(InFile, "");
} else {
strcpy(InFile, &(argv[i][3]));
}
}
break;
case '?': /* Using this for help will cause problems under UNIX */
/* because it is used by the shell for substitution. */
case 'h':
PrintUsage();
LogMsg(stdout, "OK\n");
LogClose();
remove(szLogFile);
exit(0);
case 'v': /* Undocumented command line option */
/* to print version information. */
LogMsg(stdout, "OK\n");
LogClose();
remove(szLogFile);
exit(0);
default:
LogMsg(stderr, "Option not recognized.\n");
LogMsg(stderr, "Type SEPHEM -h for help.\n");
LogClose();
remove(szLogFile);
exit(1);
}
}
}

/********************************************************************/
```

```
Name:    PrintBanner
Purpose: Prints a banner to stdout and log file.
Inputs:  None.
Outputs: None.
Returns: Nothing.
Status:  Finished.
Errors:  None known.
*********************************************************************/
void PrintBanner() {

LogMsg(stdout, "\n");
LogMsg(stdout, "***Program %s  ", szVersion);
LogMsg(stdout, "                          Written by Joe Heafner\n");
LogMsg(stdout, "***Small ephemeris program\n");
LogMsg(stdout, "***The author can be reached via Internet:");
LogMsg(stdout, "    heafnerj@mercury.interpath.com\n");
LogMsg(stdout, "\n");
}

/*********************************************************************
Name:    PrintUsage
Purpose: Prints usage information.
Inputs:  None.
Outputs: None.
Returns: Nothing.
Status:  Finished.
Errors:  None known.
*********************************************************************/
void PrintUsage() {

printf("Usage: SEPHEM [-i:FILE][-h]\n");
printf("Valid command line options are:\n");
printf("\n");
printf("    -i:FILE   Use FILE as input\n");
printf("    -h        Display this help screen\n");
printf("\n");
printf("Command line options may be in any order.\n");
printf("\n");
}

/* End Of File - sephem.c ******************************************/
```

A.20 SIDTEST.C

```
/*********************************************************************
Project:  sidtest
Filename: sidtest.c
Author:   Joe Heafner.
Purpose:  Example driver for GetGST.
*********************************************************************/

/* Header Files ***************************************************/
#include <stdio.h>
#include <stdlib.h>
#include <math.h>
#include "astrolib.h"

/*********************************************************************
Name:    main
Purpose: Main routine for sidtest.
Inputs:  None.
Outputs: None.
Returns: 0 if execution successful.
Status:  Finished.
Errors:  None known.
*********************************************************************/
```

```
int main(void) {

  double jdate;
  int NumSteps = 0, i;
  char line[1024], temp1[30], temp2[30];
  double gmst, gast, inc = 1.0;

  printf("EXAMPLE DRIVER FOR GetGST\n\n");

  do {
    fprintf(stdout, "Enter starting Julian date on TDB scale: ");
    fflush(stdout);
    fgets(line, sizeof(line), stdin);
  } while (sscanf(line, "%lf", &jdate) != 1);

  do {
    do {
      fprintf(stdout, "Enter number of steps (1 - 15): ");
      fflush(stdout);
      fgets(line, sizeof(line), stdin);
    } while (sscanf(line, "%d", &NumSteps) != 1);
  } while ((NumSteps < 1) || (NumSteps > 15));

  if (NumSteps > 1) {
    do {
      do {
        fprintf(stdout, "Enter increment in days: ");
        fflush(stdout);
        fgets(line, sizeof(line), stdin);
      } while (sscanf(line, "%lf", &inc) != 1);
    } while (inc < 0.0);
  } else {
    inc = 0.0;
  }

  printf("\n");

  i = 0;
  do {
    GetGST(jdate, 0, &gmst);
    gmst = gmst * R2H;
    GetGST(jdate, 1, &gast);
    gast = gast * R2H;
    FmtDms(gmst,4,2, temp1);
    FmtDms(gast,4,2, temp2);
    printf("JED %9.1f  GMST %s  GAST %s\n", jdate, temp1, temp2);
    jdate += inc;
    i++;
  } while (i < NumSteps);

  printf("\nOK\n");
  return (0);
}

/* End Of File - sidtest.c ****************************************/
```

A.21   SUPPORT.C

```
/***********************************************************************
Project:            fecsoftc
Filename:           support.c
Author:             Joe Heafner
Purpose:            General support routines.
Thanks to Charles Gamble for extensive modifications.
***********************************************************************/

/* Header Files ******************************************************/
```

```
#include <stdio.h>
#include <stdlib.h>
#include <string.h>
#include <ctype.h>
#include <stdarg.h>
#include <sys/types.h>
#include <netinet/in.h>
#include <sys/param.h>
#include "support.h"

/* Globals ************************************************************/
static FILE *fpLogFile = NULL;

/*********************************************************************
Name:     make_little_endian
Purpose: Reverses the byte ordering of the given block of memory IF this
         machine is BIG ENDIAN. Used to ensure that binary data written
         out to file is little-endian in nature.
Inputs:   ptr - Pointer to block of memory to reverse.
          len - Length of block of memory to reverse.
Outputs: ptr - Byte-reversed block of memory.
Returns: Nothing.
Status:  Finished.
Errors:  None known.
*********************************************************************/
void make_little_endian(char *ptr, int len) {

  if (BIG_ENDIAN_TEST) {
    reverse_bytes(ptr, len);
  }
}

/*********************************************************************
Name:     convert_little_endian
Purpose: Reverses the byte ordering of the given block of memory IF this
         machine is BIG ENDIAN. Used to convert the little-endian binary
         data read in from a file into the native endian format for this
         machine.
Inputs:   ptr - Pointer to block of memory to reverse.
          len - Length of block of memory to reverse.
Outputs: ptr - Byte-reversed block of memory.
Returns: Nothing.
Status:  Finished.
Errors:  None known.
*********************************************************************/
void convert_little_endian(char *ptr, int len) {

  if (BIG_ENDIAN_TEST) {
    reverse_bytes(ptr, len);
  }
}

/*********************************************************************
Name:     reverse_bytes
Purpose: Reverses the byte ordering of the given block of memory.
Inputs:   ptr - Pointer to block of memory to reverse.
          len - Length of block of memory to reverse.
Outputs: ptr - Byte-reversed block of memory.
Returns: Nothing.
Status:  Finished.
Errors:  None known.
*********************************************************************/
void reverse_bytes(char *ptr, int len) {

  int i;
  char *tmp;

  if ((tmp = malloc(len)) == NULL) {
    fprintf(stderr, "Memory allocation error (reverse_bytes:%d)\n", len);
```

```
      exit(1);
  }

  for (i = 0; i < len; i++) {
      tmp[i] = ptr[(len-1)-i];
  }

  memcpy(ptr, tmp, len);
  free(tmp);
}
/**********************************************************************
Name:     ucase
Purpose:  Converts string to uppercase. This emulates the BASIC function
          ucase(a$).
Inputs:   str - String to convert.
Outputs:  str - Converted string.
Returns:  Nothing.
Status:   Finished.
Errors:   None known.
**********************************************************************/
void ucase(char str[]) {

  int i;
  int len = strlen(str);

  for (i = 0; i < len; i++)
    str[i] = toupper(str[i]);
}

/**********************************************************************
Name:     left
Purpose:  Copies the first n characters of string str into dest.
Inputs:   str  - String to copy.
          n    - Number of characters to copy.
Outputs:  dest - Copied string.
Returns:  Nothing.
Status:   Finished.
Errors:   None known.
**********************************************************************/
void left(char str[], int n, char dest[]) {

  /* Safety test - make sure n is >= 0 */
  if (n > 0) {
    strncpy(dest, str, n);
    dest[n] = '\0'; /* Terminate just in case strlen(str) >= n */
  } else {
    strcpy(dest, "");
  }
}

/**********************************************************************
Name:     right
Purpose:  Copies the last n characters of string str into dest.
Inputs:   str  - String to copy.
          n    - Number of characters to copy.
Outputs:  dest - Copied string.
Returns:  Nothing.
Status:   Finished.
Errors:   None known.
**********************************************************************/
void right(char str[], int n, char dest[]) {

  int len;

  if (n > 0) {
    len = strlen(str);
    if (n >= len) {
      /* Just copy whole string */
```

```
      strcpy(dest, str);
    } else {
      /* Copy section of string */
      strcpy(dest, &str[len-n]);
    }
  } else {
    strcpy(dest, "");
  }
}

/*******************************************************************
Name:    Trim
Purpose: Removes whitespace from either end of string.
Inputs:  str - String to trim.
Outputs: str - Trimmed string.
Returns: Nothing.
Status:  Finished.
Errors:  None known.
*******************************************************************/
void Trim(char str[]) {

  RightTrim(str); /* Remove trailing whitespace */
  LeftTrim(str);  /* Remove preceeding whitespace */
}

/*******************************************************************
Name:    RightTrim
Purpose: Removes trailing whitespace from string.
Inputs:  str - String to trim.
Outputs: str - Trimmed string.
Returns: Nothing.
Status:  Finished.
Errors:  None known.
*******************************************************************/
void RightTrim(char str[]) {

  int i;

  i = strlen(str) - 1;
  while (i >= 0 && isspace(str[i])) {
    str[i] = '\0';
    i--;
  }
}

/*******************************************************************
Name:    LeftTrim
Purpose: Removes preceeding whitespace from string.
Inputs:  str - String to trim.
Outputs: str - Trimmed string.
Returns: Nothing.
Status:  Finished.
Errors:  None known.
*******************************************************************/
void LeftTrim(char str[]) {

  unsigned int i;

  i = 0;
  while (i < strlen(str) && isspace(str[i]))
    i++;

  if (i)
    strcpy(str, &str[i]);
}

/*******************************************************************
Name:    fexist
Purpose: Tests to see if a file exists.
```

```
Inputs:   filename - Filename to test.
Outputs:  None.
Returns:  0 if the file does not exist.
          1 if the file exists.
Status:   Finished.
Errors:   None known.
********************************************************************/
int fexist(char *filename) {

  FILE *fp;

  if ((fp = fopen(filename,"r")) == NULL) {
    /* File could not be opened */
    return(0);
  } else {
    /* File was opened successfully */
    fclose(fp);
    return(1);
  }
}

/********************************************************************
Name:    LogOpen
Purpose: Open a log file with the specified name.
Inputs:  filename - Name of log file to open.
Outputs: None.
Returns: TRUE if successful, FALSE otherwise.
Status:  Finished.
Errors:  None known.
********************************************************************/
int LogOpen(char *filename) {

  /* Check to see if file is already open */
  if (fpLogFile)
    return (TRUE);

  /* Open the log file */
  if ((fpLogFile = fopen(filename, "wt")) == NULL)
    return (FALSE);
  else
    return (TRUE);
}

/********************************************************************
Name:    LogClose
Purpose: Closes the log file.
Inputs:  None.
Outputs: None.
Returns: Nothing.
Status:  Finished.
Errors:  None known.
********************************************************************/
void LogClose() {

  /* Check to see if file is open */
  if (fpLogFile) {
    fclose(fpLogFile);
    fpLogFile = NULL;
  }
}

/********************************************************************
Name:    LogMsg
Purpose: Prints a message to a given file pointer and to the log file.
         Log file must have been opened previously with LogOpen().
Inputs:  fptr    - File pointer to print with.
         format  - Format string (like printf).
         va_alist - Variable length argument list.
```

```
Outputs: None.
Returns: Nothing.
Status:  Finished.
Errors:  None known.
**********************************************************************/
void LogMsg(FILE* fptr, const char *format, ...) {

  char buffer[1024];
  va_list argptr;

  va_start(argptr, format);
  vsprintf(buffer, format, argptr);
  va_end(argptr);

  /* Write to the log file if it is open */
  if (fpLogFile)
    fprintf(fpLogFile, "%s", buffer);

  /* Write to the given file pointer if it is valid */
  if (fptr)
    fprintf(fptr, "%s", buffer);
}

/* End Of File - support.c ****************************************/
```

A.22 TSPP.C

```
/**********************************************************************
Project:  tspp
Filename: tspp.c
Author:   Joe Heafner.
Purpose:  Example driver for Stat2Elem.
**********************************************************************/

/* Header Files ***************************************************/
#include <stdio.h>
#include <stdlib.h>
#include <math.h>
#include "astrolib.h"

void GetUserData(double *state, double *mu, double *jdate);
void UseThisData(double *state, double *mu, double *jdate);

/**********************************************************************
Name:    main
Purpose: Main routine for tspp.
Inputs:  None.
Outputs: None.
Returns: 0 if execution successful.
Status:  Finished.
Errors:  None known.
**********************************************************************/
int main(void) {

  char line[1024];
  int Which;
  double element[6], state[6];
  double mu, jdate;

  printf("EXAMPLE DRIVER FOR Stat2Elem\n\n");

  do {
    do {
      fprintf(stdout, "[1] Input data from the keyboard\n");
      fprintf(stdout, "[2] Use default data\n");
      fprintf(stdout, "Your choice: ");
      fflush(stdout);
```

```
      fgets(line, sizeof(line), stdin);
    } while (sscanf(line, "%d", &Which) != 1);
  } while ((Which < 1) || (Which > 2));

  printf("\n");

  switch (Which) {
  case 1:
    GetUserData(state, &mu, &jdate);
    break;
  case 2:
    UseThisData(state, &mu, &jdate);
    break;
  }

  Stat2Elem(state, mu, jdate, element);

  printf("INITIAL STATE VECTOR\n");
  printf("%+19.15f %+19.15f %+19.15f AU\n", state[0], state[1], state[2]);
  printf("%+19.15f %+19.15f %+19.15f AU/DAY\n\n",
    state[3], state[4], state[5]);

  printf("ELEMENT SET\n");
  printf("Perihelion distance (AU) %11.8f\n", element[0]);
  printf("Eccentricity             %12.9f\n", element[1]);
  printf("Inclination       (deg) %+13.8f\n", element[2] * R2D);
  printf("Long. of node     (deg) %+13.8f\n", element[3] * R2D);
  printf("Arg. of peri.     (deg) %+13.8f\n", element[4] * R2D);
  printf("T (TDT)                 %16.8f\n", element[5]);

  printf("\nOK\n");
  return (0);
}

/*********************************************************************
Name:     GetUserData
Purpose:  Routine to allow user to input desired data from the keyboard.
Inputs:   None.
Outputs:  state[].
          mu.
          jdate.
Returns:  Nothing
Status:   Finished.
Errors:   None known.
*********************************************************************/
void GetUserData(double *state, double *mu, double *jdate) {

  char line[1024];
  double mass;

  printf("\n");

  do {
    fprintf(stdout, "Enter position vector X component: ");
    fflush(stdout);
    fgets(line, sizeof(line), stdin);
  } while (sscanf(line, "%lf", &state[0]) != 1);

  do {
    fprintf(stdout, "Enter position vector Y component: ");
    fflush(stdout);
    fgets(line, sizeof(line), stdin);
  } while (sscanf(line, "%lf", &state[1]) != 1);

  do {
    fprintf(stdout, "Enter position vector Z component: ");
    fflush(stdout);
```

```
      fgets(line, sizeof(line), stdin);
    } while (sscanf(line, "%lf", &state[2]) != 1);

    do {
      fprintf(stdout, "Enter velocity vector X component: ");
      fflush(stdout);
      fgets(line, sizeof(line), stdin);
    } while (sscanf(line, "%lf", &state[3]) != 1);

    do {
      fprintf(stdout, "Enter velocity vector Y component: ");
      fflush(stdout);
      fgets(line, sizeof(line), stdin);
    } while (sscanf(line, "%lf", &state[4]) != 1);

    do {
      fprintf(stdout, "Enter velocity vector Z component: ");
      fflush(stdout);
      fgets(line, sizeof(line), stdin);
    } while (sscanf(line, "%lf", &state[5]) != 1);

    do {
      fprintf(stdout, "Enter Julian date: ");
      fflush(stdout);
      fgets(line, sizeof(line), stdin);
    } while (sscanf(line, "%lf", jdate) != 1);

    do {
      fprintf(stdout, "Enter mass in solar masses: ");
      fflush(stdout);
      fgets(line, sizeof(line), stdin);
    } while (sscanf(line, "%lf", &mass) != 1);

    *mu = (double) (GAUSSK * GAUSSK * (1.0 + mass));
}

/*********************************************************************
Name:     UseThisData
Purpose:  Subprogram to supply default input data. Data is taken from
          the paper by Mansfield (AIAA Paper No. 86-2269-CP) and is
          for Comet Halley.
Inputs:   None.
Outputs:  state[].
          mu.
          jdate.
Returns:  Nothing
Status:   Finished.
Errors:   None known.
*********************************************************************/
void UseThisData(double *state, double *mu, double *jdate) {

    double mass;

    /* Components referred to equinox/ecliptic of B1950 */

    /* Position vector components */
    state[0] = 0.7661010445554045;
    state[1] = 0.1412849664351819;
    state[2] = 0.1845468752429582;

    /* Velocity vector components */
    state[3] = -0.0101488586182795;
    state[4] = -2.485310205695914e-02;
    state[5] = 1.440200276392141e-03;

    /* Mass */
    mass = 0.0;
    *mu = (double) (GAUSSK * GAUSSK * (1.0 + mass));
```

```
    /* Julian day number (TDB) */
    *jdate = (double) 2446446.5;
}

/* End Of File - tspp.c ***********************************************/
```

A.23   MAKEFILE.DOS

```
INCLUDE=
LIBS= -lm
CC=gcc

# For normal use
# CFLAGS=-ansi -pedantic -Wall -s -O
# For debugging
CFLAGS=-ansi -pedantic -Wall -g

TARGETS = asc2eph ephinfo ephtest sephem eph geobs jdtest nuttest \
pretran rigorous rpnmat sidtest tspp coords eleprec rise

# Now the actual rules

all: $(TARGETS)

clean:
-rm *.o
-rm *.log
-rm *.exe


asc2eph: asc2eph.o astrocon.o support.o
$(CC) $(CFLAGS) -o asc2eph.exe asc2eph.o astrocon.o support.o $(LIBS)

ephinfo: ephinfo.o astrolib.o astrocon.o support.o
$(CC) $(CFLAGS) -o ephinfo.exe ephinfo.o astrolib.o astrocon.o \
support.o $(LIBS)

ephtest: ephtest.o astrolib.o astrocon.o support.o
$(CC) $(CFLAGS) -o ephtest.exe ephtest.o astrolib.o astrocon.o\
 support.o $(LIBS)

sephem: sephem.o astrolib.o astrocon.o support.o
$(CC) $(CFLAGS) -o sephem.exe sephem.o astrolib.o astrocon.o\
support.o $(LIBS)

eph: eph.o astrolib.o astrocon.o support.o
$(CC) $(CFLAGS) -o eph.exe eph.o astrolib.o astrocon.o\
support.o $(LIBS)

geobs: geobs.o astrolib.o astrocon.o support.o
$(CC) $(CFLAGS) -o geobs.exe geobs.o astrolib.o astrocon.o\
support.o $(LIBS)

jdtest: jdtest.o astrolib.o astrocon.o support.o
$(CC) $(CFLAGS) -o jdtest.exe jdtest.o astrolib.o astrocon.o\
support.o $(LIBS)

nuttest: nuttest.o astrolib.o astrocon.o support.o
$(CC) $(CFLAGS) -o nuttest.exe nuttest.o astrolib.o astrocon.o\
support.o $(LIBS)

pretran: pretran.o astrolib.o astrocon.o support.o
$(CC) $(CFLAGS) -o pretran.exe pretran.o astrolib.o astrocon.o\
```

```
support.o $(LIBS)

rigorous: rigorous.o astrolib.o astrocon.o support.o
$(CC) $(CFLAGS) -o rigorous.exe rigorous.o astrolib.o astrocon.o\
support.o $(LIBS)

rpnmat: rpnmat.o astrolib.o astrocon.o support.o
$(CC) $(CFLAGS) -o rpnmat.exe rpnmat.o astrolib.o astrocon.o\
support.o $(LIBS)

sidtest: sidtest.o astrolib.o astrocon.o support.o
$(CC) $(CFLAGS) -o sidtest.exe sidtest.o astrolib.o astrocon.o\
support.o $(LIBS)

tspp: tspp.o astrolib.o astrocon.o support.o
$(CC) $(CFLAGS) -o tspp.exe tspp.o astrolib.o astrocon.o\
support.o $(LIBS)

coords: coords.o astrolib.o astrocon.o support.o
$(CC) $(CFLAGS) -o coords.exe coords.o astrolib.o astrocon.o\
support.o $(LIBS)

eleprec: eleprec.o astrolib.o astrocon.o support.o
$(CC) $(CFLAGS) -o eleprec.exe eleprec.o astrolib.o astrocon.o\
support.o $(LIBS)

rise: rise.o astrolib.o astrocon.o support.o
$(CC) $(CFLAGS) -o rise.exe rise.o astrolib.o astrocon.o\
support.o $(LIBS)


asc2eph.o: asc2eph.c astrolib.h support.h
$(CC) $(CFLAGS) -c asc2eph.c

ephinfo.o: ephinfo.c astrolib.h support.h
$(CC) $(CFLAGS) -c ephinfo.c

ephtest.o: ephtest.c astrolib.h support.h
$(CC) $(CFLAGS) -c ephtest.c

sephem.o: sephem.c astrolib.h support.h
$(CC) $(CFLAGS) -c sephem.c

astrolib.o: astrolib.c astrolib.h astrocon.h support.h
$(CC) $(CFLAGS) -c astrolib.c

astrocon.o: astrocon.c astrocon.h
$(CC) $(CFLAGS) -c astrocon.c

support.o: support.c support.h
$(CC) $(CFLAGS) -c support.c

eph.o: eph.c astrolib.h support.h
$(CC) $(CFLAGS) -c eph.c

geobs.o: geobs.c astrolib.h support.h
$(CC) $(CFLAGS) -c geobs.c

jdtest.o: jdtest.c astrolib.h support.h
$(CC) $(CFLAGS) -c jdtest.c

nuttest.o: nuttest.c astrolib.h support.h
$(CC) $(CFLAGS) -c nuttest.c

pretran.o: pretran.c astrolib.h support.h
```

```
$(CC) $(CFLAGS) -c pretran.c

rigorous.o: rigorous.c astrolib.h support.h
$(CC) $(CFLAGS) -c rigorous.c

rpnmat.o: rpnmat.c astrolib.h support.h
$(CC) $(CFLAGS) -c rpnmat.c

sidtest.o: sidtest.c astrolib.h support.h
$(CC) $(CFLAGS) -c sidtest.c

tspp.o: tspp.c astrolib.h support.h
$(CC) $(CFLAGS) -c tspp.c

coords.o: coords.c astrolib.h support.h
$(CC) $(CFLAGS) -c coords.c

eleprec.o: eleprec.c astrolib.h support.h
$(CC) $(CFLAGS) -c eleprec.c

rise.o: rise.c astrolib.h support.h
$(CC) $(CFLAGS) -c rise.c
```

A.24   MAKEFILE.OS2

```
INCLUDE=
LIBS= -lm -lsocket
CC=gcc

# For normal use
# CFLAGS=-ansi -pedantic -Wall -s -O -Zexe
# For debugging
CFLAGS=-ansi -pedantic -Wall -g -Zexe

TARGETS = asc2eph ephinfo ephtest sephem eph geobs jdtest nuttest \
pretran rigorous rpnmat sidtest tspp coords eleprec rise

# Now the actual rules

all: $(TARGETS)

clean:
-rm *.o
-rm *.log
-rm *.exe
-rm $(TARGETS)

asc2eph: asc2eph.o astrocon.o support.o
$(CC) $(CFLAGS) -o asc2eph asc2eph.o astrocon.o support.o $(LIBS)

ephinfo: ephinfo.o astrolib.o astrocon.o support.o
$(CC) $(CFLAGS) -o ephinfo ephinfo.o astrolib.o astrocon.o support.o $(LIBS)

ephtest: ephtest.o astrolib.o astrocon.o support.o
$(CC) $(CFLAGS) -o ephtest ephtest.o astrolib.o astrocon.o support.o $(LIBS)

sephem: sephem.o astrolib.o astrocon.o support.o
$(CC) $(CFLAGS) -o sephem sephem.o astrolib.o astrocon.o support.o $(LIBS)

eph: eph.o astrolib.o astrocon.o support.o
$(CC) $(CFLAGS) -o eph eph.o astrolib.o astrocon.o support.o $(LIBS)

geobs: geobs.o astrolib.o astrocon.o support.o
$(CC) $(CFLAGS) -o geobs geobs.o astrolib.o astrocon.o support.o $(LIBS)

jdtest: jdtest.o astrolib.o astrocon.o support.o
```

```
$(CC) $(CFLAGS) -o jdtest jdtest.o astrolib.o astrocon.o support.o $(LIBS)

nuttest: nuttest.o astrolib.o astrocon.o support.o
$(CC) $(CFLAGS) -o nuttest nuttest.o astrolib.o astrocon.o support.o $(LIBS)

pretran: pretran.o astrolib.o astrocon.o support.o
$(CC) $(CFLAGS) -o pretran pretran.o astrolib.o astrocon.o support.o $(LIBS)

rigorous: rigorous.o astrolib.o astrocon.o support.o
$(CC) $(CFLAGS) -o rigorous rigorous.o astrolib.o astrocon.o support.o $(LIBS)

rpnmat: rpnmat.o astrolib.o astrocon.o support.o
$(CC) $(CFLAGS) -o rpnmat rpnmat.o astrolib.o astrocon.o support.o $(LIBS)

sidtest: sidtest.o astrolib.o astrocon.o support.o
$(CC) $(CFLAGS) -o sidtest sidtest.o astrolib.o astrocon.o support.o $(LIBS)

tspp: tspp.o astrolib.o astrocon.o support.o
$(CC) $(CFLAGS) -o tspp tspp.o astrolib.o astrocon.o support.o $(LIBS)

coords: coords.o astrolib.o astrocon.o support.o
$(CC) $(CFLAGS) -o coords coords.o astrolib.o astrocon.o support.o $(LIBS)

eleprec: eleprec.o astrolib.o astrocon.o support.o
$(CC) $(CFLAGS) -o eleprec eleprec.o astrolib.o astrocon.o support.o $(LIBS)

rise: rise.o astrolib.o astrocon.o support.o
$(CC) $(CFLAGS) -o rise rise.o astrolib.o astrocon.o support.o $(LIBS)


asc2eph.o: asc2eph.c astrolib.h support.h
$(CC) $(CFLAGS) -c asc2eph.c

ephinfo.o: ephinfo.c astrolib.h support.h
$(CC) $(CFLAGS) -c ephinfo.c

ephtest.o: ephtest.c astrolib.h support.h
$(CC) $(CFLAGS) -c ephtest.c

sephem.o: sephem.c astrolib.h support.h
$(CC) $(CFLAGS) -c sephem.c

astrolib.o: astrolib.c astrolib.h astrocon.h support.h
$(CC) $(CFLAGS) -c astrolib.c

astrocon.o: astrocon.c astrocon.h
$(CC) $(CFLAGS) -c astrocon.c

support.o: support.c support.h
$(CC) $(CFLAGS) -c support.c

eph.o: eph.c astrolib.h support.h
$(CC) $(CFLAGS) -c eph.c

geobs.o: geobs.c astrolib.h support.h
$(CC) $(CFLAGS) -c geobs.c

jdtest.o: jdtest.c astrolib.h support.h
$(CC) $(CFLAGS) -c jdtest.c

nuttest.o: nuttest.c astrolib.h support.h
$(CC) $(CFLAGS) -c nuttest.c

pretran.o: pretran.c astrolib.h support.h
$(CC) $(CFLAGS) -c pretran.c
```

```
rigorous.o: rigorous.c astrolib.h support.h
$(CC) $(CFLAGS) -c rigorous.c

rpnmat.o: rpnmat.c astrolib.h support.h
$(CC) $(CFLAGS) -c rpnmat.c

sidtest.o: sidtest.c astrolib.h support.h
$(CC) $(CFLAGS) -c sidtest.c

tspp.o: tspp.c astrolib.h support.h
$(CC) $(CFLAGS) -c tspp.c

coords.o: coords.c astrolib.h support.h
$(CC) $(CFLAGS) -c coords.c

eleprec.o: eleprec.c astrolib.h support.h
$(CC) $(CFLAGS) -c eleprec.c

rise.o: rise.c astrolib.h support.h
$(CC) $(CFLAGS) -c rise.c
```

A.25   MAKEFILE.UNX

```
INCLUDE=
LIBS= -lm
CC=gcc

# For normal use
#CFLAGS=-ansi -pedantic -Wall -s -O
# For debugging
CFLAGS=-ansi -pedantic -Wall -g

TARGETS = asc2eph ephinfo ephtest sephem eph geobs jdtest nuttest \
pretran rigorous rpnmat sidtest tspp coords eleprec rise

# Now the actual rules

all: $(TARGETS)

clean:
-rm *.o
-rm *.log
-rm $(TARGETS)


asc2eph: asc2eph.o astrocon.o support.o
$(CC) $(CFLAGS) -o asc2eph asc2eph.o astrocon.o support.o $(LIBS)

ephinfo: ephinfo.o astrolib.o astrocon.o support.o
$(CC) $(CFLAGS) -o ephinfo ephinfo.o astrolib.o astrocon.o support.o $(LIBS)

ephtest: ephtest.o astrolib.o astrocon.o support.o
$(CC) $(CFLAGS) -o ephtest ephtest.o astrolib.o astrocon.o support.o $(LIBS)

sephem: sephem.o astrolib.o astrocon.o support.o
$(CC) $(CFLAGS) -o sephem sephem.o astrolib.o astrocon.o support.o $(LIBS)

eph: eph.o astrolib.o astrocon.o support.o
$(CC) $(CFLAGS) -o eph eph.o astrolib.o astrocon.o support.o $(LIBS)

geobs: geobs.o astrolib.o astrocon.o support.o
$(CC) $(CFLAGS) -o geobs geobs.o astrolib.o astrocon.o support.o $(LIBS)

jdtest: jdtest.o astrolib.o astrocon.o support.o
$(CC) $(CFLAGS) -o jdtest jdtest.o astrolib.o astrocon.o support.o $(LIBS)
```

```
nuttest: nuttest.o astrolib.o astrocon.o support.o
$(CC) $(CFLAGS) -o nuttest nuttest.o astrolib.o astrocon.o support.o $(LIBS)

pretran: pretran.o astrolib.o astrocon.o support.o
$(CC) $(CFLAGS) -o pretran pretran.o astrolib.o astrocon.o support.o $(LIBS)

rigorous: rigorous.o astrolib.o astrocon.o support.o
$(CC) $(CFLAGS) -o rigorous rigorous.o astrolib.o astrocon.o support.o $(LIBS)

rpnmat: rpnmat.o astrolib.o astrocon.o support.o
$(CC) $(CFLAGS) -o rpnmat rpnmat.o astrolib.o astrocon.o support.o $(LIBS)

sidtest: sidtest.o astrolib.o astrocon.o support.o
$(CC) $(CFLAGS) -o sidtest sidtest.o astrolib.o astrocon.o support.o $(LIBS)

tspp: tspp.o astrolib.o astrocon.o support.o
$(CC) $(CFLAGS) -o tspp tspp.o astrolib.o astrocon.o support.o $(LIBS)

coords: coords.o astrolib.o astrocon.o support.o
$(CC) $(CFLAGS) -o coords coords.o astrolib.o astrocon.o support.o $(LIBS)

eleprec: eleprec.o astrolib.o astrocon.o support.o
$(CC) $(CFLAGS) -o eleprec eleprec.o astrolib.o astrocon.o support.o $(LIBS)

rise: rise.o astrolib.o astrocon.o support.o
$(CC) $(CFLAGS) -o rise rise.o astrolib.o astrocon.o support.o $(LIBS)


asc2eph.o: asc2eph.c astrolib.h support.h
$(CC) $(CFLAGS) -c asc2eph.c

ephinfo.o: ephinfo.c astrolib.h support.h
$(CC) $(CFLAGS) -c ephinfo.c

ephtest.o: ephtest.c astrolib.h support.h
$(CC) $(CFLAGS) -c ephtest.c

sephem.o: sephem.c astrolib.h support.h
$(CC) $(CFLAGS) -c sephem.c

astrolib.o: astrolib.c astrolib.h astrocon.h support.h
$(CC) $(CFLAGS) -c astrolib.c

astrocon.o: astrocon.c astrocon.h
$(CC) $(CFLAGS) -c astrocon.c

support.o: support.c support.h
$(CC) $(CFLAGS) -c support.c

eph.o: eph.c astrolib.h support.h
$(CC) $(CFLAGS) -c eph.c

geobs.o: geobs.c astrolib.h support.h
$(CC) $(CFLAGS) -c geobs.c

jdtest.o: jdtest.c astrolib.h support.h
$(CC) $(CFLAGS) -c jdtest.c

nuttest.o: nuttest.c astrolib.h support.h
$(CC) $(CFLAGS) -c nuttest.c

pretran.o: pretran.c astrolib.h support.h
$(CC) $(CFLAGS) -c pretran.c

rigorous.o: rigorous.c astrolib.h support.h
```

```
        $(CC) $(CFLAGS) -c rigorous.c

rpnmat.o: rpnmat.c astrolib.h support.h
        $(CC) $(CFLAGS) -c rpnmat.c

sidtest.o: sidtest.c astrolib.h support.h
        $(CC) $(CFLAGS) -c sidtest.c

tspp.o: tspp.c astrolib.h support.h
        $(CC) $(CFLAGS) -c tspp.c

coords.o: coords.c astrolib.h support.h
        $(CC) $(CFLAGS) -c coords.c

eleprec.o: eleprec.c astrolib.h support.h
        $(CC) $(CFLAGS) -c eleprec.c

rise.o: rise.c astrolib.h support.h
        $(CC) $(CFLAGS) -c rise.c
```

Bibliography

[Aoki 1982]   Aoki, S., et al., 1982. *Astronomy and Astro-physics* **105**, 359.

[Burkhardt and Danby 1983]   Burkhardt, T. M. and Danby, J. M. A., 1983. *Celestial Mechanics* **31**, 317.

[Colwell 1993]   Colwell, Peter, 1993. *Solving Kepler's Equation Over Three Centuries*. Willmann-Bell, Inc.

[Danby 1988]   Danby, J. M. A., 1988. *Fundamentals of Celestial Mechanics*, Second Edition. Willmann-Bell, Inc.

[Conway 1986]   Conway, Bruce, 1986. *Celestial Mechanics* **39**, 199.

[Danby 1987]   Danby, J. M. A., 1987. *Celestial Mechanics* **40**, 303.

[Danby and Burkhardt 1983]   Danby, J. M. A. and Burkhardt, T. M., 1983. *Celestial Mechanics* **31**, 95.

[Duffett-Smith 1988]   Duffett-Smith, Peter, 1988. *Practical Astronomy with Your Calculator*, Third Edition. Cambridge University Press.

[Fukushima 1995]   Fukushima, T., 1995. *Astronomy and Astrophysics* **294**, 895.

[Goldstein 1980]   Goldstein, Herbert, 1980. *Classical Mechanics*, Second Edition. Addison Wesley.

[Green 1985]   Green, Robin M., 1985. *Spherical Astronomy*, Cambridge University Press.

[Herrick 1974]   Herrick, Samuel, 1974. *Astrodynamics, Vol. 1*,
                             Van-Nostrand-Reinhold.

[Kaplan 1981]   Kaplan, G. H., 1981. *United States Naval Ob-
                             servatory Circular 163*. USNO Nautical Al-
                             manac Office.

[Kaplan 1989]   Kaplan, G. H., et al., 1989. *Astronomical Jour-
                             nal* **97**, 1197.

[Kovalevsky 1989]   Kovalevsky, J., et al., 1989. *Reference Frames
                             in Astronomy and Geophysics*. Kluwer.

[Lieske 1977]   Leiske, J. H., et al., 1977. *Astronomy and As-
                             trophysics* **58**, 1.

[Lieske 1979]   Lieske, J. II., 1979. *Astronomy and Astro-
                             physics* **73**, 282.

[Lieske 1994]   Lieske, J. H., 1994. *Astronomy and Astro-
                             physics* **281**, 281.

[Mansfield 1986]   Mansfield, R. L., 1986. *AIAA Paper No. 86-
                             2269-CP*.

[Meeus 1991]   Meeus, Jean, 1991. *Astronomical Algorithms*.
                             Willmann-Bell, Inc.

[Meeus 1982]   Meeus, Jean, 1982. *Astronomical Formulae for
                             Calculators*, Fourth Edition. Willmann-Bell,
                             Inc.

[Moyer 1981]   Moyer, T. D., 1981. *Celestial Mechanics* **23**, 33-
                             56 and 57-68.

[Mueller 1969]   Mueller, Ivan I., 1969. *Spherical and Practical
                             Astronomy as Applied to Geodesy*. Ungar.

[Murray 1983]   Murray, C. A., 1983. *Vectorial Astrometry*.
                             Adam Hilger.

[Press 1992]   Press, W. H., et al., 1992. *Numerical Recipes in
                             C, Second Edition*. Cambridge. Also available
                             in a FORTRAN edition.

[RASC 1990]   Bishop, Roy L., 1990. *Observer's Handbook
                             1990*. University of Toronto Press for the Royal
                             Astronomical Society of Canada.

[Seidelmann 1992]   Seidelmann, P. K., 1992. *Explanatory Supplement to the Astronomical Almanac.* University Science Books.

[Seidelmann 1992a]   Seidelmann, P. K., and Fukushima, T., 1992. *Astronomy and Astrophysics* **265**, 833.

[Standish 1982]   Standish, E. M., 1982. *Astronomy and Astrophysics* **114**, 297.

[Standish 1990]   Standish, E. M., 1990. *Astronomy and Astrophysics* **233**, 252.

[Standish 1995]   Standish, E. M., 1995. *JPL Interoffice Memorandum 314.10-127.*

[Standish 1995a]   Standish, E. M., 1995. *JPL Interoffice Memorandum 314.10-129.*

[Standish 1998]   Standish, E. M., 1998. *Astronomy and Astrophysics* preprint.

[Taff 1981]   Taff, Laurence G., 1981. *Computational Spherical Astronomy.* John Wiley and Sons.

[Taff 1985]   Taff, Laurence G., 1985. *Celestial Mechanics: A Computational Guide for the Practitioner.* John Wiley and Sons.

[Yallop 1989]   Yallop, B. D., et al., 1989. *Astronomical Journal* **97**, 274.

Index